Studia Fennica
Ethnologica 13

THE FINNISH LITERATURE SOCIETY (SKS) was founded in 1831 and has, from the very beginning, engaged in publishing operations. It nowadays publishes literature in the fields of ethnology and folkloristics, linguistics, literary research and cultural history.

The first volume of the Studia Fennica series appeared in 1933. Since 1992, the series has been divided into three thematic subseries: Ethnologica, Folkloristica and Linguistica. Two additional subseries were formed in 2002, Historica and Litteraria. The subseries Anthropologica was formed in 2007.

In addition to its publishing activities, the Finnish Literature Society maintains research activities and infrastructures, an archive containing folklore and literary collections, a research library and promotes Finnish literature abroad.

EDITORIAL OFFICE
SKS
P.O. Box 259
FI-00171 Helsinki
www.finlit.fi

Laura Stark

The Limits of Patriarchy

*How Female Networks of Pilfering and Gossip
Sparked the First Debates on Rural Gender Rights
in the 19th-Century Finnish-Language Press*

Finnish Literature Society • Helsinki

Studia Fennica Ethnologica 13

The publication has undergone a peer review.

VERTAISARVIOITU
KOLLEGIALT GRANSKAD
PEER-REVIEWED
www.tsv.fi/tunnus

The open access publication of this volume has received part funding via
Helsinki University Library.

A digital edition of a printed book first published in 2011 by the Finnish Literature Society.
Cover Design: Timo Numminen
EPUB: Tero Salmén

ISBN 978-952-222-327-2 (Print)
ISBN 978-952-222-792-8 (PDF)
ISBN 978-952-222-758-4 (EPUB)

ISSN 0085-6835 (Studia Fennica)
ISSN 1235-1954 (Studia Fennica Ethnologica)

DOI: http://dx.doi.org/10.21435/sfe.13

A free open access version of the book is available at http://dx.doi.org/10.21435/sfe.13 or by scanning this QR code with your mobile device.

Table of Contents

Acknowledgements

This book could not have been written without the help of many persons. First, I wish to thank ethnologist Riitta Räsänen and folklorist Satu Apo, whose astute observations regarding home thievery in their own research provided inspiration for the present study. I wish to thank folklorist Anneli Asplund, whose collection efforts in 1965 are responsible for the fact that today we have a solid body of source materials on 19th-century female gossip in rural communities. Although the primary focus of Asplund's research at that time was the songs sung about village gossip women, her far-sightedness led her to ask questions regarding the social context of women's gossip, for which I am immensely grateful.

Of vital importance to the completion of this study have also been the energetic research and networking efforts of literary scholar Anna Kuismin (formerly Makkonen), who, when serving as director of the Finnish Literature Society Literary Archives, created an informal research forum dealing with the previously unknown writings of self-educated Finns in the 19th and early 20th centuries. This network was quickly christened 'Anna's Salon' (*Annan salonki*) in the autumn of 2001, and is now formally known as the Research Network on Processes and Practices of Literacy in 19th-century Finland. Anyone interested in the topic who dropped by the salon was made warmly welcome, and over the past ten years, discussions at the Salon have had a broad impact on the work and perspectives of a wide range of scholars in linguistics, literature studies, folklore studies, and historical studies. The work begun in Anna's Salon is gradually revolutionizing our view of 19th-century Finnish history 'from below', as can be seen from the funded research projects which have emerged from it, and the number of new research publications written by salon-goers. One of the things that has made this research network unique is that due to the efforts of Anna and social historian Kaisa Kauranen, a treasure trove of largely forgotten and uncatalogued manuscripts written by self-educated members of the rural common folk was rediscovered in the FLS Literary Archives. Kaisa Kauranen courageously volunteered to undertake the cataloguing of this grassroots literary output, and as the texts began to emerge from the depths of the Archives, Anna made them widely accessible by transcribing them and sending them to Salon participants by email. It was this new trove of documents, never before studied, which breathed new life into my interest in 19th-century Finnish modernization.

It was the Historical Newspaper Library of the National Library of Finland, however, which revitalized my research on domestic pilfering or 'home thievery' (*kotivarkaus*), which had languished due to lack of source materials. My heartfelt gratitude therefore goes to the National Library of Finland for undertaking the ambitious – and terribly important – project of digitizing thus far all Finnish newspapers printed between 1771 and 1910. Although the general history of the Finnish press as a whole has been expertly written by the Finnish Newspaper History Research Project led by Päiviö Tommila from 1975 to 1988, the participation of the common folk in the press has remained largely unexamined. The new accessibility of historical Finnish newspaper materials calls for a renewed analysis of the history of the Finnish press from the 'bottom-up', in other words from the perspective of readers and writers who had no formal education. It also makes feasible a renewed inquiry into the content of the press, a social analysis of what was important to 'ordinary' readers and writers of the time. Finally, the electronic availability of newspapers calls for a careful consideration of the methods and approaches used in their study.

In continuing to express my thanks to those who contributed to the completion of this study, I would like to thank Pirjo Markkola for her illuminating comments during our research discussions, Heikki Kokko for his generous sharing of important newspaper source findings, Kaisa Kauranen for her insightful comments to my research on early popular participation in newspapers, Kati Mikkola for her long-time research collaboration and helpful literature references, historian Marja Kokko for comments to my early research plans, Kirsti Salmi-Niklander for pointing out, among other things, that not all writers who write under a feminine pen name are necessarily women, and Arja Turunen for drawing my attention to two articles on home thievery from the 1920s in *Emäntälehti*, which turned out to provide crucial information for this study. Anna Kuismin has continued to send me transcribed documents from the FLS Literary Archives, several of which have proven decisive in unlocking the identities of certain female newspaper authors whose writings are dealt with in this study. I am also grateful to the researchers at the Department of Cultural History at the University of Turku, who invited me to talk on this topic in the autumn of 2010 and gave valuable advice. The anonymous referees of *Naistutkimuslehti* who reviewed an article dealing with this topic and the anonymous Studia Fennica referee of this manuscript also provided perceptive insights which improved the quality of my writing.

Thanks also go to my long-time research assistant, folklorist Riikka Kiuru, for her invaluable help in gathering and copying source materials and tracking down wayward reference codes in the Finnish Literature Society Folklore Archives. I also wish to thank the ever gracious staff of the Finnish Literature Society Folklore Archives who have unfailingly helped both Riikka and myself collect the source materials and photographic illustrations for this study, as well as the staff of the National Board of Antiquity's Picture Collections, and Anneli Hänninen and Maila Vehmaskoski at the Research Institute for the Languages of Finland for help with difficult dialect terms. Thanks are also owed to the helpful staff of the Helsinki University Central

Archvies, the Rautalampi Museum, and the archives of the Kuopio Museum of Cultural History.

Last but certainly not least, I would like to thank the co-members of my Academy of Finland-funded project (2007–2010), *Strategic Practices: Hidden Histories of Gender in Finland 1880–2005*, for their enthusiasm and stimulating discussions in the course of our project. Heartfelt thanks go to my colleague Hanna Snellman, both for her support of this project and her careful editing of the preliminary manuscript of this book. Finally, I wish to thank the Academy of Finland itself, both for funding the *Strategic Practices* project which gave me the motivation to begin this research, and for the financial assistance which allowed me to spend a sabbatical year writing up its results.

Jyväskylä, the 11th of October

Laura Stark

Notes on Translations and Referencing of Texts

Principles of translation

All translations from the Finnish are mine unless otherwise stated. The translation of the texts cited as examples in this study represents a compromise between preserving as closely as possible the original meaning of the text and making it comprehensible to English-language readers who are not necessarily familiar with the Finnish language or culture. A direct, word-for-word translation has not been possible due to the considerable differences in grammatical and semantic structures between Finnish and English, and because the use of the Finnish language in the 19th-century press by writers who had little or no formal education differs considerably from modern standard Finnish. In certain cases, the term *paraphrase* would more accurately describe the renderings in English given here. This is due to the impossibility of presenting the original narratives and descriptions word for word in English in a way which would capture the most important connotations present in the original, without greatly increasing the already large number of explanations and footnotes in this study. In a few cases I have had to make an informed guess regarding the meaning of a word or phrase based on contextual cues, gained from a preliminary reading of the corpus of source texts as a whole. In addition, certain terms of address (nicknames, terms of respect or affection) have no equivalents in standard English and therefore could not be rendered verbatim. In many cases I have added terms like 'parish' or 'district' to place-names whose classification would not have been automatically understood from the text by non-Finnish readers. Grammatical and stylistic structures particular to Finnish oral speech (mixed tenses, non-standard verbal forms, gaps and 'missing' information to be supplied by the listener from context, etc.) have been modified so as to be comprehensible to the English-language reader. In many cases I have added punctuation marks such as periods, question marks and quotations marks in order to facilitate readability. Perhaps most significantly, texts in divergent Finnish dialects have all been rendered in standard English, which means that the linguistic and stylistic differences among these texts, as well as the richness of their expression, has been greatly reduced in translation.

Referencing of source texts

The referencing of articles and letters appearing in newspapers adheres to the following format: date of publishing, name of newspaper, issue number of newspaper, title of article or letter in quotes, and the name or pen name of author in parentheses. References to original texts housed in the collections of the Finnish Literature Society Folklore Archives contain information in the following order: the district or locality in which the folklore item was collected; the year the folklore item was received by the Folklore Archives, the collector's or sender's name, with his or her personal data in parentheses, sometimes followed by the acronym for the collection series (KT, KJ), as well as the number under which the folklore item is housed in manuscript form. The series of numbers following the collection series acronym (e.g. KT 24:18) indicates the volume number of the collection series (24), and the item number within that volume (18). The final entry, preceded by a dash (-), is information relating to the informant (gender, occupation, marital status, age at recording or year of birth, etc.), if different from the collector and if known. For ethical reasons (see Chapter Four), names of informants are not shown.

I
Background, Theory and Sources

1. Introduction

A major aim of this book is to contribute to current efforts toward critically rethinking the history of gender in Finland.[1] Gender scholarship within Finnish history, ethnology and folklore studies has emerged from an historical context which is unique even to Scandinavia. Finnish women were the first women in Europe to receive not only the vote but to be allowed to stand for Parliamentary elections in 1906. In this year, nearly 10 per cent of the parliamentarians elected were women. According to historians, these events occurred with little debate or fanfare, and women won these rights with apparent ease. The social and cultural factors behind this distinctive achievement are still being debated, but many researchers have surmised that 19th-century gender relations in the Finnish countryside, where over 90 per cent of the Finnish population resided, had a significant impact on this turn of events.

What precisely were the gender dynamics in the Finnish 19th-century countryside which might have left their mark on the politics of later decades? Historians, ethnologists and folklorists have already mapped out the broad contours of family relations within Finnish farming households.[2] They have shown us that the 19th-century farm master in Finland was entitled to considerable legal rights as head of the household, administrator of its material goods, and legal guardian of his wife, children and servants. They have pointed out that we must look beyond these formal and institutional privileges to the reality of daily life, where it is evident that the necessity of women's labour contribution for the maintenance of the farm meant that power had to be negotiated between farming men and women within the household. Men's and women's dependency on each others' labour skills, and the authority delegated to the farm mistress as head of the domestic sphere, resulted in an uneasy gendered balance of power within farming households. Yet significant gaps remain in our knowledge of how gendered

---

1   See Östman 1996; Markkola 1997, 2002a, 2003a; Honkanen 1997; Koivunen 1998; Juntti 2004.
2   See: Heikinmäki 1981, 1988; Markkola 1990, 1994; Räsänen 1992, 1996; Apo 1993, 1995; Rantalaiho 1994; Pohjola-Vilkuna 1995; Löfström 1998; Stark-Arola 1998.

rights were understood by 19th-century contemporaries, how perceptions of men and women were affected by the massive social changes which occurred toward the end of the 19th century, and how gendered power was experienced by members of rural farming families who may have left behind few written records.

Within Finland, recent gender history research has tended to focus on women from the middle- and upper-classes, or on working-class women in towns or cities. This research has provided valuable insights into women's roles in the public sphere[3] – in politics, waged work, organizations, and collective movements. But while the public sphere has been the context in which women's agency has been easiest to identify, the majority of 19th-century Finnish women resided in the countryside, engaged in the less visible sphere of unpaid labour inside the farm household.[4] The vast socio-economic and cultural distance which prevailed in that century between urban and rural lifestyles has meant that research into agrarian women's lives and gender relations does not always fit comfortably inside the frameworks provided by historical research on Finnish women's public roles in wage work and voluntary organizations. For this reason, Finnish ethnologists studying rural gender in the past have had to construct their own contextual frameworks, and these have centred on the *farm* as the basic unit of production and consumption in the countryside, the unit which organized economic and social relations. For most women born into the estate of the landed peasantry, the farming family was the governance structure which coordinated and monitored their work throughout their lives. It was in the context of the farm household that small storms began to brew, conflicts of interest that burst onto the public scene in the 1850s and 1860s due to the rise of the Finnish-language press. An examination of these conflicts helps fill the gaps in our knowledge of gender dynamics in the last half of the 19th century.

Long before there was any discussion of women's right to vote, before the 'women's question' was raised in the early 1880s regarding women's university education, before the rise of voluntary civic organizations and movements, even before the law allowing public primary schools in 1866, Finns were publicly debating the rights of rural women in the press. In this discussion participated not only educated elites but also landowning peasants and even farm women. The discussions began as the public condemnation of a practice known as 'home thievery' (*kotivarkaus*), in which household members and especially farm women secretly pilfered and sold the products of their farm behind the farm master's back. However, writers and meeting

---

3   I follow rhetorical theorist Gerard Hauser in defining the public sphere as 'a discursive space in which individuals and groups associate to discuss matters of mutual interest and, where possible, to reach a common judgement about them' (Hauser 1998: 21).

4   Finland during the 19th century was primarily an agricultural economy in which forest resources were exploited. In the first half of the 19th century, roughly 90 per cent of the Finnish population at that time gained their livelihood directly from agriculture and related occupations, and by 1890 this number had dropped only slightly, to roughly 75 per cent (Talve 1997: 50).

participants soon began to speculate on the causes of home thievery, at which point questions arose regarding the respective rights and responsibilities of male and female household members. The home thievery debate was thus the first documented public discussion in the Finnish language on the topic of rural women's rights. In order to understand the motives behind it and what was at stake in the discussion, this book asks: what was the nature of the 19th-century system of household power dynamics known as family patriarchy[5] in rural Finland? What responses did familial patriarchy evoke from female members of late 19th-century farming households? How did writers to the early Finnish-language press react to these responses, and to what extent did rural writers to the press participate in this discussion? Since gender encompasses both men and women, I seek to answer these questions from the perspective of power wielded by both genders, without assuming male authority and privilege as a point of departure, but treating them instead as an open question calling for closer examination.

The sources for this study are all in the Finnish language[6] and include not only archived ethnographic descriptions but also 19th-century realistic ethnographic fiction, and above all letters written to the press by individuals from a wide range of backgrounds, including self-educated commoners engaged in agrarian occupations. In terms of theory, I combine ethnological approaches to rural Finnish gender with research on peasant households from socio-economic anthropology, and utilize as my methods microhistory[7] and rhetorical analysis. Such a multidisciplinary array of approaches prevents the researcher from examining the countryside as a domain of action isolated from what was happening in urban centres of power. Instead, multiple approaches enable links to be traced among different levels of society, and between micro- and macro-level processes.

The present study takes as its point of departure a single topic dealt with in the press, namely home thievery. But it is a revealing and many-sided topic, a thematic labyrinth encompassing inheritance, rural consumption trends, child rearing methods, the function of gossip in rural society, and even traditional wedding customs. Because this study aims to describe in detail empirical materials which have never before been presented or analyzed within gender history scholarship or ethnological research on

---

5   In feminist circles, patriarchy was a concept debated widely in the 1970s and 1980s. The theory of patriarchy stipulated that male dominance was not a product of capitalism but was a system of oppression separate from class oppression that had existed before capitalism and would endure after capitalism's assumed decline. This made it clear that since gender oppression was separate from the class system of oppression defined by Marxism, the struggle must also be separate: i.e. feminism. This view formed the basis for the historical-materialist-feminist approach which has influenced this study (Delphy 1984; Jackson 1996).

6   Although a comparison with Swedish-language sources would have been potentially illuminating, it would have required an holistic analysis of an entirely separate corpus of source materials and their socio-cultural, historical and political contexts. Regrettably, such an undertaking was beyond the scope of this study.

7   I have employed microhistorical methods chiefly in discovering new sources and uncovering the identities of the actors involved in the discussions surrounding home thievery and gossip in the press.

gender, it is not intended as an overview of current discussions in the history or ethnology of gender. Although this study has direct relevance for the topics which have recently occupied scholars in these fields (i.e. women's work, gender equality, and nationalism), space does not suffice for a full engagement with these topics. It is a task which I hope will be taken up by future researchers.

Familial patriarchy

Finnish historians and ethnologists have long agreed that 19th-century agrarian farms in Finland, as in other agrarian societies of Europe, were generally under the control of the male head of household. Finnish farm households were the primary productive units of 19th-century agrarian society, encompassing ownership, labour supply, consumption and production. Rather than organized by market relationships, they were organized by kinship. This resource accumulation and distribution system represented by the farm has been named the *marital economy* by historian Amy Lou Erikson (2005). The system was organized according to the rights and responsibilities assigned to the married couple, with the husband enjoying more rights and privileges than the wife. The husband was the person primarily accountable to higher secular and ecclesiastical authorities for the smooth functioning of his household.

The term *patriarchy* has been defined by British sociologist Sylvia Walby (1990: 20) as a set of structured and institutionalized social relations in which certain men dominate, oppress, and exploit women. As Walby points out, her use of the term social relations implies a rejection of both biological determinism and the notion that all women are oppressed and all men are oppressors. Walby suggests that patriarchy in modern life is composed of six structures: (1) production relations within the household, (2) patriarchal relations in paid work, (3) patriarchal relations in the state, (4) male violence, (5) patriarchal relations in sexuality, and (6) patriarchal relations in cultural institutions. In this study, I focus on Walby's first structure, production relations within the household, for which I use the shorthand term *familial patriarchy*. From an anthropological perspective, familial patriarchy has been defined as the male head of household's control over resources that are essential to the maintenance of the family, and which form the material basis of his authority and power. Within such a system, women are dependent upon their husbands, fathers or brothers whose control of resources, although limited by their location in the class or estate system, is greater than women's due to patriarchal property and inheritance laws (Ursel 1984).

Research by historians within Finland, for its part, has provided a more specific definition of familial patriarchy (known as *målsmanskap* in the Swedish law which continued under Russian rule).[8] According to this

---

8   Pylkkänen 2009: 40.

research, the patriarch was not just any man, but one who was married, and was a landowner.[9] In Scandinavia as a whole, being the head of a farming household made a man autonomous in the eyes of the law and thus entitled him to 'represent' others (Liliequist 2002: 77). The family patriarch had authority not only over the women of his household but also over other men, including his sons, farmhands, and male tenant farmers and cottagers living on the farm's lands.

In the 19th century, Martin Luther's 'Table of Duties' in his *Small Catechism* (1529) was taught to the rural populace through sermons and was part of the Church's official catechism until the 1890s.[10] The Table of Duties departed from an assumption that God had relinquished power within the household to the male head of household. However, the wife was not considered the property of her husband, and she became the mistress of the farm upon marriage, a figure of authority within the household (Pylkkänen 2009, 40). According to the Table of Duties, certain moral standards were to be met in relations between the patriarch and his subordinates. The patriarch took on the metaphorical role of 'father' to the persons under his authority (including his wife, biological children and other relatives within the household, servants, and apprentices) with whom he was in a relationship of mutual obligations. These were in a legal and ethical sense his 'children' (Karonen 2002a: 12–18; Markkola 2003b: 135–139).

From the perspective of 19th-century officials and clergy, the function of patriarchy was to control the workforce, and the relationship between a patriarch and his 'children' was personal rather than distant, since the patriarch's role was to monitor his subordinates' lives in a holistic manner with regard to their socialization, work, morality, well-being, and obedience to the law. This patriarchal role thus implied certain rights but also responsibilities. The patriarch was subject to the norms and disciplinary measures of the state, the Church, and the informal control of the local community, and was expected to live up to a certain ideal which involved self-control and responsibility-taking (Karonen 2002a: 12–18, 2002b: 259).

The set of legal statues which most affected rural women's lives was the Code of Judicial Procedure of 1734, and it was not until the mid-19th century that women's legal status began to change. Before 1864, unmarried women had remained under the legal guardianship of their senior male relatives their entire lives. In 1864, unmarried women who had reached fifteen years of age were allowed power of decision over their own earnings, and full legal majority at age 25 (Markkola 2003b: 139–140). Until 1929, however, a married woman remained under her husband's guardianship until his death. Being his wife's legal representative entailed a number of advantages for

---

9   Although landless male labourers were also seen to be the heads of their families, in reality the fact that they owned no real wealth, and that the wife's earnings as a domestic servant or casual day labourer were vital to the survival of the family, meant that the wife of a labourer had relatively more bargaining power in day-to-day life than did a farm mistress (Apo 1993: 138).

10 Eilola 2002: 127; Karonen 2002: 15; Nygård 2002: 158–159; Nieminen 2006: 69.

married men, the most relevant one for the present discussion being that the husband controlled the entire wealth of the farm and was the only one who had the right to buy or sell its material goods. In 1889, a new law stipulated that a wife could control the money earned through her own labours, but in practice this applied only to working-class women who earned wages, not to farmers' wives.

In addition to legal advantages, farm masters enjoyed other day-to-day advantages over the rest of the farm household. First, they were more mobile than other members: most households owned one horse and cart which was used exclusively by the head of the household, or occasionally by his adult son or farmhand. Second, farm masters enjoyed the benefits of *virilocal* or *patrilocal* residence patterns, in which new couples moved after marriage to the farm owned by the husband's father, to remain there for at least the first years of their marriage. Virilocal residence meant that unless a woman married the son of a neighbouring farm, after the wedding she moved into a household of virtual strangers, without the support networks of family and friends she had hitherto enjoyed. She was forced to begin again to build the interpersonal relations that might someday give her influence or authority in the household. The new husband's social networks and support, on the other hand, remained largely intact.[11] Cross-culturally, virilocality is the most common form of postmarital residence, and has been explained as a form of social organization which maintains ties of solidarity among male kin, tends to keep land ownership in the hands of men, and enhances the authority of senior male kin.[12]

The farm master's authority was not merely confined to his household, but held sway over a large segment of the rural population. The decisions made by landowning farmers affected nearly all rural inhabitants, since between 1805 and 1865 (after which the institution of household discipline was gradually dismantled), landless persons[13] had to be in the employ and thus under the legal protection of either farm masters or master craftsmen

---

11   However, as Swedish historian Jonas Liliequist (2002: 77) points out, although the rural patriarch did not leave his natal family, he had to adjust to his new role as patriarch in other ways, since, in contrast to his freedom as a youthful bachelor, he now had significant social and familial responsibilities and was expected to display considerable self-control.

12   Warner, Lee & Lee 1986: 121; Heikinmäki 1988: 123; Coltrane 1992.

13   There were six categories of landless persons in 19th-century Finnish society: tenant farmers or crofters (*torpparit*) worked parcels of land owned by someone else. Cottagers or hill-cotters (*mäkitupalaiset*) rented plots of land which were either too small for, or unsuitable for the cultivation of crops, being, for example, too rocky or on a hill. Cottagers often survived by keeping cows and producing handicrafts. Both of these groups usually paid their rent by performing day labour for the farm on whose land they resided. Itinerant agricultural labourers (*loiset, itselliset* or *kestit*) did not even have a dwelling space of their own but lived instead as dependent lodgers, either individually or as whole families, on the farms of land-owning peasants. The dependent lodger, too, paid for his rent with his labour. The lowest social class in Finnish society was the poor who were too old, were unable, or were unwilling to work: beggars, the infirm, crippled and ailing. By the end of the 19th century, the total population of landless rural inhabitants comprised nearly three quarters of the total rural common folk.

(Markkola 2003b: 136). In addition, prior to 1859 when rural shops became legal, the farm was the primary centre of consumption and production in the countryside. This meant that most rural inhabitants, including servants, tenant farmers, cottagers, itinerant labours and beggars, were dependent upon farms in some respect. Tenant farmers and cottagers lived on land belonging to farmers, and servants and itinerant labourers received room and board from the farm. Beggars were almost entirely dependent on the charity of farms for their survival. All of these persons except beggars paid for these benefits by performing labour for the farm. Moreover, when the statute of 1865 which separated ecclesiastical and secular governments within the parish came into effect, farm masters became the primary decision makers in their local districts and thus controlled numerous aspects of local life, including poor relief, the care of orphans and widows, the founding of public schools, health care, law and order in the district, and tax matters.[14]

In his various roles, the Finnish patriarch was thus considered to be both responsible for and to 'represent' the members of his household at higher levels of political governance. If his farm was wealthy, functioned smoothly, and was capable of feeding a large number of subordinates, he was more likely to be asked to take on additional roles of public leadership and responsibility. Especially if the master was the successful head of a fraternally extended family farm (containing two or more brothers and their families),[15] he could be viewed by others in the community as a person with strong organizational abilities, which in turn meant that he could be chosen to be a senior juryman, a sexton, a parish councillor, village elder, lay assessor, tax board member, or the head of a cooperative agricultural enterprise.[16]

Gender relations within the farm household

Focusing on the rights and responsibilities of the family patriarch alone, however, results in a lopsided view of power within the household. When we take into account the farm master's interaction with other household members, it becomes clear that a distinction must be made between the patriarch as cultural ideal, and the real-life farm master unable to always achieve that ideal in the midst of conflicting demands made by members of his household and his local community. The foregoing picture of patriarchal

---

14   See also Klinge 1997a: 244–245; Olkkonen 1997: 496; Ylikangas 1986: 120.
15   Since by the 19th century, new land was not always available for the next generation to farm, surplus members of farm households were forced either to leave the farm and join the ranks of the landless as itinerant labourers, farmhands, wage labourers in railroads, sawmills, factories and logging camps, or stay at home in large extended households (*suurperhe*) whose numbers might swell to over 60 members. These large extended households offered a temporary solution to the overpopulation problem by making it possible for young men, especially younger sons, to remain on their natal farm with their wives and children rather than leave and be forced into tenant farming or casual day labour (Saloheimo 1953: 135; Jantunen 1955, 35; Stark-Arola 1998: 78–83, 96–97).
16   Kortesalmi 1975: 229; Saloheimo 1953: 136; Jantunen 1955: 68.

gender relations within the farm household must also be qualified by pointing out that survival in a culture of scarcity required a gender partnership based on shared toil, and farm production depended equally on the labour contribution of both husband and wife, a situation which resulted in interdependency in daily interaction (Löfgren 1974: 30; Rantalaiho 1994: 17–18; Julkunen 1994; Räsänen 1996: 53). It has been widely observed in ethnographic literature dealing with rural Finnish society that the gendered division of labour[17] made it necessary for a farm household to contain adults of both genders, a state of affairs most readily obtained through marriage (Stark-Arola 1998: 87–89).

The daily work of the farm was organized according to a notion of separate spheres of activity, but the farm mistress' sphere of activity was broadened by the fact that the farm master was often away from the farm ploughing distant fields, mending fences, fishing, hunting or trapping. This meant that he was compelled to relinquish much of the day-to-day decision-making and even the keys of the food storehouses to the farm mistress, who was seen to rule the domestic sphere with considerable decision-making powers, at least until the farm master returned (Pylkkänen 1990; Markkola 1990: 21; Apo 1995: 19).

The farm mistress thus enjoyed a large amount of authority in the domestic sphere, since it was she who delegated the daily tasks to other members of the household, regulated closely their use and consumption of the food stores, and acted as guardian of the household's reputation, honour, and morality (Pylkkänen 1990; Räsänen 2008: 311, 314; E. Stark 2011: 346). The farm mistress' sphere of authority was nevertheless hierarchically nested within the farm master's sphere of authority, even if due to his own activities he rarely interfered in his wife's work or decisions. Materialist feminist Christine Delphy (1984), who has studied what she calls the 'domestic mode of production' in modern French peasant households, has referred to this sort of arrangement within farming households as 'delegated autonomy'.

In 1892, a newspaper article on home thievery printed in the newspaper *Laatokka* explained the ideal relationship between the different spheres under the farm master's and farm mistress' authority:

> In this article it is our intention to say a few words about the farm mistress, who is responsible for the internal activities and takes care of, shall we say, the household economy. In the same way as the master's exclusive obligation includes all the activities outside of the farm, it is the mistress' sole responsibility to manage the household, [a responsibility] on which

---

17   In the gendered division of labour within farming households, men generally worked in the fields and forest, in burn-beat clearing, ploughing, sowing, digging ditches, scythe harvesting, grain threshing, horse husbandry, hunting, trapping, fishing and trading. The farm mistress was responsible above all for the running of the household and the food economy. In addition to food preparation and childcare, women worked in the cottage dairy industry and performed the textile and household chores including milking, spinning, weaving, sewing, laundering, and making butter and cheese (e.g. Talve 1997: 173–174). Women also worked in the fields carrying out grain binding and stacking.

In rural areas of Finland throughout much of the 19th century, farms were the main centers of food production, which gave farm mistresses a certain amount of control over the consumption of other members of the household and landless members of the community who sought to obtain food from the farm through exchange or begging. In this photo from 1926, a farm mistress in Northern Finland churns butter in the main storehouse of her farm. Photo: Ahti Rytkönen. Courtesy of the National Board of Antiquities.

no outsider may intrude [– –]. She directs the tasks of all the women in the house and takes care of the household economy. She is the mistress in the house and no one else. Her commands must be obeyed by all and no task relating to the mistress' work should be undertaken without her knowledge. And generally speaking, all the keys of the household are in the mistress' care. No person may eat, or sell anything without the mistress' permission, and whosoever does so should be given the name 'home thief' (*kotivaras*). That name is not a pretty one, but nevertheless home thievery is hereabouts so deep-rooted in the world view of the common folk, that it is one of the Karelians'[18] original sins [53].

This idealized picture painted of the farm mistress' authority describes an egalitarian balance of household power that was rarely fully realized

18   The term Karelia refers to a region historically populated by a Balto-Finnic people related culturally and linguistically to the Finns. In the 19th and early 20th centuries, Karelian speakers lived on both sides of the pre-1944 border between Finland and Russia, and two regions in Eastern Finland are named North Karelia and South Karelia. In this passage the writer seems to use the term 'Karelians' to mean Finns residing in Eastern Finland rather than speakers of the Karelian language proper.

in the daily life of 19th-century farming families. Despite the fact that the labour of both genders was vital and necessary to the maintenance of the farm household, the division of labour was unequal: women had the larger daily workload, and much of this work was extremely arduous, for example washing and rinsing laundry in ice holes in the winter, carrying water and swingling flax. The division of labour was flexible in only one direction: women helped in hay cutting and harvesting grain, and if necessary were expected to assist in men's work such as trapping and fishing, and even perform physically demanding jobs such as spring ploughing, burn beat clearing, ditch digging, and tree felling. Men, however, generally did not engage in jobs considered to be women's work (Markkola 1990: 21; Talve 1997: 173–174). In part, this was because women's work was devalued and it was considered demeaning if an able-bodied man participated in it.

Nevertheless, the interdependency that characterized the marital partnership necessitated the avoidance of open conflict (Rantalaiho 1994), and delegated autonomy gave 19th-century farm mistresses a significant amount of discretionary power in distributing foodstuffs to other members of the household as well as to landless members of the community who regularly asked for assistance. It was primarily for this reason that farm mistresses enjoyed the highest status available to rural women of the landowning peasant class. The exact rights and responsibilities which accompanied wives' delegated autonomy, however, were open to multiple interpretations, as I shall explore in Chapter Six.

In addition to the farm master and his wife, a typical farm household consisted of children and, if a son or sons had reached adulthood, usually one or more daughters-in-law, at least in the early years of a young couple's marriage. Although the nuclear household was statistically the most common form of household in 19th-century Finland, young married couples frequently went to live in on the husband's father's farm in the first years of marriage, since the division or transfer of the farm to the son usually took some time (Heikinmäki 1988: 18).

Not all rural women from the landowning classes married,[19] but married women enjoyed a much higher social status than unmarried women (see Markkola 1990: 21). Unmarried women remained on their natal farms to assist their families, or found work as domestic servants. But while their fathers or brothers might provide for them materially,[20] they had almost no status in society at large, and they were denied access to the social circles of their married peers. As gentleman farmer Elias Raussi (1800–1866), writing in the 1840s of life in South Karelia, observed:

> Women submit to being the wards of their husbands [– –] in order to receive the title of 'wife', to have her head respectfully covered, and save herself from the stigma of 'old maid', as well as a husband of her

---

19 See Stark-Arola 1998: 90.
20 SKS KRA Räisälä. 1965. Puukka KT 372:21; SKS KRA Karjala. 1962–66. Martta Arvela 63; SKS KRA Impilahti. 1961–1962. E. Jaatinen 449; SKS KRA Nurmes 1962. Elin Karjalainen 164–165.

own for security; so that there is no longer any fear of having to wait on others hand and foot against her will, or do their bidding. For if she were unmarried, that is to say, a 'girl', then she would have to do what everyone wanted and commanded, be on the spot and serve them, and would have to compete with others in earning words of thanks from both the men and married women who are her equals in terms of social class [– –]. Married women have a higher status than girls, and [– –] married women are also considered by all outsiders to have a greater share in the farm than do old maids, through the union with their husband [– –] (Raussi 1966: 314–315).

Virilocal marriage arrangements tend to give rise to patterns of behaviour in which daughters-in-law submit to patriarchal authority early in their marriages because certain positions of power and authority are potentially available to them later in life. Thus while in the 19th-century Finnish countryside, the daughter-in-law occupied the lowest position in her marital household and was often expected to perform the most laborious and menial tasks, she was willing to submit to these indignities because she could expect to someday become mistress of her own farm household, with daughters-in-law working in the domestic sphere under her authority (e.g. Heikinmäki 1988; Stark-Arola 1998: 96–100). The universal dynamics of this pattern have been noted by development studies scholar Denise Kandiyoti, who in her overview of the ethnographic and theoretical literature on gender bargaining within rural households describes women's expectations within virilocal arrangements as follows:

> [– –] women's attachment to and stake in certain forms of patriarchal arrangements may derive neither from false consciousness, nor from conscious collusion but from an actual stake in certain positions of power available to them. For instance, women's life cycle in the virilocally extended household may be such that the deprivation and hardships they experience as young brides is eventually superseded by the control and authority they enjoy over their son's wives. The cyclical nature of women's power in the household and their anticipation of inheriting the authority of senior women encourage a specific kind of identification with this system of patriarchy. This does not necessarily imply that all women will accede to this position of power but merely that it is culturally available to them [– –] (Kandiyoti 1998: 143–144).

In 19th-century rural Finland, the wife's goal of becoming mistress of the farm was usually realized if the bride and groom set up their own neolocal household upon marriage, or if the young wife happened to be the senior daughter-in-law in the family when her mother-in-law died (Korhonen 1928; Tornberg 1971; Heikinmäki 1988).

It is important to note here that the arena within which 19th-century farm women operated cannot be viewed as a domestic or private sphere in the same sense as the bourgeoisie home which functioned as an emotional haven and was dedicated primarily to biological reproduction and the socialization of children. In the middle class model of the nuclear family household, female labour is seen to be of little consequence to economic production. Finnish farm women, by contrast, were not excluded from production but were instead vital to the maintenance of the farm, even if farm masters did not always wish to acknowledge this fact in public (see Chapter Eight). As in other countries sharing the northwest European pattern of early modern marriage and household formation (Erickson 2005: 9–10), the wife's primary role in 19th-century agrarian Finnish society was not that of birth-giver but of labourer.[21]

For this reason, I follow French feminist Christine Delphy (1984) in insisting on a materialist rather than reproductive analysis of familial patriarchy. In Delphy's model, familial patriarchy is an exploitative 'domestic mode of production' in which family farming is made economically feasible through farm women's *unpaid labour*. It is this exploitation of women's labour which explains the prevalence of discourse – observed by many ethnologists and folklorists – in which Finnish women's labour contribution to the maintenance of the 19th-century farm was downplayed and dismissed by men in rural communities. For men to have openly recognized women's contribution would have given women the opportunity to make greater claims on household resources. As it turns out, women found their own means of appropriating these resources quietly, without the farm master's permission.

Women's practices behind the scenes as a challenge to familial patriarchy?

Although much is already known of Finnish agrarian gender relations, many questions remain unanswered regarding the dynamics of familial patriarchy in the countryside. What privileges – formally enshrined in law or enacted in daily practice – gave the farm master his power, and how did he retain it? How did the more dependent members of his household react to these privileges?

This study argues that rural familial patriarchy in 19th-century Finland rested uneasily on certain tacit compromises, and was beset by internal contradictions. I explore the power negotiations and struggles which took place within Finnish farm households, as well as the ways in which the activities of household members placed limits on the farm master's power. Finally, I trace out the invisible networks through which rural women circumvented patriarchal authority. Such networks consisted primarily of two practices: (1) home thievery[22] (*kotivarkaus*) and (2) news carrying

---

21   See Räsänen 1996: 58–59; Stark-Arola 1998: 199–201; Helsti 2000: 95–171.
22   Throughout this study I use the literal translation of *kotivarkaus*, home thievery, to refer to domestic pilfering carried out by farm women and other household members. Despite the fact that from a 21st-century perspective this term is both tendentious and provocative, I choose, like Danish historian Liv Egholm (2002: 276), to use the writers' own concepts, their own interpretations of actions, in order to better analyze the specific cultural meanings these terms held for their users.

The term *kotivarkaus* had two separate meanings in the 19th-century Finnish-language press. In the present study, the term 'home thievery' (*kotivarkaus*) refers to pilfering (*kontinkantaminen*), a specific form of goal-oriented gossip usually carried out by unmarried, landless women. Home thievery and news carrying were connected by the fact that *farm mistresses pilfered goods from their farms in order to pay news carriers to both spread and gather information secretly.* Both practices were documented from throughout Finland, but 19th-century writers to the press were of the opinion that home thievery was more prevalent in Eastern Finland, and indeed most of the sources available to the researcher on both home thievery and gossip were recorded in the eastern part of the country. For this reason, the present study focuses more heavily on Eastern than on Western Finland.

In 1856, clergyman Bernhard Kristfrid Sarlin (1828–1906) wrote an article on domestic pilfering which appeared in the newspaper *Suometar.* Sarlin's was one of the first letters to the press on the topic of home thievery, and he explained the phenomenon as follows:

> About Home Thievery
> 'What is this? you may ask, slightly appalled. It is something which is practiced here and there and perhaps throughout Finland on farms and in cottages, and is hardly considered a failing at all. But what do you mean, say it straight, you are thinking, my reader. It is that vile, corrupting habit among the common folk, when members of farm households, without each other knowing, embezzle, waste and squander the common goods of the farm [– –]. As soon the occasion arises that the parents, especially the father, is not looking, then they stealthily secure whatever they can get their hands on, whatever appeals to their nose for money. The farm's grain bin, butter crock, wool bushels and so forth are all in the grasp of a remorseless hand, which decides to take for itself as much as it dares, and is careful to shield it from the master's eyes, even though the heart pounds with fear. He or she then sells it to the poor, or to coffee merchants or the poor village women and presumably for half its true price, so that the buyers' mouths would be kept shut. Is not this practice in your opinion fine treachery, as well as flagrant thievery not only by the buyer but also by the seller, in whose company lies and deceit, flattery and pretence ordinarily tread? And it is natural that this sort of behaviour greatly slackens a person's conscience so that it embraces all sorts of other wickedness and wrongdoing. Womenfolk in particular are adept at this sort of cunning, due to their devious natures inherited from old Eve. For this reason young girls, usually with their mothers' help, carry out this sort of unseemly practice on their farms. [3]

Sarlin's attitude of severe moral condemnation was adopted by almost everyone writing about home thievery until the end of the century. At the same time, however, a discussion of the causes underlying home thievery

carried out by *farm family members*. The same term was also used in the press, however, to refer to theft by non-family members such as servants and apprentices. The most important difference between these two usages of the term was that while the former was only morally condemnable, the latter was punishable by law, and perpetrators, especially if they had stolen large amounts of money, were prosecuted with a substantial fine, or the alternative of 28 days in jail on bread water if the thief had no means to pay the fine.

evoked men's sympathies toward the plight of women, and motivated not only male farmers but also their adult daughters to write to the Finnish-language press in order to discuss the gender relations inside the agrarian peasant household. The public debate on home thievery, and the issues which became associated with it in the public mind such as female inheritance rights, the rise of rural consumption, and the responsibilities of the patriarch to other family members, remain a unique case in the history of the late 19th-century Finnish-language press. Like no other topic before or after it, the topic of home thievery galvanized self-educated rural inhabitants to write about the domestic power relations prevailing in their everyday lives.

The debate on home thievery in the press transforms our picture of 19th-century rural Finland in several respects. First, by illuminating the contours of the informal bargaining which took place inside farm households, it takes the investigation of rural gender power relations beyond questions of legal rights and formal institutions and highlights the complexity of 19th-century rural familial patriarchy. Second, it shifts the date of the earliest Finnish-language gender debates back by at least two decades. Finally, it calls for a renewed examination of the rise of popular participation in public life. Until now, Finnish historical research has focused on early civic participation among the rural folk by studying voluntary associations, societies and movements (*kansalaisjärjestöt, -liikkeet*) which arose in the 1870s and 1880s.[23] An examination of Finnish-language newspapers, however, suggests that farmers, crofters, landless labourers and even farm women began to began to participate in the public sphere and voice their opinions on important social issues from the 1850s onwards (see Chapter Three).

In his classic study *Domination and the Arts of Resistance* (1990), anthropologist James C. Scott asks: how can we measure the impact of power relations on personal agency in situations where the exercise of power by dominant groups upon subordinates is nearly constant throughout the subordinates' lifetimes? This question is relevant to the case of patriarchal dominance in the 19th-century Finnish countryside, because most rural women worked on farms, and thus remained under patriarchal authority, all their lives. Scott suggests that we can only begin to measure the influence of the more powerful individual's presence on subordinates when that individual is no longer physically present and is unable to monitor subordinates' behaviour. Only then, by observing how they behave in his absence, can we understand subordinates' motives for obeying the power-holder in the first place: have they obeyed him out of habit, or out of genuine respect for his character or the ideals he represents? Or have they complied out of fear of reprisals, calculating the advantages of obedience, so that when he is absent, their behaviour changes? This study provides glimpses into not only what took place within the farm household behind closed doors, but also what happened when the farm master was away.

---

23   E.g. Sulkunen 1986, 1987; Alapuro 1987; Stenius 1988; Liikanen 1995; Markkola 2002b.

2. Practices, Patriarchy and Power

Agency and cultural projects

The present study combines an ethnological analysis of two practices: home thievery and village gossip, with a socio-historical and rhetorical analysis of the discourses in the press surrounding these practices. My point of departure is that social life of the past *consisted of everyday practices implemented by ordinary persons who saw in these practices opportunities for empowerment and agency*, however weak or constrained. In a wide range of disciplines, the concept of *agency* has been viewed as useful for creating more diverse, open-ended and human-centred accounts of human life. This is not to suggest that identifying agency from historical source materials can ever be straightforward or simple, given the fact that researchers, too, are embedded in power relations that already shape and distort their views of what types of agency are possible and desirable. Nor do I suggest that the concepts of empowerment and agency should be taken at face value and applied to past societies uncritically. Empowerment and agency are historically very recent concepts, being linked to the emergence of social and political movements starting in the 1970s (Ahearn 2001). They are also concepts associated with notions of social progress, and of democratic power being spread more evenly and thus made more available to groups which were formerly oppressed, neglected and silenced.

The concept of agency is, moreover, closely tied to postmodern individualistic and reflexive 'projects of the self'. In keeping with the 'ideology of individualism' which has dominated the modern period (cf. Greenblatt 1986: 33–36), these projects of the self are often conceptualized as if disconnected from political, social and cultural contexts. From a socio-economic standpoint, agency is additionally linked to the importance of consumerism and free trade in late modern capitalism: all interference and intermediaries should be eliminated from the buyer's freedom to choose (Ortner 2006; Gordon 2005: 117). Social anthropologist Angela Cheater sees the concept of empowerment *not* as a positive and liberating one, promising potentially limitless possibilities for action available to individuals, but as a concept used to conceal the 'hard edges' of power, a 'cloak of opacity' which 'discourages any nasty questions of who benefits and how' (Cheater 1999: 7).

Applying late modern notions of empowerment and agency to our analyses of past societies, therefore, puts researchers at risk of *anachronism* – of using the ideological lenses of our own culture to interpret past behaviours and decisions. If, on the other hand, the concept of agency is understood as describing the relations between individual and society, where these relations and an individual's possibilities for action are understood to be culturally and historically variable, as something to be investigated rather than assumed, then the notion of agency can be a useful tool for understanding the forms taken by power in the past (Gordon 2005). Even then, however, the researcher must be careful in how much intention she assumes agents to possess (Ortner 2006: 130–132). Any attempt to infuse agency with too much self-determination leads us back to our modern Western ideology of individualism and takes us away from more fruitful depictions of how persons have actually operated in other cultures – or even how we operate in our own. This is because, as anthropologists John and Jean Comaroff (1992) have noted, the problem with viewing agents as fully intentional beings who carry out their carefully devised plans is that an individual's actions are only intelligible in relation to the actions of others and indeed, are constantly modified by others' actions. Moreover, many acts result in unintended consequences, and people may act without a clear vision of where their actions may lead (see also Lukes 2005: 76).

What concept of agency might therefore be useful in describing relations between individual and society in the 19th-century Finnish countryside? Here I assume that any notion of women's agency must arise from an examination of their own culturally-specific interests and goals. For this reason, I consider the most fruitful approach to agency to be that put forward by feminist anthropologist Sherry Ortner in her book *Anthropology and Social Theory* (2006). Ortner proposes that we view agency as 'cultural projects' pushed through using 'serious games' (Ortner 2006). In this model, domination over subordinates is not an end in itself, but is carried out in the service of cultural projects pursued by individuals in everyday life, cultural projects which 'infuse life with meaning and purpose', through which 'people seek to accomplish valued things within a framework of their own terms [– –]' (ibid: 145). Persons under the domination of others have projects, too, even though 'more powerful parties seek to devalue and even destroy' these projects. Indeed, resistance by subordinates against the power of dominants is, according to Ortner, really about subordinates protecting their cultural projects – or *even safeguarding the right to have projects* in the first place:

> Thus if power and the subordination of others is always in the service of some project, so too is resistance; the entire domination/resistance dialectic itself makes sense as the clash of people's projects, their culturally constituted intentions, desires, and goals (Ortner 2006: 151).

Theorizing agency and social change

Ortner represents the second generation of what have come to be known in the social sciences as practice theorists. The first generation included some of the foremost social theorists of the twentieth century, including Pierre Bourdieu, Michel de Certeau, Michel Foucault, and Anthony Giddens. Practice theories have been seen as providing a link between *actor* and *social structure* by explaining how these two analytic poles are always intertwined: individuals internalize and reproduce social structures by engaging in practices, and in order to act intelligibly, people's practices must utilize the pre-existing 'rules and resources' of social structures (Giddens 1981, 1984; Bourdieu 1977, 1990). At the same time, human practices do not have to conform *exactly* to prior blueprints: opportunities nearly always exist for creativity and reinterpretation, so that ongoing practices, over time, gradually modify the rules for action and thus the social structures themselves. By attending to these temporal aspects, practice theory also unites synchronic and diachronic levels of analysis. Ortner, for example claims that '[a] theory of practice is a theory of history' (1989, 192), and explains that

> [t]his is because the playing out of the effects of culturally organized practices is essentially processual and often very slow, the construction of social subjects, often from childhood; the practices of life of young people and adults; the articulation of those practices with larger events in the world, often moving to a very different rhythm [– –] their effects in terms of social reproduction and social transformation are often not visible, nor interpretable, until sometime after the fact (Ortner 2006: 9).

Practice theorists have been thus interested in history both because practices are viewed as having a trajectory or path of development, and because practice theory sees social change as *caused by* shifts in practices. As sociologist and practice theorist Alan Warde (2005: 139–140) sums up, '[t]he principal implication of a theory of practice is that the sources of changed behaviour lie in the development of practices themselves.'

Practice theorists have also theorized the relationship between practice and its immediate socio-spatial context, which Bourdieu terms the 'field'. Fields are specialized domains of practice such as the farm or factory, in which practices are coordinated according to the internal logic of the domain. Another way of envisioning this immediate context of action is to use the metaphor of a *game*. Drawing upon the Wittgensteinian metaphor of language as a game in which words gain their meaning through the way they are used,[24] practice theorists such as Bourdieu and de Certeau see everyday practices as an 'art', or a 'logic articulated on situations' (de Certeau 1984: xx). In games of social life, meaning arises when players demonstrate their practical competence in deciding what strategic action is most appropriate

---

24 Ludwig Wittgenstein. 1978. *Philosophical Investigations*. Oxford: Blackwell.

and effective in a given context. These two elements, action and context, are designated *moves* and *situations* in de Certeau's writing, and *habitus* and *field* in Bourdieu's. To metaphorically visualize how action and context relate to each other to produce *agency* (which may be defined here as *possibilities for action which is intelligible, culturally appropriate and advantageous to the actor*), it is useful to reflect on a game such as chess. As de Certeau points out, moves in chess are always proportional to situations (recall, for example, how the moves allowed for different chess pieces have different significances and outcomes depending on the state of play). By analogy for Bourdieu, the *habitus* of the body (meaning *the exteriorized bodily dispositions or habits produced by each individual's internalization of the social structure*) is produced and made relevant within a *field* which is defined by social, economic, and cultural *capital*. The occasional improvisation of practices employed by actors gradually alters the situation or field as a whole (except in cases where, as in rituals and games with set rules, the participants tacitly agree to strive *not* to improvise).[25] For this reason, the field or situation is in a constant state of transformation and individuals must operate within these shifting social contexts as if they were making tactical moves in a game *whose rules are always changing*. From the player's perspective, the game, or in Ortner's terms the cultural project, is a series of starts and stops in which opportunities for strategic moves arise, flourish and disappear, and in which successful strategizing depends on understanding the nature of the playing field at any given moment. Social change thus proceeds in the form of small daily 'experiments' (Giddens 1994: 59–60), in which players invent and try out new practices, and in which new layers of interpretation are gradually applied to actions, sensations, and familiar surroundings (e.g. Tuomaala 2006).

As de Certeau (1984: 21) points out, however, the inventiveness that people employ in interacting in daily situations 'is not unlimited and, like improvisation on the piano or on the guitar, it presupposes the knowledge and application of codes.' One may think of these codes as analogous to the rules of chess: players are not allowed to move a particular chess piece – pawn, bishop, or knight, for example – in just any way they choose; moves are constrained by the rules pertaining to each piece, rules which make the play between two players intelligible and strategy possible. It is precisely these *codes* – their internalization, use and transformation – that are of interest to the scholar studying gendered strategies for power. When studying the past, actual 'moves' are lost in time and no longer visible to the researcher. However, as de Certeau points out, it is common for people to give *narrative accounts* of the tactics they have used. The more distantly located narrators are (in time or circumstance) from their practical engagement in the action, the less likely they are to assume that their listener or reader is

---

25 Improvisation does occur in ritual, either when altered situations call for creative change, or when 'traditional' practices have been forgotten and ritual participants seek to reconstruct them. Although in this latter case, participants are committed to carrying out the ritual in a 'correct' or 'appropriate' fashion, their interpretations of what this means may vary, allowing modifications to creep in.

familiar with the situation or event they are narrating. For this reason, they are more likely to explain in more detail the 'rules' of the game and the ruses and devices employed therein (de Certeau 1984: 22). The researcher of historical gendered agency can use such narratives to deduce complex repertoires of codes and to reconstruct prior forms of the playing field by asking: what were the playing pieces, in other words the resources possessed by each player? How were they acquired, and what were the possibilities for action that each enabled? What combinations of 'moves' – including rhetorical ones – constituted clever tactics likely to succeed, and why?

In Ortner's terms, this is 'figuring out the game' which in her account seems to refer to the collection of tactics and moves employed to push through one's projects in a world where the projects of others constantly intrude:

> Thus the anthropology of 'agency' is not only about how social subjects, as empowered or disempowered actors, play the games of their culture, but about laying bare what those cultural games are, about their ideological underpinnings, and about how the play of the game reproduces or transforms those underpinnings [– –] once one figured out the game – that is, the configuration of practices involving the players in question, its underlying logic, and its cultural goal – the puzzling elements would make sense' (Ortner 2006, 152, 5).

Although actors use social rules and codes as roadmaps to push through their own cultural projects and negotiate, avoid, and exploit the cultural projects of others, agency itself lies not in the roadmaps but in the act of strategically manoeuvring through them. In order to answer questions regarding gendered agency and the cultural projects of 19th-century Finnish rural men and women, it is not sufficient to merely map out the social, political and economic contexts of action in which farm masters and their households lived. We need more than a theory of practice, we need a theory of power and how it is negotiated in micro-contexts.

Household bargaining and hidden transcripts of resistance

The farm master in 19th-century rural Finland was the sole person legally entitled to make decisions which affected the entire farm, but this is not the whole story when it comes to power relations within the rural household. The socio-economic model of the family[26] which prevailed in historical studies, sociology, anthropology from the late 1950s to the late 1980s treated the household as a single, cohesive unit of production and consumption, a 'black box' in which the question of what went on *inside* the family and household with regard to work and resource allocation was overlooked. If resource allocation was considered at all, it was assumed that individuals within the

---

26   E.g. Chayanov 1966. The unitary model of the household was made popular by the works of Gary Becker (1965, 1974, 1981).

household were able to make free and voluntary economic choices, and that resources and family members' tasks were rationally allocated by a benevolent household head seeking to maximize household utility for the common good. Feminist economists and anthropologists, especially those working in low income countries, have in recent decades questioned this unitary model, defining the family and farm household as a locus of political struggle and competing interests involving daily negotiations, bargaining and even conflict among household members.[27] For the researcher interested in rural gendered power relations, it is crucial to peer more closely at the *internal* organization of labour and consumption within the farm household, because one of the primary cost-reducing strategies employed by family farms has been a reliance on the *unwaged and publicly unrecognized* work of female family members (Beechley 1987; Whatmore 1991; Alston 1998). This is particularly true of 19th-century rural Finland, a society in which women notably worked alongside men in heavy farm labour when necessary (Markkola 1990; Rantalaiho 1994).

The analytic turn from the household as the indivisible unit of resource production and consumption toward the dynamics of intrahousehold resource allocation challenges us to re-examine familial patriarchy within 19th-century Finnish farm households: not as a set of legal rights or established cultural norms of authority, but as a complex system of strategic behaviours through which household members attempted to stake claims on resources both material or immaterial. This meant that in some cases the patriarch's rights and privileges were contested by subordinate persons both in the household and within the broader community who were constantly probing for weaknesses in the patriarch's power and seeking out spaces beyond his surveillance and control in order to implement their own cultural projects.

Such spaces beyond the control of the powerful have been considered in depth by James C. Scott (1990), who draws upon numerous historical examples to propose that the relations between dominant and subordinate groups can be studied in terms of a *public transcript* in which dominants emphasize the legitimacy of their rule, show a unified front and argue that they are working toward the public good. Subordinates, by contrast, must uphold their own end of the public transcript by displaying deference, humility and compliance toward the power holders. But while dominants have the capacity to define and constitute what counts as the public transcript, they are not free to redefine it at will (Scott 1990, 14). They, too, are trapped and constrained by it, compelled to put on a show of authority and self-confidence in public. As Scott (1990: 11) explains: '[i]f subordination requires a credible performance of humility and deference, so domination seems to require a credible performance of haughtiness and mastery [– –].'

At the same time they are performing the public transcript, however, both dominants and subordinates try to peer behind the masks of the other group and perceive their true intentions, strengths and weaknesses:

27   E.g. Hartmann 1981; Sen 1983; Delphy 1984; Guyer & Peters 1987; Phillips 1989; Hart 1992, 1995; Moore 1992; Kabeer 1994; Agarwal 1997; Kandiyoti 1998.

> Subordinates offer a performance of deference and consent while attempting to discern, to read, the real intentions and mood of the potentially threatening power holder [– –] The power figure, in turn, produces a performance of mastery and command while attempting to peer behind the mask of subordinates to read their real intentions (Scott 1990: 3–4).

While both dominants and subordinates act and speak in accordance with the public transcript when they meet, each group possesses a 'hidden transcript' that has been composed and practiced in spaces concealed from the other group. It is precisely this hidden transcript which each group tries to hide from the other. For subordinates, it might be a transcript of rebellion, revenge, or humor used to lessen the fear and awe surrounding the dominant group. For dominants, the hidden transcript might mean dropping their façade of strength and mastery in order to relax, drink, and revel among peers and trusted servants/employees. This hidden transcript is often verbal or linguistic in nature, consisting of speeches, jokes, parodies, folk songs, or trickster folktales. However, the hidden transcript is not always expressed through language. It can also consist of carnivalistic rituals or modes of dress, and subversive practices and acts such as poaching and pilfering from the dominant group (Scott 1990: 14). In order for subordinates to create hidden transcripts, they must be able to operate in spaces which are hidden from the watchful eyes of the dominant group, and their secret activities cannot *openly* challenge the public transcript. Thus it is clear that the organization of sequestered spaces – which can be any context allowing subordinate group members' agency to remain invisible and out of reach of the dominant group's power to suppress it – is the first necessary element in any resistance to patriarchy. In order to understand the dynamics and limits of 19th-century rural patriarchy, therefore, we must look at how spaces of activity were organized in the farm and village, as well as the kinds of discourses generated within, and around, each space.

Although gender has rightly been viewed by materialist feminists as socially constructed and therefore as a particular form of social class,[28] Scott points out that gender *is also a special case* when it comes to relations between dominants and subordinates. In most cases, as Scott explains, the hidden transcripts of dominants and subordinates are never in direct contact. But in the case of power relations between men and women, the situation is different. Men's and women's lives are rarely lived in separate spaces, as Scott points out:

> In the case of women, relations of subordination have typically been both more personal and intimate; joint procreation and family life have meant that imagining an entirely separate existence for the subordinate group requires a more radical step than it has for serfs or slaves (Scott 1990: 22).

28   See Jackson 1996.

It is one shortcoming of Scott's work that he does not further address the issue of hidden gender transcripts, nor does he ponder the implications of sequestered spaces for gendered power relations. Nevertheless, it is clear that Scott has stumbled onto something important here. Many women in history have not had the opportunity to gather in a secure space – one where men were not present – with other women who would be sympathetic to their possible oppression. Indeed, many forms of social organization throughout history have ensured that this would not happen. In 19th-century rural Finland, one such form was the nearly ubiquitous virilocal marriage pattern, in which the bride had to leave her family and friends behind and move into a house of strange women, namely her husband's relatives. These women were rarely potential allies, since they were not only strangers to the new wife, but they were also competing with her for the farm master's approval (Stark-Arola 1998: 97–100, 156–161). What is more, from the very beginning, newly married wives were so burdened with chores that it was not possible for them to leave the farm to create social networks or engage in activities that might bring them resources from outside the farm.

The usefulness of Scott's work for gender studies is hampered by the fact that he focuses only on the most dramatic instances of dyadic power relations: those between two clear-cut, hierarchically organized groups such as master-slave, lord-serf, king-subject. Real societies, by contrast, are composed of multiple and shifting power hierarchies, in which all but the most powerless persons (for example young children, prisoners, the severely disabled) are simultaneously dominated and dominant. This means that most persons in the past have been defined by the intersection of their social positions within hierarchies of gender, age, and social class. Finnish farm mistresses, for example, were subordinate to their husbands (who were in turn subordinate to officials, clergy and the gentry), but they were dominant over a wide range of persons in the countryside, including unmarried members of their household, serving maids, female cottagers, landless labourers, and the poor who came to ask for charity.

Nonetheless, the fact that Scott has identified hidden transcripts for a wide range of subordinate groups in different periods of history indicates how misleading it would be to focus on only the public transcript or *institutional framework* of power (i.e. laws pertaining to marriage, guardianship, ownership and inheritance) when seeking to understand the dynamics of gender relations in the 19th-century Finnish countryside. Without examining the hidden transcript, we cannot know how women responded to the subordination enshrined in legal documents or Church teachings. If they appeared to uphold the public transcript regarding the legitimacy of their husband's superiority, was there another, hidden transcript lurking beneath the surface? Hidden transcripts of everyday resistance provide insights into the *other side of power*: the thwarted and struggling cultural projects of subordinates which persisted just beneath the surface of the public transcript, and the tactics employed to implement these projects.

In the chapters which follow, I explore two such hidden transcripts which operated in 19th-century rural society: home thievery and paid gossip. Such transcripts were not only about gender, as we shall see. On the contrary, they were shaped by the differing interests of class and age. It is worth noting is that both of these hidden transcripts were primarily *practices*, well documented by both contemporary men and women in the period 1850–1900 (especially home thievery) and retrospectively by both genders in the 1950s and 1960s (paid gossip). As will become clear in the course of this study, the researcher has no direct access to the hidden *verbal* transcripts which women might have used to justify these practices to themselves. Hidden transcripts regarding home thievery and gossip were never described by the person who performed them, instead they were mentioned only in second hand accounts which provide mere clues to the meanings these practices held for rural women. These second hand accounts were not told by persons conveying the hidden transcript to fellow subordinates or confidantes, but by persons seeking to frame the hidden transcript *within the public transcript*, in order to explain or justify it to persons who were socially dominant, such as educated readers of fiction or newspapers. Farm daughters writing in the late 19th-century press to a predominantly educated or self-educated male audience probably assumed that these men had some knowledge of home thievery as well as prejudices against it. Other writers, however seem to have assumed that their readers had little or no knowledge of home thievery, as in the case of Adolf (Aatto) Suppanen's and Maria Jotuni's ethnographic fictions directed at least in part toward educated town-dwellers, or in the case of recollected descriptions regarding female gossips, sent to the educated staff and researchers of the Finnish Literature Society (henceforth FLS) Folklore Archives in the 1950s and 1960s.

These second-hand accounts of hidden transcripts written by intermediaries at least somewhat familiar with both transcripts are *key texts* which are valuable in their own right. Genuine hidden transcripts, even if they were somehow available to the researcher, would never be fully intelligible, having arisen as a covert means of communication within a closed cultural and linguistic community of fellow subordinates. Hidden verbal transcripts are characterized by fragmention and ellipsis because they allude to prior events, images and statements familiar to the subordinated group, which means there is no need to recount them in full, nor would it necessarily always be safe to do so. By contrast, writers to the press or authors of ethnographic fictions who described the hidden transcript couched in the terms of the public transcript, within the dominant register of accepted literary and journalistic language, had to create a bridge between the two forms of expression. It is this 'bridging' which renders the hidden transcript more accessible and intelligible to the modern-day researcher. The researcher's task is to reconstruct the hidden transcript from these cultural translations, which I undertake in the last chapter of this study.

3. Rural Inhabitants' Participation in the Nineteenth-Century Press

In 1850, the Finnish countryside had no public schools for Finnish speakers, no railroads, and few industries. The vast majority of Finnish-speaking rural inhabitants were not able to write, nor could most of them read fluently. They had never participated in civic or political life the modern sense of the word because such did not exist, and early autobiographies suggest that many rural commoners did not share a clear conception of belonging to a 'Finnish nation'[29] (Stark 2006). Finland had been ceded by Sweden to Russia in 1809 following the Finnish War between the two countries, after which Finland became an Autonomous Grand Duchy under Russian rule, with only limited powers to legislate.[30] Starting in the mid-19th century, however, rural Finland underwent a series of dramatic socio-economic transformations which have come to be referred to collectively as *modernization*.[31] At the heart of this transformation was the birth of a new kind of group culture with new social goals. These groups began to form with the rise of early 19th-century revivalist movements, and continued with voluntary organizations and movements seeking to improve society such as regional agricultural societies and fire-fighting associations in the

---

29   See Anderson 1983.
30   Swedish remained the dominant language of administration and education in Finland, and the only official language until 1863. In 1880, the total population of Finland was just over 2 million and roughly 92% of the population was rural. Swedish was spoken by 38 per cent of the urban population and 12 per cent of the rural population, with Finnish spoken by 58 per cent of the urban population and 88 per cent of the rural population. Russian-speakers accounted for less than two per cent of the urban population, and an infinitesimally small percentage of the rural population (STV 1883: 11, table 3).
31   Rural public schools began to be founded in the 1850s (formalized by a statute in 1866). Liberal laws which promoted a freer market economy were also passed in the late 1850s and 1860s. In 1865, municipal governments consisting of landowning farmers took over many of the social and administrative functions formerly handled by the Church. Debates regarding political life and social reform were catalyzed by the meetings of the Finnish Diet, at which the four Estates began to meet regularly in 1863. In the same year, Tsar Alexander II declared the Finnish language to be an official language alongside Swedish, to be used in the writing of legal documents. The Tsar allowed for a twenty-year transition period from Swedish to Finnish, after which Finnish was to be the sole language used in the administration of the Finnish-speaking members of society.

1860s, and starting in the 1870s and 1880s, the temperance movement, youth clubs, and the labour movement. Two important characteristics of these groups were that first, they channelled the energies of the common people into participation in decision-making, politics and governance, and second, they challenged the vertical structure of the estate society. The new civic organizations provided a social space for solidarity among like-minded members, including those from different estates and classes, as free and equal individuals. This was made easier by the fact that after 1865, landless workers were freed to some extent from the strict legal authority of farm masters.[32]

New civic organizations and movements arose partly in response to shifts in cultural discourse.[33] According to philosopher Charles Taylor (1989: 313), modernization and secularization do not occur simply through education and scientific progress, but because 'masses of people can sense moral sources of a quite different kind.' In Finland, new moral sources used to define people and their lives as 'good', 'decent' and 'normal' arose in part from the breakdown of the older estate society and a Scripture-based religious world view, both of which were fundamental cultural-symbolic orders in rural life. In the new order, the masses were expected to have a political consciousness of their unity as a nation, a new self-awareness of themselves as productive citizens, and were expected to improve themselves and their socio-economic situation. People became independent actors in the capitalist market economy, but this meant that individuals' subsistence and well-being became increasingly dependent on their own choices (Alasuutari 1991: 175). The modern subject was expected to be self-directed and organize his inner impulses and desires to socially productive ends and for the rational benefit of society. One of the aims shared by all of the civic voluntary societies that mushroomed in the last decades of the 19th century – regardless of their political philosophy – was the promotion of this new transformation of the individual.

The primary way in which new moral sources reached ordinary people in the late 19th-century countryside was through an explosion of new discourses: taught in the new schools, available from an expanding Finnish-language literature, and performed in the speeches and theatrical productions performed at meetings of the temperance, youth, and labour societies. Yet for the most part, these informational channels did not open up in the countryside until the late 1860s at the earliest, and often much later than that. Autobiographies written by men who were young adults in the mid-19th century reveal that the first channels of new information available to rural inhabitants were newspapers, and that the press was the primary catalyst of changing attitudes and behaviours among the common folk (L. Stark 2006; see also Leino-Kaukainen 1989). As early as the 1840s

---

32 Sulkunen 1987, 2003; Alapuro & Stenius 1987: 20–21; Alasuutari 1991; Markkola 2003b.
33 For a definition of the term discourse used in this study, see this chapter: *Changing discourses on gender in the Finnish press of the 1850s and 1860s.*

and 1850s, newspapers informed the public of vital social issues, served as forums for discussion, and stimulated people to become better readers, to become more actively interested in local and national issues, and to learn to write (e.g. Juntti 2004: 118,173).

It should be pointed out that although subscription rates remained low throughout the last half of the 19th century,[34] the sale of newspapers is not necessarily a reliable measure of their impact, since it was typical in this period for rural inhabitants to read newspapers aloud to groups of persons, for wealthier farmers to subscribe to a newspaper and then pass it on to other households, and for groups to pool their money and jointly subscribe to newspapers.[35] In one case in Häme, a group of 36 farmers, farm wives, serving maids and farmhands not only pooled their money to subscribe to newspapers, but came together as a reading group in 1862 (Salmi-Niklander 2006, 171).

When a new newspaper was founded in the 19th century, it first introduced itself to the public by explaining its aims and justifying its existence in its sample issue (*näytenumero*). A survey of these introductory sample issues from the period 1844 to 1899 reveals that the primary reason behind the rise of the Finnish language press in the mid-19th century was the so-called 'language question', in other words, the struggle for the rights of Finnish speakers.[36] It took 40 years for just fourteen Finnish-language newspapers to be founded between 1820 and 1860, and in the 1850s, only four new Finnish-language newspapers appeared. But in just three years between 1861 and 1863, eight new newspapers started up. The reason behind this optimism was the Finnish Diet. This assembly of the Estates[37] had not convened for

34　The numbers of persons who subscribed to and read newspapers in the 1850s and 1860s seems to have varied greatly from parish to parish and even from village to village. For example in 1861, a writer from Tohmajärvi parish in North Karelia stated that one half of his parish (comprising eight villages) was responsible for over 50 subscriptions, while the other half of the parish was completely without newspapers. In 1857, Johan Rännäri from Liminkä parish in North Ostrobothnia had boasted to the newspaper *Kuopion Sanomat* that 70 newspapers subscriptions had been made within his parish that year, but a rural correspondent from Pälkjärvi parish in North Karelia lamented four years later that farmers in his district had not subscribed to a single newspaper, not due to lack of reading ability, but because 'reading anything other than religious books is considered an unforgivable sin'. (February 28, 1857. *Kuopion Sanomat* no. 9, 'Limingasta' (J. Rännäri); May 11, 1861. *Tapio* no. 19, 'Pelkjärveltä'; June 15, 1861. *Tapio* no. 24, 'Tohmajärveltä' (O.F.B.).

35　Tommila 1988, 238–239; Mäkinen 2003, 316; L. Stark 2006b; Mikkola 2005, 2006. See also: February 9, 1878. *Ilmarinen* no. 12, 'Sakkolasta tammikuulla' (–s).

36　It should be noted that prior to the 1890s, Fennomanism was not a movement for national independence. Both political factions, the Old Fennomen and the Young Fennomen, presented themselves as loyal and devoted subjects of the Tsar (Nieminen 2006, 64). This is in part because the dominant language of administration and education whose privileged position Fennomen were struggling to supplant was Swedish, not Russian.

37　The three highest estates were the nobility, clergy, and burghers. The fourth estate consisted of land-owning peasant farmers, who had voting rights in the Finnish Diet. The landless members of society had no legal representation. Landowning peasants and landless rural inhabitants were the folk or commoners, and comprised the majority of the population. What distinguished the upper classes from the common folk was that the

54 years, but in 1861, word spread that Tsar Alexander II would allow it to convene in 1863. The decisions made by elected representatives within the Diet would then be conveyed to the Tsar for his consideration.

News of the upcoming Diet had a galvanizing effect on Finnish-language activists, who saw their chance to lobby for Finnish language rights. Finnish-language newspapers took on the task of developing the Finnish language and its literature, as well as urging for Finnish-language schools, and developing political awareness in rural Finns through editorials. Newspaper editors also strove to widen the scope of ordinary farmers' interests from farm and village to society at large. They did this by encouraging self-educated rural inhabitants to contribute to discussions in the press, thereby introducing them to the primary basis for civic society: a vibrant public sphere. In the process, the Finnish-language press in the mid-19th century introduced rural inhabitants to the idea of a Finnish nation as an entity with rights of its own. The story of the rise of the Finnish-language press in the early 1860s is at the same time the story of how landowning farmers, landless men and even rural women began to actively participate in the public sphere of national discussion *before* the emergence of popular voluntary movements and societies in the 1870s and 1880s.

Newspapers have not previously been analyzed systematically as source data for ethnological studies of 19th century Finland, and very little has been written on popular participation in the 19th-century Finnish press. In this chapter I examine at length the early participation of rural inhabitants in the press, and ask: who wrote to newspapers? What were the barriers faced by newspaper editors in enticing rural Finnish-speakers to subscribe and contribute to newspapers? Why did self-educated rural inhabitants participate in the press, and how was this participation shaped by their interaction with newspaper editors? What socio-cultural and socio-political discourses did writers to newspapers employ in the mid-19th century, and how did these change over time?

The National Library of Finland has recently digitized nearly all newspapers printed between 1771 and 1910 into a searchable database which makes it now easier for researchers to use newspapers as source materials for research. The availability of digitized newspapers online offers a new opportunity to examine who contributed to the press and what motivated them to do so.

---

former did not need to perform physical labour to earn a living, whereas the latter had to cultivate the land, engage in logging work, or perform skilled labour to survive.

Since landowning peasants were one of the estates which possessed voting rights, self-educated Finnish-speaking farmers, too, participated in the Diet. For instance, Anders or Antti Puhakka (1816–1893), a farmer who was illiterate until age 21 but later became an accomplished folk poet, was chosen to serve on the 'January committee' that met in 1861 to prepare for the meeting of the Diet in 1863, thereafter serving as a delegate in four different Diets. Puhakka also took part in the debate on home thievery in the press (see Chapter Eight).

Table 1. Early Finnish-language newspapers and their editors

- 1775 *Suomenkieliset Tieto-Sanomat* (ended 1776, A. Lizelius)
- 1820 *Turun Wiikko-Sanomat* (ended 1831, R. von Becker)
- 1829 *Oulun Wiikko-Sanomia* (1829–1834, 1836–37, 1840–41, 1852–1856, E. Lönnrot, later J. Bäckvall)
- 1833 *Sanan-Saattaja Wiipurista* (ended 1836, G. Wirenius)
- 1844 *Maamiehen Ystäwä* (J. V. Snellman, F. Ahlqvist, F. Serenius)
- 1845 *Kanawa. Sanansaattaja Wiipurista* (ended 1847, editor P. Hannikainen)
- 1846. *Suomalainen* (C. A. Gottlund)
- 1847. *Suometar* (A. Ahlqvist, D.E.D. Europaeus, P. Tikkanen, A. Warelius)
- 1847. *Suomi* (C. A. Gottlund)
- 1851. *Sanomia Turusta* (F. Bergstadi, G. E. Eurén, later A. Liljefors)
- 1855 *Sanan-Lennätin* (first H. K. Corander, then A. Gabriel, W. Lavonius, P. Hannikainen)
- 1857 *Suomen Julkisia Sanomia* (K. Schröder, C. E. Aspelund)
- 1857 *Kuopion Sanomat* (ended 1857, R. Krant)
- 1860 *Otawa* (ended 1863, F. M. Saukko)
- 1860 *Porin Kaupungin Sanomia* (ended 1862, K. O. Palander & A. Lindgren)
- 1861. *Tapio. Sanomia Sawosta ja Karjalasta* (A. Manninen, J. Rännäri)
- 1861. *Mikkelin Ilmoituslehti* (A. E. Landgren)
- 1862. *Helsingin Uutiset* (J. Forsman, Y. Koskinen, A. Meurman)
- 1863. *Tähti* (J. F. Granlund)
- 1863. *Lännetär. Sanomia Porista* (M. Thiesen)
- 1863. *Päivätär. Wiiko-Sanomia Helsingistä* (A. Nylander)
- 1863. *Kansakunnan Lehti* (Helsinki, D. E. D Europaeus)

The information for the above table was taken from Päiviö Tommila's (1988) Suomen lehdistön historia 1, *from the National Library of Finland's Historical Newspaper Library,*[38] *and from Antti Manninen's 1858 overview appearing in* Suometar *of Finnish-language newspapers up to that date.*[39] *In his list, Manninen included periodicals which would not today be considered newspapers in the strict sense of the word, and so are omitted from this list.*

The earliest newspapers aimed at the rural public

Although four Finnish-language newspapers had appeared before 1840 (see Table 1), it was not until the appearance in 1844 of the newspaper *Maamiehen Ystäwä* (Farmer's Friend) that a Finnish-language newspaper gained

38 http://digi.kansalliskirjasto.fi/sanomalehti/secure/main.html.
39 May 21, 1858; June 4, 1858; July 9, 1858; July 16, 1858; July 23, 1858. *Suometar* nos. 20, 22, 27, 28, 29. 'Muistelmia Suomalaisista sanomalehdistä' (A.M-n. [Antti Manninen]). This retrospective was first written in 1855 and published in 1856 in the newspaper *Sanan-Lennätin*.

a relatively broad readership among rural inhabitants.[40] *Maamiehen Ystäwä's* first editor was Johan Vilhelm Snellman (1806–1881),[41] the educated son of an Ostrobothnian sea captain and a native Swedish-speaker.[42] By this time, it had become clear to the editors of Finnish-language newspapers that if they wanted their newspapers to survive financially, they needed to increase their number of uneducated rural subscribers. The reason came down to simple economics: the elite read Swedish newspapers, but the untapped public lay in the Finnish-speakers of the countryside, who in 1880 comprised over 80 per cent of the country's total population.[43]

The problem, however, was that although the Lutheran Church had long required parishioners to learn to read the Bible and Catechism in their own language, in many cases this only meant being able to sound out words, and many rural inhabitants were unable to read with fluency or comprehension (Leino-Kaukiainen 2007; Mäkinen 2007). For example, in writing of his experiences as a youth in the 1860s, farmer Frans Fredrik Björni (1850–1930) explained in his autobiography that 'there were very few persons who could read a printed book continuously without sounding out the words', and that it was only *after* rural inhabitants began reading newspapers that their reading abilities became more fluent (Tuominen 1986, 185).

Given the harsh conditions of the 19th-century countryside where continual physical labour was necessary for survival, many rural inhabitants could not see what possible use the reading of newspapers could be to them (L. Stark 2008). Educational levels were low: parents often opposed children's schooling because time spent in school meant time taken away from productive work on the farm and from the training provided by parents in farm-related skills. Moreover, it was feared that schooling would produce lazy and arrogant 'lords' (*herrat*) who would perform no useful work and live at others' expense (Tuomaala 2004; Mikkola 2006, 2009; Mäkinen 2007, 414, 416–417).

---

40   *Maamiehen Ystäwä* had 900–1000 subscribers in its most successful years, 1844 and 1845 (Tommila 1988: 159).

41   The actual publisher of *Maamiehen Ystäwä* was printing press owner J. A. Karsten. Snellman edited only the first fourteen issues of *Maamiehen Ystäwä* (Tommila 1988: 157).

42   Newspaper editor Antti Manninen, one of the most knowledgeable men of his day regarding what was being written in Finnish, wrote in 1861 that as far as anyone knew, Snellman's editorials in *Maamiehen Ystäwä* represented the only time Snellman had ever written in the Finnish language. In the mid-1840s, Snellman initiated the language debate in his Swedish-language newspaper *Saima* (1844–1846), which served as the catalyst for a broader debate on Finnish speakers' rights, as well as the need for Finnish-language literature. With Snellman taking the lead, the Fennomans managed to push through a statute in 1863 which gave the Finnish language equal status with Swedish as a national language, to be in full use in official documents within twenty years' time (Karkama 1989; Jussila et. al. 1996). The language question remained a fundamental political issue well into the 20th century however, and in daily practice, the question of whether Finnish or Swedish would be used in government agencies or educational institutions was one of constant negotiation and debate (E.g. Jutikkala & Pirinen 1996: 339–341).

43   *Suomenmaan tilastollinen vuosikirja* (Tilastollinen toimisto). 1883. Helsinki: Finnish Literature Society, p. 11, table 3.

Snellman, like many newspaper editors who would come after him, was aware that most rural inhabitants were familiar only with the Bible, Catechism and church hymnal, which meant that potential readers in the countryside would be suspicious of anything written that was not the word of God. If Finnish-language newspapers were to receive readers and subscribers, the concepts conveyed within them needed to be couched in terms familiar to rural inhabitants. Snellman opened the first issue of *Maamiehen Ystäwä* in 1844 by explaining the usefulness of newspapers for landowning peasants. Using the question-answer format familiar to rural readers from the Finnish translation of Martin Luther's Small Catechism,[44] he sketched out an imaginary dialogue between himself (the Farmer's Friend) and the stereotypical figure of a peasant farmer whose farm he visits:[45]

> What the Farmer's Friend has to say.
> F.F. (enters the farmhouse door with a birchbark knapsack on his back).
> Peasant (sits behind the table, wearing an old fur hat, a pipe in his mouth.) [– –]
> Peasant: (Scratches behind his ear). Whence does the stranger come?
> F. F.: From Kuopio [– –].
> P.: (Pulls his fur hat down toward the other ear) What are you carrying with you?
> F. F.: I carry wisdom.
> P.: (Takes his pipe from his mouth and looks into the Farmer's Friend's knapsack). – That merchandise is sure to be expensive in our day and age.
> F. F.: For a silver rouble one receives enough for one year's needs [– –].
> P.: I've got better wisdom in that cupboard over there.
> F. F.: I see you have a Holy Bible there. And certainly it is true, more wisdom can be found from it than the human mouth can explain. But there is also learning which is not written in the Bible.
> P.: It's not likely to be very good learning.
> F. F.: You did not learn from the Bible to read or to plough, and yet it's probably a good thing for you that you learned them.
> P.: Of course those things a farmer's son learns from his father.
> F. F.: But it would be good to know where the skill to read came from in the first place and how farmers plough in other regions.
> P.: How does one become any wiser from knowing that? Is one able to read or plough better because of that?
> F. F.: Yes indeed! You must be good at reading and ploughing. But there is no man so wise, that with advice could not become wiser. The more you read, the easier reading becomes, and the more you learn, the better you understand what you read...

---

44 Tommila 1988: 159.
45 January 5, 1844. *Maamiehen Ystäwä* no. 1, 'Mitä Maamiehen Ystäwällä on sanomista'.

In the course of this dialogue, the 'Farmer's Friend' gives the farm master some examples of useful and interesting knowledge to be found in his newspaper, and suggests that if he shares the annual subscription with two other farmers living nearby, this would reduce his price of each issue to less than half the cost of a shot of vodka. At this, the farmer is finally won over:

> P.: You're not bad at praising your merchandise. But the merchandise is not completely bad. I could share with Antti and Väänänen on other farms, each paying one-fourth of a rouble, so that they would get to read this too. Half a rouble is not such a bad price after all [– –]. So be it! Give me what is in your knapsack [– –].

Commenting on the impact made by *Maamiehen Ystäwä* on rural inhabitants in the 1840s and 1850s, crofter's son and popular author Pietari Päivärinta[46] (1827–1913) gave the following description in his autobiography written in 1877 (2002: 41–42):

> At that time 'Farmer's Friend' began to spread light to a people in darkness. It was so well written, as a skilful parent would make food for his child who was sickly and weak. It was able to touch all the places so tenderly, and infiltrate into the lowest strata of the ordinary folk, that it made everyone grow fond of it. Who, for example, could be irritated at such friendly way of talking as 'Listen here, Matti, Mikko, Pekka and Paavo!' [– –] At that time there were two – yes, two! – men in our parish who read with pleasure anything they could. One of them had many years' worth of *Turun Wiikosanomia* [Weekly News from Turku] edited by Becker as well as of *Oulun Wiikko-sanomia* [Weekly News from Oulu]. As soon as Farmer's Friend appeared, both men subscribed to it. They had perceived that my empty soul longed for something which it had never had before. They promised I could read their beloved Farmer's Friend, now there was a prize! I could scarcely breathe at the end of the week because I knew that on the weekend I would be able to read Farmer's Friend. Farmer's Friend began to be subscribed to by others in the parish, and one year I was a co-subscriber. I felt I was a real man, now that 'newspapers came to me too', as I liked to explain to others.

Another early autobiographer, farmhand and later farm master Zefanias Suutarla (1834–1908), explained in his autobiography published in 1898 how it was first through newspapers that a national awakening began to be sensed by rural Finnish-speakers. Referring to himself below in the third person as 'Vani', he described his own experience of this awakening:

> Strange voices began to be heard. In newspapers began to appear, with ever more frequency and vigour, writings which shed light on the unnatural state of the ordinary people and demanded improvements, such as the right and possibility for Finnish-speakers to receive some kind of

---

46 Päivärinta later became a farm master and church cantor. He was a highly prolific writer of realistic fiction in the period 1867–1910.

learning in their own language. Oh! How those writings aroused joyful hopes and refreshed the mind. But Vani was used to believing that all the elites were unanimous in oppressing the people and wishing to keep them in a lowly state, in order to control them as they wished. 'A raven does not pluck out another raven's eye'. Thus he was astonished when he realized: what sorts of gentlemen are these, who dare to vehemently criticize the behaviour of other gentlemen and even of the government, while defending the rights and the progress of the lowly folk. Vani did not know then anything of the research made into the Finnish language nor of the cause of Finnish nationhood, not of A.J. Sjögren or of A. I. Arwidson, not even of J. V. Snellman. Those new demands for the defence of ordinary people's rights awakened a pulse of light in Vani's pessimistic mind. But whatever the reason for the elites' difference of opinion, some of them defended the rights of an oppressed people in any case and sought to obtain natural rights for them. [Vani thought:] Perhaps something will come of it.[47]

While *Maamiehen Ystäwä* was oriented toward the daily needs of rural inhabitants and strove to educate and enlighten them using language they could identify with and understand, *Suometar*, which appeared in 1847, was explicitly oriented toward a more educated Finnish-speaking audience (Tommila 1988: 164). However, *Suometar*'s circulation remained small until it began to actively request local news and opinions from rural correspondents (Tommila 1988: 166–167). Another reason for *Suometar*'s increased circulation was that in 1854, the newspaper was allowed to publish news of the Crimean war, which doubled the number of subscribers from the previous year (Juntti 2004: 152).[48] All four of *Suometar*'s young editors were university educated, but came from lower-class backgrounds. Antero Warelius (1821–1904) was the son of a farmer, as was Paavo Tikkanen (1823–1873). David Emmanuel Daniel (D.E.D.) Europaeus' (1820–1884) father was a clergyman but his mother was a milkmaid, which meant that he was largely excluded from elite circles. August Ahlqvist (1826–1889) was born out of wedlock to a serving maid, but the fact that his father Johan Mauritz Nordenstam was an officer who later became a general and a senator helped Ahlqvist gain admittance to education and facilitated his academic career.

It was Paavo Tikkanen who created *Suometar*'s network of correspondents, whose members served as both subscription agents and news reporters. By the early 1850s, Tikkanen could boast that 'Suometar has been edited by the entire Finnish nation',[49] and in 1856, Antti Manninen, who five years later would be editor of the newspaper *Tapio*, called *Suometar* 'the voice of the people', a newspaper which told 'what the Finnish people think, want, and long for'.[50] In 1856, *Suometar*'s circulation reached the record-breaking number of 4600 subscribers.

---

47   Suutarla 1898: 17.
48   War news increased newspaper subscriptions also in the late 1870s (February 9, 1878. *Ilmarinen* no. 12, 'Sakkolasta' [– –s.]).
49   Tommila 1988: 167.
50   February 2,1856. *Sanan-Lennätin* no. 5, 'Silmäys Suomalaisilta sanomalehdiltä' (A. M.-n [Antti Manninen]), in Tommila 1988: 179.

Obstacles faced by rural writers

Many of the newspapers founded in the 1850s and 1860s followed *Suometar's* example and invited rural inhabitants to send their reports and commentaries for publication. This was because in the early years of the Finnish-language press, the publication of foreign news was officially forbidden, so newspapers had to concentrate on news from local areas (Pietilä 2008: 127). Accepting written submissions from readers was also a way of increasing the amount of material for publication, since most newspapers had only one editor, for whom the newspaper was a side activity carried out in addition to his regular job (Kinnunen 1982: 58). Letters from rural correspondents did not simply contain local news. They also contained ethnographic descriptions of everyday life, opinions on issues of general interest, and replies to previously printed letters, making them similar to letters to the editor or opinion columns in modern newspapers.

Despite the difficult conditions of the countryside – recurrent famines, no public schools, very little secular literature – a surprisingly large number of rural inhabitants chose to write to newspapers. To give but one example, in its three years of publication (1856–1858), the weekly newspaper *Sanan-Lennätin* printed 178 letters of rural correspondence[51] and 63 longer essays, all of which were written by rural inhabitants. *Oulun Wiikko-Sanomia* published 846 letters of rural correspondence in the period 1852–1859, and 1355 in the period 1860–1869. In the early 1850s, writers were sending rural correspondence letters to *Suometar* from a hundred different parishes (Tommila 1979: 5). Sixty per cent of those who submitted letters to *Suometar* were educated members of the mostly lower middle classes (writers, schoolmasters, ministers and cantors) while 40 per cent were self-educated landowning peasants. In the early years of the 1860s, the proportion of writers who were landowning peasants increased (Tommila 1988: 202). Historian Päiviö Tommila (1988: 201) estimates the number of rural correspondents in the period 1847 – 1865 to have been at least 2200. Rural correspondents were so active in writing letters to newspapers that editors were unable, due to lack of space, to print all of their submissions.

The law formalizing the founding of public schools was not passed until 1866, and even after this, rural school attendance remained low. Many farm masters opposed the building of schools and hiring of schoolteachers, because it was they who would be burdened with the expense, and because they felt that schooling was unnecessary (Parkkonen 2008: 33–47; Mikkola 2009). By 1900, only 34 per cent of all school-aged children were attending public primary school (Nieminen 2006: 81, Table 4), and attendance did not become mandatory until 1921. Those who learned to write without formal schooling appear to have done so in one of two ways: either from the gentry or from other self-taught commoners. The former process occurred through informal 'writing schools' in which manor lords, military officers, secondary

51 *Sanan-Lennätin* also regularly printed letters of correspondence borrowed from other newspapers. The number 178 represents the letters sent directly to *Sanan-Lennätin* for publication.

school graduates, and assistant vicars taught writing and arithmetic to the children of wealthy farmers, manor tenants, and even factory workers' children either as a pastime or for a small fee (Häyhä 1897: 6; Makkonen 2002b: 184–185; L. Stark 2008). However, once they learned to write, the common folk occasionally set up their own schools in their homes, as Alfred Leppänen's family (1851–1908) did, an experience which he describes in his autobiography (Makkonen 2002b: 219–221; L. Stark 2008: 53).

In addition to lack of education, self-taught rural inhabitants faced a number of concrete obstacles to functional reading and writing. These included a lack of writing and reading materials, and few opportunities to practice writing, which meant that rural writers experienced difficulties in keeping up the fine motor skills which were necessary for good penmanship (L. Stark 2008: 53–54). Additionally, young persons did not always have the time needed to write. The sons of small-scale farmers and crofters were expected to participate in the unending physical work of the farm, and the children of craftsmen might be required to start work already at age five (L. Stark 2006: 79–80). Young men who carried out farm work under the watchful eye of a strict father had little time for any other activities. Impoverished rural inhabitants also had little space or privacy in which to write, since they had to share their living space with other family members (L. Stark 2008). Finally, rural readers and writers had to face the scorn exhibited by family and neighbours who valued physical labour and skilled handicraft, but saw reading and writing (which appeared to outside observers as mere idleness) as a foolish waste of time (L. Stark 2006, 2008). All of this meant that progress in learning to write throughout the nineteenth century was fairly slow. In the 1830s, roughly five per cent of the male population in the countryside was able to write (Tommila 1988: 32). By 1900, this number had only risen to 50 per cent of all Finns above the age of fifteen (Makkonen 2002a: 9). The situation was similar in many other European agrarian societies, for which reason it was long assumed that few documents written by the common people could have possibly existed before the 20th century. However, an increasing number of writings produced by the self-educated and the poor have recently been found in attics and basements, and have transformed our historical picture of the writing activities of the common folk.[52]

As social historian Pirkko Leino-Kaukiainen (2007: 434–435) has pointed out, in order for Finnish-speaking rural inhabitants to learn to write, mere interest was not enough. Rural writers needed a situation in which writing was not merely the drawing of letters on paper but represented the transmission of information useful for everyday life. As long as most official matters were carried out in Swedish, it was clear that the ability to write in Finnish could not represent a form of social capital. The aforementioned Zefanias or 'Vani' Suutarla, who was a youth at the start of the 1850s, recalled wondering what possible use learning to write could be to him:

---

52   See Makkonen 2002; Salmi-Niklander 2004, 2006; Lyons 2007; Kauranen 2005, 2007.

He grew older, his reading ability became more confident, and his world view broadened. In addition, there grew in Vani a desire to learn and gain knowledge. His ability to write had developed to the point that it produced a somewhat legible handwriting. But to what purpose? Vani could find no answer to that. Writing could be of no practical use to a Finnish speaker, since – as it appeared then – not a single meagre document could be written in Finnish (Suutarla 1898: 16).

By the end of the 1850s and during the 1860s, writing to newspapers was one of the few activities to which self-taught writers could apply their newly acquired skills (see L.Stark 2006, 2008; Salmi-Niklander 2006: 167–175). The fact that letters from self-educated rural writers were welcomed by such newspapers as *Suometar, Tapio, Sanomia Turusta, Oulun Wiikko-Sanomia, Sanan-Lennätin, Suomen Julkisia Sanomia, Hämäläinen, Pohjan-Tähti, Otawa*, and *Mikkelin Ilmoituslehti* meant that for the first time, the common folk could express their needs and interests in collective socio-political discussion, and even potentially influence public opinion and political practice.

Editors as gatekeepers to the public sphere

If uneducated rural inhabitants faced serious obstacles in writing to the press, editors and owners of Finnish-language newspapers in the period 1844 to 1900 faced their own challenges. It was often difficult to receive official permission to start up a newspaper, since like all public activity, the press was restricted by Russian censorship laws.[53] In the early 1860s, political news was allowed only if official newspapers such as *Finlands Allmänna Tidningiä* and *Suomen Julkisia Sanomia* were the source of the information (Toivanen 2000: 415).

The financial capital needed to found a newspaper was often considerable, since if there was no printing press in the town where the editor lived, it was often seen as prudent to purchase one. To print one's paper in another town often meant delays in getting fresh news to readers. Moreover, editors faced the ceaseless task of translating news from Swedish newspapers, and acted as referees between quarrelling contributors whose quarrels could possibly end in libel suits against the newspaper itself.

The most daunting challenge faced by every editor, however, was an acute lack of subscribers. In its most successful years, 1844 and 1845, the national newspaper *Maamiehen Ystäwä* had only 900–1000 annual subscriptions (Tommila 1988: 159). The regional newspaper *Tapio: Sanomia Sawosta ja Karjalasta*, to which the common folk in the Eastern Finnish countryside regularly wrote, had only an annual circulation of between 489 and 743

---

53 At times, these laws were applied more strictly, for example in the 1820s and 1830s, at the end of the 1840s and beginning of the 1850s, and in the 1890s and first years of the 20th century. At other times, they were applied more loosely, such as at the end of the 1850s, and in the 1860s and 1870s (Leino-Kaukiainen 1988: 554–560; Nieminen 2006: 100).

subscribers for the period 1861 to 1866 (Pasanen 1996: 22). A writer signing himself 'Tuiretuinen' wrote to *Tapio* in 1876 that

> [– –] the material income of newspapers is often very low because they receive so few subscriptions from the common folk. The conscience of the folk should tell them to subscribe to newspapers, if not because of their desire to read, then in any case to sustain newspapers, since they are meant for, and defend, the common folk's best interests.[54]

Editors of early Finnish-language newspapers were aware that their newspapers would likely never turn a profit (Kinnunen 1982: 52–57). As the editors of the newspaper *Tapio* explained at the end of 1861, 'even *Tapio's* main editor has received no compensation, for the money coming in from subscriptions and advertisements have barely covered the costs of paper, printing, and other small expenses.'[55] According to editors' own explanations found in the first sample issues (*näytenumerot*) of their newspapers, no one started up a newspaper in the hope of financial gain, but rather out of ideological commitment to Finnish-language rights and social progress.

While subscriptions were the primary financial concern faced by editors, their most time-consuming task was surely the proofreading and rewriting of submissions sent by uneducated writers in order to make them suitable for publication. Although a relatively small number of rural correspondence letters and cover letters survive, all of which were addressed to *Suometar's* editor Paavo Tikkanen,[56] it is clear even from these letters what a formidable task faced those editors who wished to assist self-educated writers. In these letters, the handwriting is often barely legible, there is little or no use of punctuation, and writers had difficulties in stringing together sentences together in a logical manner. Cover letters which accompanied the submissions sent to newspaper editors reveal that some writers hoped that Tikkanen would correct and improve their writing, and afterward expressed their gratitude for his editorial work. The language used by these rural writers makes it clear that having their articles published in *Suometar* was of immense importance to them, and that they were highly aware of the difference in learning and social status between themselves and Tikkanen, who held a doctoral degree. This can be seen, for example, in the following letters from North Karelia and Satakunta:[57]

---

54 July 22, 1876. *Tapio* no. 30, 'Silmäys Suomen kansan nykyiseen siwistyksen kantaan ynnä sananen sanomalehtikirjallisuuden wiljelemisestä kansassa' (Tuiretuinen).

55 December 28, 1861. *Tapio* no. 52, 'Wuoden lopuksi'.

56 Cover letters addressed to Tikkanen, of which at least nineteen examples exist, were sent to him from throughout Finland and are housed in the FLS Literature Archives. My thanks go to Hanna Karhu for her original transcription of these letters from the Finnish Literature Society Literary Archives letter collections. I also thank Anna Kuismin for giving me permission for their use.

57 The originals of the cover letters presented in this chapter follow a wide variety of orthographic conventions. For this reason I have chosen not to reproduce the non-standard forms in my translation, presenting them in standard English and adding punctuation and formatting for ease of comprehension.

Most learned doctor of wisdom sir P. Tikkanen!
If you could see the least possibility of publishing this accompanying letter in Suometar without changing the meaning of what is written there. But nonetheless I humbly ask you to repair those mistakes which exist in my unschooled writing. This I ask with respect!
Tohmajärvi 11th of April. 1861. Serkses Syrjäläinen[58]

Highly Esteemed Editor of Suometar!!!
With the greatest humility I ask forgiveness that I once again dare to send you a sequel to *Ikaalisista ihan tosia*'. But because I have seen with great pleasure that You, in your benevolence, have not only accepted my article into your newspaper, but have revised my inferior words! And have modified them for the better; so now too, I hope that Sir Magister would wish, in his benevolence, to help my essay to be good enough. The letter *Meikko repaalle* is very badly written, but as you are such an outstanding man of science and wisdom, I hope that you will amend it as you see fit, naturally you may add whatever you like, it will not offend anyone's honour...
The most humble servant of the Highly Esteemed Sir Magister,
Temu Sinervo[59]
Parkano 11th day of July 1859[60]

In a letter written in 1860, Johan Multanen, a student at the Jouhkola Agricultural Institute in Tohmajärvi, wrote to Paavo Tikkanen in the hope that Tikkanen would correct whatever was 'wrong' with his submission, since he had 'just begun to be a man of writing'. In a second letter written less than two months later, Multanen expanded on this theme and explained that he knew of no one other than Tikkanen who could correct and improve his writing skills:

Highly esteemed editorial board of Suometar!
Now I can say a thousand thanks for accepting my travelogue, *Pohjan maalle tulostani*. This has sparked a desire in me to write more stories, if you would be so good and take the great effort to correct my writing. For I am just a beginner and I do not know how to turn to anyone other than the editors of newspapers, since here is no such man who could correct [my writing] for me. Now there is this commentary which forced me to do my duty to my Fatherland. This is not good enough, which I see for myself, but because my intellect is not sharpened, I can do nothing about it, and also my hand is unpractised [– –] There would be many things to write about if I could see that Suometar would accept this.
Suomussalmi 18 29/1 61
Humbly Johan Multanen.[61]

58 Finnish Literature Society Literary Archives Letter Collection 85, Serkses Syrjäläinen, April 11, 1861.
59 One 'T. Sinervuo' also sent submissions to the newspaper *Sanomia Turusta* in 1858 and 1859. In the latter case, his submission was rejected. (November 9, 1858. *Sanomia Turusta* no. 45, 'Kirjeenwaihetusta'; September 13, 1859. *Sanomia Turusta* no 37, 'Kirjeen waihetusta').
60 Finnish Literature Society Literary Archives Letter Collection 84, Temu Sinervo, July 7, 1859.
61 Finnish Literature Society Literary Archives Letter Collection 82, Johan Multanen January 29, 1861.

As previously mentioned, newspapers tended to receive more submissions from rural writers than they could possibly publish.[62] For instance, the newspaper *Sanomia Turusta* reported in 1866 that 'the editors have received letters from many quarters which they cannot reproduce for the public in full due to lack of newspaper space. As a general rule, it would be better if these submissions were shorter.'[63] *Tapio's* editors likewise explained to their readers at the end of 1861 that '[t]his year many worthy submissions have remained unprinted due to lack of space.'[64] Earlier in the same year, *Tapio's* editors had urged readers to be brief, writing that 'with pleasure and gratitude we accept such submissions as are relevant, and which are presented briefly and clearly. The columns of *Tapio* are so narrow that we would not like to fill them with writings elaborated at length, empty decorative language or songs'.[65] Antti Manninen, the sole editor of *Tapio* starting in summer of 1862, explained that letters sent to him on the topic of home thievery, for instance, 'did not seem to stop', and that *Tapio* still had many letters on the subject which it did not intend to publish, since in the editor's opinion they did not contain any new points which had not already appeared in print.[66]

Many newspapers published brief notices under the heading of *Kirjeenvaihto* (*Correspondence*) in which they announced the rejection or acceptance of submissions from rural writers. The need for such notices of acceptance and rejection can be seen from the following letter sent in 1862 to Paavo Tikkanen by Johan Turunen[67] from Tohmajärvi parish in North Karelia, in which Turunen enquires about the fate of his submissions:

> Most honourable editor of Suometar, Doctor P. Tikkanen!
> I hereby approach you with a humble question. I have sent a few letters to be published in Suometar. I have waited with longing for them to appear in the columns of Suometar, but in vain. I do not think that Doctor P. Tikkanen would have thrown them away, that he would have at least printed a few of their points – if they in fact reached you [– –][68]

There were a number of practical and substantive criteria upon which editors based their decision to publish written submissions, as can be seen from the 'Correspondence' notices presented below. Some submissions were rejected due to their subject matter, which was considered too provocative and likely to be censored, or whose ideological outlook differed significantly from that of the newspaper. Some were rejected because they were not considered to

62   See: December 28, 1861. *Otawa. Sanomia Wiipurista* no. 51, 'Kirje-waihtoa'.
63   February 2, 1866. *Sanomia Turusta* no. 5, 'Kirjevaihtoa'.
64   December 28, 1861. *Tapio* no. 52, 'Wuoden lopuksi'.
65   April 20, 1861. *Tapio* no. 16, 'Kirje-vaihtoa'.
66   December 13, 1862. *Tapio* no. 50, 'Kotowarkauden...'
67   The only entry in the HISKI genealogical database (hiski.genealogia.fi/hiski?fi) for a Johan Turunen in Riikola village in Tohmajärvi is a farmhand who married in 1878.
68   Finnish Literature Society Literary Archives Letter Collection 86, Johan Turunen, April 6, 1862.

be of interest to the general public, while others were rejected because the editors suspected that the claims made within them were untrue. Finally, some submissions were apparently so incoherent that the editors did not even attempt to edit or correct them:

[*Tapio* 1861:] To J. Tietäväinen in Heinävesi. The poem you sent, 'Election lament hymn (*Vaalista valitus-virsi)*' is not suitable for *Tapio* due to its subject matter and its manner of address. The poetic meter, on the other hand, was somehow clear and flowing, so that we urge you not to give up practicing your poetic gift on some more innocent topic.

To O. Soininen. The story you sent about a couple of robberies was so incoherent that it contains nothing that is worthy of an audience.

To Tamminen. The writing you submitted to *Tapio*, although perhaps based in truth, is nevertheless part of such an old quarrel that few any longer remember it. For this reason it has not been printed in *Tapio*.[69]

[*Helsingin Uutiset* 1863:] To M—n! We cannot print your submission in our newspaper except to express its main point, because it is so densely shrouded in metaphor that it may be difficult to make any sense of it[– –].[70]

[*Päivätär* 1865:] To S. K. in Pielisjärvi! Your letter will be published in the next issue.

To D. M! Both of the letters you sent are of the sort that they cannot be published unless they are completely rewritten; but this would hardly be worth the trouble. What is more, what you said in defence of the poor being forced to work for others, and your opposition to the empowerment of the people and of women, do not suit the purpose of our newspaper.

To I. H. in Kihitelysvaara! We do not understand the content of your submission at all, and presumably nobody else would have understood it either.

To i— —nen in K:lahti! It is certainly allowed to write poems regarding lewdness and indecency, but one must in this, as in other things, use a decent manner of expression[– –].[71]

[*Keski-Suomi* 1871:] To J. L. in Alajärvi. Your letter of criticism about the forestry official (*metsän herra*) will not be printed. If the matter really is as you write, then send the editorial board a new explanation supported by two witnesses.[72]

[*Tampereen Sanomat* 1871:] Ero Eromäki from Teisko! We will no longer continue the quarrel concerning *boffelipaltto* [=a newfangled long padded coat]. – Gabriel Järvinen from Teisko! Nothing about *boffelipaltto*, because even without them your girls appear, as you yourself said, 'big, beautiful and plump' [– –]. A. Padenki from Virrat! Your writing could perhaps be the doom of both you and us. – A. H. H–suo Kurusta! Your writing contains nothing worthy of publicity,

69 May 11, 1861. *Tapio* no. 19, 'Kirjevaihtoa'.
70 May 4, 1863. *Helsingin Uutiset* no. 35, 'Kirjewaihto'.
71 May 6, 1865. *Päivätär* no. 17, 'Kirjewaihto'.
72 February 4, 1871. *Keski-Suomi* no. 5, 'Kirjeenvaihtoa'.

especially since all of the accidents are by now old news. – h–niemi from Teisko and A. H–lla from Kuru! Your writings are worthless. My dear fellows, please pen more relevant thoughts rather than always informing on others and quarrelling, and we will gratefully accept them to the newspaper. – K. P. from Lempäälä, M. M. R. and v–an Ruovesi, your pieces will be printed in the next issue. Others will be printed depending on available space and content.[73]

[*Sanomia Turusta* 1874:] To the sender of '*Ei hän Petteri olisikaan*'! Your piece will not be published unless, informing us of your name, your social estate, and your address, you swear that you have written the piece and that its contents are based on your own knowledge.[74]

[*Oulun Wiikko-Sanomia* 1877:] Lurjus. Yes, soon! – Leikkinen in Tornio. Did not fit this time. – Kiwinen from Puhdasjärvi. Thank you! As soon as space allows [– –]. We ask many other worthy contributors to just wait a little, and we will print [their contributions] as soon as they fit. Names will of course be kept secret.[75]

As can be seen from these notices addressed to contributors, although many decisions to accept or reject written submissions were made on practical grounds, ideological commitments played a role as well. Editors of 19th-century Finnish-language newspapers were firm on two points: those who wanted their views published in the Finnish-language press had to embrace a firm belief in progress, and they had to be committed to a desire to see the Finnish language receive equal rights and official recognition alongside the Swedish language. A political conservative or 'old timer' (*vanhalla olija*) was one of the worst things that someone could be called in the Fennoman press. Equally important appears to have been an insistence on adherence to Christian values as well as an emphasis on moral redemption. Readers were supposed to be able to discern from what they read in the press either signposts to a better life, or warning messages of what should be avoided. In other words, submissions needed to be edifying, enlightening, or uplifting in some culturally recognized fashion. A lesson of moral redemption seems to have been what was missing in one article written by 'X' which was rejected by the newspaper *Otawa* in 1862. The newspaper's editors provided an unusually lengthy explanation for the reasons behind their decision, possibly to educate other would-be writers regarding *Otawa's* own position on such matters:

[*Otawa* 1862:] To X: Your article about 'Siberia's prisoners' does not deserve to be published. In it, one must read at quite some length such brazen arrogance and hard heartedness toward those unfortunate fallen wretches who in Siberia enjoy the wages of their evil deeds, that it would only amaze every thoughtful and conscientious reader, without shedding any more light on the matter except for what each person already knows and should know – that criminals must be punished. In X's opinion,

---

73 May 15, 1871. *Tampereen Sanomat* no. 20, 'Kirjeenwaihtoa'.
74 August 21, 1874. *Sanomia Turusta* no. 34, 'Kirjeenwaihtoa'.
75 December 15, 1877. *Oulun Wiikko-Sanomia* no. 50, 'Kirjeenwaihtoa'.

those sent to Siberia are so deserving of torment that they should not be allowed the privilege and right even to hear the call to repentance nor the proclamation of God's mercy. The sender appears to be a man who little considers or deliberates before casting his stone upon the heap.[76]

The insistence on a belief in progress which permeated the Finnish-language public sphere in the last half of the 19th century was not merely a commitment to the notion that things naturally evolve toward a more refined and higher state. Instead, it was above all an affirmation that individuals and societies could and should improve themselves both morally and materially. Newspapers gave rise to a field of discourse which pondered a new kind of ideal society, set within the conceptual framework of nationalism, the new paradigm for political and social relations which had arisen at the end of the previous century (see Anderson 1983). The ideological commitment to progress propagated by the press focused on concrete improvements to be striven for such as agricultural productivity and efficiency, rational precautions taken against the sources of social and economic disorder (improved agricultural practices, insurance, fire-fighting brigades), the elimination of unnecessary suffering, the eradication of censorship, the addressing of various social injustices, education and moral refinement for the masses, and the avoidance of social evils such as alcoholism, laziness and lack of hygiene.

Local power struggles and anonymity

Editors also announced in their 'Correspondence' notices that writers were required to give the editors their full names, even if they used initials or aliases in print,[77] as editor Antti Manninen explained to the readers of *Tapio* in 1863:[78]

> Correspondence
> To all who sent contributions to us we would remind you jointly to announce to the editors your real name and place of residence, if you wish your submission to be accepted to Tapio. There already stands a pile of submissions which have not been accepted for this reason. – If the writer so wishes it, the writer's name will not be published until the courts force us to. But the editorial board must know whose letter they are putting in the newspaper.
> Tapio

76 May 16, 1862. *Otawa* no. 19, 'Kirje-waihtoa'. The reference to 'casting his stone upon the heap' is probably an allusion to the story of Jesus and the woman taken in adultery whom the Pharisees wanted to stone to death (see John 8:1–8:11).
77 See: September 5, 1862. *Otawa* no. 35, 'Kirje-waihtoa'; June 6, 1863. *Tapio* no. 23, 'Kirjevaihtoa'; October 3, 1866. *Pohjan-tähti* no. 10, 'Kirjevaihtoa'.
78 June 6, 1863. *Tapio* no. 23, 'Kirjevaihtoa'. See also: September 5, 1862. *Otawa* no. 35, 'Kirje-waihtoa'.

The reason for this request was that editors were continually concerned over the possibility of libel charges aimed at the newspaper. Newspapers were even taken to court for this reason.[79] Many writers were probably already aware of the necessity of providing their real names and the reason behind it, as exemplified in the following cover letter from Tuomas Taittonen,[80] sent from South Ostrobothnia to Paavo Tikkanen in 1863, one month before Manninen asked writers to *Tapio* to supply their real names:

> Editors of Suometar!
> I ask that a place can be found in *Suometar* for the accompanying commentary. The story of the miserable pharmacy deserves even a harsher letter. But I did not wish to insult anyone, I only described the matter as it really is. And then I ask that my name could be kept secret if possible; but if it needs to be made public, then naturally I stand behind every word and I will demonstrate that the pharmacy is as bad as I have said.
> Perho, May 1st, 1863.
> Tuomas Taittonen
> From Vähäkyrö parish, but nowadays working as a cashier for the Crown in Perho.[81]

Taittonen's reference to allegations against a local pharmacy in this cover letter points to one of the primary motivations for rural writers to submit letters to the press throughout the last half of the 19th century: in order to complain about or criticize the activities of others in their local district. A surprisingly large amount of rural correspondence to newspapers in the last half of the century contains indictments, insinuations and lists of grievances against other persons in the same district, as well as objections, rebuttals and outright accusations of slander and falsehood against the original writer of the complaint. Although rural writers generally wrote about those topics they knew best, in other words those directly connected to their own rural experience, this experience nevertheless covered a wide range of social issues with which a writer could find fault, such as farmers' distillation of alcohol, the conduct of rural clerks and officials, the moral behaviour of the youth, the finances of the parish and its clergy, the wages of servants and labourers, the situation of tenant farmers, poverty and poor relief, debates over founding a public school in the district, religious revivalism and itinerant preachers, excessive consumption of store-bought goods, and so forth. It is clear from published letters and rejection notices that rural writers routinely sought to bring their own local political struggles out of the village and into the public limelight of the press. Due to the power

---

79 E.g. April 12, 1879. *Kaiku* no. 15, 'Se painojuttu…'.
80 Tuomas Taittonen (1817–1915) was born in Vähänkyrö parish as the son of a farmer, and during his lifetime worked as a farmhand, tailor, bridge bailiff (*siltavouti*), and as the foreman and cashier of bog-draining operations in Perho parish, among other jobs. Self-educated, he was a co-founder of one of the first parish lending libraries in Finland in 1851. See: http://www.vahakyro.fi/Link.aspx?id=496419.
81 Finnish Literature Society Literary Archives Letter Collection 85, Tuomas Taittonen, May 1, 1863.

hierarchies existing in the countryside, however, rural commoners sometimes ran great risks in publishing their opinions, particularly those regarding the local elite and their activities. For instance in 1861 the aforementioned 'Serkses Syrjäläinen' from Tohmajärvi wrote to Tikkanen explaining that because of the stir created by his last letter of correspondence,[82] he had been 'subjected to the terrible fury of those who hold my entire worldly happiness in their hands' and had been forced by these more powerful individuals to write a public apology or retraction, which he hoped would be printed in *Suometar*.[83]

In another example, crofter's son Kalle Eskola (1865–1938) wrote in his autobiographical diary that when he was seventeen years old and his letters of rural correspondence were published in newspapers in the early 1880s, the articles came to the attention of the local manor lord who owned Eskola's father's croft. According to Eskola's account, 'in a violent temper, squeezing his walking stick,' the manor lord asked Eskola: 'What business of yours are our affairs? When I travel there in the city, everyone asks me: what is going on in [your] district? From now on you are not allowed to write, and if you do write, your parents will have to leave the croft'. Ignoring Eskola's protests, the manor lord turned to Eskola's father and added: 'If I see one more of that rascal's letters printed then you will leave the croft! The boy, for his part, needs a whipping.' Then to Eskola: 'Go and work for a newspaper, there you can fill the columns with your writing, as long as you don't talk about the conditions in [this district]'.[84]

According to Ilkka Mäkinen (2007: 412–413), when writers from the lowest levels of society began to send their writings to national and local newspapers, they did more than just broaden the scope of public discussion, they made the activities of the local elites subject to a new kind of surveillance, which the elites did not necessarily welcome. Previously,

> both the Swedish language and the ability to write had been [– –] the secure 'firewall' of the gentry, within which they could speak and communicate freely [– –]. But now there began to be eyes and ears in the countryside which brought to public attention those things which had previously remained secure within a small circle (Mäkinen 2007: 412).

82 'Serkses Syrjäläinen' had insinuated that 26-year-old farmer's daughter Liisa Väänänen, who had been chosen by the board of the Jouhkola Agricultural Institute to be the new instructor in cattle husbandry, was less than honorable (April 26, 1861. Suometar no. 17, 'Tohmajärveltä'. –Serkses Syrjäläinen, rahtimiehen poika). By that time, Väänänen had been a student at the Agricultural Institute for three years. Her honor and suitability for the job were defended by another rural correspondent signing himself 'Oskari Jolkkonen, son of a poor man', who accused 'Serkses Syrjäläinen' of perpetrating gossip out of envy for Väänänen's good fortune in receiving the position (May 17, 1861. Suometar no. 20, 'Tohmajärveltä'). It is not known who might have pressured Syrjäläinen into writing a retraction to be published in *Suometar*.

83 Finnish Literature Society Literary Archives Letter Collection 85, Serkses Syrjäläinen, (letter received May 23, 1861).

84 Eskola, Kalle. (written 1888–1919) *Elämän muistelmia*. Transcribed in 1999 by Raili Parviainen, AB 3661. Archive of Kalle Eskola. Finnish Literature Society Literary Archives.

It was not only the local gentry and officials who experienced the new publicity as a threat, but rural commoners as well. Farmers and other parish residents tended to resent the fact that someone from their parish might give the parish a bad reputation. Editors frequently lamented the fact that readers of newspapers were too sensitive toward the comments of others and did not understand the purpose and nature of publicity. As Paavo Tikkanen pointed out in 1860,[85]

> In our country we are not yet used to publicity when some matter concerning ourselves is made public, even if we chuckle when we read about the affairs of our neighbours. Many are wary of the most trifling matter being made public, even if they in no way hurt either by the matter itself or the telling of it.

The furore caused by letters to the press which exposed various defects in local communities meant that nearly *all* writers left their names unsigned or used only initials or pseudonyms throughout the last half of the 19th century. Writers nearly always chose to use aliases, and there is no guarantee that they used the same alias with any regularity. One writer to the newspaper *Wuoksi*, writing in 1899, described the perspective of rural correspondents on this issue as follows:

> If every newspaper correspondent [– –] would make it a habit to sign his name at the end of what he writes, then I would be happy to do so too. But now we rarely see anyone doing this in newspapers. Writers, you see, don't even write their initials at the end of what they write, much less their whole name. And so too this writer– (I confess it openly) –, who every year scribbles dozens of submissions for newspaper columns, has rarely put even his initials for the public to see, but rather uses many different aliases which vary. – What then is the reason for this sort of mystifying secrecy? The greatest reason is the newspaper reading public, which is still unfamiliar with publicity and public critique. If they see a letter in a newspaper, which in addition to describing the positive aspects of a thing also openly and remorselessly describes its darker side, many readers are furious over the latter and, without pondering further the contents of the letter or whether it contains any truth or not, they ask: who wrote it? And when they find out, then the unhappy writer, poor man, has to face the music [– –] if [the writer] is honest and working toward progress within his home district, and sees around him things which still need improving, then he mentions the negative aspects of the local area in his newspaper writings. He writes of how, in the backwoods villages of his district, brutishness, drunkenness, and ignorance still hold sway rather than progress [– –]. Of course many might guess that there might be something to the writer's blackest descriptions, but then he should not have announced it publicly to the whole world. It is that which is the unforgivable affront, of which the writer cannot be forgiven…[86]

---

85   September 21, 1860. *Suometar* no. 37, 'Kirjeitä Jukka Lintuselle. IX' (Tiitus Tuiretuinen).
86   August 12, 1899. *Wuoksi* no. 91, 'Kuka kirjoitti?' (M. P.). Parentheses in original.

Despite their exhortations that readers take publicity less personally, the fact that editors published the endless outpouring of quarrelsome letters written by rural writers suggests that these letters, which often remain opaque and baffling to the modern reader, must have been thought to be of interest the reading public. Readers, for their part, must have been impressed at least by the novelty of Finnish-speaking commoners being able to argue their points in a much broader forum than that offered by a court room or a parish meeting.

Who were rural writers and what were their motives?

The vast majority of rural correspondents in the 1850s and 1860s identified by the Finnish Newspaper History Research Project (1975–1988) led by Päiviö Tommila[87] were either members of the gentry or landowning farmers (Tommila: 1988: 202). The writings of landless men such as crofters, cottagers, farmhands, labourers and skilled artisans[88] were published to a much lesser extent, and it was not until the newspaper *Työmiehen Ystäwä* (Labourer's Friend) was founded in 1874 that the writings of landless labourers began to appear regularly in print.

Social theorist Jürgen Habermas has defined the public sphere as open to all private persons who could deliberate *as socially and economically autonomous peers*. Men who, due to their wealth or office, were not directly dependent on others were viewed as capable of deliberating rationally and being concerned for the public good. Those who were under the legal authority of others, such as wives and underage children, or those who had to sell their labour to the highest bidder (servants and labourers), were seen to have less capacity to deliberate objectively, because their livelihood was directly dependent upon someone else (Habermas 1991: 109–110). The right to participate in the public sphere as an autonomous person came down to a question of ownership: those who owned the source of their wealth were more trusted than propertyless persons, whose source of livelihood, in other words their labour, was owned by someone else. This view seems to have tacitly prevailed in the early Finnish-language press as well. It is worth remembering that the Finnish-language press gained strength in the early 1860s as a direct result of the possibility of self-representation through the Finnish Diet, and that throughout the 19th century the question of who had the right to vote for delegates to the Diet was linked to the issue of autonomy. Landless labourers, servants and women were all denied the vote until 1906, but so were a great many men who did not fall into any of these categories. The topic of how much wealth a man needed before he could be said to have 'an economically independent status in society', so that he could 'comprehend what was best for the fatherland and autonomously use

---

87 The Finnish Newspaper History Research Project (SSLH), led by Päiviö Tommila, ran from 1975 to 1988. Its archival materials are housed in the University of Helsinki Central Archives.

88 Included in this group were local blacksmiths, carpenters, masons, tailors and cobblers.

this understanding in selecting representatives to the Diet'[89] became a topic of increasing debate toward the end of the century.

Despite the clear weight given in the press to the opinions of men from the four Estates (aristocracy, clergy, burghers and landowning peasantry), it should be noted that in the five-year period from 1860 to 1864, the weekly newspaper *Sanomia Turusta* printed letters from eighteen men who had no Estate, who identified themselves as crofters (six),[90] itinerant labourers (five),[91] industrial labourers (two),[92] skilled artisans (three),[93] cottager (one)[94] and timber worker (one).[95] *Suometar*, by contrast, was less active in publishing the submissions of lower-class men. In the eleven-year period between 1854 and 1864, *Suometar* ran only six letters from men identifying themselves as labourers (two),[96] crofters (two),[97] tailor (one)[98] and cobbler (one).[99] Landless men often wrote on topics which were similar to those written by landowning farmers, but their letters also drew attention to the plight of the rural poor.

In the period under study, rural women's contributions were likewise seldom seen in newspapers. For the period 1856 – 1866, I have found only

89 May 30, 1885. *Waasan Lehti* no. 43, 'Waltiollisesta waalioikeudesta porwarissäädyssä'.

90 The numbers given in this paragraph are based on the card indexes for rural correspondents produced by the Finnish Newspaper History Research Project (SSLH). See: March 18, 1864. *Sanomia Turusta* no. 11, 'Hirwenluodosta [Maarian pitäjä]' (Torpan mies); April 17, 1862. *Sanomia Turusta* no. 16, 'Messukylästä' (Mikko Mikonpoika Haaranen, Torppari); August 17, 1860. *Sanomia Turusta* no. 33, 'Kankaanpäästä' (Torppari totuuden puhuu); May 18, 1860. *Sanomia Turusta* no. 20, 'Kiikan kappelista' (Totuuden ilmoittaja, töllin setämies J. H–n); December 14, 1860. *Sanomia Turusta* no. 50, 'Punkalaitumelta' (Jaakko Yrjönpoika Lähteenmäki, torppari); September 21, 1860. *Sanomia Turusta* no. 38, 'Loimaalta' (Jaakko Perämäki, tolppari).

91 January 2, 1863. *Sanomia Turusta* no. 1, 'Eurasta' (Matti Matinpoika ittelis-mies); November 27, 1863. *Sanomia Turusta* no. 48, 'Eurasta' (Juho Juhonpoika Saarenmaa, köyhä ittelismies Turajärwen kylässä); December 5, 1862. *Sanomia Turusta* no. 50, 'Kirje Juho Jäykkäselle' (Juho Matinpoika, itellinen); March 18, 1864. *Sanomia Turusta* no. 11, 'Nakkilasta' (Pekka Oltawainen, ittellinen); July 15, 1864. *Sanomia Turusta* no. 28, 'Hinnerjoelta' (Iloinen ittellis-äijä).

92 September 19, 1862. *Sanomia Turusta* no. 38, 'Loimaalta' (Köyhä työmies Juha Helini); November 14, 1862. *Sanomia Turusta* no. 46, 'Loimaalta' (H. E., Rautatien työmies).

93 May 13, 1864. *Sanomia Turusta* no. 19, 'Kankaanpäästä' (Frans Wahlman, Färjäri); May 27, 1864. *Sanomia Turusta* no. 21, 'Kokemäeltä' (Henrik Hentolin, pitäjän nikkari); September 16, 1864. *Sanomia Turusta* no. 37, 'Wieläkin sananen BB:llä merkitystä raudasta' (Loimaan pitäjästä Korwen kylästä seppä Juha Heliin).

94 October 2, 1863. *Sanomia Turusta* no. 40, 'Kuortaneelta' (Juha Simunanpoika Kokkila, mäkitupalainen).

95 October 21, 1864. *Sanomia Turusta* no. 42, 'Pirkkala' (Längelmäen Antti Terässaksinen [lumberjack]).

96 November 3, 1854. *Suometar* no. 44, 'Korpilahdelta' (Työmies); May 25, 1855. *Suometar* no. 21, 'Saimaan Kanawalta' (Kanawan työmies); February 4, 1859. *Suometar* no. 5, 'Uuden vuoden kirjeitä isännälle II' (–f–n K......n [self-identifies as a farmhand in his letter]).

97 October 18, 1861. *Suometar* no. 42, 'Korpilahdelta'. (Torppari A–n); October 15, 1858. *Suometar* no. 41, 'Luhangosta'(J.L [=Johan Lehtimäki, torppari]).

98 August 8, 1862. *Suometar* no. 31, 'Saarijärveltä' (H. H. käsityölainen [=Henrik Hillberg, tailor]).

99 February 10, 1854. *Suometar* no. 6, 'Petäjävesi' (K. S. [=shoemaker Kasper Sarlund Laaksonen?]).

30 letters sent to newspapers by rural women which were printed in six different newspapers.[100] Although it is impossible to determine the social estate of these writers on the basis of their names and pseudonyms alone, the content of their letters suggest that more than half were written by farm daughters. Two things are striking about these letters. Nearly half of them (thirteen) were printed in just one newspaper: *Tapio*. Second, nearly all seem to have been written by young, unmarried women.[101] Married women under the legal guardianship of their husbands were among the legally most dependent class of inhabitants in the countryside. The oppressed state of married women as opposed to widows and unmarried women of legal majority was repeatedly lamented in the late 19th century by male writers to the press [e.g. 56]. What is suggested by the age and marital status of female writers to the early Finnish-language press is that the period of early adulthood, just before a woman generally married at age 20–25, was seen as a time of relative independence in which young women, perhaps because they were soon to become wards of their husbands, could speak their minds in the press without their views immediately reflecting upon the honour and reputations of their fathers and elder brothers.

Nevertheless, in comparison to the abundance of letters written to the press by male landowning farmers, 30 letters written by rural female writers is an extremely small number. Whether this was due to the fact that rural women were being actively excluded from the press, or whether rural women simply sent fewer letters to the press than did male farmers, is not possible to know for certain. One rural correspondent from North Karelia writing to *Tapio* in 1861 speculated on the situation by saying, 'We, too, have waited that some skilful maiden from hereabouts would have undertaken to

---

100 See, for example: June 25, 1858. *Suometar* no. 25, 'Taitaako sokia sokiata taluttaa?' (Miina, nuori tyttö); September 21,1860. *Suometar* no. 37, 'Nöyrä pyyntö' (Miehelään menewä Suomen tyttö); June 19, 1861. *Suometar* no. 16, 'Karjalohjalta' (–a–l, Karjalohjan tyttö); October 18,1861. *Suometar* no. 42, 'Joen kaupungista' (Piika Miina); October 18, 1861. *Suometar* no. 42, 'Kiihtelysvaaran...' (Anna Liisa P–n); August 22, 1862. *Otawa* no. 33, 'Saarijärveltä' (Anna Liisa Laasanen); October 5, 1863. *Suomen Julkisia Sanomia* no. 76, 'Iisalmesta' (U.R., farmer's daughter from Iisalmi); September 15, 1864. *Suometar* no. 214, 'Sippolassa' (Anna Maria Kaukanen); October 21 & November 25, 1864. *Sanomia Turusta* nos. 42 & 47, 'Ulwilasta' (Wieras waimo Ulwilasta). See also: December 1, 1866. *Tapio* no. 48, 'Ilomantsi' (M. M. rokonpanijatar).
Not only female commoners but female writers to the press from any social estate were extremely rare until the 1890s. In 1883, celebrated playwright Minna Canth publicized that she would soon edit a 'women's newspaper' in Finnish, but for reasons unknown, this newspaper never materialized (June 29, 1883. *Suomalainen Wirallinen Lehti* no. 148, 'Naisten lehti').

101 The only clear exceptions are three farm wives, two of which wrote in response to a young woman who asked the readers of Tapio advice on which suitor to choose: the poor man she herself loved, or the rich man her parents and relatives wanted her to marry? Both farm wives advised her to marry for love instead of money. Given *Tapio*'s ideological stance on individual freedoms, it would have been surprising if the newspaper had allowed any other answer to be printed (November 22, 1862. *Tapio* no. 47, 'Nöyrin kysymys köyhästä ja rikkaasta kosio-miehestä' (Anna Maria Kaukanen, nuori tyttö); November 29, 1862. *Tapio* no. 48, 'Anna Maria Kaukaselle' (Kaisa Kilpeläinen [described herself as a middle-aged farm mistress]); December 27, 1862. *Tapio* no. 52, 'Sananen wastuuta Anna Maria Kaukaselle' (Liena Kaisa Hukka, vanha vaimo).

publicize her thoughts, for many already know how to write to the extent that they could write an essay. But no such writing has appeared. Might the reason be shyness or some other weakness, that we cannot say.'[102] Some newspaper editors' comments suggest that they would have welcomed more letters from rural women. For instance, a letter written in 1856 by 'Tuntematon neito Pohjanmaalla' (Unknown maiden from Ostrobothnia), who may have been the first woman from the countryside to have written to the Finnish-language press, was received by *Suometar* with the following chivalrous words of encouragement:

> We thank you for your letter, beloved maiden! Our hearts were greatly gladdened when we saw that you are able to write so well. Certainly we will try so that 'each carries the burdens of the other and avoids quarrels', particularly if it means that in this way we may win your precious favour and that of your sex (*sääty*), but please yourselves remain virtuous, and you will receive good suitors.[103]

Sanomia Turusta was another newspaper whose editors were happy to receive a lengthy letter from a writer signing herself 'Girl from Eura parish' in 1860. They introduced her letter by saying,

> [e]ven though a response to 'Boy from Kokemäki parish' has already appeared in our newspaper, we are printing this one, too, because it is written by a girl, and girls do not always write to us.[104]

Although the letter written by 'Girl from Eura parish' was intended to refute accusations of drunkenness made by 'Boy from Kokemäki parish' against the men of her own parish, she also described in her letter how she eagerly waited for the weekly newspaper to arrive:

> Every weekend my curiosity is in a tight spot, for then – and not before then, we get newspapers [– –]. And as soon as the newspaper arrives, I am in a terrible hurry to read it; especially since I am devoted to domestic news [=rural correspondence letters]. So when issue no. 18 of *Sanomia Turusta* arrived, I soon got up from my weaving loom and took the newspaper in my hands and settled myself in a suitable place in order to read in peace. And soon the news from Kokemäki parish, with the signature 'Boy from Kokemäki parish', caught my eye [– –].[105]

---

102 June 15, 1861. *Tapio* no. 24, 'Tohmajärweltä' (O.F.B.)

103 March 20, 1856. *Suometar* no. 12, 'Kirjeitä kaikilta kaikille'. Although *Suometar's* comment here may appear patronizing, it was written within a romanticist discourse which seems to have been accepted – and strategically used – by both rural male and female writers alike. Although its editorial rhetoric implied a benevolent paternal authority on the part of the newspaper in accepting women into a forum normally reserved for landowning men, this rhetoric was also used by rural women as a means of accessing the dominant discourse, and thus can be seen as enabling female agency.

104 June 8, 1860. *Sanomia Turusta* no. 23, 'Wastinetta Kokemäen pojalle' (Euran tyttö).

105 June 8, 1860. *Sanomia Turusta* no. 23, 'Wastinetta Kokemäen pojalle' (Euran tyttö).

This letter suggests that even as early as 1860, some rural young women may have read newspapers regularly, but were motivated to write to newspapers only when they wished to defend their own honour or that of their home parish. Like their male counterparts, female writers, too, wrote angry rebuttals to letters previously printed in the press. For example, two young women who wrote to *Suometar* in October of 1858 and signed themselves 'Girls from Petäjävesi parish' wrote in response to vague comments made by the parish blacksmith, Otto Lindeen about unlawful marriage and a girl who had left the parish for this purpose.[106] The female writers apparently recognized in this letter accusations against themselves, and retorted that young women who travelled by the 'Suomi' steamboat to visit Helsinki had no such 'shameful' intentions. They made it clear that their primary motivation in writing to the press was to defend their own honour:[107]

> It disgusts us to speak of these matters, but only a drunkard would have the nerve to so shamelessly trample on women's feelings of tenderness, so that they must open their mouths on such a distasteful issue to defend themselves. Look, pitiful old man, to your own baseness, and do not cast mud upon innocents!

While the content of their letter (a trip by steamboat to Helsinki some 300 kilometres distant) suggests that these girls were daughters of the local gentry, a woman writing a few months later in December 1858 to *Sanomia Turusta* who signed herself 'Kaisa Isomäki' was probably a farmer's daughter. In her letter, she responded to a previous letter written by the parish tailor regarding general local issues and writes, '[l]ong have I waited that someone would respond to him, but because there does not seem to be among the menfolk anyone who is able to take up his pen, so must I use a few words to do it, even though I am a maiden.'[108]

Letters to the press written by women – far from being rejected or scorned – were often enthusiastically received by rural young men. When a female writer from Lapinlahti parish using the pseudonym 'M. L. M.' (and signing herself in a second letter as 'M–ria Lo–sa')[109] wrote to *Tapio* to complain of rural women's ignorance and their low level of enlightenment, but also of young men's unpleasant habits such as heavy smoking of tobacco,[110] a male writer using the penname 'Matti' responded to her as follows:[111]

---

106 August 6, 1858. *Suometar* no. 31, 'Petäjäwedeltä' (Otto Lindeen, pitäjänseppä).
107 October 15, 1858. *Suometar* no. 41, 'Petäjäweden tyttölöiltä'.
108 December 7, 1858. *Sanomia Turusta* no. 49, 'Karwiasta' (Kaisa Isomäki).
109 'M.L.M'/'M–ria Lo–sa', was probably Maria Lovisa Mariasdotter Jäppinen from Lapinlahti. The HISKI genealogical database shows that she was a farmer's daughter of unknown age who married farmer's son Tobias Tuovinen from Maaninga parish in October 1861, six months after writing her letters to *Tapio*.
110 February 16, 1861. *Tapio* no. 7, 'Lapinlahdelta Helmikuussa 1861' (M. L. M.).
111 March 9, 1861. *Tapio* no. 10, 'Sananen wastineeksi neitosen M. L. M:n lempiästi ihailtawille lauseille Lapinlahdelta' (Matti).

> Cherished maiden! To my great delight I was able, in the seventh issue of Tapio, to read with pounding heart the statement sent by the maiden of Lapinlahti, which was composed with the maiden's praiseworthy intellect and was sketched most skilfully with her delicate fingers. Oh it would be joy to be able to behold that maiden's handwriting in person; and what's more her form, which I assume to be like a rose, with her slender body![112]

When, however, 'Matti' wrote a second letter to 'M–ria Lo–sa' whose tone was judged by *Tapio's* editors to be too critical, the newspaper refused to print it, and announced the same decision to another writer using the masculine penname 'Yrjö':

> To Yrjö. Your letter to 'Olga Maria' was not printed in Tapio. It is not worthwhile to begin to attack young ladies' first efforts, even if they be feeble, rather let us instead encourage them to experiment and so gradually prosper. Tapio gives the same reminder to Matti, whose letter to Maria Lo-sa was likewise not printed in Tapio.[113]

Tapio's encouragement of female writers

Tapio's defence of rural women writers in the above quote was not a unique case. In its first three years (1861–1863), *Tapio* printed at least thirteen letters written by women,[114] and in some cases the editors added their own words of support to shield female writers from potential criticism. A concern with female rural readers and writers seems to have been part of *Tapio's* official policy from the beginning. A young woman writing to *Suometar* in October 1861, whom the editors introduced as 'Anna Liisa P–n', told that when *Tapio's* first sample issue came out, it had promised that in future, the newspaper would offer advice to young women.[115] She wrote that for this reason, she had persuaded her father to subscribe to *Tapio*, and had enjoyed reading the letters in *Tapio* written by other young women. Three months earlier, *Tapio's* rural correspondent from Hämeenlinna, who signed himself

---

112 For 'M–ria Lo–sa's reply to 'Matti', see April 20, 1861. *Tapio* no. 16. 'Kunnioitettu Matti!!' (M–ria Lo–sa).

113 June 29, 1861. *Tapio* no. 26, 'Kirje-vaihtoa'.

114 These include seven personal letters published in *Tapio* in which women wrote to other women (such letters were also written by men to other men). These letters, ostensibly addressed to relatives and friends, gave advice and expressed opinions on various issues which *Tapio's* editors apparently assumed would be of general interest. Who exactly wrote these letters and how *Tapio's* editorial board soliticited them is not known. See: March 30, 1861. *Tapio* no. 13, 'Anna Marian kirje Ingalle' (waka Ystäwäsi Anna Maria); April 13, 1861. *Tapio* no. 15, 'Anna Marialle'. (Luja Ystäwäsi Inka); May 4, 1861. *Tapio* no. 18, 'Anna Marialle' (Ystäwäsi Tapiolan Munni); May 11, 1861. *Tapio* no. 19,'Hyvää päiwää sulho-pojat!' (Olga Maria Toiwotar, Ilolahden neito); June 22, 1861. *Tapio* no. 25, 'Kirje Heta Sohwialle Karttulassa' (Miina).

115 October 18, 1861. *Suometar* no. 42, 'Kiihtelysvaaran...' (Anna Liisa P–n). *Tapio's* sample issue of which 'Anna Liisa P–n' writes, no. 0 of 1861, does not exist in the Historical Newspaper Library's electronic database. Its print run may have been so small that there are no longer any extant copies of it.

'–n', had written of his approval of *Tapio's* attitude toward rural female contributors:

> Tapio has especially succeeded in receiving the favour of the young ladies, and appears to also champion them with real old-fashioned, noble-minded chivalry. It is indeed not the least of Tapio's merits that it encourages Finnish maidens towards literary endeavours, for this will arouse in them a desire to seek out knowledge and practical skills.[116]

Another rural correspondent writing from North Karelia a month earlier had noticed the same trend in *Tapio's* pages:

> Tapio seems to have found particular affection and favour in the smiles of young maidens. It is in fact quite enjoyable to see how maidens in some parts of our Finland begin to make public their inner feelings. And indeed, maidens seem to have an inner compulsion to practice virtue and refinement and live respectably. For this reason, it is not too much for young men to bear if young women reproach them a bit them for their stupidity.[117]

It is difficult to know why, among all the Finnish-language newspapers of the period, *Tapio* was the one to have attracted and encouraged the highest number of female writers. However, a key figure appears to have been its editor, Antti Manninen (1831–1866). In 1861, *Tapio* was founded by a five-man committee consisting of Manninen, notary Karl Mårten Kiljander, Erik Rudbeck (pen name Eero Salmelainen), city physician Anders Edvin Nylander, and provost Anders Gustaf Westerlund. When the committee members went their separate ways in the summer of 1862, Manninen was left to edit the paper by himself, with the assistance of printing house foreman Fredrik Ahlqvist (1829–1876), who had served as editor of *Maamiehen Ystäwä* for two years in the 1850s. In 1863, Manninen and Ahlqvist entered into a partnership to purchase the Kuopio printing press.[118]

Antti Manninen was the self-taught son of a farmer, born in the rural municipality of Mikkeli. Because his family farm was also a roadside inn, Manninen's self-education began as a youth when he worked as a horse-cart driver for the educated visitors who stopped at his childhood home. When he was young, he read every book he could find, and even learned some Swedish from the parish vicar. At age 23, in 1854, Manninen drafted a petition to the Tsar which was signed by twenty landowning farmers from surrounding parishes in Savo. The petition requested that the Finnish language be given the same rights and official status as Swedish in areas of Finland where only Finnish-speakers lived, and that within a predetermined period of time, it would become the language of higher educational institutions within Finland (Nurmio 1940). Governor-general Rokassovski

---

116 July 20, 1861. *Tapio* no. 29, 'Hämeenlinnasta 6 p:a heinäkuuta' (–n).
117 June 15, 1861. *Tapio* no. 24, 'Tohmajärveltä' (O. F. B).
118 Landgren 1988: 318; Kinnunen 1982: 48, 65.

felt that Manninen's petition had merit and sent it on to his superiors, but there is no evidence that it ever reached the Tsar. Historian Yrjö Nurmio, however, speculates that because Manninen's petition provided evidence of the difficulties faced by Finnish-speakers in the country, it may have served as a catalyst for the repeal of the censorship laws which, following the European revolutions of 1848, had been instituted to prevent the publishing of any literature in the Finnish-language except on topics related to religion or economics.

One year later at age 24, Manninen began to write rural news and small articles to *Suometar*, and its editor Paavo Tikkanen advised Manninen to open a bookshop in his parish. This gave Manninen an opportunity to read most of the books that he later sold to his customers (Laiho 1936). At this point, Manninen was already well versed in the history of the Finnish press, as can be seen from his lengthy article 'A Retrospective on Finnish Newspapers' whose instalments ran in four different issues of *Sanan-Lennätin* in 1856.[119] In his retrospective, Manninen surveyed all of the Finnish newspapers appearing after 1775 and assessed their value to the development of Finnish language and culture.

Manninen was the author of the first book in Finnish to be written by an uneducated member of the peasant estate, *Taito and toimi* (1856), a fact which received attention in the press.[120] Only after this did he briefly study agricultural related subjects at the Ultuna Agricultural Institute in Sweden,[121] the Mustiala Agricultural Institute in Finland and the University of Helsinki, and he eventually wrote at least six more books on practical agricultural improvements. In the winter of 1856–7, one of the first Finnish-language agricultural institutes in Finland was ready to be founded in Tohmajärvi, on land belonging to Jouhkola manor. Finding teachers for the Institute proved difficult, however, since few Finnish-speakers possessed up-to-date knowledge of new agricultural methods and ideas. In Helsinki, Manninen happened to meet Senator S.H. Antell, who had heard of Manninen's abilities and appointed him to be teacher and director at the Institute starting in October of 1857.[122]

In 1858, presumably inspired by what he saw at the Jouhkola Agricultural Institute, Manninen argued in a lengthy essay entitled 'Kansan Siwistämisestä (On Educating the Common Folk)' that farm women, too, should be sent to school and taught writing, arithmetic, Finnish history, and geography, as well as more practical skills such as cattle husbandry, cooking, and textile production. Manninen argued that special schools should be set up in each parish for this purpose.[123] In 1860, Manninen was offered the

---

119 January 26, February 2, February 9, February 16, 1856. *Sanan-Lennätin* nos. 4, 5, 6 and 7, 'Silmäys suomalaisista sanomalehdistä w. 1855' (A. M–n.). In 1858, Manninen's retrospective was updated and reprinted in five different issues of *Suometar*: May 21, June 4, July 9, July 16, and July 23, 1858. *Suometar* nos. 20, 22, 27, 28, 29. 'Muistelmia Suomalaisista sanomalehdistä' (A. M–n.).

120 See April 19, 1856. *Sanan-Lennätin* no. 16, 'Taito ja toimi'.

121 October 15, 1875. *Suomen Kuvalehti* no. 68, 'Antti Manninen' (A. R–dr.).

122 February 5, 1858. *Suometar* no. 5, 'Jouhkolan Maawiljelyskoulusta IV'.

123 September 3, 1858. *Suometar* no. 35, 'Kansan siwistämisestä' (A. M–n.).

A studio portrait of Antti Manninen taken by an unknown photographer in Kuopio sometime between 1860 and 1866. Courtesy of the Kuopio Museum of Cultural History.

position of director at another agricultural institute in Levänen, near the town of Kuopio, which was located nearer to his family home in Savo. Among his many teaching duties, Manninen personally taught biology, geography and the 'scientific fundamentals of cattle husbandry' to the four young women studying dairy farming at the Institute.[124] In 1861, Manninen was one of the founders of the Kuopio Agricultural Society (*Kuopion läänin maanviljelysseura*), and served as its secretary until his death (Laiho 1936: 124–127).

The 1861 meeting of the Society which was held at Jouhkola Agricultural Institute seems to have been the first regional public meeting held exclusively in the Finnish language.[125] Because historians have tended to focus on the 1870s and 1880s as the decades in which voluntary civil organizations (*kansalaisjärjestöt*) arose in the Finnish-speaking countryside, it has been easy to miss the important role played in the early 1860s by regional agricultural societies in creating a forum for civic participation. The first meeting of the Kuopio Agricultural Society was an important turning point, not just for discussions surrounding Finnish agriculture in Eastern Finland, but also in the national struggle for Finnish language rights. While

124 July 27, 1861. *Tapio* no. 30, 'Kertomus Lewäsen Maawiljelyskoulusta, Wuositutkintoon 6 p. heinäkuuta 1861'.
125 Oct. 5, 1861 *Tapio* no. 40, 'Jouhkolasta 25 p. syysk.' (-i–nen [Antti Manninen]).

meetings of other regional agricultural societies in Finland continued to be held mostly in Swedish, which frustrated Finnish-speaking farmers,[126] the Kuopio Agricultural Society's meeting in 1861 was attended by 28 members of the gentry and 127 landowning farmers, all of whom spoke Finnish at the meeting. Moreover, this meeting appears to have been one of the first public meetings in which the local elites socialized freely with the farmers, abandoning the old protocols which had kept the estates separate. As Manninen explained in the pages of *Tapio* shortly after the meeting,

> The Agricultural Society's meeting, which due to the illness of the Society's director, Governor Knut Furuhielm, was led by the Provost of Tohmajärvi, Dr. E. J. Andelin, was notable in that first, it was carried out entirely in the Finnish language, without a single word of Swedish being heard. Until now, there have been complaints that the use of Swedish in other meetings of this nature has alienated Finnish farmers from their midst. Second, the meeting was exceptionally well-ordered and lively. Confidently, freely and clearly, each spoke his mind. This was helped, in addition to other things, by the fact that during the recesses, the gentlemen wished to be in the same group with the peasants, so that there was no need for boundaries between the estates, not in speeches nor in other situations, which encouraged and greatly pleased the peasant farmers, and was congenial to all, and the honour of our gentlemen did not seem at all to be offended by this, rather it seemed to have bestowed greater distinction upon these gentlemen who dared to diverge from the usual protocol which is exactly what has kept our farmers in the low state of education and refinement in which they now find themselves [10].

The importance of agricultural society meetings in the early 1860s can be seen from the fact that their reports were published not only by regional newspapers but were quickly picked up by the national newspaper *Suomen Julkisia Sanomia* and other newspapers. For example, the 1862 meeting of the Kuopio Agricultural Society, on which *Tapio* began reporting on July 19th of the same year, was reprinted verbatim nine days later by *Suomen Julkisia Sanomia* [19, 20, 21].

Because the 1861 meeting was held to coincide with the Agricultural Institute's end of term ceremony and students' displays of agricultural skill, relatives of the students and other farming folk from neighboring parishes, including a number of women, were present when the subject of home thievery was brought up [10, 11]. Reporting on the 1861 meeting, Antti Manninen wrote in *Tapio* that 'The eleventh question about home thievery pleased everyone so much, that one girl even offered her opinion and afterwards asked the secretary [i.e. Manninen himself] for permission

126 The meeting in 1861 at the Jouhkola Agricultural Institute can be contrasted with a meeting of the Uusimaa and Häme Agricultural Society in Southern Finland a year later, in which only Swedish was spoken and less than twenty Finnish-speaking farmers participated. As the writer of the press report summed up, '[p]erhaps it was therefore good that more Finns did not come, for they would have been bored and annoyed [– –].' (September 4, 1862. *Suomen Julkisia Sanomia* no. 67, 'Maawiljeliäin-kokous Porwoossa').

to write her views in more detail and explain her thoughts more broadly for the meeting minutes.'[127] The 'girl' was 26-year-old Liisa Väänänen, a farmer's daughter from Pielavesi.[128] An excerpt from her letter was printed in Manninen's report of the meeting published in *Tapio* a month later [11], and the full version of her letter was apparently published in a booklet produced by Manninen in 1861 entitled *Kuopion maawiljelysseuran toimituksia* (*Annual Report of the Kuopio Agricultural Society*).[129]

Home thievery was also a topic of discussion at the Kuopio Agricultural Society meeting held a year later in 1862 at Levänen Agricultural Institute. After the meeting, two farm daughters, Maria Loviisa Kukkonen and 'Maria J–n', sent letters dealing with home thievery to *Tapio* (see Chapters Six and Eight). In the case of 'Maria J–n's' letter, Manninen introduced her words to the reading public by saying: 'Although not a single woman present began to speak of this matter at the actual meeting, nonetheless several expressed their opinions afterwards. For example, farmer's daughter Maria J–n from Rautalampi writes as follows...' [18]. Maria Loviisa Kukkonen's second letter printed in *Tapio* was introduced by Antti Manninen in a similar manner:

> Tapio has still many submissions [on the topic of home thievery] which it no longer intends to publish, since they contain nothing new that has not already been said. Nevertheless, we print here a couple of shorter texts sent from Rautalampi, of which the first is important because it was written by a farmer's daughter herself...[27]

At the end of her first letter printed in *Tapio*, Maria Loviisa Kukkonen had written: 'There would be more to say on this subject, but I fear that the reader will be overburdened by my inferior writing, for which reason I will finish here and bid you farewell until I greet you next time' [15]. This self-effacing comment may have been intended to shield her from possible criticism and to appeal to Manninen for his printed support, which he provided by responding at the end of her letter: 'In the opinion of the editors this submission was not written at all badly, for which reason we hope letters will be sent to *Tapio* by the same maiden in the future'.

---

127 October 5, 1861 *Tapio* no. 40, 'Jouhkolasta 25 p. syysk.' (- i–nen [Antti Manninen]).

128 Although Manninen's report, quoted in the journal *Emäntälehti* in 1925, states that Väänänen's home parish was Pielavesi, the HISKI genealogical database shows that in December of 1858, farmer's daughter Lisa Wäänänen, born 1835, moved from Kiihtelysvaara parish, not from Pielavesi, to the parish of Tohmajärvi in which the parish of Jouhkola Agricultural Institute was located. Records from Kiihtelysvaara show that a 'Hedda Lisa Wänäin' was born in Kiihtelysvaara to farmer 'Petter Wänain' and 'Lisa Wastapu' in 1835. There is no record of a Liisa Wäänänen or anyone with a similar name born in Pielavesi in the 1830s. Later in 1861, the same year that Liisa Väänänen wrote to Manninen, she was chosen to be the Agricultural Institute's instructor in cattle husbandry.

129 Liisa Väänänen's statement in *Kuopion maawiljelysseuran toimituksia* was quoted in the *Marttaliitto* organization's *Emäntälehti* in 1925 (no. 5, p. 119, 'Mielenkiintoisia lausuntoja kotivarkaudesta 64 vuotta sitten.' [A. L:s])

Manninen died suddenly of typhus (*lavantauti*) at the age of 35 in 1866.[130] After his death, the number of rural women who wrote to the press remained extremely small until the 1890s,[131] when the number of female contributors to newspapers began to rise. Manninen's encouragement of female rural writers may have arisen from the fact that he had experienced the emergent Finnish-language public sphere not as an abstract ideal but as a concrete reality in which rural women, too, participated in public discussion.

Changing discourses on gender in the Finnish-language press of the 1850s and 1860s

In order to better understand the context in which rural women's letters were accepted to newspapers in the early 1860s, Manninen's attitude toward women's written contributions must also be examined against the backdrop of mid-19th-century discourses appearing in the press, especially those pertaining to women and gender rights. Linguists define 'discourse' as any unit of connected speech or writing longer than a sentence. In this study, I use a more specific definition of 'discourse' to mean a set of arguments logically cohering around one or several premises. These arguments can be expressed directly in rhetorical statements, or they can be expressed more subtly within narratives or descriptions, for example through dialogue or plot structure. From the newspaper sources examined in this study, five prototypical discourses can be distinguished on the basis of their underlying premises. The first discourse, drawing upon conservative religious teachings, took as its premise the belief that all truth was to be found from Scripture and Church doctrine. Three other discourses addressed the question of which unit of society – individual, farm, or the nation itself? – was conceptually, politically and practically the most important, whose needs should be given priority in order for society to receive the most benefit. For instance, the individualist discourse employed by social reformers had its philosophical foundations in the liberal emphasis on personal rights and freedoms, which were thought to form the basis of a democratic and more evolved society.

130 Manninen's death was greatly mourned in the press. Johan Rännäri, who took over as editor of *Tapio* upon Manninen's death, reported that more people came to attend Manninen's funeral than had ever previously gathered in Kuopio Cemetery. Rännäri described Manninen as having been not only a highly intelligent and hardworking man, but also polite, gentle, and patient with people (October 27 & November 3, 1866. *Tapio* nos. 43 & 44. 'Kuopiosta'). See also: October 15, 1875. *Suomen Kuvalehti* no. 68, 'Antti Manninen' (A. R–dr.).

131 One exception can be found in Wolmar Schildt's (Kilpinen's) *Kansan Lehti* published in Jyväskylä for three years (1868–1870), in which the unedited letters of at least six writers signing themselves as women were printed: May 2, 1868. *Kansan Lehti* no. 18, 'Laukaassa' (A. L. L. Suomen tytär); September 4, 1869. *Kansan Lehti* no. 35, 'Kirje Siskoille!' (Siskonne Anni Moilanen.); February 26, 1870. *Kansan Lehti* no. 8, 'Mikkelistä' (Nuorin siskonne Anna Maria Alkawainen); June 11, 1870. *Kansan Lehti* no. 23, 'Kirje siskosille L–ssa.' (Teidän oma siskonne Nulpukka); July 9, 1870. *Kansan Lehti* no. 27, 'Korpilahdelta' (Nuori siskonne A. M. T–sto.); September 10, 1870. *Kansan Lehti* no. 36, 'Korpilahdelta' (Teidän siskonne E. S. –la.).

Freedom allowed individuals to improve themselves and their position in society, which from a liberal viewpoint was seen to enable social progress. The rational-functional discourse employed by some farm masters, on the other hand, assumed that the stability and continuity of the farm household was essential to agricultural productivity and thus took precedence over the individual rights of its household members. Nationalist-collectivist discourse focused on the (Finnish-language) nation as the conceptual framework within which the ideal (Finnish-speaking) society should be achieved, and to which citizens' loyalty should be owed (see Anderson 1983; Häggman 1994: 221).

The fifth discourse evident from newspaper sources derived from romanticist notions propagated by upper-class literary and visual culture which depicted women as the weaker, gentler sex, whose beauty and grace entitled them to chivalrous consideration by men. Because romanticist discourse highlighted the value of emotion as a source of moral guidance, it became associated with individual freedoms such as being able to enter into emotionally satisfying relationships, and marrying for love and mutual affection rather than marrying to promote the economic status of one's family. Romanticist discourse also laid emphasis on moral purity and decency, and could be used by writers to portray themselves as blameless and innocent. Although the gender concepts inherent in this romanticist discourse were not ideally suited to the agrarian context in which women engaged in heavy physical labour alongside men, the depiction of women as delicate maidens was not necessarily a disempowering one. Romanticist discourse enabled seemingly contradictory values – adherence to ethical and moral codes on the one hand, and individual freedoms and choice on the other – to be presented simultaneously in the discursive production of self-identity. This may be one reason why romanticist discourse was already in use by rural writers in the late 1850s and early 1860s. Another reason seems to have been that the notion of chivalrous consideration given to women was used strategically by both male and female writers to emphasize their refinement and civility, and to negotiate power and status for themselves. Men used it to construct an honourable masculine identity, and women used it to appeal to men's sympathies in order to gain access to the public sphere, to defend their public reputations and to appeal to male sympathies in this endeavour.

It was through newspapers that the rural folk first became familiar with romanticist discourses. By the early 1840s, romanticist poetry was being published in the newspaper *Oulun Wiikko-Sanomia*. Serial novellas and other fiction written by Finnish authors or translated from European literature, featuring a variety of idealized and romanticized characters both male and female, were appearing in *Maamiehen Ystäwä* by 1845. The prevalence of romantic discourses in the press meant that there was, as yet, almost no mention in public discourse of the 'strong Finnish woman' whose capacity for hard work equalled that of her husband.

Within the press, the relationship between the first two discourses in my list – Scripture-based and liberal-individualist – appears to have undergone a significant transformation at the end of the 1850s and beginning of the

1860s. Simply put, the predominant discourse shifted *from a conservative, Scripture-based perspective* in which persons were expected to seek truth from religious teachings and be content with their place within a preordained social hierarchy, to one which emphasized *individual rights and freedoms as a basis for social progress*, which entailed seeking 'truths' from sources outside the teachings of the Church (see also Leskinen 2005: 3). These new individual rights were usually argued to be based on 'natural law',[132] but they involved an expectation that the individual could improve himself and his situation in life. As such, they clearly diverged from the notion of a person's God-given place in society as spelled out in Luther's Table of Duties.

The influence of the older, Scripture-based discourse can be seen from an article sent to *Suometar* by Antti Manninen in 1857 in which he suggested a number of improvements to farming life in Finland and stressed the importance of family cohesion and cooperation in farm work and decision making. In this letter, he criticized home thievery in the following terms:

> What is required here is honesty, so that everyone looks to the interests of all, so that the common resources are used for common needs, so that a brother does not keep secret some goods from his brother, nor children from their parents, so that daughters and daughters-in-law do not carry out secret buying and selling and drain the grain bins when they pay village women to make often frivolous things for them. In this is needed above all a God-fearing mind: for piousness is the most useful of all [4].

Here Manninen appeals to religious argumentation which emphasized the importance of submission to God's authority, and he lays at least some of the blame for home thievery on younger female members of the farming family. Another contributor to the press in the mid-1850s who drew upon older religious concepts of gender in his writings was Bernhard Kristfrid Sarlin, who wrote on the topic of home thievery in 1856 to *Suometar*. Sarlin was known to be a stern, conservative and humourless clergyman (Pinomaa 1984). In his article on home thievery presented in Chapter One, Sarlin claimed that '[w]omenfolk in particular are adept at this sort of cunning, due to their devious natures inherited from old Eve'.[133]

The fact that male writers to the press in the mid-1850s wrote of home thievery and gender in conservative religious terms is not surprising. Empirical evidence from folklore, autobiographies, and personal letters strongly suggests that teachings from the Bible and the Catechism continued to be used among the common folk to organize their world view and interpret their experience until at least the end of the 19th century. What is striking, rather, is how completely the older, conservative religious discourse had

---

132 This notion of natural rights, as it appears in the press and in Finnish law and legal debates, did not signify the concept of universal rights as we understand it today, but was closely linked to a person's rank and status (Pylkkänen 2009: 38).

133 It was not long before such religious discourse regarding women began to be contested in the press, however. For a humorous approach to Scripture-based interpretations of gender, see: February 5, 1858. *Suometar* no. 5, 'Esi-äitimme ahnauden kosto'.

disappeared *from the Finnish-language press* by the early 1860s. In fact, Sarlin's and Manninen's writings appearing in 1856 and 1857 were the last time that any author who condemned home thievery in the press did so by appealing to religious-based discourse, or at least the last time that editors allowed such views to be printed. Even the farmers conversing among themselves at the Kuopio Agricultural Society meetings held in 1861 and 1862 were reported to have made only a few passing references to the general benefits of a Christian upbringing.

This same shift in discourse can be seen in how rural men wrote about rural women in the press. Take, for example, the case of a letter printed in *Suometar* in 1855 which had been written by two landowning peasants from South Savo, entitled 'A Description for Girls of How They Should and Should Not Be'. The letter was written from an entirely male perspective, and the notion of what a young unmarried farm woman might actually want from marriage or from life, or what she might deserve in terms of rights, is lacking entirely. What is emphasized instead is how she should conduct herself so as to please a man: with humility and piousness.

> Be ye pious both at church and at home, be pious in life, pious in love, pious in adversity. A pious heart is in the hands of the Lord, and the Lord never forsakes it. And be ye humble, humble towards God, towards your parents and towards the friends of your soul [– –]. And be ye silent: where the magpie makes a clamour on the roof, there nobody is at home; if the mouth is open and always speaking, there the head and heart are empty. Be ye faithful, be dedicated to God; faithful in friendship, sincere in love. Frivolity befits no one and in girls it is utterly corrupting.[134]

The publication of this letter in 1855 went unremarked by rural young men and women (at this early date we still do not have any evidence of rural women writing to Finnish-language newspapers). Eleven years later, however, when a copy of this letter was sent to the newspaper *Pohjan-Tähti* by a man signing himself 'J. W. Ä, bachelor' from the district of Muhos[135] and published as if it were an original composition, a female writer using the pseudonym 'Unknown fiia' could not take the contents of the letter seriously and responded by writing: 'What have boys done to deserve all that they appear to be demanding in us girls?' She also asked whether young men really desired these qualities, when it was clear to everyone that a plump, blond and rosy appearance and a substantial dowry were enough to attract suitors in droves. 'Fiia' urged: 'Improve yourselves first, pitiful boys, in the area of intellectual cultivation and then come to us girls to advise us regarding 'how we should be and should not be'; now it seems

---

134 September 14, 1855. *Suometar* no. 37, 'Kuwa tyttölöille. Kuinka tyttöin pitää olemaan ja ei olemaan.' (A. S. ja A. L.).

135 September 12, 1866. *Pohjan-tähti* no. 7, 'Kuvaus tyttölöille'. When the letter was printed, *Pohjan-tähti's* editors did not realize that it had been copied from a 1855 issue of *Suometar*, but they announced this in a later issue as soon as another reader informed them of it.

to me to be too hasty.'[136] The editors of *Pohjan-tähti* were slightly taken aback by 'Unknown fiia's' response, and added at the bottom of her letter that they were surprised that she had responded so haughtily to 'J.W.Ä's' contribution. Two other 'bachelors', however, who signed themselves 'E. K.' and 'I. K.', wrote to express their encouragement and agreement with 'fiia's' viewpoint:

> We are bachelors and we thank 'unknown Fiia' for her noble minded and accurately explained answer to the boy from Muhos! We hope that 'Fiia' will not forget to write to us boys in the future!
> E. K. ja I. K.[137]

Three years later, in 1869, another letter was sent to the press, this time to *Tapio*, in which a young rural man using the pen name 'a suitor' gave advice to young unmarried farm women. Although this letter, like the earlier 'A Description for Girls – –' still expressed a purely male point of view and strove to impose the author's programme of improvement upon young rural women, the programme itself differed considerably. The ideal behaviour expressed in this letter was not for young rural women to be pious, passive and silent, but to educate themselves through reading and writing, in order to benefit the future nation:

> Letter to the maidens of Maaninka district!
> Cherished maidens! Isn't it time that you, too, began to think about the demands of our times and look with a more vigilant eye to the fields of the future? Namely: you should learn to write and read all edifying books, particularly newspapers, so that you would come to know the purpose of your calling in this world. – You should strive to be ahead of boys in all areas of learning and knowledge, for in your lives you have a more precious responsibility than do boys: first with respect to knowing whom you should choose as your life's partner [– –]. Second, learning is necessary in order for you to be able to become respectable mothers of children. For then you will need to be able to advise your children on how to be noble members of our nation.
> [– –] You have no desire to read, and you say you have no time for it. Please good maidens do not speak of any obstacles to reading newspapers and other books, for the Creator did not create you to be such good-for-nothings as you now hold yourselves to be in the vanity of your lives. Many of you have noble gifts of the soul, if only they could be cultivated [– –].
> [– –] Begin to write, to obtain for yourselves better enlightenment than that possessed by your parents, for when your parents were children there were hardly any educational books, nor as many newspapers available as there are now, for which reason they cannot be blamed. But if you disdain literature and newspapers, the future nation will not bless you [– –]. [34]

---

136 September 19, 1866. *Pohjan-tähti* no. 8, 'Pieni wastaus Muhoksen pojalle' (Tuntematoin fiia).
137 October 10, 1866. *Pohjan-tähti* no. 11, 'Kirje tuntemattomalle fiialle' (E. K. ja I. K.).

By the 1860s, writings to the press about gendered relations in the countryside were no longer drawing on religious argumentation. Instead, they tended to side with either the second or third discourses outlined earlier: social reformist discourse centred on *individual* progress and *individual* rights; or rational-functional discourse centred on the continuity, stability and prosperity of the *farm household.*

In the Kuopio Agricultural Society's meetings of 1861 and 1862, it is likely that Manninen, acting as secretary, put the question of home thievery on the agenda. Everything that Manninen wrote from the summer of 1861 onward suggests that when it came to the question of home thievery and its perceived causes, his primary sympathies lay with farm women (see Chapter Eight). As early as 1858, Manninen had argued for the education of rural farm women. What happened to make Manninen so interested in the question of women and their rights? Why does Manninen's attitude toward women's involvement in home thievery appear to have changed between 1857 and 1861?

One reason may simply have been the unparalleled professionalism of *Tapio's* entire editorial committee (Kinnunen 1982: 66), as well as Manninen's role as an educator in an Institute where young farm women were among the students. Manninen is recognized to have been an eager reformer intent on educating the rural populace in numerous areas of life, and he may have found it natural to include the concerns of farm women in this mission. However, it is also clear that during this period, Manninen had come into close contact with two men born and raised in the Savo region who were active speakers and writers on behalf of women's rights. The first was Judge Karl Ferdinand Forsström (1817–1903), who like Manninen was born in South Savo. Forsström became interested already as a university student in the movement to secure Finnish-language rights, and in 1856 he became the first judge to use the Finnish language to record court proceedings. In late 1857, he was the vice director of the Jouhkola Agricultural Institute,[138] where Manninen must have met him when he arrived to teach at the Institute in October of that year. The two men are known to have been present at the same meeting of the Kuopio Agricultural Society in 1861 [12]. In early 1858, before Manninen had written his own essay on rural women's education, Forsström wrote a lengthy treatise entitled '*Naisten tila Suomessa* (The situation of women in Finland)', which was published in eight issues of *Suometar*.[139] In it, he argued for legal changes to increase girls' chances for education, wives' property rights, daughters' inheritance rights, and the legal autonomy of unmarried women. His writing of 'The situation of women in Finland' appears to have been motivated by the fact that adult unmarried women had been given legal majority in Denmark in 1857 and in Sweden in 1858. Forsström argued, among other things, that the same law should be adopted in Finland. As an avid reader of newspapers and

138 February 5, 1858. *Suometar* no. 5, 'Jouhkolan Maawiljelyskoulusta IV'.
139 February 12, 1858; March 5, 1858; March 12, 1858; April 3, 1858; April 9, 1858; April 23, 1858; April 30, 1858; July 9, 1858; *Suometar* nos. 6, 9, 10, 13, 14, 16, 17, 27, 'Naisten tila Suomessa' (F. [Karl Ferdinand Forsström]).

a regular contributor to *Suometar*, Manninen would have surely have been familiar with Forsström's writings. It is possible that either 'The situation of women in Finland' or discussions with Forsström himself may partly account for Manninen's interest in farm women's rights and his advocacy of their voices at meetings of the Kuopio Agricultural Society and within the pages of *Tapio*.

The second advocate of women's rights among Manninen's acquaintances was his editorial assistant and co-owner of the Kuopio printing press, Fredrik Ahlqvist.[140] Like his older brother August Ahlqvist, who had been one of the founders of *Suometar*, Fredrik was the illegitimate son of a serving maid.[141] Fredrik had served as editor of *Maamiehen Ystäwä* between 1853 and 1855, and his realistic fiction 'Koti (Home)' published in *Maamiehen Ystäwä* in 1853 represents an early critique of the low value placed on rural wives' work and intellect (see Chapters Seven and Eight). When the question of home thievery was brought up at the 1862 Kuopio Agricultural Society meeting, Ahlqvist gave a long and eloquent speech in defence of rural women's rights. In a style very similar to that used in 'Home', using references to everyday practical experience rather than philosophical doctrine on natural rights, Fredrik Ahlqvist argued that farm women committed home thievery because first, farm masters gave them no money for their daily necessities and second, because adult farm daughters knew that their eldest brother would inherit the farm and they themselves would receive almost nothing in return for their labour on the farm. Ahlqvist also argued forcefully that women in the countryside performed more work than men, and illustrated his point with numerous concrete examples. His speech provoked at least five responses from farmers published in the press (see Chapter Eight). In addition, the aforementioned farm daughters Maria Loviisa Kukkonen and 'Maria J–n' from Rautalampi, who were the first to respond in writing to Ahlqvist's speech even before it had been printed in *Tapio*, did not mention Ahlqvist by name but had clearly been inspired by his ideas [15, 18].

Forsström, Manninen and Ahlqvist were naturally not the only men in Finland pondering the situation of women, their role within the family and their right to learning and self-improvement. J. V. Snellman, the most influential ideological voice of the mid-19th century, had also addressed these topics in his Swedish-language newspapers *Saima* and *Litteraturblad för allmän medborgerlig bildning* (which he published both during and after his brief stint as the editor of the Finnish-language *Maamiehen Ystäwä*) (Lahtinen 2006: 233–244). However, Snellman's almost exclusive focus

---

140 Ahlqvist described himself as 'a fledgling and otherwise poor writer', although he was later an energetic translator and editor of lesser known literature (Toivanen 2000: 412, 414).

141 August Ahlqvist's father was military officer Johan Mauritz Nordenstam (who became a senator in 1857 and a general in 1868). Fredrik may have had the same father as August, but there is no proof of this, since the identity of Fredrik's father is not entered in the church records of his birth. Ahlqvist's mother, Maria Augusta Ahlqvist, brought up four children under difficult conditions with apparently little financial help from Nordenstam or anyone else.

A photograph of Judge Karl Ferdinand Forsström, most likely taken during the 1860s or early 1870s. Courtesy of the National Board of Antiquities.

on upper-class, Swedish-speaking women makes it difficult to judge the immediate effect of his ideas on Finnish-language discussions regarding rural farm women. A few letters to the press written by rural men in the 1860s, including Manninen's 1858 essay on farm women's education, follow Snellman in emphasizing the value of women's self-improvement precisely because they were to be the mothers of the next generation of Finns. On the whole, however, farm women were approached in the Finnish-language press from other perspectives: either as romanticized, as-yet-unmarried maidens, or alternately as wives and farm mistresses whose labour contribution to the farm was always a potential justification for improving their legal situation, even if not all writers wanted to publicly acknowledge this.

The extent to which Manninen, Forsström and Ahlqvist may have exerted an influence on each other's attitudes with regard to rural gender equality can only be guessed at. What *is* clear is that, as a result of the public attention which these men began to pay to the rights of women in the late 1850s and early 1860s, at least a few farm daughters were emboldened to publicly voice their opinions on issues such as home thievery, inheritance, and the rights of individual family members, and to demand greater rights for farm women.

4. Source Materials and Methods

The texts which have served as sources for this study fall into three broad categories. My primary sources are articles, letters and reports printed in Finnish-language newspapers during the period 1847–1900. These are supplemented by ethnographic descriptions, both published and unpublished, provided by rural inhabitants born between 1870 and 1929. My third source is realistic ethnographic fiction, published in the period 1881 to 1913, which appeared either in book form or as serial novellas (*jatkokertomukset*) in newspapers. Taken together, these source materials complement each other, but also call for source criticism in order to evaluate the nature of the knowledge provided by each, and how these different types of knowledge relate to each other. The researcher must also ask: how can individual agency and the dynamics of power at the local and household level be discerned from written sources which have themselves been shaped by power relations?

The answer to this question begins by distinguishing between two primary levels of analysis. First, I examine the *practices* of home thievery and gossip, as well as changing behaviours related to consumption, behaviours which made visible the extent to which home thievery was being practiced in rural areas. Second, I examine the social and cultural *discourse* surrounding these practices, which I have identified from written letters, meeting minutes, literature and ethnographic descriptions. These sources were produced by rural farmers, farm daughters, reform-minded teachers, editors, clergymen, educated ethnographers and popular authors who, starting in the 1850s and each for their own reasons, lifted the topics of home thievery and gossip out of the private sphere of the farm household and into the public sphere where they were addressed as issues of public concern.

The first level, material conditions and practices, can be inferred from reports and descriptions which I assume convey a particular picture of reality *as it was perceived and experienced* by the writer. Two things lend authoritative weight to the testimonies regarding social practices found in my source materials. The first is the *immediacy* of informants' and writers' encounters with the external social, political and material conditions in which they lived; in other words, their *proximity* to their own social context in terms of chronological time, physical presence and participation in a linguistic community. The second is *the embeddedness of these testimonies in past social relations*. In other words, because the narrators and writers were not only close to the situations they described but were also participants in them, their words carry a conviction regarding their experience and interpretation of reality which should not be ignored, and cannot necessarily be superseded by any external information available to the researcher concerning that reality. At the same time, I recognize that experience is always filtered and moulded by power relations as well as the limitations and plasticity of language (Joan Scott 1991; Hastrup 1995).

As discussed in Chapter Two, traces of past tactical 'moves', now lost from view, are often recounted in narrative. It must be kept in mind, however, that narrative accounts *are themselves tactical deployments*. The use of language – not merely to express reality as perceived but also to manipulate social reality in the mind of the listener or reader – is one of the ways in which people manoeuvre and make strategic moves within 'serious games'. This brings us to an investigation of rhetoric.

Rhetorical criticism considers the devices by which texts promote (or fail to promote) identification between writer and audience, as well as the ways in which the use of language drives wedges between readers and their unquestioned assumptions, thus facilitating cooperative action and providing room for persuasion and debate (Hauser 1998: 19, 32–33). Rhetorical critique is a two-step process. First, the vocabularies and historically-specific concepts used by writers themselves are identified. Then the researcher attempts to translate and explain these concepts for the 21st-century reader as fully as possible, recognizing that language can never provide direct reflections of, or unmediated access to, cultural reality (e.g. Hastrup 1995). This is particularly important to remember when the analytic discussion is conducted in a different language than that in which the sources were originally written.

With regard to this second level of my analysis, rhetoric and the formation of discursive concepts, my aim is to examine cultural patterns of thought and behaviour rather than to trace out historical facts. Newspaper sources were earlier treated with caution by historians because their reports were seen to be frequently incomplete, biased, and inaccurate. Yet it is precisely the fact that newspapers are value-laden and represent their writers' subjective points of view that makes them both interesting and useful for ethnologists, folklorists and cultural historians. The role of newspapers in the formation of collective cultural concerns and political stances makes them highly relevant for research into changing attitudes, meanings and concepts.

Ethical considerations

Given the growing attention given within the fields of ethnology and folklore studies to ethical considerations and the need to protect informants' privacy, several points must be made here. In the case of 19th-century research sources, the primary ethical issue which must be considered is the preservation of anonymity in cases where informants may not have intended their information and identities to become public. For the majority of my source materials, the intention of publicity is clear. The digitized newspaper materials available through the *National Library of Finland's Historical Newspaper Library* were originally intended by their authors to be public documents. Similarly, published books of ethnographic descriptions or realistic fictions were intended by their authors to be freely consumed by an ideally large audience. Reports from meetings of the Kuopio Agricultural Society in the early 1860s can also be assumed to pose few ethical dilemmas, because the farmers who gathered and spoke at these meetings not only intended their words to be public within the immediate context of the meeting, but were surely aware that the contents of these meetings might be reported in the press (as they often were).

The ethnographic descriptions housed in the Finnish Literature Society Folklore Archives in Helsinki, by contrast, pose more complex ethical dilemmas. In the case of the actual collectors, we can generally assume an intention of publicity, since such collectors voluntarily submitted their names to the Archives, often in connection with public collection contests in which it was made clear at the outset that the most successful collectors' names would be published in the print media. In the case of interviewed informants (by which I mean the human source of the data recorded), however, we cannot be certain of their voluntary willingness to have their names revealed publicly, or even that they were fully aware at the time of recording to what eventual purposes their supplied information would be put. In this study, therefore, I provide informants' background information (gender, age, occupation, home district), which is vital to understanding the context of the information they supplied, but I ensure their anonymity by withholding their names. The background information of the informants is sufficiently sparse so that discovery of their identities cannot be made on the basis of this information alone. Researchers wishing to locate the original source texts in the FLS Folklore Archives can do so on the basis of the collector's name and manuscript number provided in the reference information.

Newspapers

Finnish folklorists, ethnologists, historians and literary scholars have recently rediscovered abundant source materials from Finnish archives which reveal that in the last half of the 19th century there were many more self-educated, actively writing peasants, crofters and labourers than had previously been assumed.[142] Newspapers were one of the main forums for self-educated rural writers to express themselves from the late 1840s onwards.

Finnish-language newspapers from the period 1847–1900 represent the most important source of information on the topic of home thievery. They

---

142 See: Makkonen 2002; Kauranen 2006, 2007; Salmi-Niklander 2006; L. Stark 2006, 2008; Leino-Kaukiainen 2007; Mäkinen 2007; Kuismin & Salmi-Niklander 2008.

also provide at least ten texts mentioning female village gossips and news carriers.[143] Until now, there has been little historical research on the rise of the Finnish-language press from the perspective of readers and writers, and especially from the perspective of rural inhabitants. Likewise, the role of rural inhabitants in newspaper debates, and the impact of newspapers in the countryside have been little studied.[144] The National Library of Finland, however, has recently digitized nearly all newspapers printed between 1771 and 1910 into a searchable database which makes it now much easier for researchers to use newspapers as source materials for research. The contents of newspapers may not always provide reliable evidence of 'what actually happened' in the past, but they can help us identify what people thought, feared or hoped would happen, or at least what was important or relevant to them. Yet while the searchable electronic *Historical Newspaper Library* offers new opportunities for research, its massive and highly heterogeneous source materials pose difficult methodological challenges. There is currently no accepted methodology in place for ethnologists, folklorists and cultural historians to use newspapers as their sources. What follows are some suggestions for how research in these disciplines might proceed.

The Historical Newspaper Library may be compared to another vast and heterogeneous collection of cultural data from the 19th and early 20th centuries, namely the Folklore Archives of the Finnish Literature Society. Since Finnish folklorists have had over 150 years to develop methodologies for organizing and using the vast masses of texts in what has become one of the largest folklore repositories in the world, it is worth reflecting on their solutions as a possible point of departure. First, in using these sources, folklorists have used the method of 'corpus building' (e.g. Apo 2001: 30). In this method, the researcher demonstrates a thorough knowledge of the characteristics of the corpus as a whole dealing with a certain topic or within a particular genre or clearly delineated collection, before going on to justify the selection of a smaller group of texts for deeper analysis. Thus the relationship between the selected cases and the entire body of texts is clarified, and the researcher avoids the error of choosing only the most interesting texts for analysis with no regard for their representationality. In the case of newspaper texts, corpus-building was previously hampered by the difficulty of finding all writings on a particular topic. Now, the searchable

143 July 9, 1853. *Maamiehen Ystäwä* no. 27, 'Koti'; February 20, 1857. *Suometar* no. 8, liite 1, 'Muuan sana naimsen seikoista Pohjanmaan sopessa'; December 19, 1857. *Oulun Wiikko-Sanomia* no. 46, 'Paljaita juoruja eli epäluuloja' (E.B).; September 21, 1860. *Hämäläinen* no. 38, 'Längelmäeltä' (–br.– W.); February 23, 1878. *Sanomia Turusta* no. 16, 'Kansan elämää Lappeen pitäjästä V. Awioliiton alkamisesta.' (Lappeelainen); November 16, 1878. *Sawonlinna. Sanomia Sawosta* no. 46, 'Heinäwedelta'; April 16, 1879. *Päijänne* no. 16, 'Naapurin wirheet' (Wieno); May 15, 1883. *Sanomia Turusta* no. 74, 'Tammelasta' (A.W. L.); March 12, 1887. *Turun Lehti* no. 29, 'Ruskosta' (Närri); July 1, 1893. *Rauman Lehti* no. 52, 'Ankara eripuraisuus'.

144 The Finnish Newspaper History Research Project (1975–1988) led by historian Päiviö Tommila took a top-down approach and focused on the editors, printing presses, and political climate which shaped the history of Finnish newspapers, as well as the ideological stances of the newspapers themselves and the changes in their format and appearance.

database makes such corpus-building not only possible, but necessary. If the 'corpus' composed of all texts on a particular theme is extremely large, however, then it is acceptable to employ the 'saturation' method, in which the reader continues to analyze texts until no more new themes, topics or perspectives can be discerned from them, in other words, until a semantic 'saturation point' has been reached and the researcher can stop gathering data and treat as a corpus those texts which have already been analyzed (Apo 2001: 32).

In order to build my corpus of newspaper sources dealing with home thievery, I have used the search tool of the Historical Newspaper Library electronic database to scan for references to home thievery from all issues of the 104 Finnish-language newspapers which were printed between 1844 and 1900.[145] As a result, I have found 64 texts which specifically address home thievery by family members on farms.[146] A list of these texts can be found at the end of this study in Appendix II, and I will refer to them throughout this book by bracketed numbers (e.g. [25]). The newspaper which published the greatest number of these texts, twenty, was the Eastern Finnish newspaper *Tapio.*

Sixty-four texts on home thievery in the press may not impress the reader as a large number, given the scope of the Finnish-language press as a whole in the period under study. However, it must be kept in mind that the topic of home thievery was just one of a vast number of social concerns which were written about in the press once it became known that the Finnish Diet (*valtiopäivät*) would be reconvened in 1863 after a hiatus of 54 years. In the 1860s, only the national newspapers such as *Suometar, Suomen Julkisia Sanomia* and *Suomalainen Wirallinen Lehti*, as well as newspapers covering the country's capitol such as *Helsingin Uutiset* appeared more frequently than once per week, and most newspapers consisted of only four pages, with the last page usually devoted to advertisements and official announcements.[147] For this reason, a wide variety of issues in the press were forced to compete for very limited space. Articles dealing with rural life had to compete with official news, editors' practical advice, articles aimed at reforming and educating the less educated public, and essays on history, geography and scientific inventions.

The 64 texts in my corpus were written by less than 64 different persons, since some editors and outside contributors wrote more than one letter or report which mentioned home thievery. Of those who wrote to the press on home thievery, two were clergymen (Johan Bäckvall and Bernhard Kristfrid Sarlin) [1, 3], one was a judge (Karl Ferdinand Forsström) [5, 6, 13, 14,

---

145 Many of the 104 newspapers appearing between 1844 and 1900 were short-lived, so that for example in 1863 there were twelve in circulation, in 1870 only nine, and in 1885, 27. Some newspapers appeared weekly, others appeared 2–6 times per week.

146 In part because newspapers in the period under study were nearly always printed in fraktura font, the search function of the Historical Newspaper Library database is not infallible, and it is possible that not all of the articles and letters dealing with home thievery in the Finnish language press have yet been located.

147 In the 1870s, even regional newspapers began appearing more frequently, the norm being twice a week.

38, 39], one was a farmer's son who became a newspaper editor (Antti Manninen) [4, 30], two were male schoolteachers (Wilhelm Kukkonen and August Kuokkanen) [37, 40], one was female schoolteacher (Eva Hällström) [57], one was a female playwright (Minna Canth) [42], five were known with reasonable certainty to have been farm masters [18, 23, 24, 25, 56], and an additional four can be assumed to have been farm masters or crofters [7, 22, 26, 28, 32]. One writer was probably the unmarried son of a farmer [33, 34], and six, possibly seven, were farm women [11, 15, 18, 27, 31, 35, 41, 64]. For nine newspaper submissions, we have no information whatsoever on the writer [2, 8, 47, 48, 50, 53, 54]. Even for those newspaper submissions signed with the writer's initial or pen name, eleven writers cannot be identified [9, 36, 43, 44, 49, 51, 52, 55, 60, 61, 63]. Fourteen articles which mention home thievery are reports of meetings by farmers or clergymen [10, 11, 12, 16, 17, 18, 19, 20, 21, 30, 45, 46, 58, 59, in which 20, 19, and 21 are exact copies of 16, 17, and 18 reprinted in another newspaper].

Although only eleven of the writers in this corpus can be positively identified as having been from the rural farming population, an additional three men (Johan Bäckvall, Antti Manninen, Wilhelm Kukkonen) were raised on family farms. Of the discussants at the 1862 Kuopio Agricultural Society meeting whose opinions on home thievery were reported in the press, it is certain that three were farm masters, another two were most likely farm masters, one was a manor lord, one was described as a 'landowner', one was an innkeeper, one was an estate manager, one was a secondary school graduate, and one was a tradesman.

In continuing to outline a possible methodology for the use of newspapers as sources of socio-cultural data, I turn next to the challenge of organizing, differentiating and classifying large numbers of texts. Folklorists have chosen to distinguish the texts in the FLS Folklore Archives from each other on the basis of their form and content, resulting in categories known as tradition genres (*perinnelajit*). While different genres might deal with the same topic, each varies in the message that it conveys about that topic, and in the way in which it constrains the language used to express that topic, so that different genres can be seen as distinct channels of communication (Ben Amos 1976; Röhrich 1986; Honko 1989; Siikala 1990: 173; Apo 2001: 31–32). Similarly, the written material in newspapers cannot be treated as undifferentiated raw data. Each type of written genre (*juttulaji*) appearing in a newspaper (whether an editorial, news story, background article, book review, letter to the editor, or serialized fiction) has its own internal conventions which govern how the content of each is expressed (Pietilä 2008). Recognizing that genres are ideal types on a continuum of difference rather than clear-cut categories, the cultural researcher studying newspaper sources is well advised to take into account from the outset the particular features and communicative constraints of the genre category of any given news item.

The news items which dealt with home thievery in the 19th-century Finnish-language press can be divided into six genres: (1) editorials and solicited articles, (2) local news and commentary from rural correspondents, (3) unsolicited articles and essays, (4) opinion columns, (5) literature reviews, and (6) reports of discussions carried out at public meetings. Female gossip, for its part, was dealt with in editorials/solicited articles, and in the realistic ethnographic fiction published as serial novellas (which will be dealt with in the section 'Realistic ethnographic fiction'). I will now discuss each of these categories in turn.

Editorials and articles solicited from the editor's circle of acquaintances were usually lengthy and sought to present a broad, balanced approach to the topic at hand. The position taken was usually that of an omniscient 'voice from everywhere' and the interests claimed to be represented in the text were those of the common good, with any political arguments tending to be based on universal moral sources such as divine plan or natural law. Rural inhabitants, on the other hand, often preferred to write about what they knew best, and to couch their writings as correspondence from their home district. These rural correspondence letters were printed under the heading 'Domestic' (*Kotimaa*) or 'Countryside' (*Maaseutu*) and were generally short (or shortened by editors) and provided local news, weather and commentary on local district conditions and events, including harvests, famines, price levels for agricultural products, the building or renovation of churches, and accidents or crimes which had recently occurred in their locale. Yet, under the guise of 'local news', rural correspondents also responded angrily to prior attacks in the press on their person and home locality, and lobbied intensely for local wrongs to be righted.

Not all letters written by rural contributors were published as rural correspondence, however. Farmers and even landless labourers wrote longer essays which were published separately, outside the space set aside for domestic news. These were labelled '*Lähetetty*' (Sent). Letters sent to newspapers, both solicited and unsolicited, were also written by educated persons such as clergymen, schoolteachers, and university graduates, and were often written in response to something the writer had personally seen in his district or had read in the press, and the aim of such letters was generally either to provide practical information or to provoke discussion on a particular topic. Numerous early examples of letters sent by self-educated writers can be found in the short-lived newspaper *Sanan-Lennätin*. In its three years of publication (1856–1858), *Sanan-Lennätin* printed, in addition to 178 original letters of rural correspondence,[148] 63 essays written by fifteen rural men. At least six of these were known to be from the landowning farmer class, six more were probably landowning farmers, two were farmhands and one was a skilled artisan. These men wrote on various topics such as the language question, social reform and education, Finnish-language literature, agricultural advice, the price of newspapers, alcohol and tobacco, Christian morality, the care of orphans, the eradication of wolves from local forests, and the behaviour of farm masters and mistresses toward their

---

148 *Sanan-Lennätin* also regularly printed letters of correspondence borrowed from other newspapers. The number 178 represents the letters sent directly to *Sanan-Lennätin* for publication.

servants. With regard to the newspaper sources dealing with home thievery examined here, the genre of articles and essays sent by writers known or surmised to be self-educated rural inhabitants is represented by submission numbers: 4, 22, 23, 24, 25, 27, 28, 32, 34, 36, 43, 44, 56, and 64 printed in the newspapers *Lahden Lehti, Mikkelin Ilmoituslehti, Pohjalainen, Savo, Suometar, Tapio,* and *Uusi Suometar.*

Columns functioned somewhat like editorials in that the columnist took a stance on a particular issue and adopted the role of educator on topics assumed to concern a broad cross-section of the populace, but columnists differed from editors in that they were usually rural writers who wrote from a rural perspective and made reference to local customs and conditions. Literature reviews, for their part, could be fairly lengthy and were often written from a social reformist perspective, in which the book under review was judged by how educational or morally enlightening it was likely to be for the general public. Reports of meetings were usually summaries in which the themes of discussions were merely mentioned in passing, but the report of the 1862 Kuopio Agricultural Society meeting is interesting because it published actual speeches and comments made by meeting participants (see Chapter Eight). For this reason, the 1862 meeting report is one of the few sources in the press from which we can read both the names and the occupational/estate titles of persons who participated in public discussion. It is also one of the few sources from which we can read the opinions of men who may never have actually submitted anything written to the press, and who may not have even been able to write.

Finnish folklorists in recent decades have taken the view that source criticism means understanding not only *how* folklore texts in the archives were produced, but *why*, and *by whom* (e.g. U-M. Peltonen 1996; Pöysä 1997; Mikkola 2009). This has meant examining the reasons why rural amateur collectors produced and collected folklore texts, and the relationship between the producers of the texts and the FLS Folklore Archives' mostly male staff and researchers. These archival researchers and staff acted as 'gatekeepers' to the Archives, judging which folk traditions were authentic, valuable, and worthy of preservation, while rejecting others.[149] In the production of 19th-century newspapers, a comparable position of 'gatekeeper' to the public sphere of the press was occupied by newspaper editors, who were unable for various reasons to print all of the material submitted to them. Understanding to what extent the final printed content of newspapers reflected the interests and ideological stances of the rural public requires determining the exclusionary mechanisms of the press, in other words the criteria by which published texts were chosen over rejected texts. The reasons why some written submissions remained unpublished can be studied through editors' rejection and acceptance notices printed under the heading 'Correspondence' (see Chapter Three). Some topics, most notably complaints against the government or its officials, could not be published

---

149 Rejected texts were either sent back to the sender or placed in a file labeled 'F' for 'fakelore' where they remain in the FLS Folklore Archives to this day (Kapanen 2009).

due to censorship laws. Editors of 19th-century Finnish-language newspapers also tended to insist that submissions should reflect an ideology of progress, and that they should enlighten or educate the public. This inevitably meant that 19th-century Finnish editors declined to publish writings on certain topics. Exclusionary mechanisms have been shown by scholars to be an innate characteristic of the public sphere even when it purports to espouse openness and rational debate. Critical theorist Jodi Dean (1996: 227) has pointed out that the 'norms of the public sphere function to exclude certain topics from debate and to establish standards for what can be said and what must remain unsaid.' Topics excluded from Finnish-language newspapers in the last half of the 19th century – in addition to subject matter which might be deemed dangerous by the government – were those perceived by editors to oppose Finnish-language rights or to be at odds with efforts toward social and individual progress as defined within a liberalist ideology. In addition to this, however, editors often excluded submitted material on practical grounds such as the fact that the author had not divulged his real name, the topic of the written submission was part of a quarrel which had gone on too long or its news was already out of date, or because it was so incoherent that no amount of editing could render it publishable.

The fourth step in my methodology has been to employ multiple contextualizations in analyzing newspaper submissions (Apo 1995: 139). It must be noted that a purely intertextual or interdiscursive approach, in which texts are examined only in relation to other texts and discourses, does not produce sufficient explanatory value when the research aim is to answer questions dealing with the world outside the text. In this study, multiple contextualization has meant framing my source materials within the social, political, economic and ideological conditions prevailing at the moment the newspaper item was published, as well as within the stated mission of the newspaper itself, and the ideological leanings of its editor(s). Naturally it is also crucial, where possible, to ascertain the gender, age, occupation, social background and geographic location of the writers, and in this endeavour I have used both the archives of the Finnish Newspaper History Research Project (1975–1988), and The Genealogical Society of Finland's Historical Documents search engine (*Historiakirjojen hakuohjelma* or HisKi, http://hiski.genealogia.fi/historia) to make the best possible informed guesses concerning the identities of contributors to the 19th-century press. Additionally, it is necessary to consider the informational context of a particular piece of writing: what has been the history of discussion on a given topic in the press? It is important to note that in the 1860s and 1870s, discussions in the press were often national in scope. This is because in this period, there were still no local newspapers – at least none that were published on a printing press. *Maamiehen Ystävä, Suometar, Suomen Julkisia Sanomia, Suomalainen Wirallinen Lehti* and later *Uusi Suometar* were all national newspapers. The rest were focused on gaining a broad *regional* audience, and most regional newspapers such as *Tapio* had subscribers who lived outside their focal region. Not only did newspapers print each others' articles[150] and engage in occasionally heated debates with each other, but farmers and other rural inhabitants sometimes subscribed to several newspapers at once, thus keeping abreast of a whole range of news and ideological arguments written by contributors from all over the country. Less affluent rural inhabitants, too, could borrow issues from other subscribers or read a variety of newspapers in the lending libraries which began to appear in the countryside in the early 1860s (Kumpulainen 1983: 152; Vatanen 2002).[151] This meant that readers were often highly aware of what had been written in a number of newspapers appearing in the same week, and rural correspondents occasionally even criticized one newspaper in the pages of another.

Published and archived ethnographic descriptions

In addition to newspaper articles, the subject of home thievery was also briefly taken up in two separate books on Western Finnish rural traditions written by folklore collector and ethnographer Samuli Paulaharju: *Härmän aukeilta* (1932) and *Rintakyliä ja larwamaita* (1943). Home thievery was also mentioned four separate times in the 87-page *Kuvauksia kansannaisen elämästä maalla* (*Descriptions of Ordinary Women's Life in the Countryside*) published in 1890 by the *Suomen Nais-Yhdistys* (Finnish Women's Organization) and written by both male and female authors, of whom the female authors identified themselves only by initials or first names. According to ethnologist Riitta Räsänen (1997), this collection of texts arose in response to an article published in the 1889 *Excelsior* calendar produced by the Finnish Women's Organization. The written responses were published in the journal *Koti ja yhteiskunta* (Home and Society). In publishing these responses, the literary committee of the Finnish Women's Organization declared that although the descriptions portrayed women's industriousness and diligence, it was clear from them that '[– –] darkness still covers our land to a large degree and folk custom in many respects wages war with the fundamental ideals of Christian morality [– –]. Every person, who understands the historical truth, that nations weaken along with the weakening morals of its people and especially its women, must now, to the best of their powers, endeavour to improve the situation of women both morally and educationally' (Editorial afterword, p. 87).

For my analysis of the topic of female gossip and 'news carrying' (*kontin kantaminen*), I have located a total of 110 recollected ethnographic descriptions housed in the FLS Folklore Archives whose information was provided by 114 different informants. Nearly all of these texts were sent to the FLS Folklore Archives in the years 1965–1966. Four ethnographic descriptions of gossip and news carrying were sent to the Archives prior

150 See Tommila 1988: 204–207.
151 See also: April 20, 1961. *Tapio* no. 16, 'Rääkkylästä' (J H–n); June 15, 1861. *Tapio* no. 24, 'Tohmajärveltä' (O. F. B.).

to the Second World War: one was sent in 1889, one in 1896, one in 1928 and one in 1932. Thirteen recollected descriptions were sent to the Archives in connection with the 'Collection contest for Karelian festive traditions' (*Karjalan juhlaperinteen kilpakeräys*) in 1957, and three descriptions were sent to the Archives during the 1970s.

The texts sent to the Folklore Archives in the mid-1960s were written in response to a questionnaire compiled by folklorist Anneli Asplund in 1965 for the Archives' *Kansatieto* (*Folk Knowledge*) news bulletin. The questions dealt with village gossip women (*kylän ämmät*) and the songs composed by the youth to mock them. The *Kansatieto* news bulletin was sent to a pre-existing network of respondents, which in 1965 numbered between 1000 and 1100 individuals.[152] The exact set of questions, comprising questionnaire no. 55 in issue 19 of the bulletin, appears below:

Village women

1.	This village's women,	*Tämän kylän ämmät*
	the curly-tailed ones,	*kippurahännät*
	cuppers[153] and witches	*kupparit ja noidat*
	call me names, little maid that I am	*haukkuvat mua pikkasta likkaa*
	bark at me like mongrels	*niin kuin rakkikoirat*

Is this song familiar? What other songs do you know that tell of village women? In what situations were the songs performed, and were they sung in the village women's hearing or only among the youth at round games and dances? Were the verses to these village women's songs joined randomly one after another, whatever someone happened to remember, or were particular verses sung always in the same order? How many verses were linked together and sung to the same melody, and when was the melody replaced with a new one?
Where were these songs learned? Did people compose them themselves?

2.

In almost every village, there were at least in former times women who wished to gossip, who sifted through their neighbours' affairs amongst themselves; young persons in particular were objects of slander [literally: 'in the women's teeth']. Was the word *kontinkantaminen* known in your area, and did news carrying (*kontinkanto*) and gossiping (*juoruaminen*) mean the same thing, or did the former have some special meaning? If you know the proverb 'When there is a woman as the marriage spokesman, then [– –]' (*'Kun on akka puhemiehenä, niin on [– –]'*), how would you complete it?
When was 'news' (*kontit*) carried? Was this connected especially to courting among the youth, or was 'news' carried about other things?

152	This estimate, based on the FLS Folklore Archives' annual reports, minutes of committee meetings and the forewords printed in the *Kansatieto* bulletins themselves, was provided by the staff of the FLS Folklore Archives in a personal communication on March 11, 2011.
153	Cuppers were bloodletters who used hollow cows' horns and other implements to suction blood from small cuts made in their clients' skin. Cupping was used, for instance, to relieve the symptoms of high blood pressure.

What attitudes were adopted toward the news carrier? Did she have many enemies in the village? Was it expected that 'news' would be carried?

Who acted as news carriers? Were only women mentioned as news carriers or were men also used in news carrying? What kind of news was carried, flattering or disapproving? Did this practice make any difference, was the desired aim achieved?

Was there in the village some woman who was used particularly often, or could just anyone be sent? Were persons in certain occupations more suited to this work? Was she paid for her efforts?

Tell about other aspects of news carriers and gossip.

These questions directed at potential respondents are neutral in tone and leave broad latitude for respondents to write from their own experience and folk knowledge. Nevertheless, the amount of information pre-provided in the questionnaire is considerable, as has been necessary in the Folklore Archives' collection campaigns in order to generate interest in the topic and elicit responses. The possibility must be kept in mind that such information may have led the respondents to answer as they assumed was expected by the FLS Folklore Archive staff and researchers, or that respondents might have been reluctant to correct the assumptions embedded in the questions, such as the assumption that most village gossips were women, or that gossip women would naturally have enemies. However, since these questions did not arise from baseless assumptions but were derived from prior descriptions archived in the FLS Folklore Archives, they appear to correspond to the more or less universal features of gossip women's behaviour in the 19th-century Finnish countryside. Moreover, the corpus of ethnographic descriptions examined in this study turns out to contain little evidence that informants responded to the questions with a simple 'yes', or that they would have been reluctant to correct the questionnaire on certain points based on their own personal knowledge.

The number of recollected descriptions sent in response to this questionnaire which deal specifically with 'news carrying' is 90. The ethnographic descriptions sent by respondents to the FLS Folklore Archives were either written down from the sender/collector's own memory or were recorded from other persons interviewed by the sender/collector. In this study I use the term 'informant'[154] to refer to the person who was the original source of the information recorded. This means that the

---

154 The term 'informant' has been viewed by some scholars as problematic due to its positivistic connotations in which the researcher's own positioning with regard to knowledge production is not acknowledged. I have nonetheless chosen to use 'informant' for lack of a better term in English which would refer to persons who both narrate and describe, in other words, who provide information in the form of both narratives (a sequence of events arranged in a plot) and descriptions (general portrayals of folk life in which there is no sequence of events). For the latter, the term 'narrator' is not appropriate. I view the term 'informant' as a neutral term, since the fact that the researcher receives some sort of information from the informant is not in dispute. The term itself implies nothing about how that information is produced, negotiated or interpreted by either the informant or the researcher.

informant could either have been the sender of the information, or someone interviewed by the sender. Methodologically speaking, written ethnographic descriptions possess both advantages and disadvantages in comparison to newspaper sources. One methodological caution which applies to both newspaper sources and ethnographic descriptions is the fact that since informants and writers usually strove to present their descriptions of rural life from a general rather than personal perspective, the extent to which they are actually based on personal experience often cannot be determined. But whereas the newspaper sources analyzed here were written much closer in time to the historical moment they were describing, the FLS Folklore Archives did not express an interest in gossip until 1965, which meant that responses to the question of 'gossip women' were written as much as six or seven decades after the events and conditions they describe. Nearly all of the available information regarding gossip women and news carriers, therefore, has been subject to processes of long-term memory such as cultural filtering, selective forgetting and interpretation of the past from the vantage point of the present (see Korkiakangas 2005). On the other hand, as historian and ethnologist Michel de Certeau (1984: 22) has pointed out, temporal distance can sometimes allow the contours of cultural tactics and strategies, which are taken for granted in everyday life, to emerge more clearly and intelligibly through narrative. In fact, many of the informants who related information about gossip women were able to convey a holistic and concise picture of the practice of village gossip in prior decades, and their descriptions contain many similar elements, even if they differ in emphasis and detail.

Ethnographic descriptions of 'news carrying' reveal that the practice was known in all parts of historical Finland. Within the corpus of 110 texts analyzed here, the geographic area of South Karelia is by far the best represented, with 39 texts. The number of texts from other regions of Finland is as follows: South Ostrobothnia (14), Häme (9), Satakunta (9), North Ostrobothnia (7), North Karelia (6), North Savo (6), Central Finland (4), Ladoga Karelia (4), Kainuu (4), Varsinais-Suomi (3), South Savo (3), Uusimaa (1), and North Finland, including Lapland (1). While the specific dialect terms used for gossip women and 'news carriers' varied across these different parts of Finland, the ethnographic descriptions of the practice, its practitioners, and the social consequences of news carrying appear to have been highly similar throughout the country.

In terms of the gender of informants, 48 men and 66 women provided information on female gossips. Based on the available information regarding the ages of the informants, the oldest were born in the 1870s (three persons) and the youngest in the 1920s (four persons). Most informants for whom we have information on their date of birth were born either in the 1890s (nineteen persons) or in the decade 1900–1909 (21 persons).

Realistic ethnographic fiction

Some of the most interesting sources on gossip and news carrying are realistic ethnographic fictions such as Minna Canth's three-act play *Roinilan Talossa* (*On Roinila Farm*, 1885), Santeri Alkio's novel *Teerelän perhe* (*The Teerelä Family*, 1887), and serial fictions published in newspapers by both lesser and better known authors. E. A. Jää's *Kuolo kaikki sowittaa* (*Death Absolves Everything*) was published in eight instalments in 1881 in the newspaper *Sawo*,[155] and Eero J–nen's *Kuwaelmia sodasta walon ja pimeyden välillä* (*Depictions of the Struggle Between Light and Darkness*) was published in the newspaper *Porilainen* in 1893.[156] Successful popular author Pietari Päivärinta (1827–1913) published his *Naimisen juoruja. Kuwaelmia Kansan elämästä* (*Marriage Gossip: Depictions of Folk Life*) in 32 instalments in the newspaper *Uusi Suometar* in 1882,[157] and Johannes Häyhä's *Naimistavat Itä-Suomessa. Kuvaelmia entisiltä ajoilta* (*Marriage Customs in Eastern Finland: Depictions of Former Times*) appeared in 30 instalments in the newspaper *Wiipurin Sanomat* in 1886.[158] Häyhä's novella was later published in book form, first by the Finnish Literature Society in 1893 and again by the adult education organisation *Kansanvalistusseura* in 1899 under the title *Kuwaelmia itä-suomalaisten wanhoista tawoista. Naimistawat* (*Depictions of Old Customs Among the Eastern Finns: Marriage Customs*). The novel *Mitä Puuttui? Kertomus perheellisesta elämästä* (*What was Missing? A Narrative of Family Life*) by J. Haanpää appeared in reverse order: first as a book published by the Finnish Literature Society in 1891, and then printed in precisely the same format in the newspaper *Uusi Suometar* later that same year,[159] so that readers could cut out each instalment and reassemble the pages into a complete book of their own.

In 1888 appeared a small book entitled *Kotivarkaus. Kuvaus Itä-Suomesta* (*Home Thievery. A Description from Eastern Finland*) which described the practice of home thievery and its tragic moral consequences[160] within a single family household in Eastern Finland. Its author, Adolf (Aatto) Suppanen (1855–1898), was virtually unknown both before and after the book's publication, but the book was widely reviewed in the press and received

---

155 The first installment appeared on November 11, 1881 (no. 87) and the last on December 6, 1881 (no. 93).

156 This serial novella begins, oddly enough, at the beginning of its fourth chapter on March 7, 1893 (no. 45) and ends at the end of the fifth chapter, 'Juorukelloja', on April 18, 1893 (no. 57).

157 The first installment of Päivärinta's serial novella appeared on June 9, 1882 (no. 131), and the last installment on September 6, 1882 (no. 206).

158 The first installment appeared on January 2, 1886 (no. 1), and ran until June 29, 1886 (no. 100).

159 July 2, 1891. *Uusi Suometar* no. 149, 'Mitä puuttui? Kertomus perheellisestä elämästä' (J. Haanpää / Finnish Literature Society Press). Haanpää's book also includes a brief mention of home thievery, practiced by the son and daughter of the farm.

160 After being exposed to home thievery early in life, the second eldest son of the farm, Mikko, commits theft in adulthood and dies in a shipwreck while fleeing from the law.

praise for its 'bonafide realism' and 'warm spirit of Christian civility' [51], as well as for being a 'morally instructional and uplifting tale' [49].

What unites many of the authors mentioned above is their rural background as members of the farmer or crofter classes. By contrast, well-known Finnish author and playwright Maria Jotuni (1880–1943), who in 1913 wrote a short story about home thievery entitled *Kansantapa* (*Folk Custom*), did not come from a rural background. Jotuni was the daughter of a master blacksmith and grew up in the city of Kuopio in her grandfather's home. Jotuni's family valued learning and enlightenment, and Jotuni was allowed to pursue an education, which was unusual for a woman of her social class during this period. She graduated from a girl's school in Kuopio at the age of 20. It is unclear whether Jotuni can be said to have modelled her description of home thievery from any personal experience she might have had with farm households in the countryside. In keeping with her interest in themes regarding the battle of the sexes and her fragmented, modernist style constructed through dialogue, Jotuni describes the meetings and conversations between a farm mistress intent on pilfering and the landless itinerant woman who serves as her intermediary in selling the pilfered goods. Although the lengthy speeches given by the landless female intermediary in her story appear to be more suited to Jotuni's own views on marriage than to those which might have been expressed by an uneducated rural woman of the era, in other respects, the details and plot of Jotuni's story follow closely the depictions of home thievery which appeared in contemporary newspapers and in published ethnographic descriptions.

Although all of the above mentioned works are fictitious accounts, they nevertheless provide unique insights into the dynamics of both local gossip and women's activities within the household, insights not available from other sources. Folklorist Satu Apo, in discussing the value of ethnographic fiction for cultural and historical research, points out that as long as the author was describing the culture he or she was born and raised in, and as long as the author was committed to a realistic mode of presentation, ethnographic fiction can be considered the cultural historian's most valuable source of information, since it provides a *holistic* picture of life in a particular group or community, one in which the author has already traced out the semantic connections between behaviour and context, and has identified the meanings relevant to the members of that culture (Apo 2001: 18). One of the strengths of ethnographic fiction is that it often uses dialogue to advance the plot, thereby unveiling the dynamics of social negotiation between human interlocutors. Given most of these authors' facility with language, there is little reason to suppose that these fictive dialogues diverged significantly from the ways in which persons would have actually conversed in the cultural milieu depicted.[161]

---

161 Johannes Häyhä (1839–1913), for example, was apparently a gifted mimic who had an excellent ear and memory for dialogue. By his own account, as a young child he had been able to imitate so well the turns of phrase used by the local clergyman preaching in church that on Sundays people gathered at his home from throughout the parish to listen to the young Häyhä deliver his 'sermons' (Häyhä 1897: 4, unpublished manuscript housed in the FLS Literature Archives).

Dialogue as a means of furthering the plot allows the characters of realistic ethnographic fiction to have their own voices, which in turn provides the reader with valuable insights into what the authors assumed the characters' motives would have been, and how the characters would have understood both the world around them and their own agency. One drawback of realistic ethnographic fiction for the researcher interested in authentic portrayals of folk life, however, is that ethnographic fiction could serve a number of authorial aims beyond that of ethnographic accuracy, including moral education, social reform, and entertainment. Authors put words in their characters' mouths that advanced their own agendas, and identifying these agendas, such as the reformist agendas of many of the popular ethnographic authors listed above, adds important contextual layers to the researcher's analysis.

II
Practices of Power
in Everyday Life

5. The Rise Of Rural Consumption and its Discontents

*...Showiness flourishes in the land / Splendour on men and women alike /
If Adam and Eve were to rise again / they would not know their children...
– Finnish Lutheran hymnal of 1701, hymn no. 280*

One of the most important catalysts for social change in 19th-century Finland was the 1859 statute which legalized retail trade in the countryside.[162] After rural shops became legal, access to store-bought goods, and with it household consumption, increased dramatically.[163] Understanding the practice of home thievery in the 19th-century Finnish countryside requires recognizing the importance of transformations in personal consumption which motivated farm women to sell whatever goods they could in exchange for those items they felt they needed – items that could not be obtained directly from the farm itself.

For the gentry, personal consumption had been on the rise at least since the 18th century, with gentlefolk buying tea, coffee, chocolate, sugar, spices and wines from city shops and market stalls. Most landowning peasants, however, not to mention the landless population of the countryside, had neither regular access to, nor the money to pay for store-bought goods. There was, in fact, very little money circulating in the early 19th-century countryside. Peasant households were largely self-sufficient (although this does not necessarily mean they made everything themselves, only that they paid in grain, butter, or wool for others to make it for them), and they even paid their taxes to the Crown and tithes to the clergy in grain, butter,[164] and

---

162 The law which ensured that commerce could only take place in cities or on legal market days in the countryside was circumvented in various ways already before 1859, for instance by butter merchants who regularly travelled the countryside (e.g. Räisänen & Kumpulainen 1981: 441).

163 Just four years after rural shops were legalized, Kuopio province could already boast 58 rural shopkeepers in 21 different parishes, with an additional 17 open market stalls in Kuopio, 14–15 in Joensuu, and some half-dozen in Iisalmi, with more men applying all the time for permits. However, this still meant only 1 shop per every 2400 persons in Kuopio province. (January 3, 1863. *Tapio* no. 1, 'Maa-kauppiaita Kuopion läänissä').

164 The sale of livestock products represented an important source of monetary income for the Finnish rural population in the mid-19th century, and its importance only increased in later decades with the completion of railroads to large population centres such as Saint Petersburg, where demand for dairy products was high. Significantly for this study, it was women who primarily owned and tended cattle in the 19th century.

other farm products. Crofters and cottagers paid their rent to landowning farmers in the form of day labour, and salaries to servants were paid in grain and alcohol (Kuusanmäki 1936: 97–98; Alanen 1957: 170).

According to contemporaries writing to the 19th-century press, however, at the beginning of the 1870s there was suddenly much more money with which to buy store-bought goods. In the years directly following the great famine of 1867–8, harvests were good and butter was sold in greater quantities to towns and cities. After the Franco-German war in 1871, the European economy expanded, raising the demand for Finnish and Swedish exports, mainly lumber. In Finland, this caused a speculative boom in forest land. The price of lumber rose, bringing cash to many farmers, most of whom owned tracts of forest land in addition to their fields.[165] This particular lumber boom was brief, lasting only four years from 1873 to 1877 (Kuisma 2006: 290–291), but during these years, many who had money in their pockets were spending it faster than shopkeepers could supply the goods (Alanen 1957: 262–263). Groups with increased purchasing power included not only forest-owning peasants, but also the landless labourers who received high wages to cut and transport the lumber, as well as the farmhands and serving maids who had to be paid higher wages on farms so they would not leave to join the ranks of the lumber workers (Kuusanmäki 1936: 103; Alanen 1957: 317).[166] Another socio-economic boost was provided by the growing dairy industry, which in turn was promoted by the construction of railways and new, more efficient practices in cattle husbandry starting in the early 1860s.[167]

The goods sold in the first shops in the Finnish countryside needed little advertisement, since potential customers were drawn to them by mere curiosity (Alanen 1957: 311). By the 1870s, shops were regularly stocked with tobacco, coffee, spices, port wine, cognac, liqueurs, arrack, rum and sherry, herring, soap, rope, liquorice, fruits both fresh and dried, matches,

---

165 Concerns were raised over the ecological effects of timber clearcutting as early as 1862, when the following question was raised at the Kuopio Agricultural Society meeting: 'Since the reckless destruction of forest land will unavoidably cause damage in the future to these provinces in terms of both climate and in other ways, we ask, what are the primary causes of this destruction and how can it be prevented?' [20].

166 Newspaper articles, however, suggest that the sale of forest lumber by farmers may not always have been by choice. A bad harvest caused by a late frost in 1874, coupled with rising wages for labourers (due to the deaths of many labourers in the 1867–1868 famine and to the high demand for workers not only as lumberjacks but also in railways, iron works, and canal building) meant that some farmers, even if they might not have wanted to, may have been forced to sell off their forests in order to pay farmhands and serving maids the high wages they demanded. (August 14, 1874. *Uusi Suometar* no. 94, 'Helsingistä. Mietteitä kehnon wuodentulon ja ylenewien työpalkkojen johdosta.')

On the high cost of farm labour during the lumber boom, see: September 27, 1873. *Satakunta* no. 35, 'Ahlaisista' (– . –); May 15, 1874, *Uusi Suometar* no. 57, 'Muhokselta' (J. P. W., talokas); June 20, 1874. *Satakunta* no. 25, 'Pori. Kalliista ajoista...'; November 20, 1874. *Uusi Suometar* no. 136, 'Haapawedeltä' (A. J–nen.); February 19, 1876. *Tapio* no. 8, 'Nilsiästä' (Muu'an mies); October 13, 1877. *Ilmarinen. Sanomia Itä-Suomesta* no. 80, 'Kylmäkoski' (J. W.); October 13, 1877. *Keski-Suomi* no. 41, 'Kirje weikolleni J. E. J. Sawossa' (P–wedeltä Lokakuun t. p. 1877, G. s–sa).

167 Kuusanmäki 1936: 103; Alanen 1957: 317; Peltonen 2004: 121–122.

syrup, sweets, caps, leather, axe handles, pretzels and other baked goods, tobacco pipes, wallets, textiles and fabric, and petrol gas lamps. Shops were so attractive and interesting that people who came to buy one specific necessity often stayed to enjoy the novelties displayed on the store shelves and left with numerous things they did not necessarily need, especially since they could buy on credit and pay later.[168]

One rural correspondent from Central Finland, writing to the newspaper *Uusi Suometar* in 1878, described the dramatic change in some farmers' lifestyles brought on by the lumber boom which had just ended:

> In return for our forests, we received money by the bushel, by the barrel, but we let it go the same way it had come, why would we have saved it for the days to come? We got the money for free, and freely it left us, we didn't really need that money for necessities, since we had survived before it, survived without it. In former times we ate pine bark[169] and drank water, and we managed to get by. Now, not even unleavened barley bread and coffee are good enough in the opinions of many, now each must have his storehouse stocked with sweetbreads made from wheat and purchased from the baker, as well as expensive beverages brought from the city, at least for when guests arrive. When one adds to this fine food and drink, handsome clothing, handsome furniture, fine carts and sleighs, noble stallions which have to be fed in the stable year round, and daily food which must be bought from elsewhere [– –] one sees how this money received from our lumber slips a thousand-fold through our fingers. It taught us to enjoy life, taught us that money can be obtained for free, and we became lazy.[170]

Even after the lumber boom of the mid-1870s, heightened consumption of store-bought goods had become a daily habit which was difficult to relinquish, even to the point of leading farms and individuals into heavy debt during the severe depression which lasted until 1882.[171] A writer from North Karelia to the Eastern Finnish newspaper *Karjalatar* in 1888 gave the following account of the debt created by the boom times of the 1870s:

> Such things as we had previously no knowledge of, now became daily necessities. All clothing had been, until then, taken from the fields or from the backs of sheep. But now that began to seem so cumbersome

168 Alanen 1957: 428; See also November 2,1888. *Päivän Uutiset* no. 257, 'Palwelijain tuhlausaika'.
169 Finely ground flour from the innermost layer of the pine tree's bark, or phloem, is known in Finland as *pettu*. It was widely used as a supplement to rye flour in making bread. It was eaten not only in times of famine but, according to a survey undertaken by the Finnish Economic Administration Society (*Suomen Talousseura*) in the 1830s, was eaten more or less regularly by about half of the country's rural inhabitants (Liakka 1923: 178–183, in Haatanen 1968: 1). Pine-bark flour is now known to have been fairly nutritious when mixed with rye flour.
170 October 4–5, 1878. *Uusi Suometar* no. 119, 'Saarijärveltä'. See also: March 29, 1878. *Uusi Suometar* no. 38, 'Nykyinen taloudellinen asema'.
171 Alanen 1957: 420–429; Herrala 1999: 10; Hjerppe 1989: 56; Kaarniranta 2001: 147–148.

and old-fashioned, and the opportunity for an easier life arose [– –]. But this blissful period did not last long. The forests were sold off, and the price of lumber fell, and the credit offered by the shopkeepers began to dry up. Yet the new necessities of life had become a habit, and had to be obtained at all costs. What else was there to do but increase the mortgage on the farm, and in that way one could obtain more. Thus a great number of farms have ended up in the mortgage-fetters of the rural shopkeepers. I mention as an example that a certain shopkeeper in the city of Nurmes has over a hundred farms mortgaged against their debts to him. Since the farms are, on average, about 1/8 of a tax measure (*manttaali*) in size and the district of Nurmes contains 90 tax measures, this means that approximately 1/6 of the farms in the entire district are mortgaged to a single shopkeeper. If we take into account other shopkeepers and mortgages to private persons, how many farms in Nurmes remain free from debt? [47]

Among the goods sold in shops, those considered to be the most tempting and dangerous were various exotic varieties of alcohol beverages consumed mostly by men and offered to male visitors. Although women were blamed in the press for spending too much money on frivolities, they were not accused of consuming store-bought alcohol. Apo (2001: 104–106) has pointed out that in the older agrarian culture, in which alcohol consumption was closely linked to notions of honourable and able-bodied masculinity, women were the household members seen to be least entitled to drink alcohol. This may be why, when a refreshing new beverage became available in the early decades of the 19th century, it was farm women who embraced it wholeheartedly. Coffee was soon to be maligned in the press as the most dangerous consumer good of all.

Coffee: the necessary luxury

Sources do not provide a definitive answer to the question of when coffee drinking became commonplace in the countryside. Some suggest that coffee, made from coffee beans ground by the buyers themselves, was being drunk by peasants in different parts of the country already in the 1830s (Kuusanmäki 1936: 113), and that by the 1850s it was being consumed at peasant celebrations in many parts of inner Finland. For instance, in one fictive conversation between a farm master and his wife appearing in the newspaper *Tapio* in 1863, the farm mistress tells her husband: '[– –]when it comes to giving up coffee drinking altogether, I don't think we can make it happen any longer, now that we have been used to enjoying it every morning it for nearly twenty years'.[172] Other sources suggest, however, that although the consumption of coffee increased significantly in the 1840s, it was only in the 1870s that farm household members drank coffee every day and not just on Sundays and holidays (Talve 1997: 132). In any case, sources agree

172 December 19, 1863. *Tapio* no. 51. 'Mistä rahaa saadaan?'

Although vilified in the press as a dangerous luxury good, by the last half of the 19th century, coffee had come to be perceived as a necessity in many rural households. Farm mistresses served coffee to guests in order to enhance their social status in the eyes of their peers, and to pave the way for smooth relations with gossip women who brought information about community affairs. The rural poor, for their part, were reported to have sometimes been more willing to go without food than to give up coffee. Here, a woman from Parkano district in Satakunta brews coffee. Photo: Samuli Paulaharju, 1939.

that by the 1880s and 1890s, coffee had become the refreshment offered to guests by prosperous farming households, and that in the mornings it was offered to the entire household, including servants. Even the poor living in small cottages drank coffee, although only sparingly, when guests came to visit (Kuusanmäki 1936: 114–115; Alanen 1957: 172, 314). As one man from Satakunta explained in his ethnographic description to the FLS Folklore Archives sent in 1889:

> Coffee is offered to guests even in the smallest cottages, and on some farms it is a daily refreshment enjoyed by the farm master and mistress. This can also be seen from the new name for coffee, 'daily', by which name it is asked for in shops, especially when buying smaller amounts, and the shopkeeper seems to know this name quite well. Thus some farm masters and mistresses, and especially the latter, drink coffee three times a day, and in many cottages, when coffee runs out it creates as much distress as if bread had run out.[173]

By the last decades of the 19th century, coffee had become important to the social standing of wealthier farms. In Niilo Sauhke's description of women's social life in Salmi prior to World War II, coffee played a central role in mistresses' Sunday visits and handiwork parties. Mistresses hosted

---

173 SKS KRA. Lempäälä. 1889. J. V. Holm E 1.

the parties in their homes by turns, and since coffee was the most important refreshment offered, it was vital to a mistress' social standing among her peers to have some on hand to offer her guests (Sauhke 1971: 59–61).

Coffee was expensive, and the rapid increase in its consumption in the latter half of the 19th century led to fears that it would cause the financial ruin of farms. Because of this, coffee was vilified in 19th-century public discourse as a dangerous consumer good (Alanen 1957: 334). Already in the early 1860s, farmers worried about the effects of coffee on household economies. For example, a farmer at a parish assizes in 1863 expressed concerns that the spread of rural shops was increasing the consumption of coffee in the countryside:

> The sale of coffee – in the opinion of farm master Heikki Nousiainen from Willala farm – that is the worst of all. The drinking of coffee, as widespread as it is these days, would presumably only escalate greatly if coffee were available so close at hand [30].

As one man from South Savo (b. 1858) explained in an ethnographic description sent to the FLS Folklore Archives in 1939, songs intended to mock coffee drinkers such as the following were composed by those who 'did not dare consume it, fearing it would lead to the ruin of the farm':

Little serving maids	Piika likat pikkuset
Feeling grumpy and put out,	Päästänsä oli kiukkuiset
Being used to drinking coffee	Kahvia juomaan totunna
But their money has run out.	Kun markat heillä on loppunna[174]

Despite the widespread criticism against it, many in the countryside viewed coffee as an absolute daily necessity. Because of its 'refreshing' properties, coffee was seen as giving persons additional energy to allow them to perform heavy labour for longer periods of time, and the aforementioned fictitious farm mistress in the 1863 story in *Tapio* even claimed that servants remained content with more basic, cheaper food as long as they were given coffee, so that in fact serving them coffee saved money on the farm.[175] In 1857, the district physician of Savonlinna reported that coffee was so popular in his district that the poor preferred to go without food rather than give up drinking coffee (Kuusanmäki 1936: 114). Rural correspondent and farm master Albert Kukkonen[176] from Rautalampi likewise complained in a 1866 letter to *Tapio* that rural shops had brought coffee within reach even of the poorest rural inhabitants, who cared more for coffee than for bread and would even go so far as to beg for money in order to buy coffee (Saloheimo 1959: 334).

---

174 SKS KRA. Ristiina. 1939. Juho Oksman E 151: 284. – male labourer.
175 December 19, 1863. *Tapio* no. 51. 'Mistä rahaa saadaan?'
176 Albert Kukkonen (1835–1918) was the self-educated the master of Hinkkala manor farm and a well known folk poet. See also note 207.

New clothing styles and the critique of ostentation

In addition to coffee, many rural inhabitants also began to wear clothing in new styles which required store-bought fabrics and decorations. The appearance in shops of factory-spun cotton fabric which was both strong and cheap, first manufactured outside Finland and then, starting in the 1830s, inside the country, was a significant event, for now even a poor man's wife could afford to buy cloth she had not spun and woven herself. According to historian Lauri Kuusanmäki (1936: 110), probate inventories show that already in the 1830s, even impoverished cobblers and the wives of itinerant day labourers in the interior of Finland had factory-made cotton dresses, some even owning many such dresses, not to mention cotton scarves. By the 1850s, itinerant peddlers from Russian Karelia were carrying cheap cotton cloth in their knapsacks. Between 1859 and 1863, fabric began to be newly produced in four factories in Finland. The volume of factory-made cloth increased dramatically, whereupon the price fell, and store-bought fabrics were suddenly well within the grasp of even industrial labourers and farm servants, who began to compete with farm family members in the ostentation of their apparel.[177] The availability of affordable sewing machines, the first of which were apparently brought to Finland from Boston circa 1862,[178] meant that seamstresses could now make from factory cloth clothes which were so cheap, they no longer needed to last a lifetime (Kuusanmäki 1936: 112).

During the lumber boom of the mid-1870s, the higher wages paid to logging workers and farm servants increased the purchasing power of these groups, and this in turn was expressed in the clothes they wore (Heikkinen 2000: 143). With no land of their own to invest in, many young farmhands invested their wealth in their personal appearance. While poor farmers and crofters were still wearing homespun clothing well into the 1880s, workers in rural factories, railroads, sawmills and logging camps had no way of obtaining cloth except to buy it (Kuusanmäki 1936: 112). As Kuusanmäki (1936: 103) described, '[– –] it could be observed that the common folk, who had so recently been poor, now dressed in baize cloth and shiny shoes with no regard for their social position.' Lumberjacks and even some farmhands were able to afford stovepipe hats (ibid: 106). By the end of the 19th century, even the lowliest farmhands in peripheral areas were wearing clothes which were completely factory made. It was natural that when farm sons and daughters saw how the hired hands on the farm 'paraded like lords in such factory-made cloth', they themselves no longer wanted to wear homespun,

177 July 12, 1862. *Mikkelin Ilmoituslehti* no. 28, 'Joroisista'.
178 July 14, 1862. *Suomen Julkisia Sanomia* no. 52, 'Ompeluskoneita'. This brief news item reported that sewing machines were available for purchase in Helsinki at the shop of Mattson and Brofeldt, cost 60 silver rubles each and were already in use by a number of tailors and even private households. The article reported that while it took an ordinary tailor or seamstress at least 14 hours and 26 minutes to make a gentleman's shirt, the same shirt could be made with one of the new sewing machines in only 1 hour and 16 minutes.

but instead wore hats and store-bought silk stockings (Kuusanmäki 1936: 111). When the stiff embroidered bonnets (*tykkimyssy*) worn to church on Sundays began to go out of fashion among farm mistresses, silk scarves and shawls became 'the emblem of full standing in society' (Kuusanmäki 1936: 112; Alanen 1957: 134).

Criticism of ostentation, vanity and increased expenditure on fine clothes by rural women and youths was a favourite theme in the press throughout the period under study. This consumption was seen to threaten household economies primarily because most households were thought not to have sufficient means to afford the new fashions, as was explained by a rural writer to *Suometar* in 1865:

> Mournfully we must deplore the fact that ostentation and lordliness have become extremely common, especially among our women folk. Even though otherwise hard times are at hand, they do not care about this, but carry their last kopeck to the shopkeeper, of whom there are three here located near the church, in order to buy all kinds of frivolous items, such as crinoline hoops [– –].[179]

In 1882, a farm woman signing herself 'Liina A.' from Pielavesi district took up the topic of 'expensive foreign clothes manufactured according to elite fashions' in the pages of the newspaper *Sawo*:

> Do we have in our poor country so much money that there is enough to let so much of it slip into foreign clutches? Couldn't that money have been put to many times better use in our home country? [41]

It was not only its economically ruinous consequences which made the consumption of store-bought clothing seem threatening. The wearing of new styles was also seen to blur the social boundaries – maintained through visual performances of dress and comportment – between different classes and estates (see Mikkola 2009; Mikkola & Stark 2009). Before the coming of rural shops and rising wages, it had been possible to identify a person's social status at a glance from the clothing he or she wore. The manor lord wore lordly clothing such as stiff starched collars and shiny, delicate or tightly-fitting fabrics completely unsuited to physical labour, while the peasant wore peasant's clothing: loose fitting, homespun, durable clothing in which he could work in the fields. Gradually, however, modes of dress which no longer respected boundaries of class and estate became more common. As one rural writer signing himself 'E.W–r.' from Central Finland wrote in 1865:

> If a person comes to our parish who does not know the women of our congregation, he is often unable to distinguish the daughter of a provost from the daughter of a tailor or landowning peasant, unless a lady of the

179 July 17, 1865. *Suometar* no. 162, 'Jämsästä heinäk. 13 p. 1865' (E. W–r.).

gentry is wearing a hat, since tailors' daughters have not yet started to wear them.[180]

Another rural contributor to the newspaper *Sawonlinna* in 1878 lamented the same trend:

> The breath of these fast-moving times has blown upon the common folk so that their external, pseudo-refinement has taken the form of boundless splendour, so boundless that without an eyeglass it is impossible to distinguish the different estates from each other. Pseudo-refinement, in these fast-paced times, has already managed to draw nearly equal with the more civilized gentry, at least when seen from the outside. The only difference left is between young women, since only those of the more civilized estate can wear hats on their heads. But already in this respect, some women from landowning farm families have achieved a balance, for they are seen to wear fur hats in winter [– –]. Our hymn book says of this pseudo-refinement which scorns its true social estate: *Showiness flourishes in the land, Splendour of men and women alike, If Adam and Eve were to rise again, they would not know their children [– –].*[181]

In some situations, the violation of the symbolic boundary of dress led to more than just complaints; it created such confusion and cognitive dissonance in observers that they were forced – at least according to one rural correspondent – to categorize commoners from other districts who wore shiny store-bought clothes as complete foreigners:

> [– –] our simple and Christian way of life has had a positive influence on the population of our district. Thus our maidens have remained in quite simple dress when compared to the ridiculous foppishness of our neighbouring district's young women, their mimicking of gentlewomen, and their pursuance of fashion. Here, you see, there are very few women from the gentry who would force their wretched fashions upon our young women. [Footnote:] Our womenfolk are so behind in the pursuance of fashion that when a young hussy from a neighbouring district, who dressed in the latest fashions, happened to come here and she appeared in a public place, for example at church, our worthy farm mistresses and their daughters turned to gape at this notable miracle[182] like a cow would gawk at a new gate! And that peculiar phenomenon gave rise to speculation, conjecture and discussion for a long time. The outcome of these discussions is often very strange; for example when some time back, a young bride who married into our district from a neighbouring district appeared for the first time at church, the farm mistresses, having quickly inspected the apparel of this new social class from head to toe, had come to the conclusion that, among other things, she was of an entirely different nationality than they themselves were. If only they could have said to what nationality she belonged – but only fools tell all they know.[183]

---

180 July 17, 1865. *Suometar* no. 162, 'Jämsästä' (E. W–r.).
181 May 4, 1878. *Sawonlinna* no. 18, 'Sananen kansan oikeasta arwosta' (W. K.).
182 Probably a reference to Scripture (see Acts 4:16).
183 November 23, 1878. *Sawonlinna* no. 47, 'Heinäwedeltä' (Kipene).

Consumption and patriarchal power

The foregoing letters in the press indicate the tensions and problems experienced by rural inhabitants as trade liberalized, the money economy intensified and rural shops began to offer goods viewed by many as 'unnecessary'. On one level, newspaper writers' disapproval of rural shops can be seen as part of a general concern with rural poverty and the scarce resources of landowning peasants, which did not permit the buying of non-essential goods.[184] At the Ilomantsi Agricultural Society meeting of 1863, held just four years before the devastating famine of 1867–8,[185] the question was asked: 'Have rural shopkeepers been of any use to agriculture and domestic life?' One man present at the meeting answered:

> [– –] if rural shopkeepers would sell only those goods which are necessary to the household and for agriculture, then they could be useful. But when shopkeepers deal in all sorts of frivolous baubles, adornments, coffee and other drinks, then I don't consider them to be of any use, at least not to agriculture and domestic life; on the contrary I suspect they will bring a great deal of detriment and the corruption of behaviour [– –]. If only all these delicacies were not available for sale in every village, then I think they would oftentimes not be purchased at all, and the money would perhaps be put to more useful activities rather than going to foreign goods, as is now the case – which our poor country can no longer afford.[186]

Another rural inhabitant writing to *Uusi Suometar* in 1871 explained:

> Nobody should suppose that our rural shops are empty of customers, no indeed. [– –] They have increased the sale of infinitely useless goods to our country, goods that previously no one even knew existed. Now every Sunday people buy this and that, thinking: 'that does not cost so much', and they do not notice that there are 52 weeks in a year, and that a few marks soon become a hundred. When in former times the year's necessities were purchased once or twice from the city, then money did not go to buy worthless things, because the money was needed for necessities. People were not used to buying frivolities, or to drinking that accursed coffee at every meal [36].

Despite a high degree of self-sufficiency on farms, rural consumption had existed in various forms on a smaller scale even before 1859. In the 1840s

---

184 See also: December 15, 1888. *Laatokka* no. 100, 'Parikkalasta'.

185 Due to burn-beat cultivation and overcropping, traditional agriculture had by the mid-19th century become subject to disturbances, and years of crop failure in the 1860s led at last to a severe and widespread famine in 1867–1868 which claimed roughly 150,000 lives or approx. 8% of Finland's population. This famine, the last major famine to occur in Western Europe, has been called the final catastrophe of traditional agriculture in Finland (Soininen 1974; Häkkinen 1992).

186 Manninen, Antti. (ed.). 1864. *Kuopion Läänin Maawiljelysseuran toimituksia w. 1863*. Kuopio: A. Mannisen ja Fr. Ahlqvistin kirjapainossa (Imprimatur: C.R. Lindberg), 43–44.

and 1850s, farm masters and occasionally other household members had travelled two or three times a year to market days held in larger city centres or in the countryside, and had returned with salt, iron, coffee, sugar, pretzels, fabrics and caps. Trips to the city were not necessarily economically feasible and were in fact inconvenient, but they were undertaken because they brought variety and recreation into rural daily life (Alanen 1957: 163).

Perhaps most important for arousing and satisfying rural inhabitants' material desires prior to 1859, however, were itinerant peddlers, especially those from Russian Karelia.[187] The Karelian language was so similar to Finnish that it could be understood with little difficulty by Eastern Finns, and in 1809, when Finland came under Russian rule, the Finnish-Russian border was opened to trade. The period from 1809 to 1859 is considered to have been the golden age of the Russian Karelian peddlers, but they remained an important part of rural consumption until the end of the 19th century. Although informal peddling was illegal, rural officials did not have the manpower to interfere with the activity to any significant degree (e.g. Räisänen & Kumpulainen 1981: 441). Itinerant peddlers sold a variety of goods both practical and decorative, and like trips to urban markets, itinerant peddlers brought excitement to outlying farms. Even after 1859, it was often easier for members of farming households to buy from Russian peddlers than from local shops, which might be located many kilometres distant from their farm. Peddlers were especially important for farm women who were often unable to leave their farms due to their many chores. Most farm mistresses had to ask their husbands or some other man on the farm to buy what they needed from a marketplace or shop. Buying from a visiting peddler meant that wives, daughters and serving maids could see and choose for themselves what they were buying (Naakka-Korhonen & Keynäs 1988: 177–181).

From the farm master's point of view, however, itinerant peddlers posed a threat, both to his authority and to his wallet. At least one rural writer signing himself 'Juhananpoika' provided, in his 1857 letter to *Suomen Julkisia Sanomia*, a rare glimpse into the negotiations which took place inside the household when itinerant peddlers arrived, and the challenge they posed to the farm master's control over household spending:

> In our newspapers we discuss the common issues of our country, but nobody has said a word about knapsack traders, Russian peddlers – or how else should they be called [– –]. Probably many farm masters have already noticed how these sly, prattling fellows (*lipilaarit*) who travel around our country entice all of the money out of Finland with their inferior baubles and low-quality fabrics, especially from womenfolk and servants, down to the last cent; one would never buy these goods from a city shopkeeper, instead the money would be used for more necessary items [– –]. Buying from an itinerant pedlar only results in a reluctance to weave cloth at home and to be industrious and skilful

187 For more on itinerant peddlars from Russian Karelia, see Naakka-Korhonen & Keynäs 1988.

in handicraft, it ignites a passion for excessive ostentation by wearing trifling multicoloured garments or all sorts of scarves and skirts [– –]. But the whiskered peddler cares nothing about this, he arrives once again and opens his bag, spreads out his textiles and with honeyed words persuades the farm mistress to bring, for her part, socks, shirts, homespun woollen skirts, wool, and so forth to be bartered; to the delight of both a deal is struck, and the farm mistress and her daughters are of the opinion that it is better when no money is needed, even if they have to give a little more. If the farm master in this sort of situation forbids the purchase, saying that money is needed to pay taxes to the Crown and for other necessities, and what is more, he must still go to the city to fetch salt, iron, string, and sacks of grain, this sort of talk has no effect except to provoke angry retorts. The mistress explains that these goods, which can now be purchased at home, are never bought in the city, nor can they be bought from there more cheaply. The old grandmother mumbles that there is other work to do in the house besides weaving cloth; and what beautiful colours and fine stripes, the daughters giggle; yes indeed, agrees the mistress and snarls at the master: there's still weeks in which to obtain money before the taxes are due.

And so the barter is concluded in happy agreement, at the success of which the friendly guest smiles, and hurries to the next farm to try his luck [– –]. What I have depicted here I have myself experienced, although I do not here make public everything I have observed.[188]

This description of a pedlar's visit to a farm raises a question that was to recur throughout the late 19th-century discussion on consumption within the farm household, namely: what qualified as *necessary* goods? What were the legitimate needs of the farm and its female household members? The depiction above suggests that one reason why women were interested in buying factory-made cloth was that weaving cloth on a loom was laborious and time-consuming. As I explain in more detail in the next chapter, women also wanted to buy new, manufactured goods because these goods increased their social status in the community. From the perspective of the farm master who wrote the above description in the 1850s, however, neither women's enhancement of their social status nor the reduction of their daily workload on the farm qualified as 'needs'. Gradually, as consumer items became more familiar in the countryside, discussions intensified in the press regarding what constituted a genuine need.

There are two important reasons why the founding of rural shops in the countryside aroused the disapproval of farmers. The first was that increased rural commerce undermined their status as *heads of the only centres of consumption and production in the countryside*. Before the coming of rural shops, farms were the primary sources of food and clothing for most members of the rural community. Starting in the 1860s, new wage-labour opportunities in the logging industry and railway construction opened up for rural men in particular. Factories and rural shops began to spring up

188 December 7, 1857. *Suomen Julkisia Sanomia* no. 93, p. 378, 'Kontti-kauppiaista taikka Laukku-ryssistä' (Juhananpoika).

around the railways, and soon railway workers and factory workers became the shops' regular customers, thereby creating new centres of consumption and production which were no longer dependent on farms (Alanen 1957: 368). Indeed, workers were now forced to buy their food and clothing from these shops because they did not have the time or means to produce their own. Before 1865, rural landless labourers who did not wish to be declared vagrants and sent to military service or the workhouse had to be under the legal protection of a farm master or master craftsman. After 1865, although the poorest of the landless classes were still under the control of the district and forced to work under the poor relief system, labourers who could find work outside of farms were no longer dependent on farm masters, nor legally tied to the control of patriarchal authority. This meant that their consumption was less constrained by collective norms.[189]

The foregoing letter written by 'Juhananpoika', although it addresses itinerant peddlers instead of rural shops, hints at how rural commerce threatened the second important advantage that farm masters enjoyed over other persons in the countryside, namely the patriarch's exclusive right and opportunity to buy and sell on behalf of the farm household as a whole. Prior to the legalizing of rural trade, the distant location of markets had prevented other members of the household from travelling to participate in them. Farm masters, however, had visited them up to three times per year. The farm master was the sole owner of the only mode of transportation, the horse and cart, which meant that he alone had use of them, unless he chose to bring another member of the household along. This fact had ensured the master's exclusive right to buy, sell, and make decisions regarding the household's consumption. Although farm masters might occasionally bring home goods requested by other members of the household, at times this expectation led to bitter disappointment if the farm master returned intoxicated, having lost all his money on drink and other amusements at the market (e.g. Tiainen 1975: 312).

The spread of rural shops after 1859 meant that for the first time, household members other than farm masters had the opportunity to make choices regarding the consumption of non-necessities (Räsänen 1996: 7; Mikkola & Stark 2009). One writer to the newspaper *Uusi Suometar* in 1871 complained that 'idle youth, spendthrift servants and frivolous farm mistresses', who had earlier purchased consumer goods only on market days in the cities, and even then had brought with them only enough money for small purchases, now visited rural shops on a weekly basis and bought 'all sorts of finery and luxury goods' [36]. The irresponsible consumption of family members would continue to be lamented by male authors until the end of the century. What enabled this consumption was *home thievery*, which is the topic of the next chapter.

---

189 See Mikkola & Stark 2009; also Pöysä 1997: 75–76; Heikkinen 1997: 166.

6. Home Thievery: A Moral Evil and Practical Dilemma

A bad woman takes out in her apron what the husband brings home on his horse.[190]

After 1859, having a shop much nearer to home meant that rural inhabitants could purchase goods from its shelves whenever they wanted. But for members of farming households, finding ready cash posed a problem. Although servants could exchange the grain they received as wages for shop goods, farm wives and children received no wages and had no access to money. In many households, farm masters refused to give money to other family members or to buy for them the new consumer items they craved. The patriarchal model of authority within the farm household, according to which women were expected to work for the good of the farm as a whole but the farm master had sole legal control over the farm's products and wealth, resulted in farm women being shut out of the market and consumer economy (Räsänen 1998). In such a situation, 'necessity was the mother of invention', as one farm woman wrote to the newspaper *Savo* in 1882. According to this writer, who signed herself 'Liina A.',[191] daughters of poor farms who wanted to dress in fine fabrics like the daughters of richer farms recognized that they had in their possession 'the milk, butter, bread, wool and so forth of the farm, even grain is occasionally within reach', all of which could be sold to shopkeepers or to the poor if the sale were kept secret from their parents [41]. Another presumably female writer to the women's

---

190 This proverb comes from a woman from Eastern Finland who explained to the FLS Folklore Archives in 1968: 'Farm mistresses stole from their own households when they hired others to do handicraft work such as spinning and paid them secretly from their husband's money, from the money for household expenses. For this reason there is the proverb: A bad woman takes out in her apron what the husband brings home on his horse' (Impilahti. 1968. Elsa Jaatinen 1997).

191 Although 'Liina A.' did not explicitly state that she was a farm woman, she wrote to *Sawo* as a correspondent from the rural district of Pielavesi, and at the end of her letter mentioned that she had to stop writing or else it would be too late in the day to milk the cows in the cow shed: *'...johan olen tainnut liian kauvan istua yhdessä kohden, jonkatähden en enää jouda kirjoitelemaan, sillä navettatyöt jäisiwät liian myöhäksi...'* [41].

journal *Koti ja Yhteiskunta* (*Home and Society*), whose letter was reprinted in the newspaper *Keski-Suomi* in 1892, provided the following depiction of how farm mistresses practiced home thievery:

> In order to obtain money for small necessities, they secretly sell butter, rye, bread, salted meat, flax, and so forth to rural shopkeepers or the gentry of the district. At first, the wife practices this sort of secret selling in fear and trembling, but gradually her heart becomes hardened and she becomes a skilful thief, who uses her husband's absences as an opportunity for secret visits to the shop. Of course the shopkeeper and her neighbours, who buy her goods, often guess that the farm master knows nothing about the sale. But either they do not wish to interfere in relations between married spouses, or locals have become so accustomed to home thievery, that it is not considered a cause for shame [54].

When farm mistresses wished to sell their pilfered goods to buy items from the local shop, they had to do so clandestinely. As late as the 1940s, in his description of Ostrobothnian rural life, Samuli Paulaharju provided a description of how the wives of farmers and crofters in earlier decades had sold the goods of their household to local shopkeepers:

> Shopkeepers (*porvarit*) purchased grain throughout the autumn, mostly oats but also much rye. Many bought entire warehouses full. Side by side in the stalls were grain, seed oats and rye, even the crofters had a bit [to sell], and the crofters' good wives [– –] – and some farm wives, too – sometimes secretly filled their bundle, hidden under their aprons, from their small rye bin, and exchanged it for an even pound – the shopkeeper knew well what it was that he was supposed to weigh out. Many farm mistresses brought also butter and carried eggs, their own goods. The heart pined for coffee and sugar (Paulaharju 1943: 263).

But farm mistresses and daughters did not always go themselves to the shops to exchange the pilfered goods. They often used servants, itinerant labourers and cottager's wives as intermediaries (Alanen 1957: 334). In *Kuvauksia kansannaisen elämästä maalla* (*Descriptions of Ordinary Women's Life in the Countryside*, 1890), an anonymous, probably female writer using the pseudonym '–a.–s.' described how farm mistresses in North Ostrobothnia sent landless men and especially women to barter on their behalf, giving them a small payment in kind:

> Without the master's knowledge, the mistress brews coffee for herself and her friends. And when in this way more coffee is used than the master should know about, the mistress obtains money behind the master's back, sometimes by selling a pound of butter, sometimes a gallon of grain. But the mistress does not go to sell them herself, instead she has a good friend, a '*pussittaja*', who exchanges the goods for store-bought items and is naturally compensated for her efforts. The mistress also obtains other small necessities for herself and her daughter at the same time. From this the daughter learns in time to do the same. It's not really stealing or anything, they argue, it's just taking what is ours. Why should we tell the men about all our little needs! But the men say: that

man would still have a farm today if he had not happened to have such a merry wife [– –] (p. 28–29).

In the Köyliö district of Western Finland, farm women usually used middlemen known by the name of *huurmanni*, who conducted their business with shopkeepers under cover of night:

> These were men who, for a fee, were sent by farm mistresses, without the farm master knowing, to buy such luxury goods as for example coffee and sugar. Farm mistresses stole grain, eggs, wool, etc. which the *huurmanni* first sold, one by one, to the shops (at night with only the shopkeeper present). The payment for each set of goods was written separately in an account book and then the *huurmanni* declared with which sum of money each shop item was to be purchased.[192]

The fact that women pilfered from their own farms to pay for store-bought goods did not go unnoticed by male farm masters and other rural inhabitants. Three writers to the press stated that some farm masters tried to prevent home thievery by locking the farm storehouses and closely guarding the keys [36, 37, 61]. However, in two descriptions written as far apart as 1858 and 1900, writers explained that although farm masters were often aware that home thievery was being carried out, there was little they could do to prevent it [see also 2]:

> We have often heard, and a few times even read from newspapers complaints of how farm daughters, together with their mothers, secretly carry away whatever they can pry loose from the farm behind the father's back, and some of it they sell for a low price and their booty they either spend on useless ornaments or save it for themselves. Fathers often know about it, but they are not able to prevent it [5].

> When [the home thievery] is discovered, the home is no longer peaceful. The father gradually becomes a policeman. He does not suspect only his children, but also his wife. He guards the storeroom keys ever more closely, ever more tightly closes the strings of his money pouch.[193] But still the needs do not diminish. The wife has needs and the children have needs. They soon ally themselves against the father. Furtively, the wife takes kilo after kilo of butter to the shopkeeper. The daughter takes other things, and the capable son sells hay from the hayrack at a cut-rate price to the first who will buy it.
>
> Usually the father discovers these plots, but he often gets over it with a minor row. Getting over the hay dispute is more difficult, however. When spring comes, the farm master examines his fodder stores and notices the crime. He immediately guesses who is behind it, and [the son] must confess to him, to whom the hay has been sold. Then he has a go

---

192 Alanen 1957, 333, parentheses in original.
193 For another description of an untrusting farm master who continually carried his money in his pocket, checked on the levels of grain and flax twice per day and was ready to find any excuse to accuse his wife of home thievery in an insulting manner, see *Kuvauksia kansannaisen elämästä maalla*. 1890, p. 63.

Once threshed, grain was stored near the farmhouse in separate storehouses or granaries (vilja-aitta). It was from these granaries that family members were able to pilfer grain when the farm master was absent. This photo from 1945 shows an old granary in Sääksmäki district, Häme region. Photo: Esko Sarasmo. Courtesy of the National Board of Antiquities.

at the buyer, and it usually ends in a settlement. Unwillingness to settle generally leads to a court summons, although usually the farm master does not want to go that far, for then his own son would be arrested for theft. And where would the honour of family and home be then? [61]

Home thievery was viewed by many writers to the press as a direct consequence of the temptations of the new rural shops. One farmer expressed his concern over the spread of home thievery in a published report of the 1863 *Ilomantsi Farmers' Society Meeting* by saying that '[rural shopkeepers] promote home thievery and give rise to extravagance. The daughters and sons of the farm – even servants, try through all sorts of secret means to procure money to buy unnecessary finery, frivolous luxuries and that expensive foreign tobacco...'[194] Another anonymous contributor

194 Manninen, Antti. (ed.). 1864. *Kuopion Läänin Maawiljelysseuran toimituksia w. 1863.* Kuopio: A. Mannisen ja Fr. Ahlqvistin kirjapainossa (Imprimatur: C.R. Lindberg), 43–44.

113

writing to *Tapio* in the same year mentioned home thievery as one reason why permission should not be granted for the first shops in Kesälahti parish to open their doors:

> In recent times there have been complaints, even at public events, regarding that evil habit which has taken root in domestic life, that there are those in the family, especially women, who, without permission, behind the farm master's back, take this and that in order to obtain finery and other unnecessary things. The opportunity to buy these things near at hand, and the added temptation, have surely increased the incitement to this evil habit, and its eradication is proving more and more difficult [30].

One rural inhabitant, writing to the newspaper *Karjalatar* in 1888, described how the opening of rural shops and especially the conditions during the lumber boom of the mid-1870s were responsible for a sharp increase in the practice of home thievery:

> [– –] Now it was easy for everyone to obtain all kinds of goods, fine linen, smart broadcloth, without having to go to the trouble of making it using the old methods. And not only clothing, but everything that one fancied or tasted good, one could get from the shop without having to haggle. And what about those shopkeepers? They were most obliging! One did not even need cash when going to the shop; the purchases were just written down in a notebook! This good opportunity was too tempting to pass up, and in particular the ostentation of the youth escalated. This was an incitement to home thievery, that scourge of farm households. Without the head of the household knowing, gallons of grain and pounds of butter began to slip away to the shops [47].

The farmers of one district in Eastern Finland even expressed their hope that their representative at the Finnish Diet in 1888 would recommend new laws severely restricting the sale of consumer goods in the countryside, in essence reversing the 1859 statute which allowed free rural trade:

> Requests for the Diet
> The parish of Liperi has decided and requested to be able to present the following requests through their delegate at the next Diet: [– –] Fourth, that rural shops would be circumscribed so that they would not be allowed to offer any foreign goods except salt and, if necessary, flour; and that food and drink falling under the category of luxury consumption, even that which is produced domestically, would be completely forbidden, because experience has shown that free rural trade gives rise to the widespread and detestable practice of home thievery and economic ruin [46].

As can be seen from the above examples, rural shops were perceived to have increased home thievery to such an extent that farms were failing economically. The grand scale on which home thievery was thought to be carried out by farm women can be seen from the fact that in 1892, some farm masters were said to have claimed that the value of the goods sold secretly by wives and daughters amounted to a 'many hundreds of *markkas*'[195] [54]. Schoolteacher Wilhelm Kukkonen (1843–1908),[196] editor of *Tapio* between 1875 and 1878, argued in a similar vein in 1876:

> A certain daughter of a wealthy farm, who certainly fitted herself out as the times demanded, although the father of the family never gave her any money even for necessities, complained to her friend of what a bad year it had been, since in that year she had only been able to sell 29 barrels of grain, ten litres of fish, and a few other things [37].

Home thievery had been practiced in the countryside prior to the arrival of rural shops, when wives and daughters had traded household products to travelling peddlers while the master was away (Kuusanmäki 1936; Alanen 1957: 332; Räsänen 1998: 327–330). But it was only after rural shops opened their doors that farm women's increased consumption – their drinking of coffee and wearing of the latest fashions – began to reveal the extent to which home thievery was being practiced. As one contemporary reviewer for Adolf Suppanen's novel *Home Thievery* (1888) wrote, looking back to the 1860s: '[i]t was only with the arrival of shopkeepers that the evil habit really became visible' [51].

Ostentation and social competition

As mentioned in the previous chapter, most of the store-bought items purchased with money obtained through pilfering were directly related to maintaining or increasing the social status of farm mistresses and their daughters. One of the most important purchases was coffee, because any self-respecting farm mistress needed to have it on hand to offer guests.[197] The other important object of desire was store-bought clothing: farm mistresses strove to display their social standing through fine apparel, and farm daughters pilfered in order to gain respect in the eyes of the village youth by dressing in the latest fashions [27, 41, 52]. A columnist signing himself 'Paavo Pajumaa', writing to *Laatokka* in 1891, explained the causal connection between store-bought clothing and home thievery as follows:

---

195 One hundred Finnish markkas in 1892 was equivalent to roughly 370 euros (2006 exchange rate).
196 Wilhelm Kukkonen was the younger brother of Albert and Maria Loviisa Kukkonen whose writings to *Tapio* on the topics of home thievery and inheritance appear in Chapters Eight and Nine. Wilhelm attended the Levänen Agricultural Institute, where Antti Manninen was director, from 1860 to 1863. He graduated from the Jyväskylä teachers' seminary in 1867, and at the time of writing this editorial in 1876, was teaching in the Kuopio City Folk School. Wilhelm is characterized by historian Yrjö Blomstedt (1959: 83) as a forthright but temperamental man who had a gift for humor and storytelling.
197 Alanen 1957, 332; See also 'Kansannaisen elämä Kalajoella', in *Kuvauksia kansannaisen elämästä maalla* (1890), pp. 28–29.

We may, by way of example, assume that on a farm there are many children, especially daughters, who must without fail have the same clothes, silks, scarves, and other decorations, as they see worn by the neighbours' daughters. The farm master tries to be a strict man; he never gives his sons or daughters a penny, and now there is nothing else to be done except for them to take whatever can be taken from the storehouse, the threshing barn, or from whatever place they can find grain or some other goods, which are then sold at a cut-rate price to some dishonest person. With this money they buy from itinerant female peddlars or from shopkeepers unnecessary adornments, or other things that the spirit of the times demands from a young woman [52].

In the period under study, most of those who criticized ostentation and wasteful spending in the press were male. Rural women, too, criticized wasteful consumption and the trend toward finery, but they also provided unique insights into young women's motives for wearing the latest fashions and their willingness to pilfer from the farm in order to do so. According to these female writers, farm women wanted to wear the latest fashions in order to be seen as respectable, even superior to others, by the rest of the community. In the meeting of the Kuopio Agricultural Society held at Jouhkola Agricultural Institute in 1861, when the topic of discussion turned to home thievery, 26-year-old Liisa Väänänen,[198] a farmer's daughter and female student of cattle husbandry from Pielavesi parish, asked if women could state their mind on the issue of home thievery. When she was told that this would be welcomed, she explained that young women pilfered from their households in order to buy store-bought clothing: 'Now nothing is good enough if it is not showy. If a girl wears homespun clothing, she is not held in any esteem, rather, when she sits on the church pew, others point at her and criticize her. Those are the kind that steal if they do not get it any other way.'[199] Another farm daughter from Pielavesi, the aforementioned 'Liina A.', gave a similar explanation in 1882:

> When the daughters of large farms go to church and other public places where people gather, and they parade around in grosgrain, *vihtoorini*,[200] and other expensive fabrics, naturally the daughters of small farms want to follow their example. But – to their misfortune – their parents of lesser means require their money for more essential needs and therefore give them permission to adorn themselves in homespun clothing. – 'But that won't do at all!' – Well what is to be done? – 'Necessity is the mother of invention' [41].

198 Liisa Väänänen had already been chosen to be the official instructor of cattle husbandry at the Jouhkola Agricultural Institute upon completing her studies (April 26, 1861. *Suometar* no. 17, 'Tohmajärveltä 8 p. huhtik.' – Serkes Syrjälainen, Rahtimiehen poika). See also notes 82 and 128.

199 *Emäntälehti* no. 5, 1925, p. 119, 'Mielenkiintoisia lausuntoja kotivarkaudesta 64 vuotta sitten.' (A. L:s.). See also [11].

200 *Vihtoorini* was a black, finely woven wool fabric for dresses and aprons, similar in weight and texture to alpaca.

Maria Loviisa Kukkonen (1840–1924),[201] a daughter from Hinkkala farm in Rautalampi and sister of both the aforementioned Albert and Wilhelm Kukkonen, wrote to *Tapio* in 1862 and explained that daughters did not strive to buy fine clothing simply to stay current with the new fashions, but also in case they might not be able to obtain clothing later, especially as they did not expect to inherit much from their parents:

> And since a general passion for ostentation prevails in our country, particularly among our daughters, how can mankind's corrupted nature allow that one lags behind the others. Each strives to keep up with all the others, and somebody may think, I will not receive anything else of my father's inheritance, why don't I just procure clothing for the future, just in case, especially if she sees that her parents' wealth allows it [– –].[27]

Realistic ethnographic fiction published in the last half of the 19th and first decades of the 20th centuries suggests that dressing expensively was the primary way in which farm mistresses and farm daughters, especially those living on wealthier farms, could display the difference in status between themselves and their serving maids, who were also beginning to wear store-bought clothing (Moilanen 2008: 90–91). Women's home thievery was therefore carried out to enable farm women's public performances of dress which reinforced their standing within agrarian society. However, as is often the case with cultural projects implemented by subordinates, the cultural projects of farm women collided with the personal aims of the farm master, which I discuss in Chapter Ten.

Home thievery in public discussion

The earliest mention of home thievery in the Finnish-language press appeared in 1849 in *Maamiehen Ystäwä*. In the years 1856–1860 there appeared eight articles dealing with home thievery. The most intense period of actual debate on home thievery, however, was 1861–1863, during which

---

201 Maria Loviisa Kukkonen was raised on Hinkkala farm, a small manor house which had been purchased by her father, Gabriel (Kaapro) Kukkonen in the period when aristocrats and the gentry in Savo were selling their manor houses and moving to towns and cities (see Räsänen 2008: 247). Hinkkala farm was one of the largest farms in Rautalampi, and its household members were among the most enlightened. In her youth, Maria Loviisa was known to be a serious, open-minded and gifted girl. The university students who spent their summers as guests on Hinkkala farm practicing their Finnish language skills are reported to have enjoyed conversing with her. Maria-Loviisa's older brother, Albert Kukkonen, later became known for his self-composed folk poetry, and guests to Hinkkala farm included Julius Krohn (1835–1888), who later became a professor of Finnish language and literature as well as a pioneering folklore researcher. One year after writing to *Tapio*, Maria-Loviisa married a young man of the same age, Fredrik Halonen, who was master of Seppälä farm in Suonenjoki. As a farm mistress, she was known for her religious devoutness, her skills in a wide variety of tasks, and the fact that she served on the first public school board of directors in Suonenjoki district (Blomstedt 1959: 60–61).

time home thievery was discussed in two separate meetings of the Kuopio Agricultural Society and in at least fourteen additional letters, reports and editorials (see Chapter Eight).

In the 1870s and early 1880s, six published articles in the press mentioned home thievery. In 1886, writer and playwright Minna Canth gave a speech at a temperance meeting, published soon afterwards in the newspaper *Tapio*, in which she admonished the rural inhabitants of the Eastern Finnish region of Savo region for being lazy and dishonest [42]. Among her list of social evils peculiar to the Savonians, Canth mentioned home thievery. Her speech prompted at least one person using the pseudonym 'Inhabitant of Savo' (*Savolainen*) to write a response so lengthy that it had to be published in three separate issues of the weekly newspaper *Savo* [43]. 'Inhabitant of Savo' declared that Western Finns, too, practiced home thievery, and that in Ostrobothnia, farm mistresses and their daughters sold butter secretly to railroad workers.

In 1888, the issue of home thievery was once again in the press with the publication of Adolf (Aatto) Suppanen's 86-page novel *Kotivarkaus* (*Home Thievery*). Suppanen was otherwise nearly unknown as a writer, but was an active translator and had just been employed as a proofreader for the church periodical *Vartija*. Although there is no information available on how widely *Home Thievery* was sold and read after publication, four reviewers in the press praised the book for being morally educating, and two observed that it was an ethnographically realistic portrayal of rural life in Eastern Finland, based on the author's own observations [49, 51]. A reviewer for the newspaper *Savo-Karjala* wrote that he generally considered realistic fiction to be too secular in nature and too inventive in its portrayal of social evils. *Kotivarkaus*, however, had won his appreciation with its 'warm attitude of Christian civility' [51]. According to this reviewer, the book's topic was timely because home thievery was still a subject of public discussion in the late 1880s.

In the period 1890–1900, home thievery was addressed directly in twelve articles in which authors repeated many of the same arguments expressed in the 1860s, but also introduced new perspectives on the issue, linking the practice more explicitly to questions of gender equality within the landed peasant estate. Views were also diverging by this time on whether home thievery needed to be treated as a grave moral problem. Responding to an article printed in the newspaper *Louhi* in 1900, in which home thievery carried out in Ostrobothnia was condemned in the severest terms [62], a commentator in the newspaper *Kaleva* admitted he could not take the article seriously. 'Nyyrikki' wrote: 'Oh my, I'm drowning in such terribleness! I'm ashamed to admit that I've lived for nearly twenty years in the Ostrobothnian countryside and have never noticed that the common folk here would be as thoroughly corrupted, as thieving, dishonest, lazy and incompetent, as 'Louhi' has been able to report' [63]. A third writer who signed herself 'Farm Mistress' (*Emäntä*) described in 1901 her personal experiences regarding the secrecy practiced by the older generation of farm mistresses. Although 'Farm Mistress' made it clear she approved only of total honesty and openness between marriage partners, she nonetheless pondered the reasons why women had needed to carry out home thievery in earlier times and concluded that the wife was not entirely to blame [64].

Several additional articles in the 1890s mention home thievery chiefly as a topic selected for debates and discussions held during the meetings and social evenings of folk high schools and youth associations.[202] These discussions were meant to enlighten and civilize the rural youth, and were discussed alongside other topics such as temperance, self-education, extravagance, and the proper use of leisure time. Interestingly, these discussions seem to have taken place chiefly in Western and Southern Finland, where home thievery had earlier been perceived as less of a problem. Although home thievery certainly did not disappear after 1900 (see Apo 1993: 137), mentions of it in the press had become less frequent by the early 20th century.[203]

The perilous consequences of home thievery

Between 1849 and 1900, writers to the press pondered numerous aspects of home thievery. The consensus was that it was committed primarily by farm mistresses and their daughters, but also by sons, uncles, aunts, sons-in-law, daughters-in-law, and in the worst case, servants. The fact that home thievery was believed by rural men to be a widespread practice throughout Finland can be seen from the fact that almost without exception, male writers to the press lamented its frequency and repeatedly called for its eradication. It is clear that home thievery was perceived by rural writers to be not only an economic problem but also a serious social and moral issue. Home thievery was said to be a 'destructive', 'corrupting', 'loathsome', 'ugly' and 'shameless' habit, as well as a 'sickness', 'shameful crime' and a 'besetting sin' [1, 3, 22, 25, 27, 52, 53]. For instance, primary schoolteacher Wilhelm Kukkonen, editor of *Tapio* in 1876, described home thievery in the following terms:

> A certain vice, or more accurately a corrosive, festering wound in the body of our people is so-called home thievery. It is so well known in our country that there is no need for us to explain further what is meant by this term. We only wish to mention that this is further evidence of heathen crudity among our common folk, and that they lack a sense of honour [– –] [37].

202 July 11, 1895. *Keski-Suomi* no. 79, 'Kertomus Keski-Suomen kansanopiston toiminnasta työkautena 1894–95' (K. Kerttonen); February 24, 1899. *Kansalainen* no. 23, 'Länsi-Suomesta'; October 12, 1901. *Perä-Pohjolainen* no. 119, 'Kansan nuorisolle ja wanhemmille' (K. Kerttonen). Excerpts from Suppanen's novel *Kotivarkaus* were also read and explained by a schoolteacher at the 1891 opening of a local lending library in Jalasjärvi in order to show that novels were not all just about fun and entertainment (December 11, 1891. *Tampereen Uutiset* no. 193, 'Jalasjärveltä').

203 The debate over the husband's and wife's spheres of authority and entitlement to the resources of the farm continued in 1907 in the newspaper *Otava* between two writers, of which presumably one was female and one male. See: August 6, 1907. *Otava* no. 87, 'Kuwauksia talonpoikaisnaisen elämästä' (Epla); August 24, 1907. *Otava* no. 95, 'Talonpoikaismies maalaiswäestössä' (Juho); September 10, 1907. *Otava* no. 102, 'Nainen ja mies' (Epla).

In 1891, the aforementioned columnist 'Paavo Pajumaa' introduced the topic of home thievery by writing:

> There are countless examples of vices among the rank and file of society which are little considered to be shameful crimes, even though they, with time, impress black stains upon the human heart, and finally, deeply rooted, they become an irresistible craving and a truly shameful crime. One such vice prevailing in society is, without a doubt, home thievery [52].

In the late 1890s, when it had become common to introduce home thievery as one of the many timely topics discussed at schools and meetings of the youth, the following letter by '–w–' appeared in the newspaper *Uusi Savo*:

> In the North Savo folk high school, this topic [of home thievery] was just recently under discussion. The discussion revealed that home thievery is practiced to a terrifying degree. Nobody from among the many speakers who had the floor was of the opinion that this vice does not exist. And most of the speakers said that a poor upbringing was to blame [60].

Home thievery was seen to lead to deceit and dishonesty, as well as to a predisposition toward the theft of other people's goods [2, 3, 5, 7, 25, 37, 52]. The first person to voice this concern in the press was Judge Karl Ferdinand Forsström (1817–1903). In arguing against the practice of leaving daughters with little or no inheritance, and explaining why this was dangerous to society, Forsström was also the first writer to explain that farm daughters' lack of inheritance was a major cause of home thievery (see Chapter Eight). Forsström argued that home thievery, in turn, was undesirable because the 'wrong and evil habit is a terrible blow to Finnish integrity':

> Frankness between married couples disappears, daughters, who are used to pilfering secretly from their fathers and gradually also from their mothers, no longer distinguish between another's property and their own when they go to work for someone else, so they become accustomed to stealing, and do not raise their own children any better. People's conduct in all respects becomes corrupted [5].

A rural correspondent from Häme signing himself 'G.J.' explained similarly in 1860:

> There can be found many among landowning farmers, especially the womenfolk, who do not consider the practice of home thievery to be dishonourable at all; their children see this as well as their servants, and they think to themselves that because the mistress of the farm does not disapprove of it, then why can't we do the same; it's not such a great theft if we take here and there a little of what we need. Thus the habit is born and becomes a disease; but whose fault is it? [7]

Second, home thievery was thought to give rise to distrust within the farm household, as one writer to the newspaper *Keski-Suomi* explained in 1892 [see also 22, 52]:

> How much wickedness and moral corruption is caused by home thievery cannot be explained in a brief article. All thinking persons who have lived in the countryside have noticed this for themselves. First, it gives rise to distrust between spouses, contempt on the part of the husband, and fear on the part of the wife. Then the mother and daughter ally themselves against the father. They compete with each other in deceiving their spouse and father, in stealing from him [54].

Finally, home thievery was believed to lead to the economic ruin of the farm. As one writer to the newspaper *Laatokka* wrote in 1892:

> One does not need to live long among the local people before one notices to what horrifying extent home thievery is practiced. This vile habit is carried out by the brothers and sisters of the farm master and mistress, not to mention by their own children, who consider it their special privilege, and the same custom often leads to the ruin of the farm. For not even the riches of the wealthy would suffice to satiate the needs of everyone, instead, they come to an end before long [53].

Home thievery was thought to be economically ruinous because the pilfered goods were commonly sold at a cut-rate price to shopkeepers, itinerant traders and the landless poor, and intermediaries had to be given their own portion of the profit in order to buy their silence [2, 3, 5, 18, 34, 37, 52, 53, 54]. As Fredrik Ahlqvist explained at the 1862 meeting of the Kuopio Agricultural Society: 'grain and other goods taken in this way usually go for half price, and so there must be that much more of them to meet the [household's] needs; and still more goes to pay intermediaries' [18]. Columnist 'Paavo Pajumaa' concurred in 1891:

> When they must proceed in this way, they usually take more than they really need, and when the goods must be sold at a cut-rate price to the sorts of buyers who can keep the whole thing a secret, then the damage is twice as great... [52]

The aforementioned 1892 article in the Eastern Finnish newspaper *Laatokka* went on to explain the situation in greater detail:

> [f]armers' incomes are so small that, with frugality, they suffice only for a bare living, and they must carefully consider where each penny is spent. But if others besides the farm master have the power to use the property of the farm, then a frugal life is out of the question. Each [household member] squanders the goods of the farm as long as they hold out, and for that reason, the Karelian rarely makes it past Christmas before the entire previous year's income is spent and general deprivation follows.

Farm mistresses themselves are often a tempting example of this squandering and home thievery. They commission all sorts of small jobs, and buy themselves and their daughters more or less necessary pieces of clothing and adornments, which are paid for through the household's goods without the farm master knowing. Often the fee is paid with household goods, and since the bargain must be struck without the farm master knowing, it often happens that the person who pays must pay a price many times greater than usual. This sort of housekeeping is altogether shoddy, not only because it greatly corrupts moral concepts of justice, but because it, if anything, is likely to lead to the ruin of the farm [53].

'Great sackfuls of clothing': trousseaux and wedding gifts

With consequences as grave as those mentioned above, it was crucial to ponder the *causes* of home thievery in order to be able to eradicate it. Writers to the press expressed a wide range of opinions on what broader social phenomena were ultimately responsible for domestic pilfering. These included (1) the increased ostentation of clothing, (2) laws and practices supporting unequal inheritance between farm sons and daughters (see Chapter Eight), and (3) the miserliness of farm masters (see Chapter Nine). But blame for home thievery was also laid at the door of two traditional practices associated with weddings. In the first, daughters were expected to accumulate clothing and linens for their trousseaux, and in this they were assisted by their mothers, who helped them pilfer to pay for this accumulation (Räsänen 1996, 7–8; see also [52]). Such trousseaux were important for two reasons. First, the new bride's status in her marital home was determined in large part by the wealth she brought with her, and second, especially if she married into a large extended family household, she might not have the time or means to produce or buy textiles for her own husband and children, not to mention herself, for many years (Heikinmäki 1981: 122, 125; Räsänen 2008: 306–307). Because farm women were so occupied with their everyday chores on the farm, one of the ways in which large quantities of dowry textiles were accumulated was by hiring out the task of spinning, weaving and sewing these textiles to landless women, and paying for their services in kind [see 53].[204] At least one unnamed participant at the Kuopio Agricultural Society meeting of 1861, however, was of the opinion that farm women paid poorer women to produce textiles for them because their own handicraft skills were inadequate [11].

In his indictment of home thievery, columnist 'Paavo Pajumaa' explained how this occurred in practice:

> In some places it has become customary that daughters are obliged to have many great sackfuls of all sorts of clothing when they marry, and somebody must often be hired to make them without the farm master's

---

204 See also: SKS KRA. Impilahti. 1968. E. Jaatinen 1997.

In the summertime, farm daughters who had reached the age of fifteen or above and had been confirmed in the Lutheran Church were allowed to sleep apart from the rest of the family in their own outbuildings known as an aitta. *In these outbuildings, they received guests and displayed their trousseaux of clothing and handiwork for prospective suitors and 'news carriers' to see. Here, two such structures in Lemi district, South Savo, are shown in a photograph from 1910. The building on the right was built in 1778 and the building on the left in 1830. Photo: U. T. Sirelius. Courtesy of the National Board of Antiquities.*

knowledge. They are spun, woven and sewn by the itinerant women of the village, who often live on just this sort of work. Compensation must be paid in either grain or foodstuffs. In this sort of farm thievery matter, usually mothers assist their daughters, remembering having done the same when they were a young bride [52].

J. Räisänen, a male seminary student who in 1896 sent a detailed description to the FLS Folklore Archives regarding marriage and wedding customs in North Savo, similarly explained that in the period prior to the wedding,

> [– –] the bride 'is prepared'. Cloth is woven and sewn, and socks are knitted at home and in the village. This is the moment that 'home thievery' flourishes in the bride's home. Whatever is not nailed down is secretly sold behind men's backs to pay for bridal expenses [– –]. It is considered a matter of honour for the bride to possess five, six, even ten large sheets and bundles of clothing upon arriving at her new home. For that, pilfering is needed, and 'one had to make more than one visit to the grain bin, before that amount of clothing could be obtained'. Usually the bride's mother was doing the same thing, 'filching' grain and other goods [to pay] the village women.[205]

205 SKS KRA Pielavesi. 1896. J. Räisänen (seminarian oppilas) E 80.

A third writer in 1898 signing himself '–w–' had the following observation to make in the newspaper *Uusi Savo* regarding the practice:

> [o]ne reason for home thievery can also be found in that custom among the Savonians to accumulate enough clothing for daughters to fill all the storehouses of the world. Ordinarily one sees that the daughter of the farm has large stockpiles of clothing and linens, but usually they have arisen through more than one visit to the grain bin. It is believed that girls should have a lot of clothing, because once they marry they won't be able to obtain any more of it. And this leads to the fact that it is quite common for mothers, accompanied by their daughters, to steal whatever they can from the farm, and thus they quite simply teach their daughters to steal [60].

In addition to accumulating an impressive trousseau, brides in Eastern and Central Finland were expected on their wedding day to give hundreds of items of clothing called *antimet* to the groom's family. In order to produce enough gifts, they pilfered from their farm so they could pay poorer women to assist them [11, 18, 23, 24, 25, 26, 52, 53].[206] As 'D. H–n.' (possibly David Häkkinen from Saarijärvi parish) pointed out in the pages of *Tapio* in 1862,

> The giving of wedding gifts seems to be a more natural reason [behind the practice of home thievery], because girls begin already at a young age to quite diligently accumulate these resources. Shirts and skirts must be amassed literally by the hundreds. In Ruokolahti parish, the best girl is said to be the one who has a hundred pairs of birchbark shoes; I don't know if that is to give away as wedding gifts or for what purpose. Hereabouts, girls don't know anything about obtaining birchbark shoes, perhaps because we have scant birch forests. Instead, the amount of shirts to be given as wedding gifts must be at least a hundred, and the same number of skirts, and on top of that pillows, quilts and mattresses, socks, mittens, handkerchiefs, and so forth, if she wants to marry well. She who has no wedding gifts whatsoever to give can have no thoughts of marrying at all, for it would bring her nothing but shame. What is even more insane about this matter of many wedding gifts is that if a girl does not marry young, so that she can distribute them to the groom's relatives, they begin to rot, as has happened to many an old maid... [24, see also 16, 35].

Farm master Albert Kukkonen (1835–1918)[207] from Rautalampi parish likewise pointed out in the same year,

---

206 See also: Heikinmäki 1981; Räsänen 1996: 7–8.

207 Although he did not write his first poem until 1863, Albert Kukkonen went on to become a well known folk poet. Hinkkala farm, on which Albert was raised, was actually a small manor house which Albert's father had purchased when Albert was five years old. Albert was only 27 years old and still unmarried when he wrote to *Tapio* in 1862, but he had been in charge of running his family's debt-ridden farm since he was sixteen, due to his father's ill health (Blomstedt 1959: 62–63). Albert's younger sister Maria Loviisa and younger brother Wilhelm (who would be the editor of *Tapio* in the mid-1870s) both wrote to the press on the topic of home thievery.

I think that one remedy against home thievery would be to abandon the commonplace and needless custom of brides distributing wedding favours to the groom's relatives and to her own. In obtaining these goods, daughters cause the farm household great expense in order to receive praise and the good will of relatives and other neighbours [25].

Editor of the newspaper *Savo*, schoolteacher August Kuokkanen, wrote in 1880 that in order to enough amass wedding gifts before the wedding, the bride had to 'work night and day':

Servants and people working for servants weave and spin. Mothers, sisters, and the entire household are busy. Fathers visit the shops in order to buy the wedding gifts. If, on the other hand, fathers do not give [any money], or do not have enough money to give, the daughters go themselves 'like a mouse to the grain bin'. [– –] Who would want to remain inferior to others? Nobody. To the contrary, they strive to be better and better. 'Let Liisa Laukatar go ahead and give two skirts to her mother-in-law; but I'm not a washer-woman's daughter, I'll give three, and shoes on top of that,' thinks Mari of Mattila farm, who wants to be first in everything [40].

A. Keränen from Pielavesi suggested in 1862 that the custom of giving such wedding gifts should be outlawed, and that those persisting in it should be fined. Nonetheless, he also expressed sympathy for the young women driven to commit home thievery by the need to give *antimet*:[208]

It seems to me that the giving of gifts by the bride at weddings should be prohibited on penalty of a fine, otherwise they will not relinquish this acquired custom, which leads many a poor girl to commit home thievery. How is the hapless girl to produce such great amounts of gifts? It would be very bad to be left behind, to remain inferior. Then the poor women of the village would laugh at her, perhaps even the farm mistresses too, if she did not have gifts to give, enough for two hands to carry. I have spoken much of this matter and with many persons, and even in a few roadside inns with a constable, and he supposed that if only the men of the district would agree to it, then a parish meeting could be held about eradicating this wasteful and destructive custom [26].

In his 1880 editorial, August Kuokkanen pointed out that not only did the habit of giving wedding gifts lead to home thievery, but it was so costly that it threatened to bankrupt farms:

One often hears it said: because of daughters the farm is ruined. And this claim is not unfounded. Let us assume there is an ordinary, prosperous farm with 3–6 daughters, which is not at all unusual. These marry one after the other, even two at a time, so that within a few years all are wed. Now a cartload of dowry goods is loaded for each one (and it is better

---

208 See also: SKS KRA Pielavesi. 1896. J. Räisänen (seminarian oppilas) E 80.

to give a dowry, than to prevent someone from marrying because of it, as a few unreasonable parents do), especially if the groom is from a large, wealthy kin group. But how can an ordinary farm have enough resources to prepare clothing for each girl's father-in-law, mother-in-law, approx. five brothers, four sisters, a dozen aunts, uncles, and so forth? It is impossible! The farm must go into debt. But that too, must be paid. If the father does not want to go into debt, then the daughters must take the matter into their own hands, in plain speaking they begin to steal whatever they can from the farm and sell it for money. 'Nobody watches over a home thief' (*Eikä kotiwarasta wartioi mikään*).' This is what has given rise to this proverb and it is true, even if one can scarcely find an uglier habit...[40]

The practice of giving *antimet* to the family of the groom survived well into the 20th century (Heikinmäki 1981: 187–189). Although the practice appeared to male observers as 'wastefulness', and indeed seems to have had almost no utilitarian value,[209] it did serve several less obvious functions. First, the custom of giving *antimet* was one way in which the bride demonstrated her sewing skills to her new relations. In addition, it can be likened to the custom of *potlatch* known among the indigenous peoples of the Pacific Northwest Coast. Like the potlatch, the *antimet* custom was a ceremonial distribution of lavish amounts of gifts in which the giver validated her position as a member of the landowning class and gained prestige by outdoing her rivals in conspicuous generosity. By winning the respect of her in-laws through the mass distribution of gifts, the bride strove to increase her social capital and began building networks of support in her new marital home (cf. Bourdieu 1977: 194, 195; Agarwal 1997: 24).

Contested spheres of authority and women's justifications for home thievery

Even when the causes of home thievery could be identified and generally agreed upon in the press, however, the 'evil habit' proved difficult to eradicate. Some farm masters employed strategies to diminish the risk of pilfering, such as stacking the unthreshed grain in open fields and threshing a little at a time as needed throughout the winter, so that at any given time there was only a little grain stored in their grain bins [2]. At the Kuopio Agricultural Society meetings of 1861 and 1862, three men – a provost, an agricultural counsellor and a senior juryman – explained that one of the reasons for this custom was that it discouraged home thievery, since unthreshed grain with its stems and chaff was harder to pilfer and sell than threshed grain [12, 17].[210]

---

209 The gifts given at weddings seem rarely to have been of much use to their recipients, being often the wrong size or not to their liking [40].
210 The suggestion was made at the meetings that this custom should be abandoned, apparently because stacking unthreshed grain in the fields allowed both the grain to rot and the birds to feed on it.

*Even after factory-made
fabric became available
from shops in the 1860s,
clothing continued to be
made at home on many
farms, and landless women
were sometimes hired to
assist in the spinning,
weaving and sewing. Farm
mistresses often paid such
landless women for their
work by giving them food
or wool pilfered from
the mistress' own farm.
In this photograph from
1876, a woman from the
Häme region spins on a
spinning wheel. Photo:
A. H. Snellman. Courtesy
of the National Board of
Antiquities.*

In his ethnographic novel *Kotivarkaus* (*Home Thievery*, 1888), Suppanen describes the dilemma of the farm master who knows his wife has been pilfering but whose options for dealing with the problem are limited. In *Home Thievery*, the character who represents the coming of modern ideas to the Vaara[211] household is Liena, daughter of the village sexton who has been educated in the village public school. In the course of the story, Liena marries Matti, the eldest son of the Vaara farm. Before agreeing to marry, however, Liena sets before Matti certain conditions to their marriage. These include better hygiene in the living spaces of his father's farm onto which they will move after the wedding, and the more functional rearrangement of the farm buildings. By the time Liena moves onto the Vaara farm and begins to systematically take stock of production and consumption on the farm, the reader is already familiar with her goals of modern household reform. In order to systematize and modernize the workings of her new marital household, Liena obtains paper and pencil and receives the farm master's

---

211 The farm's name *Vaara* represents a play on words in the Finnish language: 'vaara' can refer to a high hill and so be a perfectly ordinary name for a farm, but its other meaning is 'danger', which foreshadowes the peril that home thievery would bring to the family depicted in the story.

An old lock on a farm storehouse in Puolanka district, Kainuu region. In the 19th century, farm mistresses were usually the ones who carried the keys to such locks, allowing them to feed the household when the farm master was absent. However, possession of the keys also gave farm mistresses the opportunity to pilfer farm goods and either sell them at local shops or give them in exchange for services rendered by landless women. Photo: Väinö Komu, 1953. Courtesy of the National Board of Antiquities.

permission to keep careful records of the foodstuffs in the Vaara storehouses. At first, Liena's bookkeeping nearly balances, but at the end of the third year and during the fourth, the butter accounts began to show significant shortfalls. This is because, unknown to Liena and the farm master, the farm mistress has been secretly giving butter to her married daughter whose husband is out of work. When, having taken the remainder of the farm's butter to be sold in town, the farm master realizes that the amount is much less than it should have been according to Liena's calculations, he begins to ponder how he can prevent his wife from pilfering:

> When in town he noticed the deficit of the butter to be true, just as Liena had guessed, the master thought hard all the way home by what means he could best prevent those intrigues. He thought of getting a lock and putting it on the butter container, but abandoned the idea; for even if the butter were preserved in this way, the milk, meat, and many other things would still be in danger. And in other respects, too, it did not feel right to hide the goods from the rightful mistress of the farm away behind a lock (p. 57).

128

Here the fictitious farm master, portrayed by Suppanen as a reasonable and responsible patriarch in most respects, decides against taking any concrete measures to prevent the home thievery being carried out on his farm. Since Suppanen's book was recognized by contemporaries to be ethnographically accurate [49, 51], it is likely that real-life farm masters faced similar dilemmas [see also 5, 61]. The fact that the farm master's labours and duties often took him away from the farm meant that if farm women were not given access to the farm's foodstuffs in his absence, other household members could not eat. This made it impractical to deny access to foodstuffs by locking the storehouses or hiding the keys.

The farm master in Suppanen's depiction, however, was also concerned that 'it did not feel right to hide the goods from the rightful mistress of the farm away behind a lock'. This acknowledgement of the farm mistress' delegated autonomy within the domestic sphere brings us to the heart of the dilemma: the boundaries of the husband's and wife's respective spheres of authority were not always clear. The farm household was an arena whose outwardly smooth functioning concealed an uneasy struggle over who had the right to draw such boundaries and where they should be drawn. The question of how far the farm master's authority ought to extend within the household was a key one in the moral interpretation of home thievery. From the farm master's perspective, the farm mistress was seen to be entitled to a certain amount of delegated autonomy but she was *not* seen to have the right to dispose of the farm products as she wished. This perspective is conveyed, for instance, in Samuli Paulaharju's (1932: 102) depiction of the traditional division of responsibilities within farms in rural Western Finland:

> The farm master had his own matters and responsibilities, in which the farm mistress need not interfere, and the farm mistress had her own activities, to which the farm master didn't pay much attention. The backwoods pioneers of old were told: 'when there's money and rye, one gets by', and following this advice, the farm master governed his household and worked hard. The old man made his fields, his burn-beat clearings, and his flood meadows all produce grain, hay, or whatever they produced that made money, and the money jingled in the master's money chest. The rye and the money were the master's possessions. The old man knew how much of the products of the field could be wasted, so that the farm did not go without. In some places, the mistress might begin to sell off the grain, a little at a time, behind the master's back. But this was an ugly kind of petty theft (*pussittaminen*), which led the farm to ruin…

The many references to home thievery in the press as a social evil and a moral failing suggest that male writers in the period 1849–1900 actively supported the perspective described by Paulaharju, at least at first glance. As I show in Chapters Eight and Nine, however, their real motives and aims for doing so were not necessarily to support the authority and power of the patriarch, but to promote other agendas, sometimes at the expense of patriarchal authority. Nevertheless, one point is clear: men's letters to the press never questioned the assumption that the farm master should have authority over the money and material goods of the farm. Male writers acknowledged that the farm mistress possessed authority over the activities carried out in the domestic sphere, but in most letters sent to the press before 1890, she was seen to have no rights of actual ownership over the products of that sphere. Perhaps for this reason, letters and editorials published prior to 1890 never took up the issue of how far the master's and mistress' respective domains of authority extended within the household.

At the end of the 1880s, however, the question of household authority began to be considered from a different perspective, first in ethnographic fiction, and then, starting in the early 1890s, in the press as well. Realistic ethnographic fiction provides rare insights into how the overlap between spouses' household authority provided room, if not for open negotiation and debate, then at least for women to justify their pilfering to themselves. For example, at the beginning of Suppanen's novel *Home Thievery* (1888), most of the small-scale pilfering carried out by the farm mistress is not to obtain store-bought goods for herself, but rather to give food to her impoverished sister. When the second eldest son, Mikko, inadvertently informs his father that his mother has been pilfering, the farm master quietly reprimands his wife for having given away too much food, and for keeping it a secret. The mistress, in turn, defends her actions by suggesting that they occurred within her own separate sphere of authority (pp. 15–16):

> [Farm master:] Nothing good can come of this.
> [Farm mistress]: Why do you need to be so inquisitive about everything? Those men on my home farm in the old days did not stick their noses into everything.
> [Farm master:] I'm not the men of your home farm. In former times the women of this farm, too, kept things a secret, but now I hope that would gradually come to an end. Do what you want, but do it out in the open, not always in secret [– –].

When the farm mistress retorts, 'why do you need to be so inquisitive about everything?', her self-justification echoes that of the stereotypified farm mistress and her daughter described in *Descriptions of Ordinary Women's Life in the Countryside* (1890: 29), who say: 'It's not really stealing or anything, it's just taking what is ours. Why should we tell the men about all our little needs!'

Farm women also justified their secret sale of farm goods on other grounds. Whereas male writers viewed the sale of farm goods at low prices to be irresponsible and economically ruinous, 'Liina A.' explained in 1882 that some farm daughters felt that the act of home thievery was not a 'sin' as long as the pilfered goods were sold to the poor for a low price. This suggests that home thievery could be self-justified as charity to the poor [41].

A more detailed exploration of farm women's self-justifications for home thievery is provided in the short story written by modernist author Maria Jotuni, which was first published in 1913. The realistic fiction *Kansantapa (Folk Custom)* tells of a meeting between a farm mistress whose dour husband has refused to purchase store-bought items for her, and the landless itinerant woman, Lois-Kaisa,[212] whom the mistress has asked to serve as an intermediary in selling the pilfered goods for her. In her literary works, Jotuni tended to approach society from the female point of view and often depicted marriage as merely an economic agreement between two persons, devoid of romance or idealism. In *Kansantapa*, as the two women leave the farmhouse to go to the outbuilding where butter is stored, the farm mistress complains to Kaisa that although her husband does not give her any money, he expects her to make clothing for him:

> [Farm mistress:] One may weave, but how to make cloth with no thread? And one should cover oneself with clothing, in keeping with the human custom. Except that not a penny comes from the farm. One must find a penny where one can.
> [Kaisa:] That's how it is, when you follow somebody all the way to the altar.
> [Farm mistress:] That's how it is. You keep your own council, if you wish. Well, let's keep it, it doesn't matter, there are means, those that have always been used by the common folk. Ways and means, wives have their own ways too.
> [Kaisa:] Ha ha – means.
> [Farm mistress:] Right now, next to the cellar, there is a butter crock. Take it from there, Kaisa, I, too have some business to conduct, take it and come back to visit later. Sell it for whatever price you can get. And then, under the crock I have put the key to the grain storehouse, so may Antti carry out his business. But see you, that no grain falls to the floor, when he fills the sack. Leave the key in the same place. Antti of course knows best how to go about his business, he wasn't born yesterday.
> [Kaisa:] Young Antti's a clear-headed one in these matters. He'll take care of it like before.
> [Farm mistress:] And buy coffee and sugar and take it to Reetta and ask Leena to fetch from you the money to buy thread for the loom. And buy me a shawl from the shop. I'm starting to feel naked wearing the [traditional] headdress.
> [Kaisa:] Can you imagine, poor Leena lied and put witty words in the parson's mouth.
> [Farm mistress:] What words?
> [Kaisa:] She lied and said that he claimed that home-pilfering (*kotikeh-vellys*) is a sin.
> [Farm mistress:] Ha – a sin? Maybe he was just speaking in his clerical capacity? I think he was just trying to dupe her [– –].
> [Kaisa:] Yes. But even the parson is familiar with the nature of men and likely knows how useless it is to start a quarrel with them, when one can live in harmony. Let the sulking one sulk and imagine in his mind that everything in this life is given for free...

The encounter described in this story required a *temporally* sequestered space in which home thievery could occur. The farmhouse was not a safe

---

212 Lois-Kaisa was a nickname consisting of the Christian name Kaisa with the prefix 'Lois-' from *loinen*, meaning a landless itinerant labourer.

place for two women to discuss plans to pilfer farm goods if the farm master was present, and this is what makes Maria Jotuni's short story 'Kansantapa' (*Folk Custom*) interesting, because it depicts what happened when Kaisa arrived at the farm while the farm master *was still at home*. The mistress and her guest had to sit in uncomfortable silence with the unspeaking but clearly suspicious farm master, hoping that he would soon leave to carry out his chores, until finally the mistress invented an excuse to take her guest outside to the storehouse, where the two women could discuss their plans away from the master's watchful eye.

Jotuni's fictive account of the hidden transcript underlying home thievery was produced by an educated woman who never lived as a farm wife in the countryside. As such, it is not possible to speculate to what extent the dialogue presented above represented rural women's own perspectives on the practice. It is worth remembering, however, that Jotuni was born and raised in Kuopio, where the public discussion surrounding home thievery was intense already two decades before she was born. While we cannot assume that Jotuni's story provides the same hidden transcript of self-justification that rural women would have whispered among themselves, it prompts the question of what sort of public discussions and debates on home thievery existed at the end of the 19th century from which an educated female writer could draw inspiration. One such discussion can be found in the newspaper *Lahden Lehti* in 1901, in which an author signing herself 'Farm Mistress' described how surprised she was as a young wife when older neighboring farm mistresses insisted on a pact of secrecy amongst themselves in which goods were borrowed and disposed of without their husbands' knowledge. 'Farm Mistress' wrote how, when she refused to do anything behind her husband's back, she was told: 'child, you know nothing, remain a while in the world and you will learn.' She was also given the advice: 'if you have a good husband, cover one of his eyes, if you have a bad husband, cover both.' The author of the article came to same conclusion as did Jotuni twelve years later, namely that her neighbours had gradually been forced to undertake home thievery because their surly and miserly husbands had refused to give them even the smallest amounts of money for their families' daily needs. When these women finally tired of continually asking and being criticized, they resorted to simpler means of obtaining what they needed [64].

7. Female Gossip and 'News Carrying'

What the Devil can accomplish in a year, a news carrier can accomplish in an hour.
– Man from Hämeenkyrö district[213]

Although letters in the press depicted farm women as practicing home thievery in order to purchase store-bought goods or to pay lower-class women to produce household textiles, there is a third purpose for which household goods were pilfered by farm women. Despite the silence of the 19th-century press on this matter, it appears from other sources that farm mistresses also *paid for gossip*, in other words they secretly gave goods from the farm to poor itinerant women when they wanted them to gather or spread of information on their behalf.[214] In order to understand why farm mistresses were willing to the hand over the fruits of their labours and run the risk of their husbands' disapproval, we must take a closer look at the complex phenomenon of female gossip and its social functions in the 19th-century Finnish countryside.

According to archived ethnographic descriptions sent to the FLS Folklore Archives, nearly every rural district at the end of the 19th and beginning of the 20th centuries had middle-aged or elderly women from the landless classes who possessed the ability and inclination to gossip about the affairs of others. If the gossip of these women was targeted toward young persons of marriageable age, the gossips were referred to as 'news carriers' (*kontinkantaja*). Farm mistresses could, for instance, pay these 'news carriers' to visit other farms in order to say favourable things about the mistress' son or daughter who was of marriageable age:

> News carriers were also used to carry greetings, and, with good information, to prepare the ground for a hoped-for marriage and other situations. In this case the news carrier was usually given compensation,

---

213 SKS KRA Hämeenkyrö. 1932. Martti Mattila E 97.
214 Although the cultural ideal of charity and mercy to the poor prevailed in the 19th century countryside and was reiterated in folklore and church teachings, charity was never mentioned in the source materials as a motive for giving farm products to poor gossip women and news carriers.

clothing, foodstuffs or something else. The news carrier would then praise and speak well of a neighbour girl to a boy who was wanted as a son-in-law…[215]

Farm mistresses also wanted to learn as much as possible about potential future wives for their sons, or about the young men who had shown interest in their daughters. For this reason, with promises of foodstuffs, coffee or wool, farm mistresses sent news carriers on errands to gather news about prospective sons- and daughters-in-law:

> A news carrier was paid 'in kind'. Farm mistresses rarely had money, but they could slip a piece of meat, a pat of butter, eggs, flour or hulled grain [to the news carriers] as payment.[216]

The news carrier, for her part, was able to gather information with skill and discretion. News carriers were often referred to as 'smooth talkers' or 'honey tongued' (*liukaskielinen*). Having fulfilled the task entrusted to them, they returned to the farm mistress to report whether a particular bridal candidate was rich or poor, industrious or lazy, sweet-tempered or cross, skilful or 'clumsy-fingered':

> About 65 years ago, these 'news carrying women' were quite common, especially when a young man was going about the task of finding a wife, if the proposed bride was in some neighbouring village, then the boy's mother said to some gossipy old woman, go there and visit the home of the boy's fiancée, to take a look at what the girl is like. You'll surely come up with some excuse for your visit, and I'll certainly make it up to you, I'll give you provisions to take along with you, so bring back information. Then the news carrier left and the matter was cleared up. Many marriage matches were ruined when the 'news granny' returned.[217]

Women who were paid for their gossip typically worked as masseuses, cuppers[218] and washer-women, since these occupations forced them to travel regularly from farm to farm, where they had opportunities to observe the activities of others (Asplund 1969: 189):[219]

215 SKS KRA Mikkeli. 1965. Jaakko Valkonen (schoolteacher) 1307.
216 SKS KRA Kivennapa. 1965/66. Liina Pulliainen (schoolteacher, b. 1901) 2616. – heard from her mother.
217 SKS KRA Keitele. 1965. Juha Kähkönen KT 354:13.
218 See note 153.
219 SKS KRA Ristiina. 1966. Meeri Suvikallio KT 384:158; SKS KRA Vesanka. 1965. Elsa Korhonen KT 353:21; SKS KRA Muolaa. 1966. Hilma Jussila KT 366:132; SKS KRA Impilahti. 1965. Maija Mustonen KT 356:59; SKS KRA Kitee. 1966. Eino Mähönen KT 370:45; SKS KRA Liminka. 1966. Paavo Kytökorpi KT 368:385; SKS KRA Piippola. 1966. Hilma Karppinen (farm mistress) KT 366:54; SKS KRA Metsäpirtti. 1966. Juho Hämäläinen KT 365:17; SKS KRA Kiikoinen. 1966. Jenny Leppäniemi (b. 1901) KT 368:68; SKS KRA Mikkeli. 1965. Jaakko Valkonen (schoolteacher) 1307; SKS KRA Muolaa. 1965. Aatu Virolainen (former police constable, b. 1906) 552; SKS KRA Hämeenkyrö. 1932. Martti Mattila E 97; SKS KRA Kivennapa. 1965. Liina Pulliainen (schoolteacher, b. 1901). – Heard from her mother; SKS KRA Ylämaa. 1965. Hilda Kälviäinen (farm mistress, b. 1906) 453; SKS KRA Saari. 1965. Helvi Pääkkönen KT 357:186.

Masseuses and cuppers were generally known to be news carriers [– –]. Since they covered a wide territory, they came to know the habits and stories of many farms and crofts, which they told to other farm masters and mistresses while massaging them as a pleasant way to pass the time.[220]

Masseuses, cuppers and washerwomen who travelled from farm to farm made sure that everyone's affairs were made public even as far as the next district. Farm mistresses took these gossip carriers to their chambers to drink coffee. They also gave these women the task of looking to see on their travels whether there might be any suitable marriage candidates for their sons or daughters in neighbouring districts...[221]

Although one male informant stated that men never acted as 'news carriers', others reported that although it was much less common, men, too, could gossip about the doings of others or 'carry news'. Most male gossips were tailors or cobblers,[222] although according to one informant from North Savo, other itinerant rural craftsmen such as blacksmiths, carpenters, and net weavers could be given money or alcohol to criticize someone in the district.[223] Most informants, however, were of the opinion that men looked down on gossip and discredited the practice as beneath their dignity. As one woman from South Savo put it, 'Men did not stoop to give an account of others' doings'[224]. A farm mistress from South Karelia agreed:

Men, at least in their own minds, considered themselves above this sin and said scornfully that this is just more women's gossip which cannot be trusted.[225]

Informants from Varsinais-Suomi, North Ostrobothnia, Central Finland, and South Karelia explained that men who regularly gossiped and carried news were referred to as 'old womanish' (*ämmämäisiä* or *akkamaisia*), and received very little respect in the community:[226]

Usually women retreated to the back chambers when they had something to gossip about. At least in Isojoki, men did not gossip about

220 SKS KRA Heinola. 1966. Jalmari Mäklin KT 370:11.
221 SKS KRA Jäppilä. 1965. Eila Nykänen (farm mistress, b. 1935) 392. – woman, b. 1905.
222 SKS KRA Muolaa. 1966. Hilma Jussila KT 366:132.
223 SKS KRA Varpaisjärvi. 1965. Jukka Savolainen (insurance inspector, b. 1920) 384–385.
224 SKS KRA Joutseno. 1965. Elsa Kutila KT 482:1358.
225 SKS KRA Ylämaa. 1965. Hilda Kälviäinen (farm mistress, b. 1906) 453.
226 SKS KRA Liminka. 1966. Paavo Kytökorpi KT 368:385; SKS KRA Piippola. 1966. Hilma Karppinen (farm mistress) KT 366:54; SKS KRA Kivennapa. 1966. Helena Sarvi KT 373:27; SKS KRA Vesanka. 1965. Elsa Korhonen KT 353: 20; SKS KRA Padasjoki. 1965. Väinö Korkeila (schoolteacher, b. 1907) 464; SKS KRA Himanka. 1968. Vilho Verronen (former park ranger) 169; SKS KRA Kivennapa. 1965. Liina Pulliainen (schoolteacher, b. 1901) 2616. – Heard from her mother; SKS KRA Kiikala. 1965. Helmi Laiho (female farm owner, b. 1912) 1323.

others' affairs. It was old womanish and men abhorred precisely this old-womanishness, since they wanted to be manly and brag about their strength, their fields and their horses. Men did not do women's work, it was shameful.[227]

Female gossips in written sources

Our primary source of information on news carriers comes from recollected ethnographic descriptions recorded mostly in the years 1965 and 1966, which were sent to the FLS Folklore Archives in response to question no. 55, 'Kylän ämmät (Village gossip women)' in issue no. 19 of the Folklore Archives' news bulletin *Kansan Tieto* (*Folk Knowledge*). Fourteen descriptions were also sent to the FLS Folklore Archives in connection with the 1957 *Karjalan juhlaperinteen kilpakeräys* ('Collection contest for Karelian festive traditions'), and three descriptions were sent to the Folklore Archives in the 1970s. Altogether, the corpus used in this study comprises 110 texts given by 114 different informants, some born as early as the 1870s and others as late as the 1920s. All ethnographic descriptions are housed in the FLS Folklore Archives.

Most of the 110 texts in the corpus were produced as much as a century later than the newspaper sources on home thievery, but according to those who provided information for them, they describe practices and attitudes which prevailed from the last decades of the 19th century into the 1920s. In addition, at least ten descriptions published in Finnish-language newspapers between 1850 and 1900 refer to village gossip women and news carriers,[228] and it is clear that late 19th-century writers to the press expected the stereotype of the female gossip/news carrier to be a familiar figure to rural readers.

Some of the most colourful portrayals of rural female gossips can be found from realistic ethnographic fiction. For instance, a vivid description of a local gossip woman was provided by popular author Pietari Päivärinta in his serial novella *Naimisen juoruja. Kuwaelmia Kansan elämästä* (*Marriage Gossip: Depictions of Folk Life*) which ran in the newspaper *Uusi Suometar* in 1882. As an ethnographic fiction, Päivärinta's story of two young persons in love, prevented from marrying by the young man's wealthy farming parents, is not situated in any particular region of Finland but functions as a moral allegory in which female gossip is condemned as a dangerous practice which perpetuates the ignorance of uneducated rural inhabitants. Päivärinta's plot serves mainly to promote his social reformist agenda, but his descriptions of rural life and the characters which populate it are realistic and seem to have been drawn largely from his own experience. His depiction of the local female gossip Lillu, although stylistically different from Santeri Alkio's character of Saaraleena in the novel *Teerelän perhe*, or Johannes Häyhä's depiction of Maija in his *Naimistawat Itä-Suomessa*, is

227 SKS KRA Isojoki. 1965. Johan K. Harju (b. 1910) 2838.
228 See note 143.

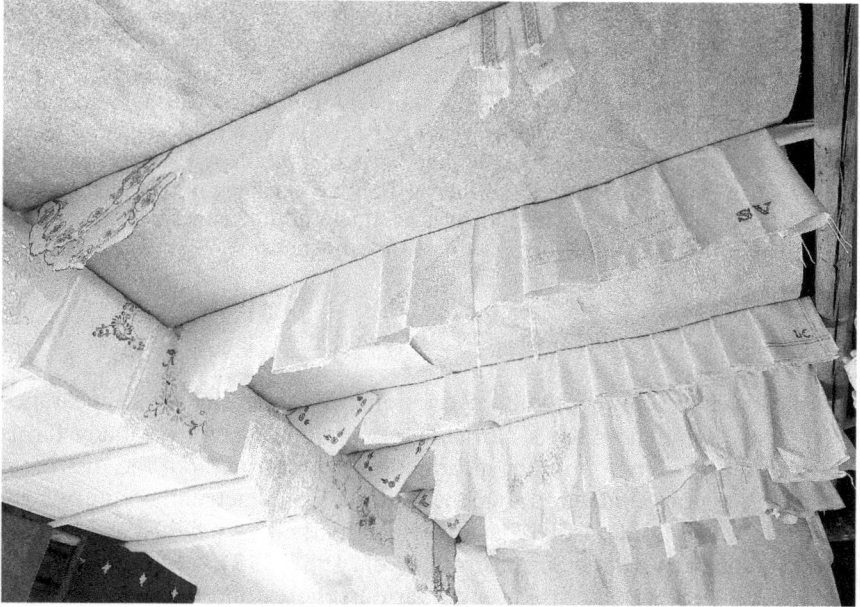

The loft ceiling of a two-storied farm daughters' outbuilding in Ilmajoki, South Ostrobothnia. The outbuilding dates from the 19th century and is now part of a local museum. The ceiling has been decorated with handmade and hand-embroidered cotton and linen textiles such as table cloths, pillow cases, dish towels, and aprons, all on display for potential suitors and 'news carriers' to admire. Photo: Matti Huuhka, 1982. Courtesy of the National Board of Antiquities.

nonetheless highly similar to both of them in terms of the gossip women's motivations and modes of operation. For instance, both Lillu and Saaraleena made themselves appear pitiful in order to evoke landowning peasant families' sympathies and extract material benefits from them, while both Lillu and Maija are depicted as modifying the information they conveyed according to the listener in order to serve their own interests. Päivärinta describes 'Lillu' as follows:

> She was roughly fifty years old, an unmarried young old maid, slender as a whipping-post and as brown as a baked turnip. She was the friend – and the enemy – of every person in the entire village; friend to their face and enemy behind their back, for if she was talking to someone, she praised them and shamelessly grovelled before them in all possible ways. The addressee was in her opinion so beautiful, that there was none other such, incomparably wise, so rich that everyone was in awe, even if the creature before her was old and one-eyed, covered with the scars of a scabby disease, and stupid as a boot; but this is how Lillu would act if she thought she would get something from him or her. However, when Lillu arrived at another place [where people had] other views on the matter, Lillu would criticize and malign to the lowest levels of damnation even the good people that she had just praised. If someone scorned her gossip and considered it idle talk, or paid her nothing for it, Lillu tried in any

way she could to wreak vengeance on the person who scorned her, and like a viper snake she slithered all around him or her, and tried to bite and poison the reputation of the scorner. She had never done any real work, for when young she had gone begging and now when older, that wretched soul lived amply from her gossip. When she became older, she considered it advantageous to limp and hobble when approaching a farm and for the duration of her visit, but when she got to a place where people could not see her, she was as fit as a fiddle! This was Lillu, whom we will get to know better as the story proceeds.[229]

Gossip as a welcome source of news

On the basis of ethnographic descriptions, it seems that the appearance of a gossip woman or news carrier was a welcome sight on many farms because these women brought information from throughout the district at a time when news and entertainment were scarce. Nineteenth-century farm households were often isolated, surrounded by their own fields, and located at great distances from other farms (Linkola 1987: 117).[230] Farm mistresses were so tied to their farms through various chores and duties, that if not for the visits of female gossips, they would have had little access to the orally-transmitted information they needed in order to manoeuvre within their social universe. For this reason, local gossip women were sometimes referred to as 'living newspapers'[231] or the 'morning newspaper'.[232] As three women from South Savo, Satakunta and Kainuu explained,

> The mistress was plagued by curiosity: what kind of stockpiles of clothing did the neighbour's household have? Had a large dowry been set aside for the daughter? How large a trousseau had each daughter-in-law brought to her [marital] household? Who better to tell them than the washer-women and cleaning women who walked from farm to farm in the spring during the spring cleaning.[233]

> I remember a certain old woman who walked from one village to another, worked as a masseuse and collected food for her daughter's family [– –] it must be said that this sort of wife who travelled around the village and parish served an important function. There were at that time not many

229 June 12, 1882. *Uusi Suometar* no. 133.
230 The old compact village settlements disappeared when a general land redistribution and consolidation occurred between 1749 and 1775 (*isojako*), in which farm buildings were removed from the communal fields and were relocated near the newly scattered fields allotted to each farm. What this meant was that especially in North Häme, North Savo, North Karelia and Kainuu, the village was not the significant unit of residence and communal identity that it was in Southwest Finland or in South Karelia, where village residence patterns were relatively dense.
231 November 16, 1878. Sawonlinna no. 46, 'Heinäwedelta (Lokakuun lopussa)'.
232 See: SKS KRA Töysä. 1970. Irja Riiho (farm mistress) 234; SKS KRA Virrat. 1965. Kyllikki Mäkinen (wife) 588; SKS KRA Padasjoki. 1965. Väinö Korkeila (schoolteacher, b. 1907) 464.
233 SKS KRA Jäppilä. 1965. Eila Nykänen (farm mistress, b. 1935) 392. – woman, b. 1905.

newspapers, nor did they come to poorer households. And when this wife arrived on a farm with her information, she was made welcome. One got to know how even distant neighbours were doing. And what the local inhabitants thought about this and that matter.[234]

[– –] When the news carrier (*juorukontti*) came to the farm, the farm mistress went with her to her chamber for many hours, no matter what busy time of year it was in terms of farm work, for she had to find out what was happening on the other farms in the village. The village's regular news carrier knew all the affairs of the village. Before she left the farm, she went with the farm mistress to the shop, to the nearest storehouse or to the food cellar and there received a bit of butter, dried meat, salted meat, salted fish or other foodstuffs in her bundle (*nyytty*)[– –].[235]

A male informant from South Karelia provided a similar explanation:

Since every village had gossip women (*juoruämmiä*), these 'information agencies' usually began unloading their information by saying: 'I would never have had time to stop by, but I've got new things to tell [– –].' In this way, news from a very broad area was spread. Other forms of media did not in those early times exist in remote villages. These were quite sufficient.[236]

In exchange for sharing their news, especially news about neighbours' private affairs, gossip women were usually served coffee.[237] According to an informant from North Ostrobothnia, 'many farm mistresses and other women fed them, offered them coffee and bribed them in order to receive the most recent news about the goings-on of the village, including love affairs.'[238] If the farm mistress had some specific task in mind for the gossip woman, however, it was mandatory to give her a gift in advance: 'if parents put a news carrier on the case, they paid her, sometimes in wool, sometimes in meat and butter, sometimes in money.'[239] As can be seen from the reference to 'parents' in the quote above, the farm master occasionally gave permission for payment to be given to a news carrier, if at stake was the successful marriage of one of his children. Nevertheless it was always the farm mistress who arranged the exchange of food for information. Other informants from South Ostrobothnia and Uusimaa explained as follows:[240]

---

234 SKS KRA Ruovesi. 1966. Sylvi Röykkee KT 373: 828.
235 SKS KRA Taivalkoski. 1965/66. Anni Karjalainen (schoolteacher, b. 1919) KT 379: 56. According to the informant, a *nytty* consisted of a white sheet which the news carrier tied around her back over her right shoulder.
236 SKS KRA Metsäpirtti. 1969. Juho Hämäläinen KT 431: 187.
237 SKS KRA Piippola. 1966. Hilma Karppinen (farm mistress) KT 366: 54.
238 SKS KRA Liminka. 1966. Paavo Kytökorpi KT 368: 385. See also: SKS KRA Luopioinen. 1978 Hilda Virtanen KT 501: 253.
239 SKS KRA Lappajärvi. 1965. Eino Hyytinen KT 365: 86.
240 Another one informant from South Karelia explained: 'Many matters were sorted out with coffee and sweet breads, but depending on the situation, farm mistresses gave them a bundle to go under their arm when they left, sometimes warm bread, meat, butter, and other such' (SKS KRA Muolaa. 1966. Hilma Jussila KT 366:132).

The most famous gossip women (*porokelloja*) in my home area were: 'Palosen Maija', 'Kurvin Maijastiina' [– –] and 'Sopasen Marialiisa', otherwise known only as 'Sopaska'. All of them had 'worked at their profession' since the 1800s and for the new information and 'secrets' they brought, they usually received a wad of wool from the farm mistress or real coffee made without chicory if the information was important, or very 'secret'.[241]

[– –] those 'village women' also played a part in the marriages of young persons. Mothers were in good relations with the women and bribed them (*pussittivat*), so that the latter would remember to praise their daughters on farms which had sons. If this sort of woman became angry, then she changed her tune.[242]

Because farm mistresses rewarded gossip women for their services, the transmission of gossip was an occupation which provided livelihoods for at least a few women in every district. As one man from Varsinais-Suomi pointed out,

[t]here was no question of paying gossip woman a 'salary'. But they were often good at psychology and were capable of, for example, vilifying a person they knew to be the enemy of their listener so cleverly that the listener might in return give a loaf of bread or two, a little butter, meat, wool, or some such. And coffee was brewed and drunk. But in former days, many cottagers lived in such difficult circumstances, in poverty, that this forced them to earn something through gossip, in order to stay alive.[243]

Gossips, 'singers' and news carriers

Many rural informants, when writing to the FLS Folklore Archives in order to describe the practice of gossip, made a distinction between ordinary female 'gossips' (*juoruakat*) and 'news carriers' (*kontin kantajat*).[244] Female gossips were those who discussed general information, usually negative and often out of malice, about absent third parties behind their backs. By contrast, news carriers went to a farm to personally inform its residents about the deeds or defects of someone in their household, most often regarding

241 SKS KRA Vehkalahti. 1966. Ville Toikka KT 375:135.
242 SKS KRA Kivennapa. 1957. Liina Pulliainen KJ 18:6134.
243 SKS KRA Pertteli. 1965. Kaarlo Aitamäki (b. 1903, driver) 257.
244 SKS KRA Kangasniemi. 1966. Tyyne Viinikainen (b. 1901) KT 484:281. – farmer; SKS KRA Saari. 1965. Helvi Pääkkönen (b. 1921) KT 357:186; SKS KRA Kiihtelysvaara. 1966. Hanna Korhonen (b. 1897) KT 381:95; SKS KRA Vuoksenranta. 1965. Lilja Virtanen (farm mistress, b. 1912) 2154; SKS KRA Uukuniemi. 1965. Eino Toiviainen (b. 1899) 2247–2249; SKS KRA Himanka. 1968. Vilho Verronen (former park ranger) 169; SKS KRA Kivennapa. 1965. Liina Pulliainen (schoolteacher, b. 1901). – Heard from her mother; SKS KRA Varpaisjärvi. 1965. Jukka Savolainen (insurance inspector, b. 1920) 384–385.

their child's desired marriage partner.[245] In other words, news carriers criticized chiefly young persons who were courting with serious intentions, and usually only sought to inform on them to persons with relative authority in marriage matters such as parents or potential future in-laws.[246] A female informant from South Savo pointed out that 'news carrying meant divulging information about some person's deeds. But gossip was empty chatter mixed with lies.'[247] Another woman from South Karelia explained:

> 'Gossip' was generally understood to mean sifting through the affairs of one's neighbours and speaking ill of one's fellow men. When one brought to light the defects of girls (and sometimes boys) of marriageable age and spread that information around the village, then it was said to be 'news-carrying' (*kontinkanto*). The 'news' (*kontti*) was said to be all the defects and negative qualities observed in a girl, which were talked about in the village. Some [girls] were said to be lazy, others lacking common sense, and so forth.[248]

Although there appear to be multiple etymologies of the term *kontinkantaja* (Asplund 1969), linguistic research on the terms associated with 'news carrying' (*kontin kantaja, kontitseminen, kontinkanto*) reveals that this practice was known throughout Finland with the exception of Varsinais-Suomi and Uusimaa in the extreme southern and southwestern parts of the country (Asplund 1969: 191). Other terms used to refer to news carriers in various parts of Finland included *kreetuämmä*,[249] *paidanpaikkaja*,[250] *juorukello*[251] and *porokello*.[252]

A third category of gossip woman was that of 'singers' (*laulajat*), who visited farms in order to 'sing' the praises of a particular young person or to spread favourable gossip concerning them. 'Singers' were usually sent on this errand by the young person's mother, but sometimes by the young persons themselves:[253]

245 News carriers did not only provide information useful in matchmaking. They could also intervene in the sale of a horse, cow or even farm by convincing one of the parties in the agreement that according to their inside knowledge, the deal that was about to be struck was not advantageous to their addressee after all. When servants, especially serving maids, were considering whether to sign on with a new farm for the coming year, 'news was carried about the farm to the serving maid and about the serving maid to the farm.' (SKS KRA Kuortane. 1966. Helmi Mäkelä (farm mistress, b. 1896) 2253).

246 SKS KRA Kivennapa. 1966. Helena Sarvi KT 373:32; SKS KRA Vimpeli. 1966. Eino Lehtoranta KT 368:2; Koivisto. 1965. Emma Lankinen KT 355:19; SKS KRA Metsäpirtti. 1966. Juho Hämäläinen KT 365:17; SKS KRA Saari. 1965. Helvi Pääkkönen KT 357:186; SKS KRA Miehikkälä. 1965. Viktor Muuronen (former policeman, b. 1887) 1533–1535.

247 SKS KRA Ristiina. 1966. Meeri Suvikallio KT 384:158.

248 SKS KRA Kirvu. Aino Heikkonen KT 364:139.

249 SKS KRA Tyrvää. 1966. Estri Viertola (b. 1911) KT 484:156;

250 SKS KRA Asikkala. 1966. Jalmari Maunula. KT 394:137.

251 SKS KRA Hyrynsalmi. 1966. Nantte Tolonen KT 375:40.

252 SKS KRA Vehkalahti. 1966. Ville Toikka KT 375:135.

253 SKS KRA Heinjoki. 1957. Lempi Vanhanen (farm mistress, b. 1906) KJ 30. – woman, b. 1880; SKS KRA Vuoksenranta. 1965. Lilja Virtanen (farm mistress, b. 1912) 2154; SKS KRA Kivennapa. 1965. Liina Pulliainen (schoolteacher, b. 1901) 2616. – Heard from her mother; SKS KRA Uusikirkko. 1964–1966. Ester Marjamaa (farm mistress) 229.

Those rumour-women did not have so many enemies. Some people even liked them, especially if some girl had been escorted home by a more distinguished boy, then quite the contrary, they were pleased when the old women spread rumours around the village that the girl had walked home with this one or that one. And that he was that kind of more distinguished escort, for example the son of a rich farm.[254]

However, 'singers' usually needed to be compensated for their efforts. If the person whose praises had been sung later married well, then he or she was deeply indebted to the singer, and singers knew how to take advantage of this:

[– –] it was a nuisance that this sort of 'singer' was never altruistic. She expected payment or something in return for her 'singing'. It was never said aloud, but everyone knew it. And the poor betrothed couple knew it better than anyone. Especially if one or the other had asked her to 'sing' about him/her to the other party. These requests were quite common. A particular person might be asked to sing something by saying: 'Sing me to Heikki, and you'll be rewarded.' These 'singers' often set marriages in motion.[255]

As is suggested by the foregoing, the most important information supplied by both news carriers and 'singers' was that which could be useful in matchmaking. Because marriage was the basic relationship which organized activities and family relations within the farm household, marriage among the landowning classes in Finnish agrarian communities was not a private matter between two individuals. Rather, it was a social and economic arrangement between kin groups. Marriages were of interest to the entire district, because through marriage, the network of relationships among community members was reorganized (Ilomäki 1998: 147).

In the second half of the 19th century, as the landless population increased and the socio-economic gap between the landed and landless widened, a nearly universal ideal concerning the contracting of marriages was for persons to marry within their own class.[256] A farmer's son was supposed to marry a farmer's daughter, and farmhands were to marry serving maids.[257] Marriage was therefore the key means through which the rural class society reproduced itself.

Since in most cases the new couple lived on the farm owned by the groom's father for at least the first years of marriage, marriage was a crucial event from the perspective of both the older farm mistress and the newly

254 SKS KRA Nurmes. 1965. Elin Karjalainen 498.
255 SKS KRA Uusikirkko. 1964–1966. Ester Marjamaa (farm mistress) 229.
256 Heikinmäki 1981; E. Stark 2011: 182–187.
257 SKS KRA Sulkava. 1967. Jossi Hopeakoski KT 389:27; SKS KRA Suomussalmi. 1935. Samuli Paulaharju 26591–26592; SKS KRA Saarijärvi. 1970. Riitta Rautiainen KT 448:40. In Eastern Finland and Finnish Karelia, however, where the boundaries between social classes were more permeable, hypergamy or marrying 'up' was more possible for both men and women (Hämynen 1984).

wed daughter-in-law who yearned to be mistress of her own household. From the farm mistress' perspective, the choice of a daughter-in-law was particularly important because the daughter-in-law would share the domestic sphere with her. The labour input, health and obedience of the daughter-in-law were vital to the perpetuation of the farm. In extended households, the daughter-in-law would also be the one expected to care for the elderly farm mistress in her old age, so that the quality of the elderly mistress' last years depended largely on the personality and diligence of the daughter-in-law. Folk beliefs and magic practices reveal that marriage was seen to be a potentially dangerous moment for the farm household, whose boundaries had to open to accept the female 'outsider' from another kin group (Stark-Arola 1998: 278). The farm mistress had no direct authority over whom her son or daughter would marry, but with the right information, she could persuade her child to marry a spouse who was hard-working and came from a wealthy farm, and persuade her husband to consent to the match.

The overriding social importance of marriage in 19th-century rural Finland and the fact that it was a topic of interest to nearly everyone in the community gave the news carrier her opportunity to ferry information back and forth to interested parties and to be rewarded for it. It was due chiefly to the activities of news carriers that the phase of courtship and especially engagement between a young man and woman were highly public affairs:

> No one was able to marry privately or peacefully or in secret. The so-called 'news carriers' (*kontinkantajat*) made certain of that, if there was anything to be said about one party or the other [– –]. God preserve them if some fault were later discovered, for then the gossip woman (*juorutäti*) would say: 'well didn't I tell you already, what kind of boy he is?'[258]

According to several informants, news carriers most commonly reported to a young woman's parents that her intended husband was in reality a drunkard, a layabout, or was by nature cruel and unpredictable. The groom's parents, for their part, were informed that the intended bride was lazy, lacking skill in handicraft, or bad-tempered. The wealth or poverty of the potential spouse was also a popular topic of gossip:

> If a suitor was poor, then it was said: how can someone feed his family who has nothing more than snotty fists? If he were wealthy, then he was called a drunkard, a layabout, and a fornicator. A girl for her part was called a harlot and a spendthrift and inept.[259]

> A girl who was the intended bride was criticized in the groom's home and, if not directly to the groom himself (nobody dared, for often he would have thrown the news carrier out of the farmhouse) then at least to his parents and relatives, for example that the girl was bad-tempered, or lazy, or '*nöppönäppi*', meaning poor at handicraft, or was unable to

---

258 SKS KRA Muolaa. 1957. V.R. Tujunen (former farmer, b. 1888) KJ 28:10513.
259 SKS KRA Sahalahti. 1965. Lauri Arra (farmer, b. 1886) 259.

perform hard labour, was '*hätkä*' (quick to run after men) and anything else that envious or malicious people could think up [– –]. News was also carried about the groom, for instance: 'he's an alcoholic, a card player, lazy, a sluggard, poor, his farm is in debt, he is a severe man, and so forth. And the mother-in-law is cantankerous, the sister-in-law is devious and the father-in-law keeps a firm grip on the whole family, he buys what he wants and nobody else has any money, the food is bad,' etc.[260]

A few informants viewed this sort of news carrying in a positive light: the news carrier informed marriage partners and their families about each other, so that surprises and disappointments could be avoided later on:[261]

> The courtship of the bride and groom before their betrothal often meant only that they knew of each other's farm and could recognize each other by sight. Gossip women, news carriers (*konttiämmät*), played a large role in matters. They praised and criticized the affairs of each to the other and everything was made clear. On the basis of this information, the bride and the groom got to know each other so thoroughly during the engagement period that afterwards, neither person experienced any very great disappointments regarding the other.[262]

But because most rural inhabitants disapproved of news carrying, the news carrier often had to carry out her task with discretion, especially if she had been paid to criticize someone by a rival. One informant from South Ostrobothnia explained how this occurred in practice:

> If the slightest negative thing is known – or is supposed to be known – about a groom or bride, then one goes to carry news about it to the other party. In other words about the groom to the bride or about the bride to the groom. This happens in such a way that one pretends to be the good friend of the person to whom one carries the news and then the conversation is steered in the desired direction and, as a good friend, one warns of great danger. Or then one pretends to know nothing at all about the young couple's relations and, with a show of indifference, mentions the negative thing that one has come to carry news about.[263]

The opinions of news carriers regarding a future match or potential suitor could differ, however, and the gossip they spread could even be diametrically

260 SKS KRA Uusikirkko. 1965. Elsa Pukonen (writer, b. 1899) 1738, parentheses in original.
261 Occasionally, 'news carriers' might be the only persons in their immediate locale who had knowledge of a proposed spouse's undesirable qualities, and they might try in good conscience to warn young persons about the faults of their intended. According to one informant from North Karelia, however, young persons blinded by love often refused to heed these warnings, and only realized the truth of the news carrier's words after the wedding (SKS KRA Nurmes. 1965. Elin Karjalainen 498; see also SKS KRA Nastola. 1965. Bertta Takala (farm mistress) 322).
262 SKS KRA Kurkijoki. 1957. Herman Poutanen (farmer, b. 1892) KJ 17:5839.
263 SKS KRA Alajärvi. 1965. Aino Hanhisalo KT 349:493. – woman (b. 1909) and man (b. 1904, farmer).

opposed. News carriers might therefore aim to rectify false gossip, positive or negative, spread by other news carriers about a future spouse (Heikinmäki 1981: 115).[264]

News carrying did not usually succeed in stopping a marriage from taking place, or even prevent suitors from coming, 'otherwise no one would ever have married, since news was carried about everyone,' as one woman from South Karelia observed.[265] However, news carrying was recognized to have sometimes 'caused trouble', [266] and it had the effect that most engagements were kept as short as possible (Asplund 1969: 188). However, in a few cases, news carrying could cause engagements to be broken off, as one farm mistress from South Karelia explained:[267]

> Sometimes it was the case that the happiness of two young persons who had been 'sung' to each other to make a match aroused jealousy and envy in others. The person who felt this envy and jealousy then paid a news carrier to sever the relationship between the two young persons. If the news carrier was sufficiently clever, she was often able to cause a separation with what she said, the disastrous consequences of which were perceived too late by the young persons and were regretted by them all their lives, since they had believed more in the news carrier than in the 'singer'.

Putting news carriers to good use

As is clear from the foregoing, news carriers were employed by farm mistresses to perform a variety of tasks. One of the most common was the spreading of a particular piece of gossip throughout the district. Gossip women were described by some informants as the most efficient form of mass media in the countryside:

> About 50–60 years ago, there was in our village a certain Mari Pöllänen who worked as a masseuse and cupper, and in her spare time she carried all sorts of information. We had no telephone in our village at that time, and newspapers came three times a week and even then, not to every house. If someone wanted some matter to be made quickly and widely known in the village, they were supposed to tell Mari about it and caution her 'never to tell anyone else', then Mari would surely not forget it. This is what my late mother told me about Mari when she needed her services.[268]

News carriers could also be sent to break up a courting couple's relationship, if the relationship was judged undesirable by one or both sets of parents. One informant from North Ostrobothnia explained, '...that sort of news

264 SKS KRA Vimpeli. 1966. Eino Lehtoranta KT 368:2; SKS KRA Nurmes. 1965. Elin Karjalainen 498; see also SKS KRA Nastola. 1965. Bertta Takala (farm mistress) 322.
265 SKS KRA Uusikirkko. 1965. Elsa Pukonen (writer, b. 1899) 1738.
266 SKS KRA Pertteli. 1965. Kaarlo Aitamäki (b. 1903, driver) 257.
267 SKS KRA Uusikirkko. 1964–1966. Ester Marjamaa (farm mistress) 229.
268 SKS KRA Uukuniemi. 1965/66. Eino Toiviainen (b. 1899) 2249.

carrier (*kontinkantaja*) could be bought off or bribed if the parents wanted to break up the relationship between their daughter or son and the person they had fallen in love with.'[269] Other informants from South Karelia described similar cases:[270]

> Those gossip-women were certainly to be found in Karelia. Some worked for their own satisfaction without any compensation, so that one had to be wary not to fall into their clutches. But others were paid for their activities. If one wanted, for example, to separate a couple, then a 'news carrier' was sent to speak ill about one person to the other, or to the young people's families. Sometimes, on the other hand, if one wanted to get a young person as a son- or daughter-in-law, then one might send out a person who spoke good things. In both cases, [the gossip woman] had to be able to speak in such a way that others did not notice that she spoke to a certain purpose. These sorts of persons caused a lot of damage, not only in young people's affairs, but in those of older persons as well.[271]

> Female 'singers' (*laulaja naiset*) were sent by a boy or girl who bribed the singer, or sometimes they came to the farm anyway, on their own initiative. Also, the parents of the girl or boy sent singers. If one wanted to prevent an intended marriage, [singers] went in the same way and criticized the girl in the boy's home and the boy in the girl's home.[272]

A farm mistress could also send news carriers to spread negative rumours concerning her daughter's *rival*, especially if her daughter had recently lost the affections of the son of a wealthy farm.[273] One recollection from Eastern Finland depicting the early 20th century describes the situation as follows:

> But in the old days there were some mistresses who, without the other members of the family knowing about it, paid 'news carriers' in kind. They secretly slipped a pat of butter, a piece of meat, a wad of wool, a kilo of flour or something of that sort to some masseuse or cupper as payment for news-carrying. If the boy whom the mistress' daughter fancied began to spend time with another girl, then carrying news about that other girl was always appropriate, and it was even worthwhile to pay some gossip woman a small fee for it.[274]

The jealous young persons themselves, too, could send news carriers to spread unflattering rumours regarding their rivals:[275]

269 SKS KRA Liminka. 1966. Paavo Kytökorpi KT 368:385.
270 See also: SKS KRA Muolaa. 1966. Hilma Jussila KT 366:132.
271 SKS KRA Jyväskylä. 1965. Elsa Jaatinen (b. 1907) 1397.
272 SKS KRA Heinjoki. 1957. Lempi Vanhanen (farm mistress, b. 1906) KJ 30:12504. – man, b. 1880.
273 SKS KRA Kivennapa. 1965. Liina Pulliainen (schoolteacher, b. 1901) 2616. – Heard from her mother.
274 SKS KRA Harlu. 1966. Maija Jaatinen 1594. – farmer's wife, b. 1871.
275 See: SKS KRA Kiikoinen. 1966. Jenny Leppäniemi (b. 1901) KT 368:68; SKS KRA Varpaisjärvi. 1965. Jukka Savolainen (insurance inspector, b. 1920) 384–385; SKS KRA Uusikirkko. 1965. Elsa Pukonen (writer, b. 1899) 1738; SKS KRA Sahalahti. 1965. Lauri Arra (farmer, b. 1886) 259.

[– –] When people heard that some boy had gone to propose marriage to a girl who had other suitors, those suitors became jealous and angry, and they paid some smooth-talking old woman to be a 'news carrier' (*konttija*) [– –]. When the news carrier went to the farm that the suitor and his spokesman had visited, at first she pretended to be ignorant of the whole matter. Usually she went first to the farm master and mistress, where she spoke of all sorts of other matters besides those related to the daughter's marriage, but gradually the talk shifted to those as well. And then the news carrier began to tell many sorts of vicious stories about the new suitor, how he is a wicked and morose man as well as a drunkard, how he has other girls that he has betrayed, and that he is said to already have children by some other girl and must pay child support. [The topic of] his wealth might also be brought up by saying that he is in debt and that his farm is poor [– –]. 'So that your daughter will end up suffering from hunger and squalor, if she marries that man. That man is indolent and inept and what's more he is lazy, I would never want to see such a good girl ending up in such misery.' These were the sorts of stories that the news carrier told, especially if the new suitor was from another village or district, so that the household members did not really know him or his farm, so they could not accuse the news carrier of lying. The girl's parents could then warn her against marrying into that farm, and if the betrothal gift had already been given, then it was returned.[276]

Finally, as already mentioned, news carriers (or rather, 'singers') could be sent and rewarded *by young persons themselves* to speak favourably of the sender (and his or her farm or dowry) either to specific persons (hoped for future in-laws) or more generally throughout the district:[277]

> Very often an unmarried girl or boy sent the news carrier on a visit for a specific purpose, to the neighbour of their sweetheart's farm, or to their sweetheart's farm itself, to praise everything about the sender. And to criticize his or her rivals. These sorts of [gossip] women, sometimes even men [– –] could receive quite substantial compensation.[278]

Although the foregoing descriptions do not tell us the manner in which the news carrier was compensated for completing her task, it must be assumed that since farm daughters and sons working on their own family farm had no access to money and were rarely given any by the farm master, the 'payment' to the news carrier consisted of farm products pilfered secretly by the young persons who arranged her errand.

Examples of using news carriers for the purposes described above can also be found from realistic ethnographic fiction. In Santeri Alkio's ethnographic novel *Teerelän perhe* (1887), Miina Kuppila, the daughter of a wealthy farm, is first courted and then passed over by Joonas, a young man much admired in the district. Miina's aunt, the mistress of Nevaluhta farm,

276 SKS KRA Padasjoki. 1965. Topias Kilpi (b. 1888) KT 353:531.
277 SKS KRA Kivennapa. 1965. Liina Pulliainen (schoolteacher, b. 1901) 2616. – Heard from her mother.
278 SKS KRA Kivennapa. 1966. Viktor Rontu KT 373:14.

wishes to help Miina win Joonas back, and to this end she invents a false rumour which she passes on to the village gossip, Saaraleena. According to this rumour, the novel's heroine, Johanna of Teerelä farm, who is Miina's rival for Joonas' affections, is actually an alcoholic (as everyone already knows her father and brothers to be). The farm mistress hopes that once this rumour has circulated, Saaraleena can convince Joonas' guardians, his uncle and aunt living on Niemelä farm, to persuade Joonas to marry Miina instead of Johanna:

> 'Tomorrow I'll go to Niemelä farm', promised Saaraleena.
> 'But of course Saaraleena understands that much, that you won't say you've been sent on Miina's behalf, will you?'
> Saaraleena's face expressed wounded dignity: 'Does the mistress think that this is the first time I...'
> 'Quite so! But as I've already said, Miina could naturally have suitors and would have received them by the dozens already, but she is choosy. I don't know what strange thing attracted her to Joonas. But the instant she heard that the boy had visited Teerelä farm, she rejected his suit and said that she's nobody's second choice.'
> 'It was well done! Nobody made him do it. The rich turn down suitors, not the poor.'
> The farm mistress went out and came back carrying wool.
> 'Here is ah...no need to give needles in return for this. Give your flagon here, I'll fill it up with...'
> 'A thousand thanks, mistress – and now for revenge.'
> The farm mistress took Saaraleena's flagon and filled it with buttermilk, and put a loaf of bread and cheese in her bundle.
> [Saaraleena] promised to carry out the matter to the best of her abilities and then wet her throat a dozen times with the mistress' gift. The farm mistress asked her once again not to unnecessarily involve her in the affair.
> Saaraleena left full of enthusiasm. After having walked a little while she burst out talking to herself: 'May God help me make this happen. – That farm mistress would pay me so well for it that I would not see another sorrowful day for a little while. Then I'll try to make Johanna agree to marry Iikka Kuppila, since Iikka always asks me to do it and has promised fifty marks. – Ho hoi! There is no sin in this, since God has clearly created me for this occupation...'
> The mistress of Nevaluhta farm remained standing in the middle of the farmhouse after Saaraleena left. Her face was beaming, and while she knotted her headscarf she said, 'This is good. If anyone can pull this off, it is she. Surely news of Johanna's drinking will soon spread, now that Saaraleena has got hold of it. As long as she doesn't lie and say that they are my words. I'm going to go to the village. Once I set my mind upon something, it would be awfully peculiar if I can't get one girl with money married off [– –]' (p. 82).

In the situations described thus far, the 'singer' or news carrier was sent upon her task by either the farm mistress or young persons of marriageable age. In some cases, however, news carriers took it upon themselves to inform interested parties of the faults or doings of others. According to one informant from Southwestern Finland, news carriers sometimes acted as though they viewed themselves as guardians of morality.[279] Especially when it came to the mores upheld by the landowning peasant classes, such as disapproval of both premarital sexual relations and courtship between young persons from different social classes, some news carriers clearly chose to act as defenders of the status quo, since they knew that it would be to their advantage to inform the farm mistress of moral transgressions committed by young persons in their households:

> There were also those sorts of gossips who deliberately monitored people's affairs and doings. For example at night, when the young men were moving around and visiting the outbuildings and lofts where girls were sleeping. When [the gossips] saw, for example, that somebody went into the room where the serving maid was sleeping, then in the morning, even before the serving maid had fully risen, the farm mistress already knew of the matter and once again the serving maid was given a lecture and had to confess. If, on the other hand, the son of the farm went to visit the serving maid of a neighbouring farm, then the same thing happened. But in this case it was the boy's ears who were burning. And naturally there were opposite cases, in which a farmhand caressed the daughter of the farm and the 'village bells' [=gossip women] found out about it and the daughter received a moral lecture. And the gossip woman received morning coffee.[280]

The power of negative gossip

It is important to note that the payments or rewards given to gossip women and news carriers by farm mistresses were not always given voluntarily. Because they were tied to the domestic sphere, farm mistresses could not know what was being said in the village behind their backs and to whom, and it was difficult for them to actively 'manage' their own reputations within the community. Gossip women and news carriers, by contrast, were forced to move around the district in order to make a livelihood. They were therefore able to both observe and reveal farm mistress' 'secrets' – often exaggerated and sometimes invented – to other persons without the possibility of being contradicted or confronted:

> I don't know whether news carriers were given payment. But there in my home village was one woman who was a real business genius in her own field. She walked from farm to farm asking for this and that sort of foodstuffs. If some farm mistress tried to refuse her, or if what she received was not good enough, she knew how to make public up and down the village all of the things that this poor mistress would have preferred to keep secret. This woman's occupation appears to have supported her well, and with it she was even able to provide for her lazy and stupid brother...[281]

279 SKS KRA Karjala Tl. 1966. Martta Arvela (schoolteacher, b. 1892) 318.
280 SKS KRA Töysä. Seidi Ylimäki (wife, b. 1905)1225.
281 SKS KRA Lappi. 1966. Fanni Ojamo (b. 1890) KT 370:8.

It was reported that gossips and news carriers often expected coffee or food in return for the news they brought on their own initiative, and if they did not receive it, they were sure to spread negative gossip about the uncharitable household around the district. Since farming families naturally wished to avoid ridicule and embarrassment, gossip women and news carriers were able to wield a certain amount of power. As one woman from South Savo pointed out, '[p]eople tried to live in such a way that there would not be anything in their lives that others could gossip about.'[282] A man from Satakunta explained:

> It was natural that when the news (*konttiasia*) carried by news carriers concerned oneself, one's farm or family, it was considered wicked, but if it injured a neighbour, one felt satisfaction at their misfortune. Often news carrying was quite effective. If the same or similar gossip was continuously repeated, even if it was supposed to have been quite impossible – people began to believe it – and the goal was achieved.[283]

Ethnographic descriptions reveal that 19th-century rural inhabitants were well aware of the danger to personal reputations posed by news carriers and female gossips. For this reason, news carriers tended to be treated with ambivalence: in some situations they were viewed as useful, but otherwise they were the objects of suspicion, disapproval and even hostility within the community.[284] As one woman from South Karelia explained: 'such persons were not held in high esteem, but no one wanted to make them angry, either. If, on the other hand, one needed information about the affairs of their neighbours, then they could be very popular.'[285] One male schoolteacher from South Savo described the caution with which the household received news carriers: 'the news carrier was usually [– –] feared and the household tried to display its best behaviour while the news carrier was there, because she might immediately go and tell the neighbours what she had seen and heard.'[286] Some persons viewed professional gossips and news carriers as motivated by laziness, since they seemed unwilling to do any other work.[287] As one woman from South Karelia summed up, '[n]ews-carriers were treated with caution and they were not as respectable as ordinary persons'.[288] In the words of another man from South Ostrobothnia, 'news carriers' (*kontiviejät*) and 'gossip women' (*juoruakat*) were usually the same person and they were hated because they left nobody in peace.'[289] Other rural inhabitants from North and South Ostrobothnia provided additional viewpoints:

282 SKS KRA Joutseno. 1965. Elsa Kutila KT 482:1358
283 SKS KRA Ylöjärvi. 1966. Reino Pihlainen 371:15.
284 SKS KRA Impilahti. 1965. Maija Mustonen KT 356:59; SKS KRA Kiihtelysvaara. 1966. Hanna Korhonen (b. 1897) KT 381:95; SKS KRA Kitee. 1966. Eino Mähönen (b. 1903) KT 370:45; SKS KRA Pertteli. 1965. Kaarlo Aitamäki (b. 1903, driver) 257.
285 SKS KRA Kirvu. 1966. Aino Heikkonen KT 364:139.
286 SKS KRA Mikkeli. 1965. Jaakko Valkonen (schoolteacher) 1307.
287 SKS KRA Vehkalahti. 1966. Ville Toikka KT 375:135.
288 SKS KRA Heinjoki. 1965–1968. Lempi Vanhanen 1520.
289 SKS KRA Vimpeli. 1966. Eino Lehtoranta KT 368:2.

Usually this kind of news-carrying was done by people who were on bad terms either with the groom or the bride, and in others' opinions it was very degrading. Usually people were of the opinion that 'marriage is a matter between two people and the news carrier gets a cuff on the ear' [– –].[290]

People reacted to news carriers with disdain. Even if someone might feel gratitude towards a news carrier who, by carrying news, had at least tried to influence a matter in the direction he or she desired, nevertheless news carriers were ultimately criticized and despised. This was because news carrying (*kontihteminen*) was considered to be sordid interference in others' affairs, and it was thought that an honourable and self-respecting person would never start to carry news about anybody.[291]

The news carrier was always hated and despised, even if she had come to tell the truth. People most often feared news carrying, for even if there had been nothing to gossip about that one knew of, [news carriers] could always invent something, and how was the listener always supposed to know whether or not there was any truth to it?[292]

Young persons in particular experienced irritation and hostility toward news carriers who interfered in their courting, and pranks played against news carriers were reportedly common:[293]

This sort of [gossip] woman had enemies, at least the youth committed all kinds of pranks against her. Sometimes stones or a pig's tail were secretly put in her bag. Usually she left her begging bag in a corner of the porch, which gave the youth a good opportunity to put something in it that did not belong there while she reported the news of the village to the farm mistress.[294]

It is clear from ethnographic descriptions that because news carriers were feared for their gossip, they used this fear to receive a negative respect that was not given to ordinary beggars (Heikinmäki 1981: 52). As informants from Varsinais-Suomi, North Ostrobothnia, Central Finland, and South Karelia reported, news carriers used farming families' anxieties over their reputations to their own advantage by coercing farm households to give them coffee, wool, and foodstuffs:

Keeping a news carrier happy meant that the one who kept her happy was left in peace. Those farm mistresses, farm masters and youths who did not keep the news carrier happy certainly got to hear which hole

---

290 SKS KRA Ii. 1966. Veikko Klasila (b. 1922) 3252.
291 SKS KRA Alajärvi. 1965. Aino Hanhisalo KT 349: 493. – woman (b. 1909) and man (b. 1904, farmer).
292 SKS KRA Vuoksenranta. 1965/66. Lilja Virtanen (farm mistress, b. 1912) 2154.
293 See also: SKS KRA Mikkeli. 1965. Jaakko Valkonen (schoolteacher) 1307; SKS KRA Kivennapa. 1965/66. Liina Pulliainen (schoolteacher, b. 1901) 2616. – heard from her mother; SKS KRA Liminka. 1966. Paavo Kytökorpi KT 368:385.
294 SKS KRA Asikkala. 1966. Jalmari Maunula KT 394:137.

the chicken pissed from. These women knew how to blacken someone's reputation, but despite this, they were not able to control the whole village with their tongues, for there were always persons who paid no attention to that sort of talk and slander.[295]

There was a certain Ieva, wife of Antti, a cupper here on the Sonkari side of the district, she carried a bundle on her arm and she begged butter and meat from farm mistresses. She was not completely indigent, for she seemed to get by with the food she was given. When a new daughter-in-law came to the district, the woman immediately went to whisper to her, give me meat, give me butter, or I'll take your reputation away with me in my bundle. One daughter-in-law had said, go ahead and take it if you think you can. After that, Ieva never went to ask for food from that person. Even many older mistresses feared that their reputations would go in that woman's bundle and they fell to giving food to Ieva behind the farm master's back. She knew her business, spoke ill of people behind their backs, but praised and flattered them when she met them. That was what those news carriers were like.[296]

If, as the above example suggests, it was possible for a farm mistress to refuse all dealings with gossip women, why did so many of them entertain and feed gossip women against their will? One of the earliest ethnographic fictions touching on farm mistresses' dealings with village gossips, written in 1853, suggests that one reason may have been the lonliness experienced by farm mistresses. The story 'Koti (Home)' was written by Fredrik Ahlqvist,[297] who served as the editor of *Maamiehen Ystäwä* from 1853 to 1855. Ahlqvist was also an early champion of rights for rural women, as I discuss in the next chapter. In his story, two fictitious farm masters discuss the proper place of husbands and wives within the farm household. Both men are already married, but Pekka is portrayed as living in relative peace and mutual respect with his wife Inka, while Martti is wealthier but has a low opinion of his wife, and is unhappy both with her and with their life of constant quarrelling. In discussing the needs of wives, Pekka implicitly suggests that gossip women may have been the only persons with whom lonely and isolated farm mistresses could share their sorrows; and that female gossips, in return for a cup of coffee, were always ready to lend a sympathetic ear:

[Pekka:] Aren't there many [men] who marry purely for money and property, the wife comes along as part of the bargain and as an annoyance, which is not as it should be; and after this she is treated accordingly, first coldly and then with contempt. Now after a time, when the wife notices that she has been disappointed, abandoned, or feels that she is not receiving the love from her husband that she expected, she grieves and mourns this. She must ease her heart, and so she seeks somebody to

295 SKS KRA Liminka. 1966. Paavo Kytökorpi KT 368:385.
296 SKS KRA Vesanka. 1965. Elsa Korhonen KT 353:19.
297 Fredrik Ahlqvist (1829–1876), like his older brother August Ahlqvist, was the illegitimate son of a serving maid.

whom she can complain of her misfortune, but since she does not always find more decent folk to whom she can trust her secrets, so the coffee and gossip women come, who listen to her complaints, express pity for her and urge her to repay evil with evil.[298]

The reference to the 'coffee and gossip women' in this passage highlights the cultural importance of coffee in the interaction between farm mistresses and female gossips. Coffee drinking was not merely a marker of social status in rural communities, it was a symbolic ritual of respect performed for the gossip woman, a means of bribing her to uphold the farm's good reputation, or to prevent her from undermining it, as informants from Varsinais-Suomi, Satakunta and Kainuu explained:

In Roismala village in my childhood there were several women who knew how to carefully weigh their words, as the saying went. I remember one of them better than the others because she would often stop at my home, because my home was conveniently situated near the village lane. My grandmother did not dare to leave the coffee unbrewed, even if it meant using her last coffee beans, and in other ways, too, we tried to please her, for it was not good to end up in this woman's teeth, she was a real aristocrat among gossip women, a dignified looking creature (in her youth she had been the famous beauty of the district, who had ended up 'under a leaky roof'), and her vocabulary came out in a fluent stream, juicy and colourful. If only someone present had possessed a tape recorder.[299]

It was well known that news carriers (*juorukontti*) were not liked, they were talked about a bit behind their backs but people were friendly to their faces, for they held each person's reputation on their tongue. For this reason, farm mistresses always took them to their private chamber and brewed strong coffee in small coffee pots which they drank with cream, even if [the farm mistress] herself did not normally go so far as to drink coffee with cream.[300]

When the coffee was ready and good, and there was good cream in the cream jug and a big lump of sugar (if it was too small, one got a reputation for being stingy), the [gossip] woman had a blissful smile on her face. Her good mood and the glibness of her tongue increased with the number of cups of coffee she drank. The norm was two cups, but it was the extra ones thereafter which did the trick. One had to pour at least a third cup, regardless of the other's protestations. This third cup was also a question of the farm mistress' reputation. The [gossip] woman would go to another farmhouse and say, 'I received three cups of coffee from that farm'. But if the farm mistress for some reason did not brew coffee, she was criticized in other farmhouses. The better hospitality the [gossip] women received, the more contented they were. They might

298 July 16, 1853. *Maamiehen Ystäwä* no. 28, 'Koti'.
299 SKS KRA Tyrvää. 1966. Esteri Viertola (b. 1911) KT 484:155.
300 SKS KRA Taivalkoski. 1965/66. Anni Karjalainen (schoolteacher, b. 1919) KT 379:56.

even praise the mistress to the skies in the next farmhouse. Most farm mistresses in their hearts did not approve of them. But they preferred to give them hospitality rather than to be the object of their anger.[301]

Gossip as a threat to the reputations of the youth

At stake in gossip and news carrying was not only the reputations of farm mistresses. Gossip women and news carriers posed an even more serious threat to the reputations of young unmarried girls and their chances of contracting a good marriage. As we have seen from the foregoing examples, gossip in 19th-century rural Finland was not merely the conveying of news about absent persons behind their backs. It was also the strategic manipulation of opinion used to discipline people, assert values and define community standards (see White 2000; Stewart & Strathern 2004). Gossip was an important means by which lower class women (and to a lesser extent lower-class men) exercised power over persons from the landowning classes and compelled them to adhere to their own professed ideals of social superiority. Even if the gossip woman herself did not necessarily tell her stories in order to uphold social mores but rather for her own immediate material gain, the farm mistresses who listened to her gossip were very interested in the moral transgressions of others, since moral conduct was an important basis for the rural social hierarchy, especially among women of the landowning classes. In particular, farm mistresses were interested in 'news' concerning farm daughters of marriageable age, since they were naturally concerned that only the most deserving young women should join their ranks.

In order to marry, and especially to marry well, young women generally needed to be able-bodied and healthy, and have a reputation for industriousness, skill, and obedience. Wealth was often an important criterion, and beauty was an added benefit. Young women who fell short of these cultural standards – at least according to female gossips – might soon gain a bad reputation and were not courted by suitors (see Stark-Arola 1998: 90–91). Although some informants maintained that it was rare for gossip women to permanently ruin a girl's reputation, others explained how mere gossip, if malicious, could suffice to harm or even ruin a girl's chances on the marriage market:

> A girl who remained an old maid was either ugly in appearance, or among the local people, evil had begun to be spoken about the girl on account of hostility, envy or poverty, she was slandered and gossiped about, and these disparagements were brought to the attention of the village boys, and the village women took part in this defamation, and the girl's enemies even paid the village women to slander the girl. The girl's own family was of the opinion that the village women had performed magic (which the village women did, in fact).[302]

301 SKS KRA Kiikala. 1965. Helmi Laiho (female farm owner, b. 1912) 1323.
302 SKS KRA Kontiolahti. 1966. Onni Kettunen KT 367:34–35.

Special 'news carriers' (*konttijat*), gossips, began to spread all kinds of malicious rumours about the bride's character – that was 'news carrying'. She was denounced as useless in all possible ways regardless of whether or not there was any truth to it. Many girls became victims of news carriers even before they had any intention of marrying – all that was needed was a skilful news carrier, some malicious and glib wife, which had for some reason or another become angry with the girl.[303]

According to one male informant from South Ostrobothnia, a sentence of 'unmarriageability', once passed, was very difficult to escape, since no self-respecting boy would court a girl who had already been judged unsuitable by others in the community.[304] On the other hand, parents could take certain measures to improve their daughter's chances of marriage, namely by increasing the size and value of her dowry in order to entice reluctant suitors:

> [– –] if suitors did not appear or were not in the least satisfactory, then parents began to take special measures. They let word get out that the girl would be given, for example, two cows (usually only one was given), a sum of money, or some portion of the farm. In this case, 'peat moss was put on the girl's back', even though there might have been sons on the farm as well. In this way, the desired result was achieved: the girl did not remain an old maid.[305]

The prevalence of news carrying in rural districts meant that young women of the landowning classes had to be extremely careful that their outward behaviour did not provide any cause for gossip, any 'news'. One woman from South Karelia added that girls had to be cautious especially around female masseuses and cuppers, because these women's 'territory' for the spread of gossip was so broad.[306] News carrying thus placed constraints on the behaviour of young rural women, as is suggested in the following example from South Karelia:[307]

> At home, people had to be constantly on guard for their daughters' sake, so that such and such a matter would not become 'news'. The vigilant eyes of neighbours monitored a young girl's life at all times. Close attention was also paid to aspects of character. Being cross and snapping angrily at people indicated a lack of sense, about which 'news' was spread. In order to avoid being gossiped about, the girl had to prove herself diligent and active in both household and outdoor work. In handicraft as well, she had to be clever, otherwise it would be gossiped that she was 'clumsy-fingered'. Illnesses, even minor ones, which the family tried to keep secret by all possible means, also became 'news'. [– –] Since the criticism was so severe and such close watch was kept, it

303 SKS KRA Lavansaari. 1957. Verner Hannula KJ 51:19254.
304 See SKS KRA Evijärvi. 1966. Matti Järvinen KT 366: 111.
305 SKS KRA Vuoksenranta. 1957. Aino Heikkonen KJ 2:315. –woman, b. 1873.
306 SKS KRA Vuoksenranta.1957. Aino Heikkonen KJ 2:315. –woman, b. 1873.
307 SKS KRA Uusikirkko. 1957. Elsa Pukonen KJ 17:5879.

is understandable that there were not many girls about whom 'news' was not spoken. The only ones spared were those who were so looked down upon that no one bothered to mention anything about them [– –].[308]

Gossip and news carrying thus functioned as a mechanism of control and surveillance over those young women who sought to join the ranks of farm mistresses. Young women who were judged unfit to preside over the resources of the farm were weeded out already before marriage, or at least prevented from marrying the most eligible young men of the district.

Yet news carriers' gossip did not only have the potential to destroy the reputations of young women in the community. It also posed a real danger to *young men's* honour and reputation, if to a somewhat lesser degree than for young women. Gossip most commonly threatened men's reputations during the crucial phase of courtship. Aside from owning land, marriage was the primary way in which a man could establish himself as a farm master and patriarch. A young man's social status could be improved by a partnership with a hardworking woman whose family possessed wealth and status in the community. If his reputation was damaged by a news carrier, however, he could have little hope of marrying such a young woman. This was because during courtship, the same basic logic applied to young men as to young women: unless she knew him personally, no self-respecting girl or her parents would accept the suit of a boy who had already been judged unfavourably by others in the community. Nor could the young man challenge his accusers, since the identities of village slanderers were nearly always impossible to determine after the fact. Thus, for young men as for young women, the stigma of being gossiped about and rejected was difficult to escape, as one male informant from South Karelia explained:

> A boy who had been turned down greatly lost his standing in the eyes of the other girls. Many girls were ready to reject a boy who had already received a refusal even though, if he had come to ask for her hand in marriage first, she would have been ready to become his wife. Because she didn't want to be considered inferior to the other girls.[309]

There seems to be little doubt that rural young men from landowning families recognized the danger to their reputations posed by female gossips. According to a woman from South Savo, '[t]he youth did not particularly like these gossip women. The boys very nearly hated them.'[310] Young men and women alike expressed their resentment of gossip women's slander through a tradition of mocking songs known as *ämmälaulu* which flourished throughout Finland in the latter half of the 19th century. These songs were sung by the youth during their labours or in their places of meeting and socializing such as the village lanes (Asplund 1966: 10). Informants from

308 SKS KRA Kirvu. Aino Heikkonen KT 364:139.
309 SKS KRA Uusikirkko. 1957. Herman Sirkiä KJ 25:8996.
310 SKS KRA Jäppilä. 1965. Eila Nykänen 392.

Satakunta, Häme, South Ostrobothnia, South Karelia, and Ladoga Karelia[311] told how the youth even sang mocking songs publicly so that gossip women could hear them, 'when we were quite cross about their gossiping,'[312] and that 'when older women happened to be present at the occasion, then the words were sung with particular emphasis.'[313] In *ämmälaulu* songs can be identified a wide range of motifs used by the youth to complain about gossip women's meddling in their courtship, of which some examples can be seen below (Asplund 1966: 135, 138, 139, 146):[314]

I looked out the windows of the garrison,	*Katselin kasarmin lasista*
at the waves on the lake	*kun lammi se lainehteli.*
Darling, don't believe the women's gossip,	*Älä usko heilani ämmäin juttuja*
the village women are lying.	*ämmät ne valehteli.*
I will now leave this village	*Pois minä menen tästä kylästä*
and slam its gates behind me,	*niin että portit paukkuu*
I can't stand listening anymore	*En minä jaksa kuunnella*
to the village women's slander.	*kun tämän kylän ämmät haukkuu.*
The women's tongues of this village wag	*Tämän kylän ämmäin kieli se pelaa*
like an aspen leaf in a tree	*kuin haavanlehti puussa.*
I, poor boy	*Minä poika vaivainen*
am in every village woman's mouth	*olen joka ämmän suussa.*

One man from North Ostrobothnia described how these mocking songs were sung by young men at the top of their voices if they met a female gossip while driving their cart along the road:

> It was not possible to retaliate against these [gossip women] except by composing harsh songs, which were not very commendable to the ear, but were sung nonetheless. If, while driving a horse-drawn cart, a farmhand or son of the farm happened to perceive that this sort of gossip woman was coming toward him on the road, he struck up a song, and the sound of the song did not have much of a tune, instead it was a terrible shouting like the Trumpet of God [– –].[315]

The same informant conceded, however, that gossip concerning a young suitor's faults or shortcomings might have had a basis in reality, as in the case of possible illegitimate children or various vices such as drink and

311 SKS KRA Orimattila. 1965. Aino Huisko (b. 1913) KT 351:73; SKS KRA Pyhäjärvi Vpl. 1966. Matti Viskari (b. 1891) KT 362:11; SKS KRA Impilahti. 1965. Maija Mustonen KT 356:44; SKS KRA Lappi. 1966. Fanni Ojamo (b. 1890) KT 370:8); SKS KRA Lappajärvi. 1965. Eino Hyytinen KT 365:48–51; SKS KRA Töysä. 1970. Irja Riiho, farm mistress.
312 SKS KRA Orimattila. 1965. Aino Huisko (b. 1913) KT 351:73.
313 SKS KRA Pyhäjärvi Vpl. 1966. Matti Viskari (b. 1891) KT 362:11.
314 Examples of these songs were recorded from numerous areas in Western and Central Finland, and from a few districts in Eastern Finland (Asplund 1966: 135–146).
315 SKS KRA Rantsila. 1966. Eino Linna 1047.

gambling that he might try to hide from his intended bride.[316] In ethnographic fiction, by contrast, the claims of gossip women against young men are always presented as unfounded. For instance in Minna Canth's three-act play *Roinilan talossa* (*On Roinila Farm*, 1885), the female village gossip Sanna is not necessarily seeking material compensation for her news, but nonetheless her tendency to exaggerate nearly leads to the ruin of a respectable young man. Sanna claims to have seen two men throw the body of Eero, son of Roinila farm, from a bridge into the river rapids. She shows everyone Eero's cap, fetched from the riverbank, as evidence. One of the men she claims to have recognized on the bridge is Mauno, who is secretly loved by Eero's sister Anna. Mauno is subsequently sought for murder, caught and bound as a prisoner awaiting trial, until Eero reappears at Roinila farm, in perfect health, having lost his cap while standing on the bridge spanning the rapids.

In his account of a news carrier in *Naimistawat Itä-Suomessa. Kuwaelmia entisiltä ajoilta* (*Marriage Customs in Eastern Finland: Depictions from Former Times*, 1886),[317] Johannes Häyhä (1839–1913) implies that it would be misleading to view news carriers who spread gossip on their own initiative as having acted from altruistic motives. Instead, news carriers were skilful in setting into motion dramas from which they hoped to eventually benefit, and they were adept at persuading farm mistresses to entrust them with – and compensate them for – news carrying tasks which they themselves invented. *Naimistawat Itä-Suomessa* describes rural southeastern Finland in the period of Häyhä's childhood and youth (1840s–1850s). Its fictive narrative recounts the courtship and marriage of the handsome daughter of a wealthy farm, Kaisa Niemelä. Kaisa has received four suitors, all of whom are farmers' sons in the district: first Juhana Lippola, whom Kaisa herself wishes to marry, and then Martti Junnola, Mikko Miehikkälä, and Matti Lahtela. Each man has given Kaisa a ring as a pledge of his suit. This unusually large number of suitors reflects well upon Kaisa's reputation in the community, and now Kaisa and her family must decide which suitor's offer to accept, and which rings to give back. This was precisely the sort of situation which gave news carriers their window of opportunity,[318] and two instalments of the story published in the newspaper *Wiipurin Sanomat* mention the strategic gossip of Maija, the local cupper, who takes it upon herself to carry news – much of it invented by Maija herself – back and forth among the farms involved. Because Maija wishes to test the waters and discover in advance which suitor is likely to be accepted by the Niemelä family, her strategy when talking to Kaisa's mother is to criticize Juhana Lippola:

---

316 SKS KRA Rantsila. 1966. Eino Linna 1046–1047.
317 This serial novella appeared in *Wiipurin Sanomat* starting on January 2, 1886 (no. 1), and ran until June 29, 1886 (no. 100). It was later expanded and published, with significant changes to the plot, as a book entitled *Kuwaelmia itä-suomalaisten wanhoista tawoista. Naimistawat* (*Depictions of Old Customs Among the Eastern Finns: Marriage Customs*) in 1893.
318 Asplund 1966.

After a few days, Maija the cupper visited Junnola farm. When she returned, she praised the suitor from Junnola and his farm to the farm mistress of Niemelä farm, saying that there was not such a good place in the whole parish as Junnola farm. [Kaisa's father], too, appeared to listen with pleasure to Maija's eulogies and decided to go on foot to examine Junnola farm.

'To whom do you intend to give Kaisa in marriage, since she has so many suitors?' Maija asked the mistress of Niemelä farm.

[Mistress of Niemelä farm:] 'I can't really say, since we have not yet decided, but I would prefer her to go to Lippola farm',

[Maija:] 'Really…Lippola of all places. Dear mistress, you wouldn't believe what an inflexible man is the suitor of Lippola farm. Your daughter would have her hands full waiting on him hand and foot to the end of her days. Even though the farm master has commanded him for two or three autumns to marry, he hasn't so much as lent an ear. How would such a man treat his wife, if he doesn't obey his father?' chattered Maija.[319]

When the mistress of Niemelä farm refuses to listen to criticism against Juhana Lippola, who is a neighbour already well known to her, she accuses Maija of having been 'sent to carry news'. Maija hastily leaves the farm and, on her way to Junnola farm, meets Juhana Lippola himself working in the fields. In the ensuing monologue (Maija leaves him before he has a chance to respond), Maija slanders the reputation of Martti Junnola, whom she had just praised to Kaisa's mother:

[Maija:] You will get Kaisa Niemelä. I'm just coming from there. You won't believe how the mistress praised you to the skies. I suggested in vain that you were of stiff and unyielding character, even though I know you to be as pliable as skein of yarn. She became angry and began to call me a news carrier. May God help her, don't I have other things to do than carry news. Just now I must hurry to Junnola farm to massage their suitor, he is so sickly that he does not see a day of health [– –] thank God that the master and mistress of Niemelä farm are such wise people that they won't marry their daughter off to such a wretch.[320]

In the expanded version of Häyhä's story first published as a book in 1893, Maija's role likewise broadens, and in the course of a single day, she has conversations with five different women. These include Kaisa's mother and the mothers of three of the suitors for Kaisa's hand, as well as Kaisa herself. By manipulating the truth according to the interests of the listener, Maija manages to ingratiate herself to the suitors' mothers and concoct new errands for herself (such as suggesting new brides for those suitors she predicts will be rejected by Kaisa's family), and receives foodstuffs from all of them in advance. In the book version, instead of meeting Juhana Lippola after talking to Kaisa's mother, Maija runs into Kaisa herself on her way

319 February 19, 1886. *Wiipurin Sanomat* no. 27, 'Naimistawat Itä-Suomessa' (-yhä [Johannes Häyhä]).
320 February 19, 1886. *Wiipurin Sanomat* no. 27, 'Naimistawat Itä-Suomessa' (-yhä [Johannes Häyhä]).

to Lahtela farm. Kaisa, who wants to marry Juhana Lippola, deliberately misleads Maija to protect the secret love between her and Juhana (Häyhä 1898, 30–31):

> [Maija] ran into Kaisa in the village lane and said:
> 'You are so beautiful, like an angel, it's no wonder those suitors are vying for your hand! Your mind must be in a whirl, poor girl, when the first suitor is good, the next one better, and you don't know who to take and who to leave. Have you thought it over, who is the best in your opinion?'
> Kaisa, who knew Maija from before and was familiar with her tricks, answered laughingly:
> 'I guess the first offer [from Matti Lahtela] might be the best one. The suitor from our neighbour's farm I know best, and on that farm I can be the mistress right away; on another farm I know not when it might happen.'
> 'Ah dear Kaisa, that is indeed a wise choice', said Maija. 'So would I do if I were you. You see, because I travel around the parish, I know the habits of every man and his farm. Juhana Lippola is stubborn and unyielding, even if your mother just a moment ago became angry when I said it to her, but it is true. Martti Junnola, for his part, is a good-for-nothing layabout and in other ways, too, discord prevails on that farm.'

From the foregoing scenarios sketched out by Häyhä, it is easy to see how a news carrier could find it useful to slander male suitors even if she had not been paid to do so. Such slander was useful because the news carrier could use it to flatter other young men and to elicit responses from those in a position to assist the news carrier materially, responses which revealed to the news carrier what her interlocutor really wanted and would be willing to pay for.

A situation in which the gossip woman had been *paid* to slander a particular suitor is illustrated in Santeri Alkio's *Teerelän perhe* (*The Teerelä Family*, 1887). Here the village gossip Saaraleena realizes that in order to prevent the heroine Johanna from marrying Joonas, the young man Miina Kuppila wants to marry (a task entrusted to her by Miina's aunt), it would be easiest if Johanna could be convinced to marry Miina's brother Iikka, who already desires such a match. Saaraleena goes to Teerelä farm where she urges Johanna to marry Iikka Kuppila instead of Joonas. In order to do this, however, Saaraleena resorts to suggesting that Joonas, an upright young man, is actually himself prone to alcoholism. When Johanna begins to protest loudly that she cares nothing for Iikka, the old woman answers, surprised:

> [Saaraleena:] 'How stubborn you are, and unwise in the matter of your own interests!'
> [Johanna:] 'It's my own affair!'
> [Saaraleena:] 'Has some evil person attached you to Joonas? – Apparently you think that he will always remain as blameless and sober as he is now, but wait! He will start drinking like the other men and I've heard he already does, secretly–'

'You're lying through your teeth!' shouted Johanna, red with rage.

[Saaraleena:] 'Don't shout at me! I did not invent that, I've heard it from better persons than you or me. – So, lying am I? When have you ever discovered me lying?'

[Johanna:] 'A hundred times already! And you still dare to ask the question.'

[Saaraleena:] 'Learn to speak courteously to an elderly person! Even though I am poor, no one has ever, ever [– –] accused me of lying, even though I have lived this long. My conscience – thank God – has always been clean; nor has anyone so shamelessly accused me of lying as you have – uh uh uh uuh!' and the old woman began to weep pitifully.

[Johanna:] 'Don't cry your eyes out, tell me, who told you that Joonas drinks, and I'll let it go.'

[Saaraleena:] 'I'm not a snitch and I won't say who told me, but I'm not a liar, I want you to admit that!'

'I'll bet!' said Johanna with mock seriousness and continued: 'Have you said your piece?'

[Saaraleena:] 'I'll just say this, and mark my words, the world will yet crush your pride. Crush it! You're not going to get as good a husband as you think.'

'Goodbye now!' laughed Johanna and put potatoes in the pot.

[Saaraleena:] 'Goodbye, goodbye! But you'll regret that you treated me this way, you impertinent bigmouth.'

[Johanna:] 'You probably still expect me to put in your sack butter, cheese, and bread as payment for your slander, and what's more to thank you!'

Saaraleena moved as fast as her sore legs could take her, huffing and muttering as she went (pp. 86–87).

In all of the ethnographic fictions discussed so far in this chapter, the male victims of gossip were young and unmarried. In 'Eero J–nen's' serial novella *Kuvaelmia sodasta valon ja pimeyden välillä* (*Depictions of the Struggle between Light and Darkness*, 1893), however, it is a married man who is portrayed as the target of malicious slander. Pekka is a hardworking, honest and abstaining young man, married to a virtuous wife named Elli. The couple become objects of village gossip when Pekka goes to North America to seek his fortune, leaving Elli to await his return. While he is gone, village gossips invent the tale that Pekka has killed a man and is wanted for murder. When Pekka returns to Finland both blameless and a richer man, gossips tell the vicar that he is a drunk who beats his wife, and he is called before the vicar to be reprimanded without the possibility of speaking in his own defence. The author ends his tale with an image of Pekka and Elli standing together, resolute against the evils of the world, especially gossip:

'Elli my dear', comforted [Pekka], 'the entire world is full of falsehood, but the worst place must be this district. We are not the only ones to have been the target of gossip women's interest. Here one person is painted one colour, another black and the third red. No one can escape the gossip women's teeth. And gossip itself is a vestige of the era when heathenism held sway, but it is being overthrown by increasing education and enlightenment, just like other vices which are evidence of savagery. Of that you can be sure, my dear Elli.'

'You are right, Pekka my darling. Even if we have been made the scapegoats of the world, we are nonetheless happy. Aren't we?'

'Indeed we are!'

And Elli wrapped her arms, trembling from emotion, around Pekka's neck and he pressed Elli to his chest, both of them knowing in their hearts that no storms would separate them.[321]

From the perspective of ethnographic fiction with a social reformist agenda, female gossip was a channel of information that operated outside of the male-controlled public arenas of meetings and courtrooms, with their institutional norms and procedures for evaluating trustworthiness, for establishing consensus on verifiability, and for maintaining accountability (see Eilola 2009). The fear harbored by these writers – shared also by men writing to late 19th-century press[322] – seems to have been that gossip, which flourished in the absence of any official controls, would leak out into public life and insidiously blacken the reputations of men with property and social standing who could not to defend themselves against a nameless, faceless accuser.

Gossip as a domain of intersecting cultural projects

Gossip has long been of interest to anthropologists and sociologists due to its universality and complex social nature (e.g. Gluckman 1963; Paine 1967). In any analysis of gossip, attention can be paid to a number of aspects, including (1) the content of gossip, (2) the network of actors engaged in gossip, (3) their resources and motivations, and (4) the concrete social situation in which gossip is transmitted. In this chapter I have touched briefly upon the content of gossip, but it is the actor network, motivations and situations which provide the most important insights into social power relations in rural 19th-century Finland.

Gossip can first of all be examined as a transfer of *social capital*. Sociologist Alessandro Portes (1995: 12) has defined social capital as 'the capacity of individuals to command scarce resources by virtue of their membership in networks or broader social structures [– –]. The resources themselves are *not* social capital: the concept refers instead to the individual's ability to

---

321 April 18, 1893. *Porilainen* no. 57, 'Kuwaelmia sodasta walon ja pimeyden wälillä' (Eero J–nen).

322 Men writing to the press occasionally expressed severe condemnation of village gossip and slander. For instance, one author argued in an 1891 article entitled 'What is a news carrier?' that '[– –] [s]uch a news-carrier, in other words the minion and the person who sends her, can cause even fits of insanity, nor would it be too severe if a millstone were hung from their necks and they were drowned in the depths of the ocean. It would be a loss, to be sure, but only because of the millstone.' (February 19, 1891. *Keski-Suomi* no. 20, 'Mitä on kontinkantaja?' [Recreatus]). See also: March 2, 1861. *Porin Kaupungin Sanomia* no. 9, 'Kielittäminen ja herjaaminen'; March 18, 1876. *Tapio* no. 12, 'Kieliminen ja panetteleminen'; October 17, 1882. *Sanomia Turusta* no. 161, 'Mietteitä panettelusta'.

mobilize them on demand'. If we examine the network of actors involved in rural gossip, the various resources at their disposal and their motivations, it is clear that in 19th-century rural life, ownership of land enabled farming families to acquire vital resources such as foodstuffs and raw materials for textiles, resources needed by nearly everyone in the countryside. Since these resources were stored on the farm and the farm mistress was given access to them in order to feed and clothe her household, she was also able to distribute them to members of the landless population as charity or as payment for their labours, with little monitoring or intervention from the farm master. The farm mistress also had access to coffee, often obtained through home thievery, which she offered as bribes and rewards to cottagers, beggars, and day-labourers.

The spatial organization of society, however, limited the amount of *information* to which farm mistresses had access. To function efficiently in any social environment, humans require information about the other persons around them. Due to the sparse spatial distribution of farms and crofts in 19th-century Eastern Finland, most persons who were actively engaged in agriculture at their place of residence were members of a thinly spread 'low accessibility network' (Hannerz 1967: 57), which meant that nearly all social knowledge was valuable because it was difficult to obtain. Tied to the farm by her many chores and tasks, the farm mistress had the least opportunity of anyone in her household to gather information that would be useful to her.

Cuppers, masseuses and washerwomen, by contrast, were forced by their occupations to walk from farm to farm and from village to village. This created an opportunity for them to gather information from their locale and and to provide listeners – for a price – with a 'map of their social environment' (Hannerz 1967). But since they lacked the land needed to cultivate their own food, female gossips needed the goods that only the farm could provide. Farm wives and local gossip women thus worked together to create a secret network of commodity and information exchange in which gossip women gave the local information they had gathered in exchange for consumable goods pilfered by farm wives, in a transaction which paralleled traditional forms of exchange (see Rosnow & Fine 1976). This network of exchange circumvented the legal and economic authority of the farm master, and allowed women to pursue their own interests behind the scenes.

However, this mutual interdependence between farm mistresses and landless female gossips should not necessarily be seen as voluntary or as evidence of harmonious cooperation. Female gossips were compelled to trade in the only commodity they had access to – information. Farm mistresses, for their part, needed the social information brought within their reach by female gossips, but they were often forced to acquiesce to female gossips' demands for material rewards simply in order to avoid negative gossip spread about themselves and to preserve their hard-won reputations.

With regard to the social situation or encounter which engendered gossip, only a few archived ethnographic descriptions supply this information. Realistic ethnographic fiction, on the other hand, provides detailed descriptions of the gossip setting and the dialogue between gossiper and listener. It is these descriptions which suggest that rural gossip was not merely the casual imparting of information regarding an absentee third party. It was a strategic manipulation of conversational and cultural conventions which appealed simultaneously to the listener's self-interest and self-image (through flattery) and to social expectations of what constituted moral and acceptable behaviour.

The gossip situation, like visits from intermediaries who sold pilfered farm goods to rural shops, required a space which was *temporally* sequestered from patriarchal power by the absence of the farm master. Ethnographic descriptions make it clear that gossip women and news carriers, especially if they expected food or coffee from the farm mistress, visited only when they knew the farm master would not be at home. It was the farm master's *absence* which rendered the communal working space of the household a safe one for gossip, as two women from Central Finland and Varsinais-Suomi pointed out:[323]

> [News carriers] didn't usually carry news for farm masters because they didn't receive any payment from them. Farm mistresses were sensitive about their own reputations and paid [the news carriers] behind the farm master's back. When the farm master was not at home, this was possible.[324]

> The men hated [gossip] women. But usually the [gossip] women knew when the men would be away from home. It wasn't every farmhouse in which the coffee pot would be put on to brew for the [gossip] woman, if the men were at home.[325]

In Scott's model of public versus hidden transcripts, gossip is presented as a weak weapon for criticizing the dominant group. Yet, as Scott points out, gossip can sometimes serve to draw attention to the hypocrisy of powerful individuals, in other words to the fact that the dominant members of society have fallen short of the moral ideals they themselves profess to follow as the foundation of their authority and superiority (Scott 1990: 105–107). With respect to the gossip encounter in 19th-century rural Finland, however, this is only part of the story. Finnish rural gossip was a highly complex intersection of cultural projects linked to class and gender. Farm mistresses' payments of pilfered farm goods to female gossips was an act of defiance – however self-justified – against male patriarchal authority, but the gossip conveyed to the farm mistress was rarely about the farm master or any established and respected patriarch. The bulk of the gossip concerned young persons who, although they were nearly always from the landowning classes, wielded no power over either the female gossip or the farm mistress – hence the need among the youth to resort to indirect protest in the form of derisive songs. In this sense, the female news carrier was not helping the farm

---

323 See also Suppanen 1888.
324 SKS KRA Vesanka. 1965. Elsa Korhonen KT 353: 20.
325 SKS KRA Kiikala. 1965. Helmi Laiho (female farm owner, b. 1912) 1323.

mistress to devise a hidden gender transcript of resistance, but was assisting her in policing her household and the class boundaries of her social group against improper behaviour, as well as against potential spouses who were unsuitable for the roles of farm master or farm mistress. According to the source materials examined here, everyone in the countryside was aware that gossip women and news carriers acted ultimately from self-interest and that their strategies involved morally questionable acts such as breaking promises of secrecy and intentionally misleading the listener. However, the fact that female gossips helped farm mistresses to uphold and reinforce the public transcript of rural society, which in turn bolstered the power and reputation of landowning heads of household, may be one reason why farm masters seem to have looked the other way and allowed female gossip to continue.

III
The Emergence of Public Discussion on Rural Gender in the Press

8. Inheritance, Labour Incentives and the Value of Women's Farm Work

A man's life depends on his horse, the maintenance of the farm depends on his wife.[326]

Home thievery was one of the few topics in the 19th-century press which elicited rural inhabitants' opinions on power relations within the rural Finnish family. An analysis of the discussions surrounding home thievery therefore offers possibilities for examining more closely the discourses pertaining to gender, equality, and women's roles in work and family which were promoted or disputed by writers in the late 19th-century press. An examination of newspaper discussions in the 1850s and 1860s reveals that even at this early date, such discourses were already multiple and even contradictory. It is impossible to state definitively whether writers to the press considered rural women to be strong or helpless, whether women's individual rights should be reflected in law or subordinated to the needs of the farm, or whether women's labour was seen as vital to the productivity of the farm or of lesser value than men's labour. It is impossible, because all of these alternatives were simultaneously being voiced – or at least implied – in the writings of the late 19th-century press.

In newspapers, as in daily face-to-face verbal interaction, discussants employed rhetorical strategies to bolster their particular cultural projects. Each of the five discourses outlined in Chapter Three was culturally acceptable to at least some dominant group in society and thus represented alternative public transcripts. Their use depended on the writer's ideological commitments but also on the context of the discussion: who was expressing an opinion, and to what purpose, in other words what practical or ideological agenda was being served by writing to the press. For example, it is clear that there existed tensions between, on the one hand, the ideological obligation to support women's rights as a means of promoting the concept of the (Finnish-language) nation, and on the other, the practical need to subordinate women's individual rights for the benefit of the household's stability and prosperity. By the time they wrote to the press, most men had already decided which of these stances deserved more emphasis in the particular context of their

---

326 *Hevosessa miehen henki, vaimossa talon pidäntö* [25].

argument. Some male writers, however, wavered and equivocated between the two, even within the same piece of writing. Where this can be seen most clearly is in the intense newspaper debates sparked by the question of how to eradicate home thievery, which was brought up at the Kuopio Agricultural Society meetings of 1861 and 1862.

The 1862 debate in Tapio

Shortly after Antti Manninen founded the Kuopio Agricultural Society in 1861, the Society's first meeting was held at the Jouhkola Agricultural Institute, whose directorship Manninen had vacated one year earlier. The 1862 meeting was held at the Levänen Agricultural Institute where he was then serving as director. Those present at both meetings included not only uneducated (and self-educated) landowning farmers but also male members of the gentry who were interested in improving agricultural conditions and thus social life in their rural locale. Some members of the clergy, minor rural officials, and merchants also attended. The newspaper report regarding the 1862 Kuopio Agricultural Society meeting was especially lengthy, probably because the discussions were intended to inform the debates expected to take place at the Finnish Diet in 1863. The discussions followed a predetermined list of questions such as 'In what way can current methods of farming be changed?'; 'In what way can cattle husbandry be improved so that revenues do more than just meet our own needs, but would produce great benefits for our country?'; or 'Is digging ditches for field drainage of any use, and has it been practiced in our region?'. In 1861 and 1862, but apparently not in subsequent years,[327] the question of how to eliminate home thievery was included in this list. On July 26, 1862, *Tapio* published a lengthy account of the discussions surrounding home thievery which had taken place at the 1862 meeting. This report was reprinted only three weeks later in the national newspaper *Suomen Julkisia Sanomia*. In order to show how the discussion progressed and in what order, it is reproduced in full below:

> 14th question. How can we eradicate the evil and in all respects harmful custom by which daughters steal from their parents in order to assemble a nest egg for themselves?

> **Innkeeper A. Rahikainen** considered it best if daughters were not allowed to have their own separate outbuildings and separate stockpiles of goods, for when they have them, then they want to accumulate separately from the household economy and to that end, they steal from the goods of the farm. – **Farmer H. Jaatinen**[328] from Hiitola decided

---

327 The 1861 and 1862 discussions produced so many letters to the press on the topic of home thievery – some of which were never published – that by 1863, Manninen may have felt the topic to have been sufficiently debated.

328 H. Jaatinen from Hiitola parish was probably Henrik Jaatinen (1829–1879), master of Ruisselkä farm.

that the entire problem lay in children's upbringing. Children should be raised with a better knowledge of Christianity. Fathers should always give their daughters what they need in moderation. But our laws already look down on womenfolk by giving them less inheritance than is given to men, which prompts them to take possession of the household goods with their own hands. Even our farm mistresses do not ordinarily receive the full respect and share of the household which is their due. – **Manor lord Westzynthius** agreed and desired that there should be one master in the household, who looks after his storehouses better and gives to each what they need, as well as keeps written accounts of the household economy. – **A. Kolehmainen** criticized also the farm master's habit of not giving even to his own wife enough for her ordinary needs, which results in her taking it on her own authority. **O. Räsänen**, for his part, desired that excessive zeal for ostentation among the youth could be eliminated through better child rearing. – **M. Puustinen** said he had earlier built his farm in an entirely new place, and, having throughout his life experienced much there, he had also observed that the more a child is suppressed and constrained, the more prevalent is home thievery. – **Estate manager Pehkonen** expressed the wish that better child rearing methods would become the custom and complained of the lamentable fact in this matter of home thievery that every father surely knows that his children are stealing, and sees his children wearing store-bought clothing, but he never chastises them for it or even asks from where they have received it. There are also said to be fathers who say 'go ahead, children, and steal, as long as I don't see it!' – **H. Jaatinen**, for his part, criticized the pointless custom in which brides distribute gifts at their weddings, which for its part has greatly contributed to home thievery; for one had to obtain a great many goods, both by purchasing them and paying the village women to make them, since there must be gifts for nearly all of the guests at the wedding feast. – **Landowner H. Aminoff** said that there are folk in this parish who wear the expensive blue colour and their daughters have too many clothes, with hundreds of shirts and dozens of skirts each, and that home thievery plays a role in their procurement.

Then the subject arose of whether sons and daughters should already start receiving equal inheritance. On this issue there were differences of opinion, with some wanting the shares to be equal because wives did as much good for the farm as men and were many times more industrious than men. But others were of an entirely different mind and firmly desired that things remain as they are. **A. Kolehmainen** thought that sons would abandon farm work, if they were not given a larger share than daughters, and secondary school graduate **M. Jaatinen**, for his part, did not think that it was yet the time to change the inheritance law, because the common folk were still of the opinion that daughters should not inherit as much as sons, which meant that even if the law were changed, it would be circumvented by selling or giving away the farm, or through special wills that would benefit the son. – **H. Jaatinen** also reminded the participants of the fact that so far only home thievery committed by daughters had been spoken of; but sons did the same and that was just as bad. – **Tradesman Fogman** suggested that parents should give their children proper annual wages in return for their labour just as is given to non-related servants, and having received this, children could then spend it as they wished. – **Farmer Europaeus** said that in order to thoroughly eradicate this evil habit, everyone had to combine their efforts and set to work to establish public schools in every locality, so that the common folk would learn to consider this habit a shameful one.

Then it was asked of the group of women present, did they not have, for their part, anything to say regarding this question, but they were inclined to think that it was not proper for them to speak on this matter which especially concerned them, and even though it was made clear to them that they were permitted to speak their mind on this issue, still they did not speak, but merely said they were 'ready to listen' [16].

There is much of interest to the researcher of 19th-century rural gender relations in this summary account published in the press, but here I wish to draw attention to several themes which gave rise to their own debates in the press after the 1862 meeting. These topics were: the injustice of daughters' unequal inheritance, the possible threat posed to the farm by reduced inheritance for sons, and the problem of miserly fathers refusing to give money for their family members' daily needs.

According to the law existing before 1878, daughters were entitled to receive one-half of the inheritance that sons did, but in Eastern Finland, they rarely received that much in practice. Daughters usually received only a dowry consisting of a cow or sheep, spinning implements, clothes and bed linens, and a sickle and other tools (Voionmaa 1915: 481–492; Jutikkala 1963: 60). Young women received this inheritance only if they married, and a significant number of rural Finnish women never did.[329]

The connection between home thievery and lack of inheritance was first made in 1849 by Vicar Johan Bäckvall (1817–1883) from Oulu, who signed himself '—kw—' and who would later serve as the editor of the newspaper *Oulun Wiikko-Sanomia* from 1854 to 1865. Bäckvall explained that home thievery arose because adult children guessed that they would receive very little inheritance from their father:

Children who remain at home begin to illicitly look to their own interests: they begin to pilfer and steal from their own parents and in this way begin to accumulate the fruits of their labours which they will not otherwise receive. In landowning households what usually happens is that the father, in striving to keep the farm intact, saves all the land for one child, usually the eldest child, and arranges for him pay a small sum to the other children. If there are many children on the farm, then the youngest ones start to fear this, and when they become adults they either rush off to work on other farms or begin to secretly amass something for themselves from the farm's common stockpiles. How ruinous this is, each can perceive for himself. For when the children of the household are of the opinion that they will come to suffer, the desire to promote the common good completely dies within them [– –][1].

---

329 Between 1880 and 1910, for instance, 30% of Finnish women aged 30–34 had never been married (Strömmer 1969: 46).

In his article Bäckvall did not, however, make a distinction between the inheritance of sons and daughters. This was left to Karl Ferdinand Forsström, who in his 1858 serial overview 'The situation of women in Finland', explained that no one in the press had yet mentioned the real reason for home thievery, which was that

> women have gradually come to feel that their lack of inheritance is a clear injustice, which they themselves have tried, and still try, to rectify in the aforementioned manner. When they were girls, mothers proceeded in the same way; men received a share of these ill-gotten goods when they married, and so it goes unto this day, everyone winds up in the same skein of wrongdoing, and the thievery committed by daughters is considered normal. Daughters themselves say: 'we're not going to receive any other inheritance'; fathers, for their part, perhaps knowing in their conscience that an injustice is being committed against daughters, do not wish to really prevent this in earnest; nor do neighbours hesitate to receive what daughters steal and sell: for it is a familiar and blameless thing [5].

One interesting point made by Forsström in the passage above is that because the wife's dowry came under the control of the husband upon marriage, newly married husbands stood to benefit when their brides pilfered before the wedding in order to amass great quantities of clothes and textiles. It should further be pointed out that this benefit was not only economic in nature. With great quantities of fine clothing, the new wife could look the part of a wealthy farm mistress and thus draw attention to the husband's social standing in the community.

Starting in the early 1860s, the issue of farm women's inheritance rights began to arouse more debate within the press. This was because the topic was also being discussed within the committee debates preceding the Diet (*Tammikuun valiokunta*, 1861–62), as well as within the Finnish Diet itself (1863–64, see Pylkkänen 2006).[330] Judge Forsström monitored these discussions closely over a period of two decades until equal inheritance was legislated for farm daughters and sons in 1878. According to Forsström's own account, he was not interested merely in the letter of the law, but also in what rural landowning farming families actually did with it, and the discussions surrounding rural inheritance which preceded the 1863 Diet apparently led the pragmatic Forsström to conclude that although equal inheritance represented a worthy ideal, it was not yet practical for the rural masses in Finland.[331] This was because the rural farming folk still did

---

330 Four years later at the 1867 Diet, a highly influential delegate for the landowning peasant estate, bilingual farmer Johan Keto (1826–1882), argued at length in favor of daughters' equal inheritance, basing his argument on the notion of women's 'natural rights.' However, at this sitting of the Diet his views did not prevail within his own Estate. For a transcript of his speech, see: April 27, 1867. *Tapio* no. 17, 'Yhdenlaisesta perintö-oikeudesta'.

331 August 13, 1877. *Uusi Suometar* no. 97, 'Uusi laki naima-osasta ja perintö-oikeudesta' (F. [Karl Ferdinand Förström]). The editor of *Sanomia Turusta*, Anders Liljefors, disagreed with Forsström's conclusions and offered a number of arguments for why the proposed law mandating farm daughters' equal inheritance with sons should be passed [14].

not abide by the older law which specified that daughters should receive one-fourth of the total inheritance, choosing instead to sidestep it through various means:

> Even now the [current] law is not completely familiar [– –]. And if it is, it is not followed, but is circumvented whenever possible [– –]. Even if in my opinion it is quite important that we begin to treat women justly in terms of inheritance, and Sweden's new inheritance law, which makes sisters equal with their brothers, has been established on the premise of natural justice; nevertheless I do not think that it is suitable for us in Finland to follow their example, as one newspaper recently reminded us. You see, it would not immediately be adhered to, since the general public opinion is not in support of it [– –]. Nevertheless, the fact that this question will be discussed in the Finnish Diet will presumably be a good inducement for many men to consider more carefully what is required by natural rights and justice with respect to women. And it is also good that men think of the causes underlying home thievery and their elimination. For this reason I, too, brought up the subject a few years ago in Suometar [13].[332]

Many of those who wrote to the press about home thievery in the 1860s and 1870s followed Forsström's 1858 arguments by pointing out that daughters who contributed their labour toward the good of the farm as a whole until they married were motivated to steal from the farm the fruits of their labours, knowing full well that they would never receive them by any other means. Home thievery and inheritance were perceived to coexist in inverse relation to each other: the smaller the amount of inheritance bequeathed to daughters, the more likely they were to practice home thievery. This was the stance taken, for instance, by the first woman on record to state her views on home thievery. At the 1861 meeting of the Kuopio Agricultural Society, when the conversation turned to home thievery, 26-year-old Liisa Väänänen[333] first asked permission to speak and then to send additional comments in letter form after the meeting so that they could be added to the minutes. Antti Manninen published these comments in a small printed booklet entitled *Kuopion Maawiljelysseuran Toimituksia* which contained the minutes of the meeting.[334] In her letter, Väänänen explained:

> Here I may respond at more length to the eleventh question regarding farm daughters' home thievery and its eradication, which was discussed in Jouhkola at the Agricultural Society meeting on the 23rd of September. The home thievery committed by farm daughters could be eliminated if parents would bequeath inheritance to daughters as they do to sons. Then daughters would not steal. But when nothing is given other than

---

332 Forsström is referring here to his overview 'Naisten tila Suomessa (The situation of women in Finland)' which was published in *Suometar* in 1858 (see note 139).

333 See notes 82, 128 and 198.

334 I have not been able to locate an extant copy of the actual report, but it is quoted in *Emäntälehti* no. 6, 1927. See also [11]

one cow or sheep, then daughters take more by stealing, so that there would not be so much of the parents' estate left for her brothers.[335]

A year later, at the 1862 discussion on home thievery and inheritance at the Kuopio Agricultural Society meeting, one participant's name which had not been mentioned in *Tapio's* July 26 report of the discussion was printing press foreman Fredrik Ahlqvist.[336] That same summer, Ahlqvist had begun helping Manninen by being responsible for *Tapio's* public notices and advertisements (Kinnunen 1982: 65; Toivanen 2000: 399), and a year later in 1863 he became part owner of the Kuopio printing press with Manninen.[337] In the fifth instalment of the meeting report printed in the August 16th issue of *Tapio*, Antti Manninen explained: 'Even though we have already briefly written of the answers to this question [of home thievery], we still wish here to especially publish two contributions [18].' The contributors were Fredrik Ahlqvist and a farm daughter from Rautalampi signing herself 'Maria J–n'.

Although Ahlqvist's speech was not published in *Tapio* until six weeks after the meeting, it was most likely presented during the actual discussion on home thievery, where other participants were allowed to comment on it. The speech was long, covering not only the topics of home thievery and inheritance, but also fathers' treatment of daughters and women's labour contribution to the farm. Ahlqvist argued that as long as daughters were treated ill before the law in terms of inheritance, they would be predisposed to think that it was not worthwhile to labour for the good of the farm, regardless of how much they might otherwise value hard work [18]. Farm master Adolf Kolehmainen from Karttula seems to have objected to Ahlqvist's views during the meeting itself, arguing that if sons could not inherit their home farm or at least most of it, they would not be motivated to stay and work there, since they always had the alternative to go to work on another farm as a farmhand for wages. Kolehmainen apparently also expressed the opinion that sons were entitled to a greater share of the farm's inheritance because they performed the heaviest labour on the farm. By contrast, Fredrik Ahlqvist argued that the *quantity* of farm work performed by women equalled, or even surpassed, that done by men:

> [– –] What Kolehmainen said to refute me, that men supposedly plough and perform heavier work, and that for this reason daughters should not receive as great a share of the inheritance as sons, to this I would answer briefly that men were made for [such work] already at the time of Creation. And another thing, men in the countryside never do more, and rarely as much, work as wives. When women are already spinning or caring for the cows, one often sees the men still resting. On Sundays,

---

335 June 1927, no. 6. 'Mielenkiintoisia lausuntoja kotivarkaudesta 64 vuotta sitten', *Emäntä-lehti*, 119–121. (A. L:s).
336 See notes 140, 141, 297.
337 The name(s) of the owners of the Kuopio printing press, which always appeared at the end of the last page of *Tapio*, changed from 'P. Aschan and company' to 'A. Manninen and Fr. Ahlqwist' on May 23, 1863.

too, the men are left in peace to rest while the wives have just as much work as on any other day of the week; they must feed and give water to the cattle, and prepare food for the family. In the summer in the hay meadows, wives are nearly the equal of men, and in cutting hay they even leave the men behind. Even then, they are not more prone to fatigue than men, even though they hardly get a break to eat and rest compared to the men, since men, as soon as they have eaten, go to lie down, whereas the women must still put away the food, wash the dishes and other chores. Nonetheless they leave again to labour in the fields at the same time. In the threshing barn, too, the wife is the equal of her husband. Ploughing, tree felling and other work using horses may well be the only tasks to which a man is more suited, has better endurance and is stronger [18].

Ahlqvist's speech is significant because it marks the first mention within the discussion of home thievery of what would later become the stereotype of the strong Finnish woman working alongside her husband for the survival of the farm.[338] Ahlqvist's speech seems to have derived from his own observations, rather than from the philosophical notions of natural rights and equality widely used by male writers both before and after him. Ahlqvist's mother was a serving maid in Kuopio who raised four children alone and in poverty, and Ahlqvist's appreciation both of women's potential and the injustice of their situation may derive from this experience. Ahlqvist may have made reference to his mother's situation in his fictitious tale 'Koti (Home)' published in 1853 in Maamiehen Ystäwä, when the character of Pekka, a farm master, praises a hardworking widowed mother with four children. Pekka tries to explain to his friend, a more conservative farm master named Martti, that the significance of a wife's work and common sense should not be underestimated, whereas Martti considers women to be lacking in judgement and therefore well-suited to being the subordinates of their husbands:

> [Pekka:] But you have certainly seen many wives who have gone from poverty to prosperity through their hard work. Take Liisa Lampela, for example; she was left in destitution with four children when Olli died, because their entire wealth was auctioned off by creditors to pay their debts, and only through hard work and diligence did she raise her children, so that now all of them are prosperous and highly respected men. Yes, yes, that may well be, said Martti, but one example does not prove much.[339] [Pekka:] Do not say so, dear brother; we are surrounded

338 The notion that rural wives could be strong and sensible, and that their calling in life was to perform physical labour alongside their husbands, had been presented already in 1840 in Oulun Wiikko-Sanomia (March 14, 1840. Oulun Wiikko-Sanomia no. 11, 'Työn kunnia. 3. Luku. Waimon-puolet tarwittewat harjauwa monenlaiseen työhön'). Yet when the Finnish-language press began to flourish in the early 1860s, this concept of Finnish agrarian womanhood was overshadowed by other discourses which viewed women as vulnerable and ill-treated, passive and even weak. Ahlqvist's speech appears to have been one of the first to resurrect the notion of the strong Finnish farm woman.

339 In the original Finnish, this is expressed: '...but one stone does not heat much water' (mutta ei yksi kiwi paljoa wettä lämmitä).

by many good and industrious wives, even if no notice is taken of them, nor is it appreciated that they do whatever work they can while we men live as we wish, and try to always conceal our shortcomings [– –].[340]

How was Ahlqvist's notion of the strong Finnish woman received by the other rural men present at the 1862 meeting? H. Jaatinen agreed with Ahlqvist that 'our farm mistresses usually do not receive the full recognition and share of the household which is their due' [16]. As previously mentioned, Adolf Kolehmainen had apparently disagreed with Ahlqvist regarding the value of women's work on the farm, saying that sons were entitled to a greater share of the inheritance because the ploughing and other farm work carried out by men was more laborious than that performed by farm women [18].[341]

Writing three months after Ahlqvist's speech was published in *Tapio*, farm master Albert Kukkonen (1835–1918)[342] agreed with Kolehmainen by saying that the existing inheritance law was the most appropriate one, since sons were stronger and their work more important to the maintenance of the farm than that of daughters, 'even though Mr. Ahlqvist maintains that womenfolk are just as strong and steadfast in work as men' [25]. Kukkonen argued that it was understandable that men worked harder on the farm than women, since women left their birth farm to marry and inherited less than their brothers:

> Of course, women must not be oppressed, in other words due to the nature of their work, put in the situation where they now are; but on the other hand, extravagant praise in which women are claimed to the equal of men in outdoor labours is not appropriate [– –]. I do not say that it is to be wondered at, if daughters are less concerned with the work of the farm, for they know they are destined to marry and will otherwise receive less inheritance [25].

Although Kukkonen's letter was careful in its wording, Antti Manninen took issue with Kukkonen's view that women's work was less important to the maintenance of the farm than men's work. In an 'editorial reminder' at the end of Kukkonen's statement, Manninen criticized Kukkonen and defended the image of the strong farm wife introduced by his assistant editor. Manninen wrote that more enlightenment and education were needed among the common folk so that 'justifications and explanations such as the foregoing regarding the worthlessness of wives' work will become a thing of the past. Then perhaps people will give credence to the proverb: 'a man's life depends on his horse, the maintenance of the farm depends on his wife'' [25].

Yet despite the objections that were raised by Ahlqvist's speech soon after it was published, echoes of his arguments can be found in articles written years later, as in the case of a letter written to the Central Finnish newspaper

---

340 July 9, 16. 1853. *Maamiehen Ystäwä* nos. 27 & 28. 'Koti'.

341 Kolehmainen nevertheless agreed with Ahlqvist that farm masters should be more concerned with the daily needs of their wives [16].

342 See note 208.

Kansan Lehti in 1870, which was purportedly written by a woman [35]. *Kansan Lehti* (*The People's Newspaper*) was an unusual newspaper for its time, both because it was more religious in tone and subject matter than other newspapers of the period, and because its editor, medical doctor and ardent Fennoman Wolmar Schildt (who often used the Finnish-sounding surname Kilpinen), seems to have published rural correspondence letters with almost no editing.[343] This may have contributed to two interesting features of the newspaper: first, *Kansan Lehti* printed at least six letters written by women during its three year existence (1868–1870), a number comparable to *Tapio's* publishing of thirteen women's letters during the six-year period 1861–1866. Second, the correspondents to *Kansan Lehti* appear to have imagined themselves as a fellowship of discussants and routinely referred to each other as 'brothers' and 'sisters'. This situation apparently provided the opportunity for a writer using the pseudonym 'Teidän oma siskonne Nulpukka (Your own sister, Flower-bud)' to address her fellow 'sisters' publicly and to express a remarkable sentiment: that home thievery should not be too harshly condemned.

The purpose of 'Flower-bud's' letter was to urge rural young women to sell their accumulated dowry clothes and linens rather than display them in outbuildings or let them rot from disuse, and to place the money thus obtained in the savings banks which were just beginning to appear in the countryside. 'Flower-bud' opened her argument by praising rural young women's diligence, and in doing so used several of the points made by Ahlqvist in his 1862 speech regarding women's work, home thievery, and farm daughters' inheritance:

> Dearest sisters, I now approach you in this letter, because we have no other place of meeting than the church hill and Sunday morning [– –]. I have often thought of your diligence and hard work in domestic tasks. And I have especially been amazed at your genius in obtaining for yourselves 'trousseau goods'. In itself, this deserves no reproach. For first of all, you produce the greater part of them yourselves, you weave and spin while the men are lying down and resting. It is thus to your credit. And second, even if you were to take [the goods needed to amass a trousseau] on your 'own authority', as the boys say, even that is not so very blameworthy, even if it is just a little, because the law stating that daughters do not inherit equally with sons still prevails [35].

---

343 When the newspaper announced that it would cease publishing, one writer lamented this news and explained that *Kansan Lehti* had been loved by its readers because of the freedom it gave Finnish-speaking commoners to express their ideas and opinions in their own words:
  'But what was it that made this newspaper to us so beloved above all others? It was the freedom that it used in printing each person's ideals, concepts and truths in the form in which that person had conceived them. It was precisely this freedom granted by *Kansan Lehti*, which made it so loved by us, and, I believe, will make it dearly missed. For, although there are other newspapers in our country, and in other ways surely more worthy ones, yet the yearning for *Kansan Lehti* will be considerable, because there will no longer be the freedom to publish thoughts and ideas which do not suit the opinions of newspaper editors' (December 24, 1870. *Kansan Lehti* no. 51, 'Hywästi jättö weikoille ja siskoille' (J. H–n).

'Flower-bud's' letter is the only newspaper text dealing with home thievery in the last half of the 19th century which makes the point that home thievery should *not* be condemned, and it thus deserves closer attention. Who was 'Flower-bud'? Was the writer even female, was she self-educated? If written by a woman, the letter is unusual in that it not only strives to enlighten rural women about the benefits of abandoning traditional customs and putting their savings in a bank, but also does so in a highly confident manner. Such confidence may be accounted for by the forum in which 'Flower-bud' wrote, since other letters ostensibly written by women and printed in *Kansan Lehti* display a similar attitude of self-assurance. What is clear, however, is that 'Flower-bud' was highly knowledgeable about the daily lives and attitudes of farm daughters in rural Finland:[344]

> The question therefore is simply: how can we make better use of this work and these goods than we have so far, goods which now cover the rafters and walls of our outbuildings to be guarded, with great anxiety, in the summer against moths and in the autumn against thieves and robbers? I know of storehouses in which these goods have been stored for nearly twenty years, where energetic mothers began storing goods while their daughters were still growing, and in this way so much is accumulated that the lower layers rot. Of what use, then, is all your efforts? I think it would be better to sell the handicraft work, and to accumulate the money in a savings bank, where it would increase [– –]. 'But can anyone get by without clothing? If one is not well-dressed, she is hardly considered human. And what then would we show to the suitors if they happened to visit the farm? [The clothes] must be ready before one marries, for one has no time to make them afterwards.' This is probably what each of you is thinking. Yes indeed. Certainly each person needs clothing, but just not so very many as is now the custom [– –]. A suitor who comes to look at your trousseau will be even happier to look at your savings book. A decent man will care nothing for these things [– –] [35].

The amount of detail provided in 'Flower-bud's' letter suggests that he or she, if not an actual member of a farming household, then at least lived in the countryside and was in close contact with farm women. The reason why 'Flower-bud' chose not to condemn home thievery may be that, unlike the other newspaper sources in my corpus whose primary audience was assumed to be men, 'Flower-bud's' letter was expressly directed at rural women. The writer, in wanting to persuade these women of the benefits of selling their handiwork and accumulating their savings in banks, naturally would have wished to win their trust, and attempted to do so through the rhetorical device of siding with farm daughters on the issue of home thievery. What is interesting here is that 'Flower-bud' did not produce any new or original justifications for why farm women were entitled to pilfer from their home farms, but instead seems to have drawn upon Ahlqvist's arguments which had appeared in the press eight years earlier.

344 The pseudonym 'Nulpukka (Flower-bud)' suggests that the writer was from Eastern Finland, more specifically from an area to the north or northwest of Lake Ladoga, since those were the only regions in which this particular dialect term was known (KOTUS, Lexical Archive of Finnish Dialects, personal communication October 10, 2011).

Inheritance as a labour incentive for sons

As discussed in Chapter Two, anthropologists and socio-economists studying peasant agricultural societies have shown that gender is a key factor in the internal dynamics of family farming households. One important finding is that family farms tend to reduce their costs by relying on the unwaged work of family members, especially women.[345] The work of wives, daughters and sons on 19th-century farms was not unpaid *because it was devalued or unproductive*. On the contrary, every service that these family members provided could also be bought on the labour market – and such services were in fact commonly purchased from farmhands and serving maids when there were no family members to perform them. Family farm work was therefore unpaid *as a result of the specific social relations in which it was performed* (cf. Delphy 1984). In other words, the farm master's direct claim upon the labour of his household members arose from the concept of a household economy created through the institution of marriage, as well as from the patriarch's legally established rights of control over the group of persons who were formed through this institution (his wife and legitimate children). This arrangement can be seen as an institutionalized means for masking relations of power. As Pierre Bourdieu (1977) has shown, in order for domination to be exerted in a lasting and credible fashion without the need for physical violence (which is costly both to the power holder and to society), it must disguise itself as a set of moral relations. Domination therefore relies on a public transcript in which strategies of subordination are transformed into relationships of kinship, loyalty, generosity, and so forth (Kandiyoti 1998: 148, note 4).

Using family labour on farms had additional benefits to the farm besides the fact that wages did not need to be paid. Ties of loyalty and a sense of belonging served as a way of motivating family labourers to work harder for the common good, and family members also lowered what social economist Robert Pollack (1985) has called the farm's *transaction costs*, meaning the costs of negotiating, monitoring and enforcing agreements between worker and employer, as well as the costs of mitigating the higher risks of short-term labour relationships. The fact that labourers from within the family were socialized from childhood into the particular working culture and tasks specific to that farm meant that farm masters and mistresses did not have to monitor family workers for mistakes; and where surveillance of non-family labourers was needed to ensure their hard work, sons and daughters could do this. It follows from this that family members were not interchangeable with non-family workers: each able-bodied family member was more valuable than a hired hand. An editorial in the newspaper *Tampere* in 1883 summarized this idea as follows: 'If there is no other bond between master and servant than the terms of service (*palvelussääntö*), then that servant will become very expensive for his master. He will never do any extra work, even if a minor effort would result in great benefit for his master [– –]. He

---

345 E.g. Chayanov 1966, Beechley 1987; Whatmore 1991; Alston 1998.

feels himself in no way responsible for carrying out his tasks in the proper manner or at the proper moment.'[346]

Already in 1857, Antti Manninen, in arguing for improvements to farming life and for the division of large estates into smaller, more productive parcels, wrote that servants were usually considered to be careless, untrustworthy and lacking in diligence, but that this arose from their lack of motivation to work hard when they could not be sure they would be treated well in their old age. The mid- and late-19th-century Finnish-language press contains many letters from farm masters who complained that labourers employed from outside the family were scarce and expensive in economic boom times, and problematic even when hired. One writer to the press in 1876 lamented that hired servants had become strangers to the landowning farming class: they were no longer part of the family, they no longer ate at the same table nor worshipped together. Servants, having seen the disparity in wealth between themselves and farming families grow during the rise of the lumber economy, had become more selfish.[347] Other writers to the press in the period 1862 – 1878 mentioned the common complaints made by farm masters regarding servants, for instance that they were lazy and careless, possessed insufficient skills for farm work, displayed lewd behaviour, made unreasonable demands on their employers and even stole from them.[348]

In part, these complaints arose from the fact that social transformations were driving a wedge between servants and the farming family.[349] In the older rural society, family members and servants had worked together, eaten at the same table, and even – for example in the case of some farm daughters and female servants – slept in the same beds. The farming family and servants together made up what was called an 'eating community' (*ruokakunta*), a concept with powerful symbolic connotations of harmony and internal cohesion. However, due to the increased educational opportunities for landowning farmers and their sons but not for the landless population, as well as new wage labour opportunities and a heightened political consciousness among the labouring population, farming families and landless workers could no longer perceive themselves as working together toward common goals.[350]

346 October 3, 1883. *Tampere* no. 115, 'Isäntäin ja palwelijain wälinen suhde – sana ennen muutto-aikaa.'

347 February 15, 1876. *Sanomia Turusta* no. 13, p. 1, 'Satakunnan maanwiljelysseuran johtokunnan lausunto 1863:en wuoden palkkaussäännöstä'. See also: October 3, 1883. *Tampere* no. 115, 1–2, 'Isäntäin ja palwelijain wälinen suhde – sana ennen muutto-aikaa.'

348 January 31, 1862. *Suometar* no. 5, 'Rääkkylästä'; June 7, 1865. *Suometar* no. 129, 'Helsinki 7 pnä kesäkuussa. Suomen Maatalouden parannuksesta'; October 31, 1866. *Pohjan-tähti* no. 14, p. 1, 'Palkollisten tilaisuudesta'; December 21, 1878. *Pohjois-Suomi* no. 102, 'Palkkawäestä' (*Työmies*). See also [4] and Mikkola & Stark 2009, 6.

349 This was noted in the press as early as 1860: (January 5, 1860. *Hämäläinen* no. 1, 'Työwäen olo').

350 See: January 5, 1860. *Hämäläinen* no. 1, 'Työwäen olo'; October 3, 1883. Tampere no. 115, p. 1, 'Isäntäin ja palwlijain wälinen suhde – sana ennen muutto-aika'; August 11, 1883. *Keski-Suomi* no. 64, 'Keskusteluista Keski-Suomen maanmiesten yhdistyksen ensimmäisessä kokouksessa Petäjäwedellä, 2 päiwänä elokuuta 1883'.

The desirability of keeping one's own children working on the farm meant that incentives had be provided for adult children to remain in their birth household rather than leave to work for wages as a farmhand or serving maid on another farm. This was pointed out already in 1849 in *Maamiehen Ystäwä* by Vicar Bäckvall:

> Not all the children of a tenant farmer who lives on the Crown's lands have any hope of inheriting immovable property, meaning land, which the eldest son alone inherits and other children must go their own ways without. For this reason, the children of a [Crown tenant] do not stay together, but try as soon as possible to be hired onto other farms, from which they receive a wage for their labour. In their stead, the father must now hire strangers, who are usually more careless in carrying out the work of the farm and looking after its interests than his own children would have been, if he had cared about their troubles. Thus both are deprived: the maintenance of the farm is carried out poorly, and the children lose their home and often their parents' love as well [1].

In 19th-century rural Finland, the primary form of labour incentive which kept sons, and particularly eldest sons, working on the farm was the inheritance they received upon either their father's death or his retirement from active control of the farm. Inheritance to sons was also seen to be crucial to the survival of the farm because dividing the farm into smaller equal shares for all siblings threatened to reduce their viability, an argument which was used both within the Finnish Diet and in the press starting in the early 1860s (see Pylkkänen 2006: 386).

In 1877, when it appeared likely that the new law for equal inheritance between rural sons and daughters would soon become a reality, Judge Forsström was careful to explain that whereas some members of the 1877 Diet had claimed that 'men's work was generally of much greater worth than that of womenfolk', in his opinion this was an idle claim because on a family farm it was nearly impossible to judge whose labour played a greater role in promoting its wealth. Nevertheless, continued Forsström, the new law was likely to be a detriment to farming, especially on farms where there were many sisters and only one or two sons. Forsström explained that if daughters inherited in equal measure with sons, this would lead to the ruin of the farm because the son of the farm would be less motivated to work toward the day when he would inherit the farm. Even if he worked hard and the value of the farm increased, it simply meant that he would have to go deeper into debt to buy his sisters out of their share of the farm in order for the farm to remain intact [39]. He might be tempted instead to work as a farmhand on another farm where he would receive wages, leaving his birth farm without a proper master [38]. At the very least, Forsström argued, equal inheritance laws were likely to cause quarrels among siblings, destroying the harmony of the family [38].

Fifteen years earlier, a writer signing himself 'J. K–n.', who was probably a farm master from Savo, had described how a son might feel if the law were to mandate equal inheritance: '[he] begins to feel negligent in his labours, thinking: I won't receive any more from the farm than my sister will, let her go and plough or chop down trees [– –]' [22]. In the same year, farm master and folk poet Anders (Antti) Puhakka (1816–1893), who was at that time representing the estate of landowning farmers at the committee debates preceding the 1863 Diet (*Tammikuun valiokunta*), wrote to *Tapio* that a farmer's son who inherited the same portion as his sisters could not hope to compete for a bride with those suitors who had no sisters and so would inherit a larger share of their father's farm [23].

In these letters published in the press, the question of younger sons' inheritance – or lack of it – was rarely mentioned. Writers and meeting participants may have neglected to mention younger sons in order to avoid diluting their arguments, but one reason for the omission might also have been that in Eastern Finland, where *Tapio's* primary reading public resided, it was sometimes possible for younger brothers to remain with their wives and children on their birth farms in fraternally extended households (*suurperheet*). Such extended households, containing usually two or three brothers and their families, might later decide to divide the farm into smaller parcels among the married brothers, but in this case the immediate question of brothers' inheritance was not as acute as it was for daughters, who nearly always had to move away from the farm when they married.

Male writers and meeting participants did not merely focus on the labour incentives provided to sons of the farm, however. They recognized that farm wives and daughters, unlike serving maids, were not paid for their work. While it is true that the farm relied on the unwaged work of all family members, sons were given the incentive of farm inheritance, whereas female family members were not. At the 1862 meeting of the Kuopio Agricultural Society and in one letter to the press, men even compared the situation of farm women to that of slavery [16, 17, 18, 56].

To remedy this situation, the suggestion was made by Vicar Johan Bäckvall as early as 1849 that daughters and sons should receive a wage like non-family farm labourers:

> If we examine the common situation of farm sons and daughters in their own homes, there is no doubt that parents, too, are at fault for this habit [= home thievery] of their children. The farm master pays his farmhand and serving maid a wage, and also gives them some clothing because otherwise he would never get them to work for him; but even the wealthy father often gives to his own fully grown sons and daughters nothing more than the most essential clothing; but [his children] work alongside the servants and monitor their work as well. When they see the servants either saving their wages for the future or spending this well earned sum on something useful or on self-adornment, this creates in farm sons and daughters the desire to do the same, and when there is no other way to get [money], they start to steal from their parents' stockpiles [1].

The suggestion to give family members wages was repeated in the press by a merchant named Fogman at the meeting of the Kuopio Agricultural Society in 1862, again by columnist Paavo Pajunmaa in 1891, and by an anonymous, presumably female writer in 1892 [16, 52, 54].

The question of farm women's daily needs

In his 1862 speech, Fredrik Ahlqvist also made it clear that one cause of home thievery was fathers who refused to give their daughters the little money they required for daily necessities:

> There is probably no scarcity of farms on which no notice is taken either of the daughter's, or of the farm mistress' needs. And it is nonetheless natural that all human beings have needs, if for nothing else then at least for a decent set of clothes. If a daughter asks her father for money to meet her needs (and sometimes it is the eldest brother in charge of the money), she sees either that he is inclined to grumble, or she receives the reply: 'what would you do with money? You have bread ready for you to eat.' After receiving this brief and not very well thought out reply, she has no wish to renew her request. Instead, [– –] [h]aving taken the keys to the storehouse and avoided the watchful eyes of anyone concerned, a sack of grain or a pound of butter now leaves the storehouse and ends up in the wrong hands. But if she had received the little for her needs that she had requested, and which would possibly have satisfied her, then her conscience would have surely prevented her from committing this evil act [– –] [18].

After the 1862 Agricultural Society meeting, the debate on home thievery continued when five men and two farm daughters wrote to newspapers (mostly *Tapio*) to respond either specifically to Ahlqvist's comments or to add their views to the discussion as a whole. The first to write was 22-year-old farm daughter Maria Loviisa Kukkonen (1840–1924)[351] from Rautalampi. Maria Loviisa was the younger sister of Albert Kukkonen, as well as the older sister of Wilhelm Kukkonen who would later become the editor of *Tapio* between 1875 and 1878. Although Wilhelm received a formal education, both Albert and Maria Loviisa were self-educated, and from their letters it is clear that they identified with the landowning farmer class. However, due to their family's reputation for interest in literature and learning, they also had acquaintances among the university students who spent their summers on Hinkkala manor farm in order to practice their Finnish language skills. One year after she wrote to *Tapio*, Maria Loviisa married a young farmer and became mistress of Seppälä farm in Suonenjoki parish (Blomstedt 1959).

Maria Loviisa's letter appeared in *Tapio* on July 26, before the publication of Ahlqvist's speech. This means that she must have heard Ahlqvist's speech, whose argumentation she follows closely, either in person or from someone who had been present at the meeting. Maria Loviisa's younger brother Wilhelm was a student at the Levänen Agricultural Institute where the meeting was held, so it is possible that Maria Loviisa had attended Wilhelm's end-of-year ceremony and had therefore been present at the discussion on home thievery. In her letter, Maria Loviisa cited the unwillingness of farm

---

351 See note 201.

masters to provide for the daily needs of their daughters as one reason why farm daughters pilfered from their home farm [15]: [352]

> When I heard that, at the year-end examination at Levänen, there was a question about why daughters dispose from their parents, or rather, steal from them, I would like to say a little about this. To my mind, the primary reason for this is that fathers do not give their daughters money for their ordinary needs if the daughters, who are already frightened and timid, go and ask them. When [the daughters] present their case, they immediately perceive the condescension and reluctance which makes even a child sad and downcast, so that she does not dare to tell all her needs, fearing his increasingly cold response, and when another need arises, then she no longer goes to ask, but rather trusts in her own devices and in the habit learned from, and familiar from her ancestors. And when in a sullen and dissatisfied mood she pilfers, she does not only take what she would ordinarily need, rather, she takes extravagantly, thinking that 'because you will not give, I will take as much as I want!' ('*koska ette anna, niin minä otan niin että piisaa!*'). But if parents were to gently forbid daughters already in childhood from such a wasteful and wicked habit and were to gladly and humbly give them the little that they needed, then daughters would be better led by the law of their conscience, and would ask before they stole, since they would not need to be subject to any slavish dread. Then asking would be easier than taking without permission, for this latter is in no way a cheerful or amusing undertaking. For this reason, I too would hope that this detestable habit would vanish completely so that we young girls of today, as well as those who will come after us, will be allowed to see the fruits of civilization and enlightenment in this area as well. – There would be more to say on this subject, but I fear that the reader will be overburdened by my inferior writing, for which reason I will finish here and bid you farewell until I greet you next time [15].

At the end of Maria Loviisa's letter, Antti Manninen added the following encouraging comment:

> In the opinion of the editors this submission was not written at all badly, for which reason we hope letters will be sent to *Tapio* by the same maiden in the future.

Writing four months later, Maria Loviisa's older brother Albert Kukkonen[353] stated that the problem, in his view, was not the relative amount of inheritance received by daughters, but the fact that their everyday needs were not being met. Echoing Maria Loviisa's arguments, Albert wrote that daughters' receipt of twice as much inheritance would not resolve this dilemma:

352 The argument that home thievery could be avoided if parents gave their children more money for decent clothes was also mentioned by 'Liina A.', a farm woman who wrote to the newspaper *Sawo* in 1882 [41].
353 See note 208.

> [– –] if the farm master himself is not reasonable and fails to give the household members, his sons and daughters, what they ordinarily need on different occasions, then how can daughters stop themselves from taking without permission, even if they know they will receive twice as much inheritance, if they are not openly given what they need from the farm to meet the demands of the times? [25].

The debate over which should be given priority, the needs of farms as the primary socio-economic entities of the countryside or the needs of individual farm women, was played out not only in the press between writers, but also within the minds of individual writers, as can be seen from the aforementioned letters by Karl Ferdinand Forsström. An internal mental struggle is also evident from two letters written by the writer signing himself 'J. K–n.'. In his first letter written in 1862, chiefly in response to Ahlqvist's speech printed one month earlier, 'J. K–n.' stated that 'it is not possible, from whatever perspective one looks at this matter, for sons and daughters to receive equal inheritance, for our poor agriculture would be left in an even worse state' [22]. 'J. K–n.' argued that if each sibling were to receive an equal share of the farm, the son would have no incentive to work, and since none of the siblings would be motivated to run the farm as a whole, they would probably end up selling the farm to a third party and go their separate ways. 'J. K–n.' also asked whether anyone could guarantee that a law mandating equal inheritance would eradicate home thievery. Daughters would only receive their share of the inheritance upon their parents' death, whereas they needed it much earlier, when they left home to marry, since it represented their dowry [22].[354]

However, in a second letter written thirteen months later, the same 'J. K–n.' had changed his mind:

> This matter appears to be already much debated back and forth, but if we look at this issue conscientiously, it can be perceived that it is wrong that daughters are not allowed to inherit half along with sons, for daughters are just as much the children [of farm masters] as sons, so that in the matter of inheritance they should be the same, for in this way our women are quite callously demeaned and are denied equal merit of citizenship with men, which results in their being looked down upon. [– –] [I]f we look more closely, we see that women are deprived of many things and

---

354 'J. K–n.' also objected to another theme in Ahlqvist's speech, namely Ahlqvist's practical suggestion that under a law mandating equal inheritance, inheritance shares would balance themselves out when sons married girls who had received their own share of their birth farm, since the wife's property automatically came under the husband's control. 'J. K-n.', who otherwise employed a pragmatic discourse in his own objections to equal inheritance, now countered with a religious-based argument, maintaining that Ahlqvist's suggestion amounted to marrying for money, which was against God's will. 'J. K–n.' also asked: what if a young man had three sisters, should the law be changed to allow him to marry three wives, thereby amassing the wealth needed to pay off his own sisters' share of the farm? [22]. Another writer who took exception to Ahlqvist's suggestion was Albert Kukkonen, who wrote that this would mean that young men would start to marry purely for money, and that love could have no place in the marriage [25].

bear many hardships of which men will never know anything. And this is precisely the reason why women should inherit equally with men and have control over property like men. Many persons say that the farm will be ruined if both sons and daughters inherit equally, but the assumption that it would lead to ruin is baseless: instead, it would be of benefit, for in this way women would give up their evil addiction to home thievery, which now appears to be common throughout our country, and it is not to be wondered at when the womenfolk of our country are in the position they are [32].

What caused this complete reversal in 'J. K–n.' views on female inheritance? While the persuasive rhetoric used by proponents of equal inheritance may have at least caused 'J. K–n.' to reconsider his original stance, he himself provides an important clue to his change of heart at the end of his second letter:

> I have known many wives who would not have carried out home thievery if they had openly received something from their husbands, but needs often come up for which money is needed, which are just as necessary for men as for women, but men give nothing and yet they demand from their wives a full set of clothing, among other things, and all of these must be obtained by the wife on her own, even though they are for the common good. But if women were to receive equal inheritance and equal legal control then it would lead to immense benefit [32].

Here 'J. K–n.' implies that he had actually discussed the topic of home thievery and inheritance with more than one farm wife, and that these discussions had given him a new perspective on the debate. Since home thievery was an unlikely topic to have arisen on its own in the course of an acquaintance between unrelated farm men and women, we may reasonably assume that 'J. K–n.' was either informed on this matter by a wife or sister, or that he intentionally inquired into the matter by asking the farm women he happened to know. His letters suggest that the public debate on home thievery made him curious enough to delve deeper into the matter, and that it had the potential to transform the attitudes of rural men on the question of equal inheritance and women's rights.

Testaments and wills as an unjust circumvention of the law

In 1877, Judge Karl Ferdinand Forsström argued that daughters were not pilfering because their legal share of the inheritance was too small, but because they were not even receiving the one-fourth of the farm's value to which they were entitled. Legislating a larger share of inheritance would mean that daughters would feel entitled to more, but since they were still not likely to receive it in practice, they would steal even more from their birth farms [38]. The reason that farm daughters were not receiving the share to which they were entitled was because their parents drew up contracts which took legal precedence over the inheritance law, leaving the entire farm and its contents to their (eldest) son.

Already in 1858, Forsström had commented on how parents used special wills and testaments to circumvent the existing law which granted daughters half the inheritance of their brothers. Forsström pointed out that young women were awakening to the fact that this represented an injustice against them, and repeated this argument in another article published in 1861:

> [– –]parents who feel it is a shame to give real inheritance to daughters, draw up a special will (*lahja- eli testamentti-kirja*) for their son. This dispossession has gradually begun to feel to women like an injustice, and they try to avenge this injustice by committing another wrong, when they take what is not given to them. How widespread this habit may be, can be surmised from the fact that at the Jouhkola [=Kuopio Agricultural Society] meeting, even though a great many common folk had assembled there, nobody refuted what the girl [= Liisa Väänänen] said who spoke about it. But it is a sordid and lamentable situation [13].

Forsström's claim that farm daughters were dissatisfied with existing inheritance practices received support nine months later from a farm daughter who responded to the Kuopio Agricultural Society's 1862 discussion on home thievery. In the same August 16th issue featuring Fredrik Ahlqvist's speech, Antti Manninen introduced a letter written by a farm daughter from Rautalampi parish signing herself 'Maria J–n'.[355] Because the full report of the Society's meeting was reprinted less than three weeks later in the national newspaper *Suomen Julkisia Sanomia* [21], Maria's letter was read by persons throughout Finland.

'Maria J–n' had personally attended the year-end exhibitions of the students at Levänen Agricultural Institute in order to learn how to better make cheese and butter. In order to get out of the pouring rain, she had stepped into the hall where the Kuopio Agricultural Society meeting was taking place just as the question of home thievery began to be discussed. 'Maria J–n' reported being at first surprised and offended by the topic:

> As soon as I stepped through the doorway, the question of daughters' home thievery was brought up. Here perhaps I need not explain how I felt, I only remind the reader that if anyone, for example an innocent person, is accused in court of thievery, how much it costs their dignity, especially for us farm daughters [18].

After listening to the discussion, however, and apparently perceiving that its purpose was not to blame or criticize farm women, she changed her

---

355 'Maria J–n' was most likely Maria Jalkanen. According to the HISKI genealogical database, there were three young women named Maria Jalkanen in Rautalampi in 1862. Two were farm daughters in Hanhitaipale village (their fathers being Petter and Lars Jalkanen), who would have been 21 and and 23 years of age in 1862. A third Maria Jalkanen, aged 17 in 1862, was daughter of farmer Johan Påhl Jalkanen in the village of Kerkonjoensuu. Farm master 'G. Jalkanen', probably 35-year-old Gustav Jalkanen from Hanhitaipale village, also had his letter printed in the same issue of *Tapio* as Maria's, and he, too, criticized the special wills written in order to deny farm daughters their rightful inheritance [18].

mind and realized that she might be able to add her own perspective to the discussion:

> Then when they discussed the issue in a very natural manner, of how this blameworthy matter could be rectified, I soon came to a different realization, that this portends something good, to which I, for my small part, would like to add my explanation [18].

Although 'Maria J–n' had remained silent at the meeting itself, she wrote to *Tapio* afterward. She argued that while she did not object to the existing inheritance law which granted daughters one half of the son's share, and in fact found it 'very natural', since 'men's work is heavier and more necessary to the maintenance of the farm household than is the work of daughters', she objected to the fact that parents often circumvented the existing law by leaving nearly the entire farm to the son in separate wills. 'Maria J–n' explained that this was one way for parents to ensure that their son would treat them well when they were elderly and living on farm as pensioners (*syytinkiläinen*):

> [– –] sons begin to reduce the daughter's share in ways that I cannot explain. Parents listen more to them, since they will be with the sons, will live and die with them, and in the hope that [the sons] will reward them (which they may do badly), they have a contract drawn up, by which the daughters' share is reduced to as little as possible. Sons control the entire farm. Daughters are given hardly anything from it [– –] [18].

'Maria J–n' argued passionately that the making of such wills should be made illegal. In her argument, she drew upon a variety of rhetorical sources, including the emergent discussion of Finnish nationhood, and social reformist discourse according to which the rural common folk should learn from more educated members of society. She also made reference to a Scriptural verse from the New Testament. 'Maria J–n' explained:

> It would be best if the law would declare these sorts of special contracts (*väli-kirjat*) utterly illegal, because they have such evil consequences. Or are we merely the daughters of bondwomen?[356] Are the devalued daughters of our country utterly useless in the great family of our nation? In my view, daughters are the best asset or metal ore that our country has to offer, if only we are properly prepared in the forge of civilization by those who are more learned! We will not become any better by being rebuked in a disgraceful manner, if we are not taught better and generally given what we need [18].

---

356 This is a reference to the passage in Galatians 4:30: 'Nevertheless what saith the scripture? Cast out the bondwoman and her son: for the son of the bondwoman shall not be heir with the son of the freewoman' (*Mutta mitä Raamattu sanoo? aja palkkavaimo poikinensa ulos; sillä ei palkkavaimon pojan pidä perimän vapaan pojan kanssa*, Biblia 1776).

One interesting aspect of Maria's letter is that she implicitly challenged the dominant rhetoric regarding farm masters' motives for leaving the entire farm to their sons. In the arguments put forward by farm masters and other male writers in the 1861–1863 debate, measures to ensure that the eldest son would inherit the farm were justified as being for the good of the farm as a whole, for its continued stability and prosperity. 'Maria J–n', by contrast, accused farm masters (and farm mistresses) of acting instead out of selfish interest, essentially bribing their sons with a generous inheritance so that they would be well cared for by them when they were pensioners.[357]

Maria's letter received support from two sources. The first was a letter from a Rautalampi farm master 'G. Jalkanen', who may have been Gustav Jalkanen from Hanhitaipale village and a relative of 'Maria J–n' (see note 355). *Tapio* printed the paraphrased version of Jalkanen's letter directly after Maria's letter in the same issue. 'G. Jalkanen' stated that home thievery would continue so long as special wills gave sons the entire inheritance and daughters were left with almost nothing. Antti Manninen himself then added a concrete example at the end of Jalkanen's statement:

> We have received word that on a certain farm where the parents are estimated to have an estate of roughly 30 thousand roubles as well as two sons and two daughters, these parents have had a contract drawn up which specifies that the daughters should receive nothing more than 400 roubles each, even though according to the current law they should inherit 5 thousand roubles each! These sorts of examples are still a daily occurrence hereabouts, for which reason this country would do well to awaken people to a better sense of justice [18].

Although, in his 1862 letter, Albert Kukkonen disagreed with Fredrik Ahlqvist, he nonetheless agreed with 'Maria J–n' on the topic of inheritance, saying that he did not believe that daughters were necessarily dissatisfied with the inheritance allowed them by law, if only they were to actually receive it, 'but even this share is often reduced through promises and testaments' [25]. Judge Forsström predicted in 1877 that if the law for equal inheritance were passed, it would merely continue to be circumvented through legacies and separate wills [39]. His prediction apparently proved accurate, because twelve years after the law for equal inheritance was passed in 1878, blacksmith and popular author Heikki Meriläinen explained in *Descriptions of Ordinary Women's Life in the Countryside* (1890) how daughters in Ostobothnia were still being cheated out of their rightful inheritance. Fathers signed over the farm and its possessions to a son or son-in-law in return for being supported in their old age, and gave daughters only a small sum of money, a cow and a sheep when they married. According to Meriläinen,

> daughters feel bad about this, they feel as if they have been robbed of their entire wealth and even their home. Everything feels alien. Their

---

357 On the other hand, in the absence of any other pension system, the *syytinki* life annuity arrangement whereby elderly parents remained on the farm to be maintained by the new farm master meant that bequeathing the whole farm to one son was the only realistic option for many parents.

home does not feel like home, their father does not seem like a father, nor their mother like a mother. Bitterness fills their soul. The daughters beseech their father, but their father feels he has done the right thing. Their mother comforts them and makes small promises that their inheritance will be supplemented [– –] years go by and more and more the daughter sees that she must work like a slave without receiving any sort of wages. A serving maid's position would be better, since she would receive a wage from the farm. Now gradually arises the thought to take [money] without permission from the farm's cash box in order to obtain a pound of yarn for weaving. In this task, she is assisted by her mother. But if the new farm master [=the brother] has a [wife who is now the] farm mistress, who out of sheer anxiety keeps a close eye on the doings of the family members, then this effort is a failure and the girl receives a harsh warning. But if it happens again, then the farm master, too, soon comes to know of it. Now she must learn to be a bit wiser, and it is true what the old proverb says: 'one cannot guard against a home thief' (p. 84).

At the beginning of her letter, 'Maria J–n' described the moment at which 'I soon came to a different realization, that this portends something good, to which I for my small part would like to add my explanation'. Here, she seems to describe her realization that the public transcript regarding home thievery, even if it condemned pilfering as 'theft' and thus insulted her sense of dignity, could nonetheless be useful as a point of departure from which to criticize unjust practices against farm daughters. If home thievery was an evil to be eradicated, then this justified a closer examination of its causes, even if the fault might be found to lie with farm masters themselves. From this point onward, farm daughters who were otherwise helpless to defend their legal inheritance rights within the local context suddenly had a legitimate forum for protest – namely the topic of home thievery in the press – within which they could insist upon the importance of their legal rights being honoured in practice.

Farm women's entrance into the public sphere also allowed them to express support for other legal changes which would improve their economic status. This can be seen from a letter written by a woman who signed herself 'U. R., farm daughter from Iisalmi'. 'U. R.' wrote to *Suomen Julkisia Sanomia* in 1863 to express her delight at the fact that the questions of both daughters' inheritance and women's legal majority were being taken up for discussion at the Finnish Diet. Like nearly all other farm women who wrote to the press on the topic of home thievery, 'U. R.' criticized home thievery as a deplorable vice in order to argue for the importance of rural women's rights:

> We daughters are rejoicing now that we have heard that the Finnish Diet is looking out for us in terms of inheritance so that the shameless practice of home thievery would disappear, as well as the fact that at age 25 we would attain legal age so that legal guardians cannot squander our property if we remain old maids. May God grant happiness, success and wisdom to our dearly beloved ruler and to all of the Estate representatives in order that they may decide everything for the benefit of our fatherland! [31]

191

Was home thievery silently approved of in rural communities?

In autumn of 1862, a writer signing himself 'D. H–n.'[358] sent to *Tapio* a letter entitled 'On the home thievery of daughters' in order to give his opinion regarding the primary cause of home thievery:

> This matter has already been discussed in the Economic Society's [= Kuopio Agricultural Society's] meetings and in many newspapers, but in seeking the reasons behind this theft, there have arisen a number of different opinions and claims. One says that the cause lies in the paucity of inheritance, another in the giving of wedding gifts, and a third in the unreasonable strictness of parents. This last was complained of by Maria from Rautalampi as the reason, to which A. J. Puhakka[359] replied that '*konttiinsa päin teini laulaa* (the student sings to fill his knapsack)'[360] but did not explain any further. I don't know how it might be, but the paucity of inheritance seems to me a lesser reason, because ordinarily even a daughter who is an only child, and will inherit her parents' entire property, will steal nevertheless. The giving of wedding gifts (*antimet*), by contrast, seems the most natural reason, for girls must already at a young age begin to very diligently amass these stores [of clothing] [24].

Having explained this, 'D. H–n' went on to additionally accuse young women of committing home thievery in order to give gifts to gossip women who would then be more likely to spread word of the girl's 'wisdom' and 'cleverness' in stealing from her household. 'D. H–n.' maintained that young women thought they would be more likely to find a good husband if they had the reputation of being 'clever', whereas it was thought that if a girl did not steal from her farm, it was because she was incapable of it. Such a girl was not considered to be a fit wife for a decent young man:

> And to pay for this waste of goods, if the parents are too strict to give money for actual needs and thus do not give her any, then she steals, and this is for girls very agreeable and honourable work, for in her own opinion and that of our community, the person who is capable and quick enough to steal the most becomes quite renowned and esteemed. Then especially if bribes are given, the village women will take word to the next farm, and in each farmhouse [they visit], they praise and extol her,

358 'D. H–n' might have been David Häkkinen from Saarijärvi parish (archived notes of *The Finnish Newspaper History Research Project* (SSLH) led by Päiviö Tommila).
359 Anders (Antti) Puhakka (1816–1893) was a farmer and a celebrated folk poet. See also note 37.
360 Puhakka's reply was apparently intended for Maria Loviisa Kukkonen, since 'Maria J-n' did not complain in her letter about the strictness of parents per se. Puhakka's only response to Kukkonen was to write: 'When it comes to the answer given by Mari from Rautalampi, one might say that 'the student preaches to fill his sack (*säkkinsä pain teini saarnaa*)' [23]. In the 19th-century, students funded their studies by begging for money to be put in their sacks when they performed student songs. The proverb and its variants were used to indicate that the speaker had a personal agenda in presenting a particular argument.

saying that on that farm there is a very clever and ingenious girl. She can steal from her father and brother while standing still. And each girl does this with the heartfelt opinion that she deserves to marry well. By contrast, the girl who does not begin to steal, nor in this way to seek honour for herself, she is said to be a stupid oaf, who does not know how to look after her own interests, and what is worse, they say that she is not good enough to be the farm mistress of a young and honourable man, no matter how wise and hardworking she might be in her conduct and labours [24].

At first glance, 'D. H–n.'s' claim that pilferers were admired in rural communities for being clever and ingenious seems out of place in the context of the overwhelming moral condemnation that surrounded home thievery in the press. Yet if we consider that young women pilfered in part to display or maintain their social status in rural society, and that newly married husbands stood to benefit from their bride's pilfering prior to marriage, this claim may not be so implausible. Similar observations were made by another writer signing himself '–w– ' in 1898, who claimed in the pages of *Uusi Savo* that some farm masters were even proud that their children had learned to secretly pilfer in order to satisfy their personal needs:

> The farm master on his farm might know that his children steal, but even then it does not occur to him to try to prevent it. He might even secretly be pleased that those daughters or sons are so clever that they know how to take advantage of the situation. Sometimes one even hears it spoken out loud: 'I don't give them anything, but they seem to be able to obtain it for themselves' [60].

In fact, the letter from 'D. H–n.' suggests that an attitude in which farm daughters were silently acknowledged to be entitled to the goods they pilfered through home thievery may have been common in rural communities. Rural inhabitants seem to have recognized the contradiction between, on the one hand, the expectation that a bride bring many gifts of clothing to her husband's family, and on the other hand, her having no time to spin, weave and sew them all herself, nor any resources with which to purchase cloth and the labour of others. In such a situation in which everyone tacitly understood that pilfering was necessary, the girl who could do it quickly, efficiently but above all quietly, may have been covertly applauded. However, the publicization of this contradiction and its tacit solution in the press posed a problem for farm daughters who wanted to present themselves as morally upright within the prevailing public transcript. It was therefore nearly inevitable that 'D. H–n.'s exposé would be challenged by a rural female writer who felt that it dishonoured her and her fellow farm daughters.

The challenge came from Maria Loviisa Kukkonen, who in a second letter to *Tapio* published in December 1862 used the pseudonym 'M. L. K–n'.[361]

---

361 Manninen introduced 'M. L. K–n's letter by saying that it had been sent from Rautalampi parish and had been written by a farm daughter.

In her response to 'D. H–n.'s letter, Maria Loviisa expressly disagreed with the idea that daughters sought more honour for themselves through home thievery. In order to bolster her argument, she used the rhetorical strategy of ending her letter by appealing to religious truths couched in traditional Kalevala meter. But in her letter Kukkonen also provided insights into women's own attitudes towards home thievery:

> D. H – n writes of daughters' home thievery and says that in searching for its cause, many different opinions have arisen. He says that one claims the cause to be paucity of inheritance, another the giving of gifts at weddings and the third the strictness of parents, and it is of course natural that this might occur for a number of reasons. But D. H – n thinks that this habit exists because daughters are seeking a good reputation. Here, however, I think that he is mistaken, or how does this appear to those who are wiser; but to my mind among the daughters of our country there is probably not one who has been raised in such blindness that she would not be able to distinguish good from evil, and so how can she then hope to obtain honour for herself by committing an evil act, for each person is aware while undertaking this act that it is an wicked undertaking and wrongly done; but since usually necessity demands (perhaps at times not such a great necessity) and she has heard from olden times the proverb: 'a father's thief will not be hanged' (*ei isän warasta hirtetä*), so she, on the basis of this time-honoured guarantee, takes [goods from the farm] on her own authority rather than bother and anger her parents by pleading, which is usually to no avail [– –].
>
> Again comes to my mind that reproachful statement of D. H-n, and I do not understand with what purpose he may have done it, when he castigated the daughters of our country in such a disgraceful manner, saying that they seek honour for themselves through stealing, and hope that the village women's' praise will bring them good fortune in marriage. But this is not the case. *The reins of fortune are in God's hands, the keys to luck in the Creator's, they not under the arm of the envious nor at an evil person's fingertips (Jumalalla on onnen ohjat, Luojalla lykyn awaimet; waan ei kateen kainalossa, wihan suowan sormen päässä)* [27, emphasis in the original].

Although Maria Loviisa's defence of farm daughters' honor is understandable within the demands of the public transcript, it appears from other sources that home thievery was in fact often tolerated within farm households. Forsström's 1858 claim [5] that fathers knew in their hearts that an injustice was being committed against daughters and therefore did not wish to really prevent home thievery in earnest is supported by enough evidence that we may reasonably conclude that this was the perspective taken by at least some farm masters in rural communities.

Although it was often easier for farm women to pilfer butter from the farm than grain, sayings which referred to farm daughters as 'another mouse to the grain bin', or the acquisition of the daughter's trousseau as requiring 'more than one trip to the grain bin' expressed the common assumption that the farm's grain, once stored in the granary, was in jeopardy of being pilfered by the women of the farm. This photo from the late 1920s shows the corner of a farm's granary in Maaninka district, North Savo. Photo: Ahti Rytkönen. Courtesy of the National Board of Antiquities.

Home thievery as a hidden labour incentive for daughters

One premise of recent socio-economic bargaining models is that when family members are also potential labourers for the family farm, the more able they are to survive outside the family, the greater is their bargaining power over resources within the family.[362] On 19th-century Finnish farms, sons had the option of leaving their family household and receiving wages in exchange for their labour on other farms. Therefore, their bargaining power was significant, and the inheritance of the farm as a whole was the incentive intended to discourage them from desertion. In practice, this left the farm with no incentives for daughters, who in Eastern Finland, at least, could never be sure that their future claims to legal inheritance would be honoured. Under normal circumstances, the 'threat point'[363] at which family members believed they would be better off outside the household than inside it was less likely to be reached with daughters than with sons,

362 Agarwal 1997, 8–9.
363 See Agarwal 1997, 4–5.

for two reasons. First, daughters were less motivated to hire themselves out as serving maids, because a female servant's wages were generally only between one-half and two-thirds of a farmhand's wages.[364] Second, the highest social status that could be achieved by most farm daughters was that of farm mistress through marriage to a landowning farmer, and this depended on her receiving a dowry from her parents (Markkola 1990: 21). Although a daughter's dowry was often meagre in comparison to what she was legally entitled to, it was still necessary for her to marry well. It may have been possible, but certainly would not have been easy, for a daughter to acquire this dowry for herself on a serving maid's salary.

Nevertheless, unwed farm daughters sometimes did leave their home farms to take up work elsewhere. After 1864, an unmarried woman who had reached the age of fifteen had the right to control her own earnings, and historian Pirjo Markkola (2003b: 139–140) has shown that in rural districts of Häme, 28 per cent of the farm women in her source materials who had been born in the 19th century eventually went to work for other farms. Often they were compelled to do so, for instance if their own father ceased to be the master of their birth farm through death or poverty (ibid: 141). In some cases, however, they may have seen employment outside their home farm as an opportunity. How, then, did their parents react to the possibility of their desertion?

In the mid- and late 19th-century press, mothers were widely reported as having assisted their daughters in home thievery [2, 3, 5, 13, 52, 56, 60].[365] For example, in the following description of a typical inheritance situation, 'Maria J–n' explains how, after the son of the farm had inherited the farm with his mother staying on as a pensioner, the mother, who no longer had access to the goods of the farm, might advise her adult daughter to secretly pilfer the goods of the farm:

> The mother begins to think aloud to her daughter, 'you're going to have to take it without asking, because your brother is not going to give it to you; I don't have anything to give you because I'm not allowed to access to my old nest-egg.' Well, what other advice can daughters take. She goes to the farm's joint stores of goods [18].

In 1891, columnist 'Paavo Pajumaa' explained that mothers assisted their daughters in home thievery because they themselves had pilfered as young brides in order to acquire the clothes and textiles needed for their dowries:

> In some places it has become customary that daughters are obligated to have many great sackfuls of all sorts of clothing when they marry, and somebody must often be hired to make them without the farm master's knowledge. They are spun, woven and sewn by the itinerant women of

---

364 Soikkanen 1981, 10–11; Heikkinen et. al. 1983, 122, table 4.
365 See also: SKS KRA Pielavesi. 1896. J. Räisänen (seminarian oppilas) E 80; *Kuvauksia kansannaisen elämästä maalla*. 1890. Suomen Nais-Yhdistyksen ulosantama. Porvoo: Werner Söderström, 61, 84.

the village, who often live on just this sort of work. Compensation must be paid in either grain or foodstuffs. In this sort of farm thievery, mothers usually assist their daughters, remembering having done the same when they were a young bride [52].

Other male writers, too, assumed that mothers assisted their daughters in pilfering because they themselves had pilfered as young women before their marriage in order to amass their dowries, and therefore saw it as natural to assist their daughters. However, mothers' assistance in pilfering can also be interpreted in another way. Mothers may have valued and needed their daughters' work in the domestic sphere, and therefore intentionally arranged incentives for their daughters to remain on the farm. In *Descriptions of Ordinary Women's Life in the Countryside* (1890), the writer from Ostrobothnia signing herself '–a. –s.' explained that when daughters had more lucrative options for taking their labour elsewhere, for example by emigrating to North America, mothers in particular strove to assist their daughters in home thievery so that daughters could amass large trousseaux of clothing, precisely in order to discourage them from leaving:

> It has become a bad habit [for daughters] to accumulate more clothing than their poor parents can provide for them [– –]. The outbuildings where the clothes are displayed are often a topic of conversation among girls, as well as their pride and joy. The mother must aid her daughter in procuring clothing, otherwise the girl will go and work as a servant in another household or leave for America. There is always some acquaintance or relative [in America] who can buy a ticket for her. That's why she must be kept happy.[366]

Mothers clearly tolerated their daughters' home thievery, but as we have already seen, there is evidence that fathers did as well. Male writers to the press reported that farm masters often turned a blind eye to the pilfering going on around them, and took few measures to prevent it. In fact, they seem to have expected that daughters would help themselves to goods from the farm's storehouses. Clergyman Bernhard Karl Sarlin, writing to *Suometar* in 1856, commented on cultural reactions to home thievery by claiming that when a daughter was born, it was common for the father to say, half in jest and half in annoyance: 'here comes another mouse to the grain bin' [3]. According to the report in *Tapio* covering the 1862 meeting of the Kuopio Agricultural Society, estate manager Pehkonen who was present at the meeting

> complained of the lamentable fact in this matter of home thievery that every father surely knows that his children are stealing, and sees his children wearing store-bought clothing, but he never chastises them for it or even asks from where they have received it. There are also said to be fathers who say 'go ahead, children, and steal, as long as I don't see it!' [18].

366 *Kuvauksia kansannaisen elämästä maalla* 1890: 26, Kansannaisen elämästä Kalajoella (–a –s.).

The walls of this outbuilding, which was occupied by a young farm woman from Kuortane, South Ostrobothnia, are covered with handmade textiles arranged for display to guests. Photo: Oskari Kivistö. Courtesy of the National Board of Antiquities.

Fredrik Ahlqvist, too, noted with puzzlement that parents seemed to not take any notice of the store-bought goods that their adult children had clearly obtained through pilfering: '[– –] it is amazing that parents have no inkling of the whole matter; they seldom ask where a particular item comes from or in what manner it was procured' [18]. The editors of the newspaper *Savo* similarly explained in 1880 that in some farm households, both parents deliberately ignored their daughters' home thievery: 'One finds many parents, who in their 'wisdom' say: 'let the girls obtain for themselves what they think they need', and give them not a penny' [40].

All of the above suggests that as long as domestic pilfering was kept secret and not brought to the level of explicit discourse, it provided an incentive with which to keep daughters working hard on the farm. Yet when dramatic changes began to transform the countryside, this tacit compromise could no longer remain hidden. After 1859, the greater availability of consumer items combined with farm women's lack of money deepened the inequalities upon which the system of familial patriarchy rested. These inequalities became visible to the public eye primarily because women were actively circumventing the farm master's authority in order to pilfer even more household goods, and the rise of the Finnish-language press provided a forum in which writers lamented the fateful consequences of this practice.

Although daughters' inheritance continued to be circumvented through wills even after the 1878 law mandating equal inheritance was passed,[367] the law itself marked an important turning point in the official recognition of the need for rural gender equality. As can be seen from the aforementioned debates, however, this legislation was not necessarily a foregone conclusion. The arguments against it, whether moral (the smaller labour contribution of daughters did not entitle them to equal inheritance) or practical (equal inheritance would lead to the ruin of farms), reflected the realities of agrarian life as experienced by at least some farm masters. The debate over the causes of home thievery and solutions to eradicate it played an important role in raising new perspectives on the issue of farm inheritance, making the moral and practical questions surrounding it more concrete to the Finnish-speaking public already in the late 1850s, and lending an added urgency to its discussion within the Finnish Diet in the 1860s.

---

367 The law nonetheless stipulated that if the land and farmhouse to be inherited could not be suitably divided, then the brother had the right to take the farmhouse and reimburse his sister for her share. If, however, the brother was unable to buy his sister out of her share of the house, then in that case the sister did not receive her share of the inheritance (*Nainen ja naisen työ* 1893:4).

9. The Unenlightened Rural Patriarch

Fathers, do not exasperate your children; instead, bring them up in the training and instruction of the Lord.

Martin Luther's Table of Duties in his Small Catechism (1529)

Despite the overwhelming condemnation of home thievery in the press, it is clear from the previous chapter that many male writers did not write merely in order to condemn the practice or to point an accusing finger at farm women. Although writers to the press – both male and female – nearly always wrote of home thievery in disapproving terms, their subsequent arguments rarely ended in condemning farm wives and daughters. In fact, criticism of home thievery in the press appears to have been a rhetorical moral platform from which writers could lecture their audiences on more controversial social problems related to the relationship between individual and society.

Granted, these perceived problems differed depending on the writer. Within practical discourse which prioritized the needs of the farm, the topic of home thievery was used by farm masters to argue against the consumption of non-essential goods and finery, and against the wastefulness of producing dowry textiles and wedding gifts on a massive scale. But these were systemic criticisms aimed at rural society as a whole rather than at specific farm women. In liberal-progressive discourse prioritizing the needs and rights of individuals, on the other hand, home thievery was brought up by social reformers in order to complain about unequal inheritance for sons and daughters. At least one man stated that home thievery could only be eradicated through the founding of public schools for the rural masses [16].

When writers and meeting participants discussed who was primarily to blame for home thievery, fingers were pointed in several directions: farm mistresses were blamed for not setting a better example [3, 8, 51, 53], and both parents were seen to be partly responsible for home thievery when they were aware that their adult children were pilfering but did nothing [3, 16, 17]. Two female writers and two male writers blamed home thievery in part on young women's frivolity and desire for fine clothing [27, 34, 41, 52], and two writers mentioned that the buyers of pilfered goods were also to blame [3, 52]. But one target of blame stood out above the rest. Overwhelmingly, it was farm masters who were faulted for being miserly and neglecting the needs of their household members [1, 3, 11, 16, 17, 18, 25, 32, 37, 52, 53, 57, 61, 64]. It is not surprising, therefore, that in addition to the issue of equal inheritance for farm sons and daughters, a major theme which arose in the 1862 debates over home-thievery was criticism of farm masters who failed to take sufficient care of the daily needs of their family members.

Although it would still be half a century before Finland achieved the status of independent nation, liberal-minded writers to Finnish-language newspapers were warming to the new idea of nation-states as founded not on families or farms but on *individual citizens*, whose consent to be governed was the foundation for democratic legitimacy.[368] For this reason, traditional forms of familial patriarchy which focused on the interests of the farm at the expense of its individual members began to lose their justification toward the end of the century. Of course, not all individuals were seen as equals or even potential citizens: personal rights throughout the 19th century were dependent on a person's position both within society and within the farm household. Both in the Finnish Diet and within the press, discussions regarding women's rights focused on farm wives and daughters, and rarely mentioned the situation of servants, daughters-in-law, or women from landless families (Pylkkänen 2006: 386–7).

Earlier, the farm master's primary duty to society had been to uphold the social order through the control of his household. This was done out of obedience to a Church and Crown which desired above all the stability of the realm, and stability required that each member of society kept to his or her proper and predetermined place. By the middle of the 19th century, however, it was not stability but *change* and *improvement* which were the watchwords of educated elites. In this new world envisioned by social reformists, the individual was expected to make his or her own contribution to social progress through self-improvement (see L. Stark 2006, 76–79). In order for this to happen, it was necessary that individuals be freed from their roles as subordinate members of a corporate group such as the farm household, and be afforded greater freedoms and rights than were previously seen desirable. In the modern era, social rights became individual rights, to which only individuals, not families, could lay claim (Beck 1993: 15; Pylkkänen 2009: 39–42, 46).

When writers to the press discussed the social contradictions and dilemmas arising from this altered relationship between individual and society, one of the perceived problems was the figure of the rural patriarch himself, who represented the power structure of an older order no longer responsive to the needs of society. The topic of home thievery, for its part, functioned as a kind of Trojan horse, a ploy disguised as a discussion on farm women's wrongdoings which was actually aimed at introducing into public discourse sensitive issues regarding the failures of patriarchs. In a

368 Cf. Beck 1994, 15; Räsänen 1996, 6; Pylkkänen 2006, 385.

rhetorical twist used by writer after writer, the arguments used to condemn farm women's home thievery were turned instead against farm masters.

Criticism of farm masters can be found early in the discussion on home thievery. Even clergyman Bernhard Kristfrid Sarlin, whose 1856 criticism of pilfering farm women was harsher than any that would come after him in the press, concluded in the end that it was farm masters who were primarily responsible for the practice of home thievery:

> But on this point we cannot blame only womenfolk. Often, just as much blame lies with the men as well, with the farm masters. Among them there are many who are so uncivilized, so unreasonable, so stingy, that they do not understand, or do not want to understand to give the goods from their own hands which would be needed for essential things such as food and clothing [3].

Schoolteacher Wilhelm Kukkonen had been a student at Levänen Agricultural Institute when home thievery was discussed there at the 1862 Kuopio Agricultural Society meeting. Fourteen years later, as editor of *Tapio*, he described how home thievery led household members and even servants to steal the possessions of others outside the family. He did this by addressing not his fellow readers but the farm master in whose household pilfering occurred. It was the farm master whom Kukkonen accused of being ultimately responsible for his household members becoming habituated to theft:

> [– –] But look you, farm master! – Whither come those blue skirts, silk shawls, and so forth that your daughters are wearing, whither those good boots, caps and jackets worn by your sons, which present-day expectations force each young man and woman to procure for themselves in order to have the courage to meet their friends, and at the same time to protect you from the shame of not having taken sufficient care of your children. Have you ever asked or wondered how your children have obtained them, because you yourself have not bought them – they must have had some means of obtaining them and perhaps you yourself suspect, if you have not seen it with your own eyes, that they have not been obtained through entirely proper means. You notice this, and yet you still consider yourself to be a Christian family man who is working toward your children's future, you speak of public schools and children's education, but how? You are knowingly educating your children right before your very eyes, even forcing them, to become thieves [– –].
>
> Just think how much grain and other products of the farm are sold by your children every year at a cut-rate price in order that they might in this way obtain for themselves some fabric in order to appear as the times demand, think of the corrupting company and the discussions into which your children are forced and of the contempt which you gradually bring upon yourself through your children's high-handed behaviour; think finally of how many poor servants who assist in this sort of activity become tempted sooner or later to finger the property of either the farming family or of their other fellow men. We know of at least a few such cases, in which servants, having at first assisted in the secret selling of the farm's property, finally began to do it to their own advantage and thus, through others, ended up receiving the penalty for it [37].

Not all farm masters were targeted by such criticism in the press, only those referred to as being over-authoritarian and miserly. These were never the writer himself nor any specific person addressed by him. A clear delineation was made between farm masters striving for education and progress, and those 'others' who were referred to using the terms '*wanhoilla olija*' (conservative old-timer), '*rajatoin waltias*' (absolute sovereign), '*tyranni*' (tyrant), or '*kaikkiwaltais hallitsija*' (all-powerful ruler). The use of these terms in the context of the home thievery discussion indicated that these farm masters had fallen short of the patriarchal ideal outlined in Luther's Table of Duties, in which authority was to be maintained through earning subordinates' trust and respect rather than through coercion (Liliequist 2002: 76, see also [7]).

In this chapter, I use the term *unenlightened patriarch* to refer to the stereotype of the farm master blamed for the home thievery in his household. Patriarchs were also criticized for their behaviour in other contexts, for example that they encouraged servants to drink alcohol or even paid them in alcohol [7, 8].[369] In the context of the discussion surrounding home thievery, however, at issue was the patriarch's behaviour toward his wife and children.

In a broader sense, the unenlightened patriarch had been a useful stereotype in the press ever since Snellman's knapsack-carrying figure went to visit him in the first issue of *Maamiehen Ystäwä* in order to convince him to buy and read newspapers (see Chapter Three). The image of the unenlightened farmer provided a useful target of improvement without, however, stigmatizing all farming men. Through their own efforts, rural men could construct for themselves an 'enlightened' identity by actively promoting education and improvements in their community, or by writing newspaper articles, poetry, fiction, or autobiographies in which they presented their personal struggle for individual and social progress (L. Stark 2006). The unenlightened farm master, by contrast, was the very embodiment of crudity and obstinacy, a figure who was seen to impede progress and who required the civilizing efforts of the educated elite and middle classes.

One of the earliest Finnish-language portrayals of the unenlightened farm master, in which this stereotype is contrasted with the image of a more thoughtful, rational and progressive patriarch, was Ahlqvist's story 'Koti (Home)' appearing in 1853 in the newspaper *Maamiehen Ystäwa*. Ahlqvist's tactic of appealing not to philosophical argumentation but to practical everyday experience in arguing for the rights of rural women anticipates his speech in defence of women's rights which would spark a lively debate nine years later (see Chapter Eight). In 'Home', which is constructed almost entirely through dialogue, the farmer-protagonist Pekka tries to explain to his friend, a more conservative farm master named Martti, that the happiest household is one in which the husband and wife live in harmony and even have joint authority over the running of the household:[370]

---

369 See also: July 20, 1860. *Suometar* no. 28, 'Maawiljelijäin kokous Haminassa'.
370 July 9, 16. 1853. *Maamiehen Ystäwä* nos. 27 & 28. 'Koti'.

Martti and Pekka visited each other often. It was a relief for Martti to be able to complain to Pekka of his sorrows and quarrels at home; and many was the time that Pekka had to act as an arbiter between Martti and his wife. One Sunday afternoon Martti invited Pekka over to visit in order to smoke pipe tobacco, he was alone, because his wife and children had gone to a wedding; but Martti had not wanted to go there with them. When the men had spoken of this and that, the talk turned to their wives. 'It cannot be denied that Inka is a good wife', said Martti, 'but if she were my wife, I would not explain all my actions to her.' 'Well, why not?' asked Pekka. [Martti:] 'Wives don't understand all the things that belong to a man's affairs, nor do men's affairs concern them.' 'How so?' asked Pekka. [Martti:] 'What do they understand of teaching and rearing children, and what do they understand of household affairs, except what concerns making food and their own chores?' 'But what if we don't understand much about child rearing either?' said Pekka. 'Oho,' swaggered Martti, 'a man is a man and understands more than his wife.' 'Ah so you think,' answered Pekka, 'is that what you suppose, Martti, that we men always have a greater comprehension than women?' 'Just so,' answered Martti, wondering at Pekka's question [– –]. 'The man *is* the head of the wife,' said Martti. [Pekka:] 'If that is so, then why is the head so often inferior? Don't you suppose God put as much capacity for reason in a wife's head as in a husband's, and if the wife is allowed to always use her capacity for reason, it would be a great blessing to husbands?' 'Hoh, what man would actually forbid his wife to use her capacity for reason?' said Martti. [Pekka:] 'But many men let their wives have no power at all, and care nothing for the wife's good advice, even if the wife understands a thing many times more clearly than the husband.' [– –] [Martti:] 'Oh my dear Pekka, they are already so full of cunning and every sort of intrigue; we'd be trampled upon if wives got the upper hand.' Pekka: 'Sometimes those poor wives must take refuge in cunning and all sorts of stratagems, since they are not allowed to think, speak and act freely; he who cannot advance on a straight path must take a circuitous route to where he wants to go. Men should place the same value on wives as on husbands, but instead many men treat their wives badly, speak of her inferiority and gossip about her faults even in front of strangers.' 'That's no worse than a wife deserves,' said Martti, a trifle indignant. Pekka: 'Well, is it always the case that we men are not at fault, that we are always innocent of the wrongs of which we blame our wives?' [– –] Martti: 'A wife should be obedient to her husband in all things.' Pekka: 'So I too thought at first and believed it to be so, but the more I have read the Bible and historical books, the more I have come to understand about this matter; what is more I have inquired from learned men and received clarification.' [– –] 'Well, dear Pekka,' asked Martti, 'what kind of person do you want a wife to be?' Pekka: 'The equal of us men, not a bit inferior.' Martti: 'But now if both [spouses] have equal say in the household matters and what is more, differ in their opinions, whose wishes should determine how they should live?' 'The will of the more sensible spouse,' answered Pekka [– –].

The rhetorical tactic of constrasting the image of the unenlightened farm master with the ideal of the enlightened farm master was also employed in Wilhelm Kukkonen's aforementioned editorial in 1876. In this thorough and severe condemnation of the unenlightened patriarch, Kukkonen outlined the model of the benevolent, enlightened patriarch to which every farm master should aspire, and explained how the widespread occurrence of home thievery demonstrated that in practice, this ideal was rarely being achieved. Drawing upon nationalist-collectivist rhetoric as well as liberal-individualist notions of the desirability of freedom and happiness, Kukkonen went on to explain how in many cases the farm master acted as a tyrant who wielded his power over the money and goods of the household purely for his own benefit, in order to show the community how rich he was, when he could have invested the money in his family's well-being and his children's future. The tyrant-patriarch neglected his family's needs and so forced them to commit theft from their own home. In this way, the unenlightened patriarch was responsible not only for the moral degradation of household members, but also ultimately for the collapse of social order and well-being:

> The family is the smallest association of individuals in society, but within it, the responsibilities of its individual members are so great, that the whole kingdom falters if the responsibilities of the family are neglected and the wrong spirit prevails among them. Every builder of the family, that is, the father, is therefore committed to the sacred obligation of loyalty towards his family members, his society, his fatherland, and his Maker [– –]. Ordinarily the farm master is the patriarch, or more aptly the despot, the tyrant of this whole community. He leads his small flock in a manner which leads persons with the least human feeling to experience shame and scorn – since it is the opposite of a happy and free civic life – and therein lies the reason why so many farms are abandoned, the reason for inheritance disputes, the reason for the disappearance of a home life of friendship and love, the reason for the bad treatment of parents at the hands of their children, the reason, finally, for all dishonesty in life [37].

The patriarch and household members' needs

In specifying the faults of the unenlightened patriarch, writers to newspapers in the period 1850–1900 blamed farm masters for three types of behaviour which were seen to be ultimately responsible for home thievery: (1) the patriarch's selfish and miserly use of resources, (2) his incorrect methods of child rearing, and (3) his inability to manage his household in a rational manner, due to insufficient knowledge.

The first problem, namely that farm masters did not meet the needs of their family members even though they might have the resources to do so, was cited most often, and the person who explained this problem in greatest detail was Fredrik Ahlqvist. At the 1862 meeting of the Kuopio Agricultural Society, Ahlqvist even compared the situation of daughters to slavery:

> The slavery of daughters is in many parts of the countryside what drives them to this evil habit that is now under discussion. Nor is this habit (which is, of course, vile) really to be wondered at, if the matter is examined more closely and calmly [– –]. There is probably no scarcity of farms on which no notice is taken of either the daughter's or the farm

mistress' needs. And it is nonetheless natural that all human beings have needs, if nothing else then at least for a decent set of clothes. If a daughter asks for money to meet her needs from her father (and sometimes it is the eldest brother in charge of the money), she sees either that he is inclined to grumble or she receives the reply: 'what would you do with money? You have bread ready for you to eat.' After receiving this brief and not very well thought out reply, she has no wish to renew her request, instead, the thought and act just now under discussion occurs to her and has its effect. Having taken the keys to the storehouse and avoided the watchful eyes of anyone concerned, a sack of grain or a pound of butter now leaves the storehouse and ends up in the wrong hands [18, parentheses in original].

The Kukkonen siblings from Rautalampi all had something to say regarding the topic of the patriarch's neglect of his family's needs, and in contrast to their dissimilar views on inheritance, on this topic they were all in agreement. Wilhelm Kukkonen's views regarding the miserly patriarch were unambiguously expressed in his aforementioned editorial from 1876. Maria Loviisa Kukkonen wrote a letter to *Tapio* in July of 1862 which closely followed Ahlqvist's speech even before it was published, and in a direct response to Ahlqvist's published statement in *Tapio*, Albert Kukkonen argued along similar lines in November of the same year:

> Fathers themselves are to blame for many habits which are corruptive and degrading to human dignity. As is often seen, the farm master is a strict saver of goods, and gives nothing for the ordinary needs of his sons and daughters [– –] [25].

The topic was still current in the 1890s, when 'Paavo Pajumaa', the rural columnist writing to *Laatokka*, brought up the topic in 1891, as did an unknown writer in the same newspaper a year later:

> Whose fault is home thievery, and how can it be eradicated?
> To this we can answer briefly, that the fault lies with the farm master himself, and it is this problem which must be immediately rectified. The farm master does not give the slightest amount of money for spending to his younger brothers, sisters, sons-in-law, daughters-in-law nor to his own children, nor does he himself purchase for them even the essential needs required by the current times, so they take [what they need] on their own authority, reckoning that even a horse gets to eat from the common load. In this, they cause great harm [– –] [52].

> [– –] it is not appropriate for the farm master to refuse to buy for his family those essentials that they truly need, for in such cases they are forced to buy these things without his knowledge and naturally using the goods of the farm. If the farm master acts in this way, he himself promotes home thievery, to the ruin of the household finances, for it is clear that every person has essential needs and that the farm mistress and the other family members have no place from which to obtain money if the farm master does not provide it. But each family member must adapt his needs to the wealth of the farm [53].

In 1901, a female writer to the newspaper *Lahden Lehti* signing herself 'Emäntä (Farm Mistress)' agreed:

> There are to be found men whose dispositions can be said to be dour and sullen. These sorts of men, by being unreasonable, have made their wives home thieves. If, for example, the wife asks her husband for money for some small need, then the husband loses his temper, and the same happens with larger purchases. If the wife needs money for the ordinary needs of the family and hears only criticism and harsh words over this, then — if she does not have a extremely resolute and at the same time honest disposition — she abandons the whole exhausting chore of asking for money and begins on her own to procure the money for her purchases [64].

As late as 1927, two years before the old marriage law was repealed, the topic of the unenlightened farm master who ignored his family needs was brought up yet again, this time in an issue of the journal *Emäntälehti* produced by the *Martat* home economics organization:

> I know of a case in which a father – the master of a rich farm – gave his daughter so little that in order to survive, she had lapsed into pilfering from the food stockpiles. When the father was told of this, he said, 'I didn't think that a girl-child needed more than that'. Presumably pilfering had been carried out earlier on that farm right under the farm master's nose and perhaps precisely in order to survive. In such a case, the father's 'purse strings have been too tight', which is just as bad as if they had been too loose, for those tightly knotted purse strings lead his family members into temptation, which is all the greater the wealthier the farm and the more dependent and timid is the mother of the family with respect to the family's wealth. It is natural that a farm mistress who works toward the good of the farm and home views the farm and its goods as joint property, to which she has the right of use. But if her husband is a man who neither notices nor understands her or her reasonable needs, but rather becomes angry at the wife's slightest personal expenditures and makes her ask for every penny, then the wife, in order to avoid having to plead, which is humiliating, embarrassing and disturbs domestic peace, might use other means to satisfy her most essential needs. In this way, she soon becomes in the eyes of her husband an evasive so-called 'home thief' (*kotivaras*). [371]

As can be seen from the above excerpts, whereas discussions of unequal inheritance laws centred on the question of *rights,* discourse on home thievery *per se* revolved around the question of *needs*: whose needs were legitimate and what qualified as a need rather than merely a desire or whim? How much – and what – did farm wives and daughters really need? Although the discussions in the early 1860s dealt with material needs, mainly for clothing, by the mid-1870s some social reformers were arguing

---

371 June 1927, *Emäntälehti. Suomalaisen Marttaliiton Äänenkannattaja* no. 6, p. 169, 'Mistähän se joutunee?' (Edla Kojonen, headmistress of Lahti folk high school).

that what counted as a 'need' had changed from the previous generation. The writers below argued in 1876 and 1898 that needs constituted more than mere physical requirements for survival. Changing times had created new emotional and intellectual needs:

> [– –] these sorts of proceedings [=home thievery] are usually the farm master's own fault. We have heard that farm masters are to be found who do not dare send even their own wife, much less their children, to fetch something needed from a storehouse, nor do they ever give their families as much as a penny for their needs, but nevertheless the family goes about well dressed and manages in other respects as well. The reason for the farm master's fear may be well justified, for naturally in this case he can have no other intention than that his family should go about naked – with even less thought given to any enlivenment for their intellectual or spiritual life through books or newspapers. Such an old-timer (*wanhallaan olija*) no longer remembers the days of his youth, nor keeps up with the changing times, but views everything new, the innocent amusements of the youth and even their comely, modest behaviour, through his old sour ideology, and in his firm conservative Finnish stubbornness considers it all to be madness, vanity and pride [– –] [37].

> It is also a common assumption that even when they are adults, 20–25 years of age, children need nothing more than the food and clothing they receive from the farm. But this is an utter impossibility. A person's non-material side surely needs something. In other words, everyone who wants to keep up with the world's progress needs money to some extent. A person must try to procure for his intellectual and spiritual (*henkinen*) side some refreshment, and this cannot always be had for free. But the fact is that many parents cannot understand this. And when children are poorly reared from the beginning, then these circumstances together understandably lead to home thievery [60].

Among those who blamed the persistence of domestic pilfering on the conservative nature and backwardness of male heads of household were at least five farm masters [16, 25, 32, 56]. According to Scott (1990: 55–58), under normal circumstances it is to power holders' advantage that they remain unanimous in their actions and attitudes in order to uphold the force and legitimacy of the public transcript – in this case the discourse which emphasized the patriarch's total authority and his right to control the household's wealth. At first glance, therefore, it seems surprising that some farm masters in the last half of the 19th century broke rank to criticize their peers for their stubborn conservatism. But changing circumstances in the late 19th century were giving rise to new alliances of power. Finnish-speaking farm masters may have been the dominant group within their local communities, but they occupied an inferior social position with respect to the language used in education and administration, and the wealth and privileges of the higher estates such as aristocrats, landed gentry, clergy, and government officials. Farmers who had to perform physical labour in order to survive were well aware that they were at the mercy of famines and early frosts, whereas educated elites were neither forced to carry out physical labour, nor were dependent for their income on the vagaries of the weather (L. Stark 2006). At the same time, Finnish-speaking members of the educated lower middle classes were eager to change the structure of social privilege and opportunity in 19th-century Finland. Official positions for even university-educated men had been scarce since the 1820s, and the problem had only worsened by the 1850s (Nieminen 2006: 60–64). The dissatisfaction was exacerbated in the early 1860s by the wealth-based system of voting rights, according to which members of the middle classes possessed votes according to their wealth, which meant that a small number of wealthy merchants and factory owners controlled most of the votes for delegates to the Diet. Those who had risen to the gentry through education, including lower-ranking civil servants, schoolteachers, younger university faculty and lower-level clergy, were effectively disenfranchised, and these lower-middle classes moved to align their own interests more closely with those of the landowning peasants and to take up the role of their educators. It was this class of persons who appear to have been particularly active in nationalist Fennoman pursuits and in agitating for Finnish-language rights, so that more positions in the spheres of health care, courts, schools, government, and trade would open up to Finnish-speakers, giving them greater influence in society (Ylikangas 1986: 127–128; Juntti 2004: 111–112).[372] Some landowning farmers thus perceived reformist-Fennoman pursuits as an opportunity to climb the social ladder, and allied themselves to these efforts (Stark 2006).

The father and his children's upbringing

The second area in which some writers felt that farm masters were at fault was child rearing [36, 57, 60, 61]. In the 19th century, most rural parents reared their children according to conservative, Scripture-based principles. They viewed themselves as having God-given authority over their children, and bodily punishment was the norm.[373] Heeding the Biblical exhortation 'He that spareth his rod hateth his son: but he that loveth him chasteneth him betimes',[374] parents strove to raise their children to be honourable, God-fearing adults in an evil world which, it was feared, would try to corrupt them. Any expression of independence or obstinacy in a child could be taken as a sign that the child was already in the grip of the world's influences. Total obedience to the patriarch-father was expected and in many cases given.[375]

Yet many of the men who lived through this period, and who were among the first to write their autobiographies in the Finnish language, viewed the strict discipline experienced in their childhood and youth as evidence of their parents' lack of self-control and pedagogical understanding (L. Stark

---

372 See: April 15, 1885. *Suomalainen Wirallinen Lehti* no. 85, 'Waltiopäiwät'; January 4, 1897. *Savo-Karjala* no. 1, 'Naisten waltiollinen äänestysoikeus ja raittiusasia'.
373 Pulma 1987, Häggman 1994; Latvala 2005; Tuomaala 2004: 83–84.
374 See Proverbs 13:24, 22:15, 23:13, 29:15.
375 Päivärinta 2002/1877; Suutarla 1898; Östman 2005; L. Stark 2006.

2006, 60–65). While some writers to the press in the last half of the 19th century continued to write of a religious upbringing in a positive light, they increasingly made a distinction between parents who merely fed and clothed their children, neglecting them in other respects and showing them little respect or trust, and those who spent time with their children, patiently explaining to them the difference between right and wrong [e.g. 25]. Faulty child rearing practices perpetuated by neglectful farm masters were ultimately seen to cause innocent children to lose their trust in parents and become predisposed to steal from their own homes [e.g. 61]. For example, in his lengthy speech on home thievery given at the Kuopio Agricultural Society meeting in 1862, Ahlqvist named traditional child rearing methods as one of the causes of home thievery committed by daughters:

> Education is another thing which would eradicate this evil habit to a large degree. Nothing is helped by hiding the keys or keeping them hidden, as someone here suggested, not even were the farm master to wear them around his neck, for he who wants to go will go and he who wants to take will take, even if he were imprisoned. [Parents] should raise their children in total freedom: through guidance and persuasion rather than hard discipline and imprisonment. [Children] should be allowed to go everywhere [on the farm] and see it all, so that especially when they are older, they will know the affairs of the farm at least somewhat, and know what kind of life the farm can really sustain. They should not be allowed to think that their parents mistrust them, which nevertheless is the case when the keys are hidden from them and the common storehouses are locked [– –]. Slavery deadens the mind and dulls common sense. Freedom lightens the mind, and the knowledge and familiarity which comes from joint participation, as well as seeing and knowing everything in the household, in addition to gentle and benevolent reminders, are the things which allow the child to see everything around him but touch nothing, especially when he knows he will receive from his parents what he needs [36].

Similar arguments were being made thirty-six years later in an article entitled 'Kotiwarkaudesta (On home thievery)' written by '–w–', which appeared in the newspaper *Uusi Savo* in 1898:

> This vice [=home thievery] is caused to a large extent by poor upbringing. In the countryside there are very few families in which the relationship between children and parents is what it should be. They are not able to teach the child to approach the parents or to inform them of their needs. Thus children remain somehow strangers to their parents, at least to the extent that collective deliberation remains largely out of the question even when they are grown. The way in which parents address their children is normally harsh, imperious, which arouses in the child the feeling that he is not able to obey any other kind of command. Parents do not know how to condone children's play, which is thought to be an utter waste of time, they try to force the children into an adult mould. It is clear that in such circumstances, hardly any tender feelings will develop in the child toward his parents, but in their place only a peculiar tendency toward stealth and avoidance [60].

Eva Hällström, the first female schoolteacher at the Otava provincial college in Savo, introduced a letter in which she condemned unenlightened patriarchs by explaining to her readers in 1896 that

> our common folk do not demand that we, the more educated members of society, flatter them or praise them unnecessarily. Now, when concern over the advancement of the common folk is at its height, now when a foundation is being laid for their future enlightenment, now when thousands of men in the backwoods awaken and thirsty souls turn to us, now it is important that we know and are familiar with those to whom we give [57].

In order to illustrate the darker side of the lives of the common folk, Hällström brought up the topic of the unenlightened farm master who reared his chidren using the wrong means:

> The father is the almighty ruler of the home, who, without trying to understand the youth, maintains strict discipline often with curses and the switch! The mother wavers between the father and the children, is a sort of vacillating creature, showing first one side and then the other; the children, who have been raised with the magic phrase: 'Wait until your father comes, then you'll know', become used to acting always in secret, always going behind their parents' backs. Is this what gives rise to trust, compassion, affection? What are home thievery, and night courting, and all other secret behaviour, which are so very commonplace, if not precisely an expression of the lack of understanding, the stifling of a young person's natural wants and needs, which make the relations between family members so tense? [57]

The foregoing letters published in the press not only offered a new vision of the father's proper role and responsibilities within the family and household. They also indicate the increased value placed on children within society at large. According to the new ideology of social and individual progress, properly reared children – whose needs and rights were taken into account – were seen as the future builders of a successful and enlightened nation. Home thievery, by contrast, was taken as proof that this ideal was not yet being achieved.

The farm master and the rationalized household

Finally, writers turned their attention to the need for farm masters to run their households in a rational manner. This topic was taken up already in the discussion on home thievery at the 1862 Kuopio Agricultural Society meeting, when 32-year old manor lord Birger Westzynthius argued that the master of the household should keep written accounts of the household economy, and senior juryman Pelkonen urged the same, in order to monitor home thievery in the household [16, 17]. However, the issue of proper household management received its most detailed treatment in Suppanen's novel *Kotivarkaus* (*Home Thievery*, 1888).

The fictional protagonist in Suppanen's story diverges from the stereotype of the unenlightened patriarch in the sense that Suppanen did not describe the master of Vaara farm as a one-sided tyrant, but constructed him as a more nuanced and ambiguous figure, a man who was stern and conservative on the one hand, but capable and reasonable on the other. In creating this ambiguity, Suppanen left open to the reader's interpretation the question of who in the story was ultimately responsible for the home thievery carried out on Vaara farm, as well as for its tragic consequences. One contemporary reviewer of the book, for instance, felt that the author himself had laid the greatest blame for home thievery on the farm master's doorstep, yet drew his own conclusion from the book that it was the farm mistress who was ultimately to blame:

> Aatto S. distinguishes different reasons for the rise of home thievery in this book. From it we see that the primary blame lies with farm masters, who are not so quick to give money to farm mistresses to meet their needs. The result is that wives must somehow work out a way to obtain what they need. The grain bins and butter tubs of the farm have been under their control and there they find goods which are worth something [– –].
>
> The farm master is a sensible man, who does not wish to use his authority like a tyrant – on the contrary, he was ready to give his adult son Matti, who works hard around the farm, some spending money when Matti asked for it. And in the same way, even though he is an exacting and frugal man, he bought for the womenfolk all sorts of small luxury goods from the city which they considered necessities. So, you see, on that farm there was certainly no need to pilfer secretly. But the mistress had brought the habit from her birth farm and boldly defended it when the deception came to light. It is no wonder, then, that the farm master's more sober teachings and discipline were futile with regard to the children, who followed their mothers' example. The daughter Anna Maija was already fully versed in pilfering. At home she would say that 'water has made the butter trickle out' when, while visiting the shop to sell the butter, she had used two pounds of it for her own small necessities [51].

According to this anonymous reviewer, the book *Home Thievery* emphasizes the farm mistress' culpability for her children's predisposition to theft. Yet with the hindsight provided by the twelve decades of history, it may be suggested that the real target of the book's criticism was not the women of the farm but the conservatism of all its members – including to some extent the farm master himself – which made them resistant or indifferent to the demands of progress. This can be seen in the fact that the co-protagonist in the book alongside the farm master is the educated and confident daughter-in-law Liena, who helps the farm master understand the extent to which home thievery is being carried out in his household. In his story, Suppanen made use of the distinction between 'enlightened' and 'unenlightened' which in newspaper discourse was applied to farm masters, but mapped it instead onto the farm women occupying different positions in the family. The daughter-in-law Liena represented education and reason, whereas the farm mistress and her daughter represented backwardness and lack of foresight. The farm master, for his part, is portrayed as having to decide which of the female examples in his household he should follow.

The master of Vaara farm stands in need of a modern education in the running of a household, which he receives through his daughter-in-law Liena.[376] She does this by demonstrating to him the new form of control and surveillance afforded by the modern practices of bookkeeping and accounting. Already in the early 1860s, systematic accounting procedures were being mentioned in the press as a superior method for keeping track of the production and sale of farm products [9, 16]. In 1860, the newspaper *Suomen Julkisia Sanomia* published a letter entitled 'The importance of agricultural schools for the education of Finns' which explained how

> [a]t any moment of the day [the farmer] can look up in his account books and see how much of this or that resource he possesses. When he is in his grain storehouse, he can quickly determine, by looking at the grain bin and doing some arithmetic, whether there is as much grain as there should be, or whether the grabbing hands of home thievery, that evil habit which damages both morals and wealth, have reduced the stores of grain. For he has measured how much grain he puts in the bin every time, and measured how much he has given for the household to use, and written all of this in his book [9].

In Suppanen's story, the same causal connection is made between bookkeeping and home thievery: modern accounting practices are presented as the only way to determine the extent and gravity of domestic pilfering. After moving to the farm as Matti's wife, Liena obtains paper and pencil and begins to keep careful records of the foodstuffs in the farm storehouses, which puzzles the farm master and irritates the farm mistress. Although the farm mistress does not really understand the reason for Liena's monitoring and measuring of the milk and butter stores, she resents her daughter-in-law's interference. Undeterred, Liena turns her attention to the grain stores:

> The master loaded sacks on his arms, intending to fill them with dry rye. 'Won't you take the measuring scoop?' asked Liena, who was in the yard, where the farm mistress also happened to be busy with something.
> [Farm master:] 'What, are we to measure the grain as well? I always bring it here to the storehouse without measuring it.'
> [Liena:] 'Then you don't know how much there is all in all.'
> [Farm master:] 'Well, I guess we could measure it, even though it seems to me a waste of time.'
> [– –] From the master's last words, the farm mistress had received welcome support for her own dissatisfaction.

---

376 In 19th-century rural Finland, daughters-in-law sometimes brought innovations to their marital farms, since they had learned alternative – and sometimes superior – ways of carrying out tasks on their birth farm. According to an elderly farm master from Satakunta, 'new ways of doing things always came to the farm through the new daughter-in-law' (SKS KRA Mouhijärvi. 1939. Eero Järventausta E 150:117. – old farm master, b. 1852).

[Farm mistress:] 'There, now you see what a waste of time this constant measuring is, when it happens to you.'
[Farm master:] 'Well, this is entirely different from weighing out the butter. All the grain is put into the bin and from there it is eaten, it doesn't disappear.'
[Liena:] 'Mice might eat it.'
[Farm master:] 'It's not mice I'm worried about, as long as no two-legged mice come around. But they can more easily get to the butter and milk containers' (pp. 47–48).

On the following New Year's Eve, Liena asks the other members of the household, as if in jest, whether anyone can say how much bread has been eaten at home during the preceding year. When no one is able to hazard a guess, she reads aloud from her account book how much grain has been consumed in total, how much has been ground into flour, how much purchased in the summer, and how much grain was still left in the storehouse bins. 'So that's why you measured everything?' says the master in amazement. Liena is also able to tell them how much milk and butter the farm has produced, and how much of that has been sold and how much eaten at home. To which the farm master asks, 'has that much butter really been eaten? How can that much have been consumed, even though butter is not on the table at every meal?'

Although contemporary reviewers hardly mentioned the character of Liena at all in their reviews of *Kotivarkaus*, and chose to see the book chiefly as a morality tale, this particular side plot of Suppanen's book illustrates the increased importance of *knowledge as a form of power* in the modernizing era (cf. Foucault 1977; 1978). Although the farm master had the *right* to monitor and control the activities taking place on the farm, Suppanen makes it clear that without systematic use of bookkeeping, there were no real *means* by which he could effectively do so. Without careful recording of all the food produced and stored on the farm in the first place, farm masters had no idea how much pilfering was going on behind their backs.

In real life, Liena as the daughter-in-law would have most likely occupied the lowest status in the farm household (Heikinmäki 1988). In the fictive world envisioned by Suppanen, however, Liena becomes, by employing systematic record keeping, the only person in the story who possesses information regarding the quantities of goods produced, consumed and stored on the farm. Liena's knowledge even causes the farm master to have doubts about his role as head of the farm and – in a surprising literary move on the author's part that would surely have been out of the question in real life – the master offers to turn control of the money over to Liena:

[Liena:] 'But guess, how much money was received from everything we've sold this year.'
When no answer came, Liena listed all of the goods with their prices and at the end mentioned the total sum.
[Farm master:] 'Then where in the world has all the money gone?'
That Liena could not say, since the money had been in the farm master's keeping and she had not gone to him to demand an account of all the purchases and other expenses. Nor did the master himself remember

anything other than the largest sums: the sacks of flour, taxes, the serving maid's salary and such. He also remembered precisely the sum of savings which was hidden in the corner of the grain bin. But it was somehow small in comparison to the total sales reported by Liena, so that the master truly regretted that the expenses were not in the account book, whereby he could have seen what had been spent on necessities, and what on frivolities. He thought it over a while. He didn't really, after all, want to turn the control of the money over to Liena, since, you see, it would have felt inappropriate to a farm master's status, but he couldn't come up with a better solution.

[Farm master:] 'I guess it would be best to give you the money, then you can put every penny in your book.'

[Liena:] 'I don't want that responsibility. And what if somebody stole it, then it would be thought that I had lost it. Keep the money yourself.'

[Farm master:] 'How will you remember the expenses then?'

[Liena:] 'I don't need the money in order to write it down, as long as you let me know.'

[Farm master:] 'Well, that's alright. That's a good idea' (pp. 50–53).

Although Suppanen did not depict his farm master as an unreasonable tyrant, he clearly hoped his readers would draw from his tale the conclusion that rational knowledge was superior to traditional patriarchal authority. Modern learning represented power even when in the humble hands of a young daughter-in-law, whereas lack of such learning rendered even a patriarch helpless.

The unenlightened patriarch as an obstacle to modern social reform

By the late 19th century, farm masters had enjoyed a long tradition of authority within agrarian communities. After 1865, when the Church's civil administration of rural areas ended and municipalities became self-governing, it was farm masters who decided affairs at the district level. For this reason, they represented a potential obstacle to those who sought to reform and educate the rural population. As many writers in the press implicitly argued during this period, a farm master could only continue to lay claim to traditional authority – and be respected by the educated members of society – if he did not stand in the way of reforms implemented by Finnish-language educators and activists. As we have seen in this chapter so far, farm masters whose actions and attitudes were viewed as backward and conservative frequently came under fire from social reformers writing to newspapers. The farm master's power as an obstacle to social progress was most clearly highlighted in the debates which erupted in some districts in the last half of the 19th century over the building of public schools, the expenses of which the landowning farmers of the district were expected to bear (Parkkonen 2008: 33–47; Mikkola 2009). For example in 1896, the aforementioned schoolteacher Ewa Hällström wrote of a meeting she attended in which the possible construction of a public primary school was discussed:

[– –] I have seen farm masters who have supported such issues, even sacrificed donations for them, but they are few. The money pouches of the vast majority remain firmly closed, both money pouches and hearts [– –]. The district meeting in which the matter was discussed was a truly sad example of the backwardness of our common folk. With their fur coats on, their tobacco pipes between their teeth, spitting and cursing, the men responded to all of the chairman's questions by shouting in absolute fury: we will not pay, we will not pay [57].[377]

Generally speaking, when it comes to criticism of the unenlightened patriarch, women's rights *per se* were not necessarily the primary motive. For example, censure of the unenlightened patriarch in the press never mentioned unequal rural inheritance practices, even if these were at the centre of debates which focused on home thievery. In other words, the legal circumventions which denied farm daughters their rightful inheritance were never included in the usual list of wrongs perpetrated by fathers against their children. This may have been because most social reformers in Eastern Finland had a fairly close acquaintance with the agrarian way of life and participated in the tacit understanding that the practical needs of the farm household outweighed the demands of rural gender equality. Whatever injustice it might have represented on a philosophical level, unequal inheritance did not pose a direct threat to the cultural projects of social reformers, nor was women's equal inheritance in the countryside seen to be necessary for the progress of the nation.

Nevertheless, in urging farm masters to look after the well-being of their families and invest in their children for the sake of social progress, social reformers implicitly drove a moral and ideological wedge between the farm master's own individual interests (especially his wealth and standing in the eyes of the community) and those of society at large, since these two were no longer perceived within educated circles to be one and the same. In conceptual terms, the new reformist rhetoric aimed to extract from the private sphere of the household those members whose needs and rights had earlier been subordinated to the priorities of the farm. These household members were now presented in the public sphere as individuals with natural rights and personal needs which were of consequence to the nation's future (see Pylkkänen 2009: 41–42, 46).

Individual rights in the modern era were conceived as inseparable from new forms of accountability and responsibility. An individual's subsistence and well-being was increasingly seen as dependent on his or her own choices (Alasuutari 1991: 175), and modern subjects were expected to be self-directed and organize their behaviours in new ways to socially productive ends (L. Stark 2006; Tuomaala 2004). Farm women under the authority of the farm master, however, were unable to exercise their new responsibilities as citizens for the betterment of Finnish society. The labour and resource structure of agrarian society necessitated that most household members remain physically within the bounds of the farm household to

---

377 See also: December 10, 1866. *Suometar* no. 99, 'Tammelasta' (Tammelan asustelija).

carry out their tasks. The responsibility of ensuring the rights and freedom of household members to develop their talents and become more productive citizens thus fell to the head of the household. Yet many rural patriarchs did not seem to recognize or implement this sacred duty, a fact which vexed social reformers. As Wilhelm Kukkonen explained in 1876 regarding farm masters who cared nothing for the material needs of their children:

> At the same time that this sort of farm master accumulates assets to satisfy his own desires with the help of his family, his family must content themselves, especially with respect to their material needs, with either designated charity or, as usually happens, with almost nothing at all except for their daily bread and whatever clothing they need for their tasks and labours [– –].
>
> But why do you proceed in this way with your family? Your children are the renewal of your life, the hope for our future! Allow them then, according to your means, the few needs they have, and adornments, even though to your stern eyes they may sometimes appear frivolous, in this way you can keep the trust and respect of your family and uphold a sense of honour among your family members [– –]. [37]

Public discourse regarding women's rights underwent a crucial transformation in the 1890s, when the effects of the moral wedge driven between the personal interests of farm masters and those of society at large become more evident, not only in letters written by educated reformers, but also in those written by the farming population. For example, a letter from a farmer from Laihia, Mikko Iiponen, entitled 'What are the rights and responsibilities of women?' appeared in 1895 in the newspaper *Pohjalainen*. Iiponen's letter draws upon a wide range of discourses (Scripture-based, liberal-progressive, and nationalist-collectivist) in order to argue that women should receive equality with men:

> Who would dare to claim that our Redeemer, when he freed humanity and redeemed them, did not also free wives from the subordinate position and state of slavery to which they had been condemned by the Fall? But women's weakness and their need of men's custody is firmly entrenched in the minds of men even in civilized nations, not to mention in barbaric and less civilized societies, in which the man considers himself the absolute master and ruler over his wife's and daughter's freedom, even their lives [– –] women have neither power nor money, for the man has usurped and laid hold of both power and money, leaving to women only the status of a servant [– –] Thus it is clear that it is men's responsibility to ensure that women receive before the law the same rights they themselves possess. If a man wishes to act as an honest man and not just solely in social and governmental affairs, then he must, without delay, allow women to stand alongside him before social and national law. Calls have occasionally been made to give rights of citizenship in Finland to the Jews, but not to first free the other sex of our own people, women, from their current state, from their slavery and the fact of being wards of their husbands, even though a woman's help is just as important, just as necessary to a man as sunlight is to nature, it is: the precondition for life [56].

217

The new emphasis on individual rights also caused the practice of home thievery to be perceived and interpreted in new ways. This can be seen from an article entitled 'A word about so-called 'home thievery'' which originally appeared in the women's journal *Koti ja Yhteiskunta* (*Home and Society*) and was reprinted in the newspaper *Keski-Suomi* in 1892. Because this article represents a fundamental shift in the discourse regarding home thievery away from the assumption that the patriarch had rightful control over all of the resources of the farm and toward a female perspective and expectation of equal ownership within the household, I quote it at length below:

> It is often said there is no sense in speaking of a wife's right to possess property, for joint ownership is much better. Everything should be shared jointly in a marriage, including ownership rights.
>
> But do ownership rights in marriage truly mean joint ownership? Does not the husband in most families consider himself the owner, who gives his wife what she needs when she needs it, money, clothing, etc. If this were not so, then surely such a term as home thievery would never have arisen in [our] language. For what does this term mean if not that the wife secretly takes this and that from her husband, who owns the goods of the household, and then furtively sells the purloined items in order to obtain money? If the husband sells the household goods without his wife's knowledge, his methods are not referred to as home thievery, even though it naturally would be thievery, if joint ownership truly existed. Why is it not called theft? Naturally for the reason that the man himself is the owner, and no one can steal goods from himself.
>
> Legal experts may explain these matters in whatever way they wish, but the truth remains, that the wife's economic status is generally understood in the aforementioned manner. If the wife in her own mind was the owner of goods just like her husband, she would never be content, as is now common, with the sort of status in which she has not a penny to spend as she wishes. If, in the husband's opinion, the wife were equal owner of the household's property alongside himself, then he would not let her plead for money to buy medicines, coffee, and clothing, nor – as is now frequently the case – would he scold her when she asks for money. Often even a good husband, who does not answer his wife's requests for money by rebuking her, nonetheless keeps all the money of the farm to himself, without allotting even the tiniest amount for his wife to use. In a few more civilized families, a change has been made in this respect, so that the wife has her own fund of money, but the great majority of wives in our country, especially those in the landowning peasant estate, own nothing [– –]. Perhaps many men might say boastfully: 'yes, it is precisely that accursed desire for coffee and ostentation that leads to home thievery! We men would never do that!' Good. But let each man try to put himself in his wife's place. Let him try to be so utterly without money, that he cannot even buy a handful of tobacco, trouser buttons, a hunting knife or a cap to wear to church for himself, but rather must always ask someone else for the money with which to buy them. Would not his situation feel degrading and would he not better understand why women fall into the sin of home thievery?
>
> [– –] Let, therefore, each husband remove this temptation from his wife by allotting for her use either some small annual sum of money

Home thievery was made possible by the fact that farm mistresses had constant access to the contents of the outbuildings where the farm's grain, butter, and meat were stored. Here, a farm mistress stands at the door of a storehouse in Ylihärmä, South Ostrobothnia. Photo: Samuli Paulaharju, 1929.

or some part of the grain, milk, etc. Let each husband remember that children, too, desire to own something. The desire to own something is inborn in humans, nor is this desire in itself a bad thing, unless it becomes avarice. On the contrary, it demonstrates that a person wants to earn their own daily bread rather than live on charity. Until we receive the sort of law which safeguards the economic situation of the mother of the family better than the present one, let each husband consider it his duty to promote it as much as possible. Even the poorest servants own something. It is unnatural therefore, that the mistress of the farm, the mother of the family, who should be the ruler and manager of the household, has not a penny to spend without asking for it from her husband or – stealing it from him! [54].

In the 1860s and 1870s, social reformers had not been able to ponder the difficult contradictions implicit in the term 'home thievery' so long as they had needed the term to retain its rhetorical force as an 'evil', 'sickness' or 'sin'. This rhetoric, in turn, was needed to justify explorations into the causes underlying home thievery. When these were identified to be the very attitudes which had proven resistant to change and which had troubled both social reformers (the miserliness of farm masters, resistance to public schools) and farmers (over-consumption of store-bought goods, wasteful wedding customs), the notion of home thievery as a corrupting vice justified even harsher criticism of these attitudes.

By the 1890s, however, the public sphere of the press had fragmented into a number of more specialized readerships based on age, gender, class and political affiliation, so that journals existed which were both written by and directed toward women. This seems to have been the first time that writers could call into question the taken-for-granted premise underlying the word 'home thievery', namely that the husband-father owned everything in the home, and that any unauthorized disposal of household goods by other family members represented theft.

Objections to this premise were still cautious, however. In 1898, a writer to the newspaper *Uusi Savo* called into question the assumptions behind the term 'home thievery', but diverged from the public transcript only for a moment before returning to it to condemn women's pilfering:

> We still speak of a wife's home thievery, but never of the husband's. If a wife sometimes takes something out of the common fund, even if for their common needs, it is already home thievery, but the husband is allowed to take as much as he likes without his wife knowing, he can squander whole countries and continents, and it is both just and reasonable. I do not wish to suggest here that among wives there exist no true home thieves. Naturally it is each person's responsibility to avoid this vice, and under no circumstances to start stealing the wealth of their home, for that makes them a thief nonetheless, and no mitigating circumstance can free them of blame [60].

This circumspection continued into the 1920s. In an article published in the journal *Emäntälehti* in 1927, the writer urged mothers to teach their daughters greater responsibility with household money. When it came to mentioning home thievery, the female author paused in her essay to scrutinize the contradictions implied within the term 'home thievery', but then returned to a moral condemnation of its practice:

> A peculiar word by the way, if I do say so. For if we admit that the mother and mistress of the family has her home where her husband has his, and 'what is mine is yours', then how can we say that a mother is *stealing* when she makes use of their common property? But nevertheless that mental state in which she does so is dangerous. It is akin to the state of mind of a thief, in the sense that it is at least servile and secretive, and drags a person down. But it is not only dangerous to the mother herself, it is also dangerous to her children. Before long they, too, begin to figure out that one should go behind father's back [– –].[378]

Despite the fact that discussions of home thievery continued to be couched in a framework of moral condemnation well into the 20th century, social reformers and educators had made their position clear: the farm master could no longer act as a tyrant with unlimited power, but now had to use his position to further the aims of the new society. How was this new

---

378 June 1927. *Emäntälehti* no. 6, p. 169, 'Mistähän se joutunee?' (Edla Kojonen, head-mistress of Lahti folk high school, emphasis in original).

patriarchal ideal conceived? With regard to relations within the household, it was described already in Fredrik Ahlqvist's 1853 story 'Koti' (Home). It was also described in the early autobiographies of rural men who lived in the last half of the 19th century (L. Stark 2006), as well as in Pietari Päivärinta's *Naimisen juoruja. Kuwaelmia Kansan elämästä* (1882) and in Eero J–nen's *Kuwaelmia sodasta walon ja pimeyden välillä* (1893). In all of these accounts, the young farm master marries not for money, but for compatibility of character. Ideally, mutual respect and affection were to continue throughout the marriage and were not to be marred by the drunkenness or violence of the husband (see e.g. Päivärinta 2002/1877, 69–74). In the new model of marriage which respected both spouses' rights, husband and wife were expected to share the running of the household and its day-to-day decisions, even if the master still had the final word over larger household matters. The ideal of this shared-decision making is explained, for example, in the 1892 article 'One person in charge, one farm mistress':

> In a well organized household, it is not fitting for the master or the mistress to sell or squander the goods of the household without the other's knowledge. If something is to be sold from the farm, then they should together consider how it can be most advantageously changed into money. It is same with purchases. Let the farm master and mistress decide together what should be purchased and what can be done without [53].

Although new responsibilities for a well-managed household would also fall upon the farm mistress in the late 19th century, it was the role of the farm master which came under the most pressure to change. The patriarch-father was now expected to consult his family members regarding the rational maintenance of the farm, and to look after not only the material needs but also the emotional and educational needs of his children. What made it difficult for the family patriarch to meet these expectations was that they ran counter to his own cultural projects, the forms of agency which represented the ambitions of generations of farm masters in the Finnish countryside. It is these forms of patriarchal agency, and the factors which constrained them, which I address in the next and final chapter.

10. Hidden Transcripts and the Limits of Rural Patriarchy

A father's thief is never hanged.[379]

This study began by suggesting that when we take into account women's activities carried out behind the scenes in 19th-century agrarian Finnish culture, we obtain a more nuanced and multifaceted picture of the system of power negotiations known as familial patriarchy, of which the legal and normative framework is only one part. An examination of home thievery and news carrying not only enriches our view of the marital economy in 19th-century Finland, but also reveals the limitations of an approach focusing solely on the formal constraints imposed by society on individual agency. Formal controls on female agency in the form of laws, traditions, and religious teachings certainly existed in the 19th-century Finnish countryside. Yet the circumvention of these constraints was not only possible, it could even be tolerated as long as it did not openly challenge the normative framework of power. The reason it was tolerated was that occasionally such circumvention could benefit patriarchs themselves: for instance when a new husband prospered from his bride's pilfering of goods from her father's farm, or when gossip women brought information to the farm mistress that was also of interest to the farm master.

No system of domination is without its weaknesses and internal contradictions, and the structural weaknesses of the farm master's power were exploited by other household members to further their own cultural projects. These cultural projects were not necessarily intended to block the projects cherished by the farm master, but in the case of both family members' home thievery and the gossip of landless women, the cultural projects of subordinates collided with the aims of patriarchs. It is clear from the discussions in the foregoing chapters that the farm master's actual power to enforce his authority was restricted, attacked and forced to compromise on a number of fronts, which I shall now discuss.

379 See [27] and [60].

The spatial organization of resources and the practised hidden transcript

One of the assumptions underlying this study is that agency must be examined within the historical context of individuals' own interests and goals, in other words, in light of their own cultural projects. As I argue in Chapter Two, the cultural projects or serious games whose implementation comprise agency can be broken down into the following levels of analysis: (1) project resources, their distribution in time and space, (2) individuals' access to them, and (3) the tactics or moves made by the actor in maximizing use of these resources. In other words, the tactical deployment of cultural projects is dependent first upon the arrangement of resources in physical space, and second upon the practices which organize, facilitate or hinder access to those resource-spaces.

The four groups in the countryside examined in this study – farm masters, farm mistresses, poorer landless women, and youth of marriageable age from the landowning classes – naturally do not cover the agrarian population in its entirety. Mentioned only briefly in my analysis have been the patriarch's younger brothers, daughters-in-law, landless men, serving maids, and workers in early rural industries. Nevertheless, the four groups which form the focus of this study were all centrally connected to the system of family patriarchy, representing the patriarch, his dependents related by blood, itinerant women dependent on the goodwill of farm households, and future aspirants to positions of power within the farm household. Each of these groups had resources – both material and immaterial – at their disposal, which they used strategically to further their own aims.

In the period prior to 1859, a primary resource possessed by farm masters was mobility. This mobility was both a necessity and an opportunity: farm masters were forced to hunt, fish, and plough distant fields, but were also able to travel to other households, villages and towns to establish extra-household networks which could enhance their status. Mobility also enabled them to carry out their duties as household heads (paying taxes to government authorities, serving as jurymen, and so forth). Exclusive access to transportation by horse and cart did not necessarily result in increased personal gain, since market trips, for instance, were not always economically lucrative. But the farm master's exclusive mobility did constrain the use of household resources by other family members, who could not squander the goods of the farm on consumer items if they had no access to markets and tradesmen.

The advantages of the farm master's mobility were counterbalanced by certain disadvantages, however. The farm master's activities often took him away from the farm house and its outbuildings, where the productive resources and wealth of the farm were stored. Farm mistresses, although constrained in terms of mobility, carried out their daily tasks in a space which offered constant access to the farm's resources. In the period before 1859, farm women were dependent on random visits from itinerant peddlars in order to exchange those goods for new items which might enhance their status, but after 1859, access to store-bought goods increased dramatically when the appearance of shops in the countryside significantly altered the arrangement of resources in social space.

The cultural projects of farm wives and daughters included promoting the success and wealth of their marital farms, which would ensure them a relatively high status in the eyes of the community (see Stark-Arola 1998: 98–99). But equally important to female family members were opportunities for external display which distinguished them from servants and landless rural inhabitants, and earned the high regard of their peers. To this end, one of the most important cultural projects pursued by women of the rural landowning class was public consumption of store-bought goods, especially coffee offered to guests and the wearing of new fashions in clothing. Farm women, however, could not achieve these public displays alone. They needed the assistance of intermediaries who enjoyed greater mobility, but who in turn needed the resources only farms could provide.

The hierarchical class organization of rural life meant that landless or itinerant women who worked as masseuses, cuppers, and washer-women, as well as beggars without any occupation at all, were forced by necessity to travel from farm to farm on foot seeking charity or payment for services. This mobility, however, gave them access to rural shops (in order to act as intermediaries for farm women in selling the goods of the farm) and access to information about their local social milieu, which farm mistresses lacked. Farm mistresses and their daughters needed information regarding their neighbours and other residents in their districts in order to construct a map of socially relevant knowledge. For a farm mistress, this included information regarding moral transgressions by those in her household, as well as knowledge of potential marriage partners for her children which enabled her to influence the decisions of her husband and adult children in a direction beneficial to herself and her household. For a farm daughter, such relevant knowledge might include how large a dowry or how many wedding gifts other brides in her district had brought to their marital home, so that she could strive to outshine them when her own turn came to marry. Landless gossip women tactically deployed their knowledge of these matters to gain for themselves a measure of respect (even if this meant negative respect based on fear and resentment) which they might not otherwise have commanded. Within this symbiotic relationship, both farm women and lower-class women learned to be adept in converting the resources each had at their disposal (goods versus information) into resources to which they did not have direct access. The question of what function was performed by gossip in 19th-century rural Finnish life thus depends on the perspective from which the matter is considered: for farm mistresses, the function of gossip was undoubtedly the social maintenance of both communal morality and their own personal standing in society. From the perspective of the female gossip, by contrast, it was concrete material gain.

Farm women's wearing of fine clothing and their drinking of coffee represented a *public transcript* which demonstrated their status. But this public transcript could only be maintained through the enactment of a *hidden transcript*, namely home thievery. Women who practiced home thievery did not merely slip into the storehouse to grab some butter or

Most farms had only one horse-drawn cart, owned by the farm master, which meant that the family patriarch usually enjoyed more freedom of mobility than other members of his household. The farm master's responsibilities away from the farm became a disadvantage, however, when his absence enabled other members of the household to pilfer from the farm's food stores. This photograph from 1910 shows a farm master from Taipalsaari district, South Savo, in his low, four-wheeled cart known as a rospuski. Photo: U. T. Sirelius. Courtesy of the National Board of Antiquities.

a sackful of grain. They needed to carefully orchestrate networks of cooperation with lower class men and women who acted as go-betweens in the selling of farm products to local shopkeepers. Although determining the nature of farm women's hidden *verbal* transcripts regarding home thievery poses a significant challenge, the existence of the *practices* themselves is well documented and demonstrates that women did not accept the public transcript of patriarchal authority at face value. In other words, it may be impossible to determine what rural inhabitants thought, felt and said to each other when they carried out home thievery, but we know the consequences and effects of the practice: in the sequestered spaces where farm mistresses and lower-class men and women met and carried out home thievery, the farm master's legal control over farm products was ignored, with the result that the farm master lost the potential wealth generated by their sale. In this same space, the farm master also lost farm goods which were paid to gossip women in exchange for social information vital to the farm mistress, information which enabled plots to be hatched behind the farm master's back in order to manipulate marriage agreements and social opinion. These plots had very real consequences for both individual honour and reputation, and for the social organization of the rural marital economy.

225

Moreover, gossip women posed a threat to the social standing of individual men, particularly to that of young male candidates for future patriarchy. This was because in small communities in which honour and reputation were primary determinants of landowning men's social status among their peers, female gossips could temporarily control the field of social information in which male honour and reputation were negotiated. It is not surprising, then, that male farmers and reformers writing to the press were outspoken in their disapproval of local gossip by women, since female gossip was not subject to official controls of verifiability. To sum up, if we understand family patriarchy to be *domination disguised as a set of moral relations of loyalty owed to the patriarch*,[380] it is clear from the existence of home thievery and news carrying that rural women were capable of both seeing through this ideology and recognizing where their best interests lay.

On the trail of the verbal hidden transcript

The notion of a shared and practiced hidden transcript already assumes the existence of verbally communicated discourses by the practitioners, since without language, the perpetuation of subversive practices cannot be ensured under conditions of control and oppression. As can be seen from the foregoing chapters, most letters to the press on home thievery were written by persons who had most likely never carried out the practice themselves (although we cannot exclude the possibility that adult male writers may have pilfered from their fathers' farms when they were young, or received goods pilfered by their own brides upon marriage). Taken as a whole, writings to the press on the topic of home thievery represent the *public transcript*. Although this public transcript contained multiple viewpoints on the causes of home thievery and was itself employed in a wide variety of rhetorical stratagems, it unanimously condemned home thievery as damaging to household harmony and prosperity, as well as morally dangerous and corrupting to those who engaged in it. As such, it emphasized the importance of both a strong patriarchal authority, as well as the moral authority of the Church and Christian community.

Three tacit assumptions, only rarely articulated in full, underpinned the farm master's authority in the countryside, and these discourses, having achieved the status of unquestioned truths, persisted in spite of the rhetorical shift in the press towards notions of progress and reform in the last half of the 19th century. The first of these assumptions was that most farms functioned at subsistence level and were barely able to scrape out an existence for themselves, which meant that the purchase of non-essential goods posed an immediate threat to the financial stability of farms. Although poverty in 19th-century rural Finland was indeed widespread and many persons lived at subsistence level (Haatanen 1968, 1981; E. Stark 2011), on wealthy farms there seems to have been a significant amount of money spent on

380 See Bourdieu 1977, 1990, 126; Kandiyoti 1998, 148, note 4.

non-essentials, and much of this was spent on farm masters' own personal consumption of goods such as tobacco and expensive alcoholic beverages (Kuusanmäki 1936: 102–103; Alanen 1957, 332).

According to the second assumption, men's work was more valuable to the maintenance of the farm than women's work. The third assumption was that only the farm master had the common sense and self-discipline to be concerned for the welfare of the farm as a whole. The vitality of these assumptions explains why the general attitudes of condemnation expressed in the press regarding home thievery, upon which all writers agreed, changed only slightly over the half-century examined here. On the other hand, as the patriarchal ideal began to shift toward the notion of the patriarch as a progressive citizen, guarantor of his household members' rights and freedoms and thus facilitator of a new kind of society, the public transcript began to include an element of criticism toward those farm masters seen to be acting as tyrants within their household. The increased emphasis on individual self-improvement as the foundation for social progress meant that by the 1890s, writers to the press were emphasizing the importance of socio-economic gender equality within the household, so that family members of both genders could fulfil their potential in contributing to society. Social reformers and educators strongly advocated a new kind of ideal patriarch who would put the material and emotional welfare of his family, as well as the progress of his nation, before his own personal desires.

Within the public transcript, allusions to farm women's attitudes regarding home thievery were made by a number of writers both male and female. What emerges from these glimpses is an ambivalent picture of how women themselves understood the act of pilfering. According to many writers, there existed a large section of the rural populace who saw nothing wrong with home thievery [3, 4, 7, 24, 41, 42, 50, 52, 53, 54, 55, 57, 59, 60]. Recurrent remarks such as 'home thievery is hereabouts so deeply rooted in the world view of the common folk that it is one of the Karelians' original sins' [53]; 'the common folk still live in such darkness that they do not know what is good and what is evil' [24]; and 'there can be found many among the farming population, especially womenfolk, who do not consider the practice of home thievery to be shameful at all' [7] were clearly intended to justify the role of educator adopted by social reformers on such a private issue as home thievery which would normally have lain outside their domain of concern and experience. Reformist writers may have also recognized that individual property ownership remained a hazy concept in the countryside when family members functioned as components of a corporate whole rather than as individual citizens, and wished to draw the lines of individual rights and responsibilities more clearly [see 2].

Because the picture of deep-rooted tolerance surrounding home thievery painted by social reformers was intended primarily as an instrument of rhetoric rather than an attempt to portray the perspective of rural inhabitants, writers rarely clarified what this tolerance among the rural folk was supposed to signify. Did it mean that women felt themselves entitled to take whatever goods they wanted from the farm, and were ready to justify their own actions? This seems to have been the intent behind a statement reportedly made by an unnamed participant to the Kuopio Agricultural Society meeting in 1861, who said: '[i]n view of this oppression, wives see nothing wrong with compensating themselves with their own hands for that which is denied to them by the law and the oppression-mindedness of men' [11]. Other writers seem to have been of the opinion that women pilfered out of habit rather than out of conscious resistance to patriarchal authority. Such an alternative was suggested in an article by '–w–' published in *Uusi Savo* in 1898:

> Among the Savo peoples there still flourishes an audacious vice, which is so deeply etched into the thinking of the common people that it is not really considered a vice at all. It is home thievery. Our people are able to place value on honesty and honest persons, but they can also look on with equanimity, even respect, upon those persons who steal so much that an ordinary thief, who would take the same amount of grain from somebody else's storehouse, would have to spend years in prison to atone for his crime. But when it is taken from home, from the stockpiles of one's own father, then the act is given quite another face, for 'a father's thief is never hanged' [60].

The frequent assertion that home thievery was not perceived by rural inhabitants to be shameful was contradicted, however, by claims in the press that farm women experienced fear and a guilty conscience when pilfering. As clergyman Bernhard Kristfrid Sarlin maintained in his 1856 article regarding home thievery, '[t]he farm's grain bin, butter crock, wool bushels and so forth are all in the grasp of a remorseless hand, which decides to take for itself as much as it dares, and is careful to shield it from the master's eyes, even though the heart pounds with fear...' [3]. A presumably female writer, whose 1892 article on home thievery in the women's journal *Koti ja Yhteiskunta* was reprinted in the newspaper *Keski-Suomi* the same year, observed that '[a]t first, the wife practices this sort of secret selling in fear and trembling, but gradually her heart becomes hardened and she becomes a skilful thief, who uses her husband's absences as an opportunity for secret visits to the shop...' [54]. Maria Loviisa Kukkonen, writing from Rautalampi parish to *Tapio* in 1862, was another writer who asserted that young women knew they were doing wrong when committing home thievery:

> [– –] to my mind among the daughters of our country there is probably not one who has been raised in such blindness that she would not be able to distinguish good from evil [– –] for each one is aware while undertaking this act that it is an evil undertaking and wrongly done [– –]. [27]

It must be kept in mind, however, that all of the above claims of women's fear and shame were still part of the public transcript. Indeed, such claims may not have reflected how female pilferers experienced home thievery at all. Instead, they may have simply served the rhetorical aims of writers who wished to remind their readers of farm master's legal rights and how women *ought* to have felt when committing home thievery.

This leaves the researcher with only two places from which to seek more direct insights into farm women's verbal hidden transcripts on home thievery. First, some men writing within the public transcript added fragments of female pilferers' own self-justifications – possibly imagined or overheard – to their arguments. The first to do this was Karl Ferdinand Forsström, who in his 1858 treatise on the situation of women in Finland explained that daughters pilfered while saying to themselves: 'we're not going to receive any other inheritance' [5]. In 1860, 'G. J.' from Janakkala imagined the self-justifications made by adult children and servants for pilfering to be as follows:

> There can be found many among landowning farming folk, especially the womenfolk, who do not consider the practice of home thievery to be shameful at all; their children see this as well as their servants, and they think to themselves that because the mistress of the farm does not disapprove of it, then why can't we do the same; it's not such a great theft if we take here and there a little of what we need [– –] [7].

Fredrik Ahlqvist, for his part, claimed in 1862 that farm daughters reasoned the following to themselves [18]:

> [– –] of course it would be good to do work and be diligent, but what good would it do, since we won't gain anything more by it, we won't even receive equal inheritance and scarcely a decent inheritance in any case. For this reason let us take while we can, so we'll know we've at least received something.

Ahlqvist's perspective was given support by Maria Loviisa Kukkonen four months later, who explained in her second letter to *Tapio*, '…and somebody may think, I will not receive anything else of my father's inheritance, why don't I just procure clothing for the future, just in case….' [27].[381] Writing in 1863, 'J. K–n' hinted that farm women had told him why they committed home thievery [32]:

> I have known many wives who would not have carried out home thievery if they had openly received something from their husbands, but needs often come up for which money is needed, which are just as necessary for men as for women, but men give nothing and yet they demand from their wives a full set of clothing, among other things, and all of these must be obtained by the wife on her own, even though they are for the common good.

One unique fragment reminiscent of a hidden transcript which was not brought up anywhere else was mentioned by 'D. H–n.' in 1862. 'D. H–n.' argued that young women pilfered in order to amass large dowries and that 'each girl does this with the heartfelt opinion that she deserves to marry well' [24].

---

381 Even the unusual letter by 'Flower-bud' which refused to condemn home thievery [35] falls under this category, since, although ostensibly written by a woman, it did not offer any justifications for home thievery which were not already expressed by Ahlqvist.

It is possible that these fragments of the hidden transcript were constructed for rhetorical convenience in order to express support for women's rights and win the sympathy of the reader. Nevertheless, what is important here is that male writers' mention of these fragments indicates their interest in the point of view of rural women, as well as their recognition of rural womens' right to harbour grievances against the patriarchal system. The rhetoric employed in the discussion on home thievery served to extract farm women from their invisible roles as self-sacrificing members of the corporate farm household, and within this discussion women began to take shape as individuals with socially-relevant goals and motives. The hidden transcript began to gradually enter the public transcript, which marked a subtle but significant shift in rural gendered power relations.

Our second source of information on the hidden transcript of home thievery comes from farm daughters who wrote to the press. It is important to point out that even letters from farm daughters (except for the unusual letter from 'Flower-bud' in *Kansan Lehti* [35]) conformed closely to the public transcript which described home thievery as 'shameless', 'evil work', and 'loathsome'. Because of this, it is impossible to speculate on what these women *really* thought or believed, except to note that farm daughters seem to have conformed to the dominant male judgement on home thievery in order to manipulate the public transcript for their own ends. Because farm daughters could present themselves as possessing unique insights into the motivations behind domestic pilfering, the debate regarding home thievery gave farm women access to the public sphere. When female writers upheld the public transcript condemning home thievery, they did so in order to argue against injustices which they claimed were causally linked to home thievery, such as unequal inheritance and the poor treatment of daughters by miserly fathers.

Despite their adherence to the public transcript, farm women's accounts in the press contain scattered hints that a hidden transcript *did* exist among rural farm women. These hints include women's fleeting reactions of surprise which may have arisen from the conflicting moral demands made by the public and hidden transcript which were suddenly thrust upon them. When, in writing to *Tapio* in 1862, 'Maria J–n' declared that she had felt surprised and offended when the topic of home thievery was introduced as a topic of discussion at the Kuopio Agricultural Society meeting, or when, at the same meeting, the woman present were asked if they had anything to say about home thievery and replied that since they were directly concerned with the issue, it was not proper for them to speak about it, we glimpse a transcript which is hurriedly hidden, to be kept safe from the eyes and ears of male patriarchs [16, 18].

But hidden transcripts were also expressed verbally by female writers. The anonymous, probably female writer '–a.–s.' in *Kuvauksia kansan-naisen elämästä maalla* (*Descriptions of Ordinary Women's Life in the Countryside*, 1890) provided a fragment of the hidden transcript when she put the following words into the mouths of a hypothetical farm wife and her daughter who were selling farm goods behind the farm master's back: 'It's not really stealing or anything [– –] it's just taking what is ours. Why should we tell the men about all our little needs!' Farm daughter 'Liina A.' from Pielavesi similarly provided a piece of the hidden transcript when she stated in 1882 that when the parents of poorer farms refused to buy their daughters the expensive fabrics worn by the daughters of wealthier farms, the daughters thought to themselves: 'but that won't do at all!' – Well what is to be done? – 'Necessity is the mother of invention.' [41].

From farm daughters' own letters can be found only one true example of outright resistance, however. The first letter sent by 22-year-old Maria Loviisa Kukkonen to *Tapio* in the summer of 1862 was written before the discussion at the Kuopio Agricultural Society meeting was reported in the press. Because Maria Loviisa's younger brother Wilhelm was a student at Levänen Agricultural Institute from 1860 to 1863, it is likely that Maria Loviisa herself was present at the meeting of the Society and heard the debates regarding home thievery first hand. In the letter she sent after the meeting, Maria Loviisa explained the reasons behind home thievery by creating a hypothetical farm daughter who verbally justifies the practice to herself [15]:

> To my mind, the primary reason for [home thievery] is that fathers do not give their daughters money for their ordinary needs if the daughters, who are already frightened and timid, go to ask them, and when they present their case, they immediately perceive the condescension and reluctance which makes even a child sad and downcast, so that she does not dare to tell all her needs, fearing his increasingly cold response, and when another need arises, then she no longer goes to ask, but rather trusts in her own devices and in the habit learned from and familiar from her ancestors, and when in a sullen and dissatisfied mood she pilfers, she does not only take what she would ordinarily need, rather, she takes extravagantly, thinking that 'because you will not give, I will take as much as I want!' (*'koska ette anna, niin minä otan niin että piisaa!'*).

Despite the fact that the outburst 'because you will not give, I will take as much as I want!' is embedded within the public transcript of disapproval surrounding home thievery (Maria Loviisa continues by writing 'I too would hope that this detestable habit would vanish completely [– –]'), it is nonetheless a palpable display of emotion equalled only by 'Maria J–n's' impassioned plea for justice against separate wills which invalidated daughters' legal inheritance, and it is a genuine glimpse into a hidden transcript of resistance against patriarchal injustice. It provides momentary insight into the anger that farm daughters must have felt when they experienced the farm master's refusal to grant access to the resources of the farm that they themselves had laboured to produce.

While only the merest glimpse of the hidden transcript on home thievery can thus be read from writings to the press, farm women provided a very clear voice of resistance on other issues. The letters of farm daughters may have conformed to the public transcript and affirmed that home thievery was a social evil which needed to be eradicated, but this was done in order to establish a common rhetorical ground with their male readers, so they could protest the farm master's neglect of family members' needs and the moral and legal wrongs attached to private inheritance contracts. What is worth noting here is that, of the three farm daughters whose opinions on home thievery and inheritance appeared in *Tapio* in the 1860s, we know for certain that Liisa Väänänen and 'Maria J–n' had seen Antti Manninen in person at meetings of the Kuopio Agricultural Society, and it is highly likely that Maria Loviisa Kukkonen had been present at this meeting as well. Even a superficial acquaintance with the sympathetic Manninen may explain why these young women were less hesitant to submit their opinions to Manninen for publication than other farm women seem to have been.

Who really perceived home thievery to be a problem in the countryside and why?

As hard as it is to find evidence of women's verbal hidden transcripts on home thievery, it is equally hard to find traces of farm masters' own views on the practice, the sort of opinions they might have expressed within their own local communities. In other words, we know very little about what farm masters, as the locally dominant group, might have wanted to say on the topic of home thievery if they had been able to discuss it privately among themselves. The fact that there is very little evidence of such discussion can be partly explained by the fact that the vast majority of farm masters could not write, and among those who could, there would have been little reason to write about home thievery among themselves. An equally important consideration is that the Finnish-language press of the 1850s and 1860s was dominated by reform-minded members of the educated middle classes. These editors and writers to the press had immediately perceived the potential of home thievery as a rhetorical tool, and in the early 1860s began to actively assign their own meaning to the practice, which quickly transformed the discursive field within which farm masters could publicly express themselves.

Because it was one of the few topics upon which everyone could be assumed to take the same moral stance, home thievery was a useful platform from which to launch into a discussion of more controversial and divisive issues. Writers to the press, by first establishing that they, like their readers, wanted to eradicate home thievery, could justify their next, more delicate move, namely delving into the painful and private causes of home thievery which might have otherwise been expected to offend some readers. For social reformers seeking to 'enlighten' the rural populace, and for whom home thievery was evidence of backwardness and ignorance, such controversial issues included rural inheritance practices, incorrect child rearing methods, and the tyrannical and miserly treatment of families by farm masters. It should be noted that the farm daughters who wrote to *Tapio* in the 1860s immediately grasped the rhetorical possibilities offered by the topic of home thievery for bringing up these very same issues.

Our only insights into the practice of home thievery within 19th-century rural households have thus been filtered through the discussions dominated by reform- and education-minded editors. The primary question raised by this dilemma is whether or not home thievery was truly perceived to be problem among rural inhabitants in their local communities. In other words, was home thievery considered in farms and villages to be a 'wicked habit' to be condemned and eradicated? Or were the attitudes of moral condemnation attached to home thievery a post-hoc invention of social reformers writing to newspapers, with which farm masters saw it as advantageous to agree?

As previously noted, writers to the press frequently remarked that home thievery was a habit deeply rooted in rural practice, which was not recognized by rural inhabitants to be a vice or sin. Some writers suggested that farm masters, although surely aware of the fact that home thievery was being practiced on their farm, seem to have chosen to look the other way. Yet farm masters clearly agreed with social reformers that the best way to discuss home thievery was in terms of harsh condemnation, which prompts the question, why? In asking why farm masters themselves referred to home thievery as a problem in their letters to the press, we arrive at a set of reasons which differ from those which motivated social reformers and educators.

The first reason was linked to the rising cost of hidden labour incentives for farm women. As discussed in Chapter Eight, 19th-century Finnish households were plagued by structural inequalities. The traditional system of land allocation to sons, which was seen to keep the farm intact and safeguard it from debt, gave farm daughters no reason to work for the good of the farm as a whole. Although the labour of farm wives and daughters was vital to the farm, unlike serving maids they did not receive any wages. The conflicting needs of the farm household (female family labour input versus continuity in the form of male inheritance) created the need for alternative incentives with which to keep wives and daughters working hard on the farm. Prior to 1859, when women occasionally pilfered to obtain goods from itinerant peddlars, the hidden incentive of home thievery did not represent a significant cost to farm masters, nor did farm women need to spend much money on store-bought fashions when lower-class women were not yet wearing them. But the dramatic rise in consumption starting in the 1860s placed new pressures on farm households which practically ensured that home thievery would be carried out to a greater degree than before. It also made the hidden incentive of home thievery much more costly to farmers.

It may well be that the topic of home thievery, when discussed at the meetings of the Kuopio Agricultural Society, caused just as much discomfort to farm masters as it did to the farm women present. Domestic pilfering was becoming increasingly public as everyone could see farm women wearing the latest fashions and drinking coffee regularly, and this made it clear that farm masters did not exert full control over their households' consumption and use of money. Home thievery after 1859 represented not only a drain on the farm master's money chest, but also an embarrassing challenge to the public transcript of familial patriarchy.

Cultural projects of the patriarch under threat

For this reason, farm masters seem to have been happy to express their condemnation of home thievery in the press and in the Kuopio Agricultural Society meetings, and their specific concerns focused on *three related areas of rural life*: (1) ostentation through consumption, (2) the ruinous effects of proposed equal inheritance laws on farms, and (3) the traditions that involved extensive stockpiling of clothing and linens by farm daughters before their weddings.[382]

The reason for farmers' criticism of rural shops and consumption of store-bought goods has been examined in Chapters Five and Six. By bringing possibilities for consumption within reach of nearly all household members, the rural trade in retail goods eliminated the advantage that mobility had given farm masters in being the only person to travel to distant markets and make consumption decisions on behalf of other household members. With the coming of rural shops, the farm master found it difficult to restrict both household members' secret sale of farm goods, and their consumption of goods which he perceived as unnecessary.

With regard to the second concern, farm masters wanted sons to inherit the farm as a whole so that it would not be broken up into parcels that could not be maintained by daughters, nor driven into debt when the son reimbursed his sisters for their share of the farm. Inheritance to sons was also the basis of the life annuity system known as *syytinki* in which parents were allowed to continue living on the farm, and the inheriting son was obliged to not only house and feed them, but also give them an agreed amount of land, pasturage, grain, and/or money each year, even though they had retired from active labour in the maintenance of the farm (Talve 1997: 174–175). A situation in which daughters would have actually inherited equally with sons would have, in the view of male farmers, disrupted the entire virilocal system of marriage and land division which was the basis for agrarian production, for the reproduction of social power hierarchies, and for the social security of the elderly.

Finally, farmers condemned as wasteful the traditional wedding practices in which young women amassed vast trousseaux of clothing and linens for display in their outbuildings, and distributed hundreds of items of clothing to the groom's family during the wedding. These wedding traditions had represented less of a drain on the household's resources prior to 1859, when nearly all clothing was spun, woven and sewn at home from wool and flax grown domestically. After 1859, however, the new fabrics sold in shops raised the standards for acceptable clothing among self-respecting farm women, and homespun fabric was no longer seen as sufficiently dignified to reflect the status of belonging to the landowning class. Since the farm master was often not prepared to spend money on his daughter's trousseau

---

382 These concerns were voiced only twice by middle-class reformers: in 1861 by Forsström (who was concerned with the impact of equal inheritance on farms [38]), and in 1880 by August Kuokkanen, editor of *Sawo* (who was concerned with the drain on household wealth represented by trousseaux and wedding gifts) [40].

or her wedding gifts to villagers, these had to be financed through home thievery.

Farm masters' resistance to endorsing social transformations such as rising consumption and equal inheritance laws should not be viewed as mere conservatism, for farm masters were happy to argue against the 'old ways' and call for modern enlightenment when the old ways hurt their pocketbook. For example, 'J. T-r-n.', writing to *Tapio* in 1861 on the subject of wedding gifts, criticized this custom by saying: 'It is just like many other useless, old-fashioned customs [– –]. Perhaps the peasant farming folk will see from now on that these harmful customs are more corrupting than civilizing, for now times should be different than they were before.'[383]

All three targets of criticism by patriarchs – inheritance, consumption, and the accumulation of clothing prior to weddings – were part of the same general anxiety: that the economic capital of the farm would be wasted, divided, or allowed to gradually trickle away. This points to a fundamental cultural goal of farm masters which formed the foundation of their social status: *material accumulation*. Until 1929, the patriarch had sole legal control over the wealth of the farm, even if this wealth came from his wife's inheritance or earnings, which meant that the conceptual boundaries between household wealth and personal wealth were in practice irrelevant. Despite the fact that the farm master was responsible for paying certain expenditures such as taxes to the Crown and servants' wages, the remaining household wealth remained in essence his personal wealth, and it was in his interests to ensure that the entire household worked together to increase it. Wilhelm Kukkonen provided a detailed portrayal of the patriarch's cultural project in 1876:[384]

> The farm master is the one in the family who [should] naturally stockpile the wealth, not for his own greed nor to satisfy the desires of others, which is nowadays often commonplace, but to use it for the progress, the success, the happiness and the blessing of the whole family collectively; and even though thrift is good when it stays within the bounds of moderation – this is not always the case. This absolute sovereign often amasses thousands [of Finnish *markkas*] which he either keeps safe in his money chest or lends to others so that neighbours can tell of and praise his riches, or sometimes he himself boasts and swaggers about it – this is delightful to the old Adam, but this same ruler does not seem to notice that these thousands could be half as much again and richer in blessings if his behaviour had worked to increase the happiness of his whole family, not only that of his own independent interests. At the same time that this sort of farm master accumulates assets to satisfy his own desires with the help of his family, his family must content themselves, especially with respect to their material needs, with either designated charity or, as usually happens, with almost nothing at all except for their daily bread and whatever clothing they need for their tasks and labours [37].

383 March 2, 1861. *Tapio* no. 9, 'Morsianten antimista naimis-asioissa' (J. T-r-n.)

384 Criticism of the miserly farm master who neglects the needs of his family members is a theme which unites the letters written by all three Kukkonen siblings who wrote to the press.

In Kukkonen's description, which may derive from his youthful observations as a member of a large farm household, the farm master's status is bolstered by the visible wealth and prosperity of his farm, as well as by his capacity to loan money to his neighbours. It has been pointed out by sociologist and ethnologist Pierre Bourdieu (1977: 191–197) that in pre-capitalist economies, accumulation of material resources and the generous lending of these resources to others were means by which local male heads of society acquired the symbolic capital needed to receive legitimate authority. In the 19th-century Finnish countryside, although farm women and the youth were criticized for their ostentation and for wasting money on finery, farm masters too, 'were happy to smoke foreign tobacco in handsome, store-bought pipes and [drink] their beer bottles by the dozen' (Alanen 1957, 332). Reports of farm masters' conspicuous consumption in the press confirm that they purchased fine furniture, new clothes, expensive livestock, and exotic food and drink, in part so that their wealth would be visible to their neighbours and guests (Kuusanmäki 1936: 102–103).[385]

The farm master thus sought to bolster his status through first, demonstrating to the community his capable management of his own household, and second, amassing wealth to be displayed and lent to neighbours. Prior to 1859, these cultural projects were enabled and sheltered by the general inaccessibility of consumer goods. After 1859, rural shops offered new possibilities to household members for pursuing their own goals of status display, which meant that the cultural projects of wives, daughters and sons collided with those of the farm master. The increased use of finery and store-bought clothing by women and youths, financed through pilfering, undermined not only the visible boundaries of class and estate in the countryside but also the farm master's project of economic accumulation.

The fact that material accumulation seems to have been the goal of many farm masters makes it all the more puzzling that the farm master apparently preferred his household members to pilfer secretly rather than having to give them money or buy them what they needed. Pilfered goods were often sold for a much lower price than what the farm master could have sold them for on the open market, which meant that giving household members a small allowance to prevent them from pilfering would have saved the farm master money in the long run, as many writers to the press pointed out. Why, then, do farm masters seem to have preferred the cat-and-mouse game of home thievery to the alternative of consulting with their families about the household's use of money, or giving household members cash for daily necessities? Social reformers, at least, were of the opinion that farm masters should have chosen the latter path. For example, the newspaper *Wiipurin Sanomat* printed an article in 1894 entitled 'Farm masters, discuss matters at home with your families!' In it, a writer signing himself 'S' urged that farm masters should share the decision making with other family members:

---

385 See note 170. Young unmarried men from farms, too, were criticized for their consumption of unnecessary goods such as clothing made from baize cloth, fine tobacco pipes, pocket watches and alcohol. See: June 25, 1858. *Suometar*, 'Taitaako sokia sokiata tallutaa?' (Miina, nuori tyttö).

Family discussions can eliminate so-called home thievery on the farm. When all family members receive what they need, and come to have a precise knowledge of household affairs, then they will not begin to steal for themselves in order to obtain small necessities. Even if they do not receive what they want immediately, at least they know that they will get what they need at the nearest opportunity. But when necessities are forbidden a son or daughter, they try, together with their mother, to obtain those necessities through theft, and thus some are forced to tear down what others build. If each family member tries to build his or her own nest egg and pulls on a different rope, then it is clear what the result will be [55].

Three years earlier, columnist 'Paawo Pajumaa' had expressed similar arguments:

If the farm master would now [– –] explain in a fatherly manner, at least to his own children, the shamefulness of home thievery and its evil consequences, and would give them permission to come and freely tell him of their needs, [– –] and would promise to try to grant their wishes as moderation and his resources allow, then this evil habit would certainly disappear completely before long. In places where farm masters do this, home thievery no longer exists at all [52].

Despite such exhortations in the press for fathers to engage in family discussions that would save them money, farm masters behaved as if there existed a taboo against his consulting with his wife or children on the use of money. The explanation for this taboo can be found from the public transcript of patriarchy. In order to be seen as a powerful patriarch, the farm master had to sustain an identity as an autonomous, self-determined actor who could make decisions not only for his own farm but also on broader local issues without having to ask the permission of his subordinates. Having full powers of decision making over the members of his household was part of the playbook of mastery and dominion, the show of independence and control upon which the patriarch's authority and masculine identity depended (see Liliequist 2002: 76–77). In actuality, this autonomy was an illusion: farm masters were highly dependent upon female household members' labour not only inside the domestic sphere but also in the fields, yet in the prevailing discourse these female farm family workers were nearly invisible (see Östman 2004: 326). As long as home thievery was carried out in secrecy and never displayed or articulated explicitly, it continued to maintain this illusion and support the public transcript of patriarchy. Home thievery seems to have remained the compromise condoned by farm masters, because it contradicted neither his reputation as autonomous patriarch nor the legal and cultural norms according to which the head of the household had total control over household production and consumption.

But while farm masters may have tolerated the compromise inherent in home thievery, it was a sore point for social reformers. This was not only because the increasing visibility of household members' illicit consumption was starting to render the whole enterprise both ludicrous and objectionable in the eyes of reform-minded observers, but also because the compromise offered by home thievery rested on, and was seen to perpetuate, problematic practices which contravened modern ideals of individual rights. As we have seen, these problematic practices included women's unwaged labour, unequal inheritance, and child rearing methods based on secrecy, threats and mutual distrust. By condemning the practice of home thievery, it was possible for social reformers, including the farm masters who joined their ranks, to argue for the eradication of these injustices without polemicising the discussion and alienating a large section of the rural reading public.

New perspectives on gender history

What new insights are provided by the foregoing examination of women's behind-the-scenes practices within farm households and the discourses surrounding them? To start with, it reveals how rural power relations in the household can be most fruitfully examined from a broader perspective than simply that of privileges enshrined in law or custom, by taking into account the forms of agency available to persons other than the patriarch. Second, discussions on home thievery in the press point to the diversity of gender discussions going on within the same society. While upper-class Swedish-speaking authors and writers to the press were pondering the roles of wife and mother within the bourgeoisie family ideal, Finnish-speaking writers from the countryside had different issues with which to grapple, namely the question of how to ensure the productivity of a system which relied on unpaid female labour, while at the same time aspiring toward the individual rights and equality demanded by the ideal of a modern Finnish-language nation.

As home thievery became more visible after the rise of rural consumption, it was lifted from the private sphere of the farm master's authority and taken up as a topic for public deliberation by numerous writers to the press starting in the late 1850s. Observers of rural life recognized that farm masters had few means of preventing home thievery in their households. Using home thievery as their case in point, reform-minded writers implicitly argued that familial patriarchy was not an all-powerful institution, nor one which ultimately promoted social harmony and progress, but one riddled with internal conflicts and weaknesses. Home thievery became the rallying point for writers who were critical of the patriarchal household structure which denied farm women their rights as productive citizens in the new modern order, with the most vocal criticism in this debate coming from Karl Ferdinand Forsström and Fredrik Ahlqvist.

Antti Manninen, for his part, facilitated women's participation in the discussion, which meant that suddenly social reformers were not the only persons calling for more rights for rural women. Rural women themselves complained of the miserliness of patriarchs and the practices which disinherited farm daughters, and advocated legal changes that would improve their own economic situation. In the most intense period of debate taking place between 1861 and 1863, the key concepts in the discussion centered on *human dignity* (lack of inheritance was degrading to women), *citizenship* (laws denied women full membership in the nation), and above all, *natural rights*, which moderation and reason dictated should belong equally to all persons, regardless of gender – as long as they were of the same social estate or class, a qualification which was unspoken but implicit.

A survey of the 64 letters written to the press touching upon the topic of home thievery suggests that the discourse of the 'strong Finnish woman' had not yet fully emerged in the early 1860s, being overshadowed by both romanticist discourse on gender (which is often assumed to have penetrated the ranks of the common folk at a much later date), and by the afore-mentioned emancipatory rhetoric produced by liberal male writers who emphasized women's natural rights and legal vulnerability. This latter discourse was used in an effort extract rural women from their traditional role as subordinate member of the corporate farm and to assign them a new role as citizen-individual. By the mid-1860s, the nationalist-collectivist discourse which emphasized women's roles as mothers of the future citizenry had also been adopted from bourgeoisie and upper-class discourses by some writers discussing rural concepts of gender. This discourse never predominated in discussions of home thievery, however, because it ran counter to the tacit, if seldom expressed, recognition that farm women's primary contribution to the marital economy lay in their physical labour and especially their textile and dairy skills, rather than in childbearing. But nationalist discourse could be useful when social reformers wished to undermine the authority of farm masters. This was because women could only take their place as responsible citizens and mothers once they had been freed from the shackles of *unenlightened* patriarchy. Women's subordinate place within a patriarchal structure whose male head was 'enlightened', however, was never in question.

Rural inhabitants' early participation in the press was crucial to the development of a broad-based modern civil society. Only through lengthy discussions in the press on what sort of society was desirable, and how this ideal could be achieved, was it possible to arrive at a loose consensus regarding national goals, standards of truth, and moral ideals such as equality, decency and progress, all of which enabled the rapid growth of civil society and its voluntary forms of participation starting in the 1870s. The topic of home thievery, being of concern not only to social reformers but also to farm masters and their household members, served as the lure which attracted writers and meeting participants who were unused to publicly voicing – or perhaps even reflecting upon – their opinions regarding the conditions prevailing in rural society. The discussion surrounding home thievery also provided a means of prying open the 'black box' of the rural household and examining farm women's own views and experiences regarding familial patriarchy, which was a first step toward conceiving of rural farm women as individuals with a vital contribution to make toward society and the nation.

Appendix I: Map of Historical Provinces in Finland

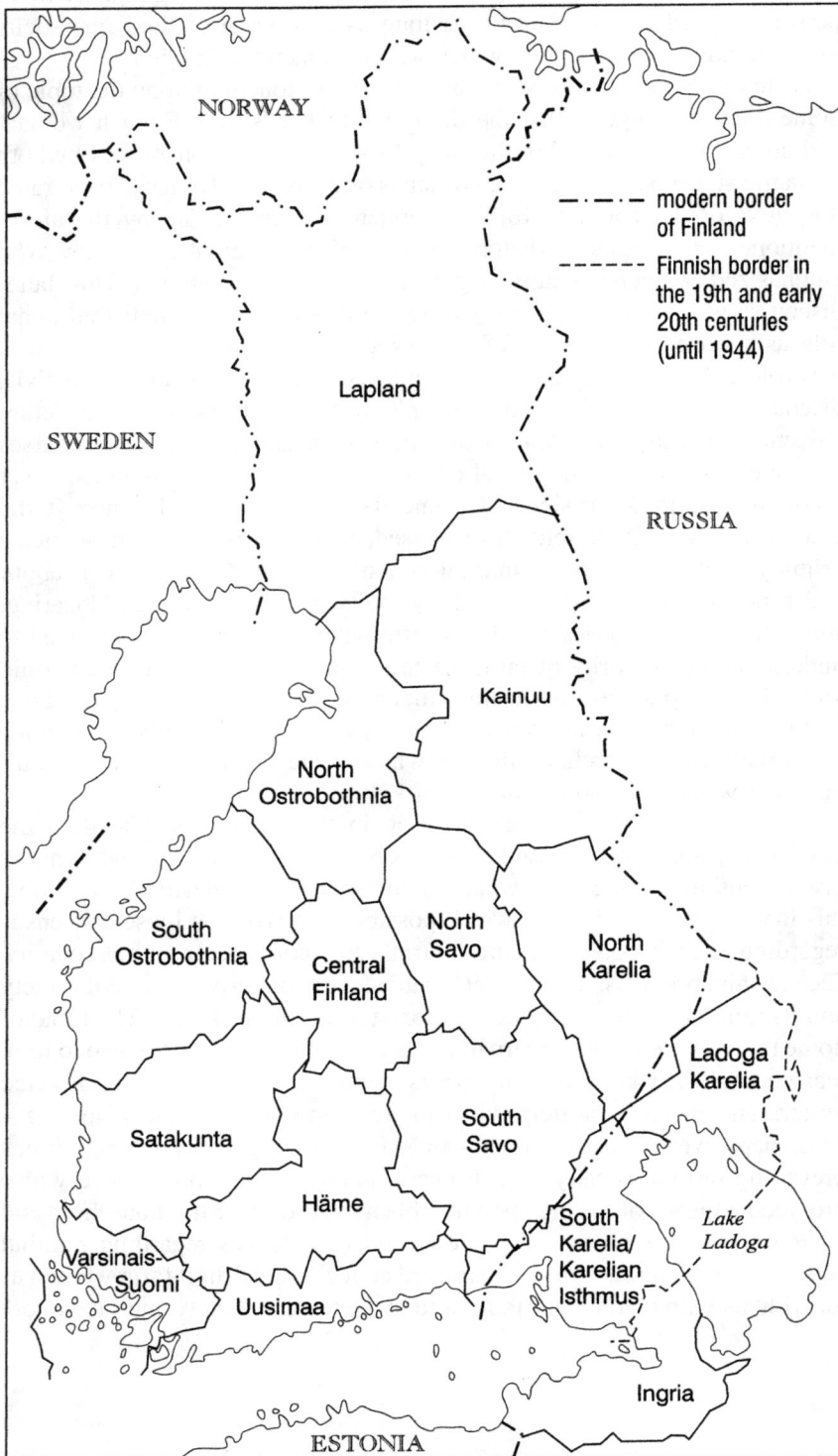

240

Appendix II: Finnish-Language Newspaper Sources on Home Thievery

(http://digi.lib.helsinki.fi/sanomalehti/secure/main.html)

(1) Nov. 24, 1849. *Maamiehen Ystäwä* no. 47, 'Muutamia talon asioita' (–kw– [pastor Johan Bäckvall]); (2) Oct. 4, 1856. *Sanan-Lennätin* no. 40, 'Eräs kansan tapa joka on paha tapa' [Translated from a Swedish-language article entitled 'En folksed som är osed' appearing in *Kuopio Tidning* no. 31 on September 6, 1856, which was probably written by its editor Z. J. Cleve]; (3) Nov. 28, 1856. *Suometar* no. 48, 'Koto-warkaudesta' (B. S. [Bernhard Kristfrid Sarlin]); (4) March 20, 1857. *Suometar* no. 12, 'Talon elämästä' (A. M–n. [Antti Manninen]); (5) April 3, 1858. *Suometar* no. 13, 'Naisten tila Suomessa. IV: Waimon osa pariskunnan yhteisistä tawaroista ja naisten perinnöstä' (F. [Karl Ferdinand Forsström]) (6) July 9, 1858. *Suometar* no. 27, 'Wielä neitoin omasta wallasta' (F. [Karl Ferdinand Forsström]); (7) Aug. 24, 1860. *Hämäläinen* no. 34, 'Janakkalasta' (G. J.); (8) Sept. 28, 1860. *Hämäläinen* no. 39, 'Hämeestä'; (9) Dec. 3, 1860. *Suomen Julkisia Sanomia* no. 94, 'Maawiljely-koulujemme arwosta Suomen siwistykselle' (C. E. A); (10) Oct. 5, 1861. *Tapio* no. 40, 'Jouhkolasta 25 p. syysk.' (–i–nen [Antti Manninen]); (11) October 26, 1861. Tapio no. 43, 'Karjalan Maawiljeliäin kokouksesta wiime syyskuun 23 ja 24 päiwinä' (A. M–n. [Antti Manninen]) (12) Nov. 2, 1861. *Tapio* no. 44, 'Karjalan Maawiljeliäin kokouksesta wiime syyskuun 23 ja 24 päiwinä' (A. M–n. [Antti Manninen]); (13) Nov. 15, 1861. *Suometar* no. 46, 'Olisiko laki perinnöstä muutettawa niin, että tyttäret pääsisiwät perimään yhden werran kuin pojatkin?' (F. [Karl Ferdinand Forsström]); (14) Nov. 22, 1861. *Sanomia Turusta* no. 47, 'Olisiko laki perinnöstä muutettawa niin, että tyttäret pääsisiwät perimään yhden werran kuin pojatkin?' (F. [Karl Ferdinand Forsström]); (15) July 26, 1862. *Tapio* no. 30, 'Rautalammilta 22 päiwä Heinäk.' (Talon tyttö Maria Loviisa Kukkonen); (16) July 26, 1862. *Tapio* no. 30, 'Maawiljelijäin kokouksen keskustelemuksista Lewäsellä 4 ja 5 p:nä Heinäkuuta'; (17) Aug. 9, 1862. *Tapio* no. 32, 'Maawiljelijäin kokouksen keskustelemuksista Lewäsellä 4 ja 5 p:nä Heinäkuuta'; (18) Aug. 16, 1862. *Tapio* no. 33, 'Maawiljelijäin kokouksen keskustelemuksista Lewäsellä 4 ja 5 p:nä Heinäkuuta' (F. Ahlqvist, Maria J–n, G. Jalkanen); (19) Aug. 18, 1862. *Suomen Julkisia Sanomia* no. 62, 'Maawiljeliän kokouksen keskustelemuksista Lewäsellä 4 ja 5 p:nä heinäkuuta'; (20) Aug. 25, 1862. *Suomen Julkisia Sanomia* no. 64, 'Maawiljeliäin kokouksen keskustelemuksista Lewäsellä 4 ja 5 p:nä heinäkuuta'; (21) Sept. 4, 1862. *Suomen Julkisia Sanomia* no. 67, 'Maawiljeliäin kokouksen keskustelemuksista Lewäsellä 4 ja 5 p:nä heinäkuuta'; (22) Sept. 13, 1862. *Mikkelin Ilmoituslehti* no. 37, 'Muutama sana poikien ja tyttärien tasa perinnöstä' (J. K–n.); (23) Sept. 20, 1862 *Tapio* no. 38, 'Kotowarkaudesta. Wähän wastausta herra Ahlqvistin...' (A. J. Puhakka [Antti Puhakka]); (24) Nov. 1, 1862. *Tapio* no. 44, 'Tyttärien koto-warkaudesta' (D. H–n.); (25) Nov. 15, 1862. *Tapio* no. 46, 'Muuan sana kotowarkaudesta' (A. K–n.); (26) Nov. 29, 1862. *Tapio* no. 48, 'Pielawedeltä' (A. Keränen); (27) Dec. 13, 1862. *Tapio* no. 50, 'Wähän wastunta Tapion 44:nroon "Tyttärien kotowarkaudesta"' (M. L. K–n.); (28) Dec. 13, 1862. *Tapio* no. 50, 'Wielä muutama sana tyttärien kotowarkaudesta' (J. L.); (29) Jan. 3, 1863. *Tapio* no. 1, 'Tapion lukioille'; (30) May 30, 1863. *Tapio* no. 22, 'Eri mieliä maa-kauppioiden tarpeellisuudesta'; (31) Oct. 5, 1863. *Suomen Julkisia Sanomia* no. 76, 'Iisalmesta' (U. R., talontytär Iisalmesta); (32) Oct. 31, 1863. *Tapio* no. 44, 'Onko tyttäret mahdolliset perimään sen saman kuin pojatkin?' (J. K–n.); (33) Dec. 26, 1868. *Tapio* no. 52, 'Maaningalta' (R. J–nen); (34) Jan. 23, 1869. *Tapio* no. 4, 'Kirje Maaningan neitosille' (kosio-mies [R. J–nen.]); (35) June 11, 1870. *Kansan Lehti* no. 23, 'Kirje siskosille L–ssa.' (Teidän oma siskonne Nulpukka); (36) Nov. 29, 1871. *Uusi Suometar* no. 141, 'Matkamuistelmia Jyväskylästä Tampereelle' (Matkustaja tärkeillä toimilla); (37) Feb. 19, 1876. *Tapio* no. 8, 'Eräs kansamme pahe!' [editor Wilhelm Kukkonen]; (38) Aug. 10, 1877. *Uusi Suometar* no. 96 (Lisälehti), 'Uusi laki naima-osasta ja perintö-oikeudesta' (F. [Karl Ferdinand Forsström]); (39) Aug. 15, 1877. *Uusi Suometar* no. 98, 'Helsingistä. Uusi laki naima-osasta ja perintö-

oikeudesta' (F. [Karl Ferdinand Forsström]); (40) May 14, 1880. *Sawo* no. 37, 'Kaunis tapa, waan sietäisi parantamista' [August Kuokkanen]; (41) Feb. 28, 1882. *Sawo* no. 16, 'Pielawedellä helmikuun 24 pn:a' (Liina A.); (42) March 24, 1886. *Tapio* no. 23, 'Esitelma' [Minna Canth]; (43) April 10, 1886. *Sawo* no. 42, 'Kirje Sawolle. Rouwa Minna Canth'in 21/3 pitämästä esitelmästä' (Sawolainen); (44) April 29, 1886. *Sawo* no. 50, 'Onko maakauppa tosiaankin maallemme niin wahingollinen, kuin sitä monen kuullaan wäittäwän?' (Kansalaisen); (45) Jan. 3, 1888. *Wiipurin Sanomat* no. 1, 'Waltiopäiwätoiwomuksia'; (46) Jan. 9, 1888. *Sanomia Turusta* no. 6 'Waltiopäiwätoiwomuksia'; (47) Oct. 19, 1888. *Karjalatar* no. 83, 'Joensuusta. Maataloudelliset olot läänissämme'; (48) Jan. 6, 1889. *Uusi Suometar* no. 5, 'Kirjallisuutta'; (49) Feb. 2, 1889. *Laatokka. Sanomia Sortavalasta ja Itä-Karjalasta,* no. 10, 'Kirjallisuutta' (K. R.); (50) Feb. 8, 1889. *Hämeen Sanomat* no. 12, 'Kirjallisuutta'; (51) April 5, 1889. *Savo-Karjala* no. 40, 'Kirjallisuutta' (I.); (52) Jan. 24, 1891. *Laatokka* no. 7, 'Paawo Pajumaan pakinoita V. Pahe yhteiskunnassa'; (53) Feb. 13, 1892. *Laatokka* no. 12, 'Yksi edeskäypä, yksi emäntä' [probably one of *Laatokka*'s editors]; (54) October 8, 1892. *Keski-Suomi* no. 120, 'Sananen n.k. 'kotiwarkaudesta''; (55) June 9, 1894. *Wiipurin Sanomat* no. 130, 'Käyttäkää, isännät kodissanne perheneuwotteluja!' (S); (56) Feb. 12, 1895. *Pohjalainen. Sanomia Vaasasta ja Pohjanmaalta* no. 18, 'Mitkä owat naisen welwollisuudet ja oikeudet?' (Mikko Iipponen); (57) July 28, 1896. *Turun Lehti* no. 89, 'Kansanihailu' (Ewa Hällström); (58) Oct. 30, 1896. *Savo-Karjala* no. 123, 'Kertomus seurakuntain tilasta Kuopion hiippakunnassa. Annettu äskeiseen pappeinkokoukseen'; (59) Nov. 15, 1896. *Louhi. Tietoja Oulusta ja Oulun läänistä* no. 137, 'Kertomus seurakuntain tilasta Kuopion Hiipakunnassa. Annettu äskeiseen kokoukseen'; (60) Jan. 27, 1898. *Uusi Savo* no. 21, 'Kotiwarkaudesta' (–w–); (61) Nov. 15, 1900. *Karjalatar* no. 134, 'Kodin kunnia' (–o–el); (62) November 23, 1900. *Louhi* no. 138, 'Epärehellisyys maaseudulla' (S. [Gustav Stenwik]); (63) November 24, 1900. *Kaleva* no. 276, 'Oulun kirje' (Nyyrikki); (64) March 20, 1901. *Lahden Lehti* no. 22, 'Muutama sanoja kotiwarkaudesta' (Emäntä).

Archival Source Abbreviations

KOTUS = Research Institute for the Languages of Finland, Helsinki.
SKS KRA = Texts housed in the Folklore Archives of the Finnish Literature Society, Helsinki.

Unpublished Sources

Asplund, Anneli. 1966. *Tämän kylän ämmät...Havaintoja ämmälaulujen struktuurista ja funtiosta.* Unpublished Master's Thesis, Folklore Studies Department, University of Helsinki.
Eskola, Kalle. (written 1888–1919) *Elämän muistelmia.* Transcribed in 1999 by Raili Parviainen, AB 3661. Archive of Kalle Eskola. Finnish Literature Society Literary Archives.
Häyhä, Johannes (kirjoitettu 1897). *Oma elämäkerta.* Typewritten copy made in 1939 from the original manuscript in the collection of the Finnish Antiquarian Society. B434. Finnish Literature Society Literary Archives.
Jantunen, Elli. 1955. *Parikkalan suurperhelaitos vv. 1820–1850.* Unpublished Master's Thesis. Department of History, University of Helsinki.
Juntti, Eira. 2004. *Gender and Nationalism in Finland in the Early Nineteenth Century.* Unpublished doctoral dissertation, Sociology, Birmingham State University. UMI no. 3151765.

Kapanen, Maiju. 2009. 'Toivoisimme, jos keruuta jatkatte, että vähitellen oppisitte erottamaan tuon täysin arvottoman aineksen hyvästä ja kunnollisesta'. Suomalaisen Kirjallisuuden Seuran Kansanrunousarkisto perinnepoliittisena ja perinnettä arvottavana toimijana vuosina 1934–1939. Unpublished Master's thesis, Department of History and Ethnology, University of Jyväskylä.

Kauranen, Kaisa. 2005. Luettelo kansankirjoittajista, heidän aineistoistaan ja käymästään kirjeenvaihdosta. Finnish Literature Society Literary Archives.

Parkkonen, Tero. 2008. Kansakoululaitoksen perustaminen 1800-luvun puolistavälistä 1900-luvun loppuun. Kuntakokouksen suhtautuminen kansakoulukysymykseen tasa-arvon ja alueellisuuden kannalta. Unpublished Master's thesis. Department of History and Ethnology, University of Jyväskylä.

Pasanen, Kari. 1996. Sanomalehti Tapion suhtautuminen yhteiskunnallisiin kysymyksiin vuosina 1861–1888. Unpublished Master's thesis, Department of History, University of Oulu.

Literature Cited

Agarwal, Bina. 1997. 'Bargaining and gender relations: within and beyond the household', *Feminist Economics* 3(1): 1–51.

Ahearn, Laura. 2001. 'Language and Agency', *Annual Review of Anthropology* 30, 109–137.

Alanen, Aulis. 1957. *Suomen maakaupan historia*. Helsinki: Kauppiaitten Kustannus Oy.

Alapuro, Risto, Ilkka Liikanen, Kerstin Smeds & Henrik Stenius (eds.). 1987. *Kansa liikkeessä*. Helsinki: Kirjayhtymä.

Alasuutari, Pertti. 1991. 'Individualism, self control and the Finnish temperance movement', *Ethnos* 3–4: 173–188.

Alkio, Santeri. 1923/1886. *Teerelän perhe*. Helsinki: WSOY.

Alston, Margaret. 1998. 'Farm women and their work: why is it not recognised?', *Journal of Sociology* 34(1): 23–34.

Anderson, Benedict. 1983. *Imagined communities: reflections on the origin and spread of nationalism*. New York, NY: Verso.

Apo, Satu. 1993. 'Orjatytöstä oman kodin valtiaaksi: näkemyksiä kahdeksasta maalaiselämän kuvauksesta'. In Ulla Piela (ed.), *Aikanaisia. Kirjoituksia naisten omaelämäkerroista*. Helsinki: Finnish Literature Society, 125–148.

Apo, Satu. 1995. 'Aleksis Kivi ja talonpoikainen erotiikka'. In *Naisten väki: tutkimuksia suomalaisten kansanomaisesta kulttuurista ja ajattelusta*. Helsinki: Hanki ja jää, 50–72.

Apo, Satu. 2001. *Viinan voima. Näkökulmia suomalaisten kansanomaiseen alkoholiajatteluun ja -kulttuuriin*. Helsinki: Finnish Literature Society.

Asplund, Anneli. 1969. 'Kannakselainen kontinkanto', *Kalevalaseuran vuosikirja* 49: 187–195.

Beck, Ulrich. 1994. 'The reinvention of politics: toward a theory of reflexive modernization'. In Ulrich Beck, Anthony Giddens & Scott Lash (eds.), *Reflexive Modernization: Politics, Tradition and Aesthetics in the Modern Social Order*. Cambridge: Polity Press, 1–55.

Becker, Gary. 1965. 'A theory of the allocation of time', *Economic Journal* 299(75): 493–517.

Becker, Gary. 1974. 'A Theory of Marriage: Part II', *Journal of Political Economy* 82(2): 11–26.

Becker, Gary. 1981. A *Treatise on the Family*. Cambridge, Mass.: Harvard University Press.

Beechley, V. 1987. *Unequal Work*. London: Verso.

Ben-Amos, Dan. 1976. 'Introduction'. In Ben-Amos, Dan (ed.), *Folklore Genres*. Austin: University of Texas Press, ix–xlv.

Blomstedt, Yrjö. 1959. *Kukkonen – Sukukirja*. Mikkeli: Sukuseura.

Bourdieu, Pierre. 1977. *Outline of a Theory of Practice*. Cambridge: Cambridge University Press.

Bourdieu, Pierre 1990. *The Logic of Practice*. Cambridge: Polity.

Chayanov, Aleksandr V. 1966. *The Theory of Peasant Economy*. Daniel Thorner, Basile Kerblay, & R. E. F. Smith (eds). Homewood, IL: Richard Irwin (published for the American Economic Association).

Cheater, Angela. 1999. 'Power in the post-modern era'. In Angela Cheater (ed.), *The Anthropology of Power: Empowerment and Disempowerment in Changing Structures*. New York & London: Routledge, 1–12.

Coltrane, S. 1992. 'The micropolitics of gender in nonindustrial societies', *Gender and Society* 6: 86–107.

Comaroff, John & Comaroff, Jean. 1992. *Ethnography and the Historical Imagination*. Boulder, CO & Oxford: Westview Press.

de Certeau, Michel 1984. *The Practice of Everyday Life*. Trans. Steven Rendall. Berkeley: University of California Press.

Dean, Jodi. 1996. 'Civil society: beyond the public sphere'. In Rasmussen, David M. (ed.), *The Handbook of Critical Theory*. Oxford: Blackwell, 220–242.

Delphy, Christine. 1984. *Close to Home: A Materialist Analysis of Women's Oppression*. London: Hutchinson.

Egholm, Liv. 2002. 'Peasant diaries as a microhistorical investigation'. In Klaus-Joachim Lorenzen-Schmidt & Bjørn Poulsen (eds.), *Writing Peasants: Studies on Peasant Literacy in Early Modern Northern Europe*. Odense: Landbohistorisk Selskab.

Eilola, Jari. 2002. 'Cuckoi päällä curjanakin; cana alla armaisnakin' – patriarkaalisuus, puolisoiden välinen suhde ja auktoriteettien muodostuminen. In Piia Einonen & Petri Karonen (eds.), *Arjen Valta. Suomalaisen yhteiskunnan patriarkaalisesta järjestyksestä myöhäiskeskiajalta teollistumisen kynnykselle* (v. 1450–1860). Helsinki: Finnish Literature Society, 100–127.

Eilola, Jari. 2009. 'Gossip, social knowledge, and the process of social stigmatisation'. In Petri Karonen (ed.) *Hopes and Fears for the Future in Early Modern Sweden, 1500–1800*. Studia Historica 79. Helsinki: Finnish Literature Society, 159–183.

Erickson, Amy Louise. 2005. 'The marital economy in comparative perspective'. In Maria Ågren & Amy Louise Erickson (eds.), *The Marital Economy in Scandinavia and Britain 1400–1900*. Aldershot & Burlington, VT: Ashgate, 3–20.

Foucault, Michel 1977. *Discipline and Punish: The Birth of the Prison*. Trans. Alan Sheridan. London: Penguin Books.

Foucault, Michel 1978. *The History of Sexuality: An Introduction*. Volume one. New York: Vintage Books.

Giddens, Anthony. 1981. *Central Problems in Social Theory*. Berkeley: University of California Press.

Giddens, Anthony. 1984. *The Constitution of Society*. Berkeley: University of California Press.

Giddens, Anthony. 1994. 'Living in a post-traditional society'. In Ulrich Beck, Anthony Giddens and Scott Lash (eds.), *Reflexive Modernization: Politics, Tradition and Aesthetics in the Modern Social Order*. Cambridge: Polity Press, 56–109.

Gluckman, Max. 1963. 'Gossip and Scandal', *Current Anthropology* 4: 307–316.

Gordon, Tuula. 2005. 'Toimijuuden käsitteen dilemmoja'. In Anneli Meurman-Solin & Ilkka Pyysiäinen (eds.), *Ihmistieteet tänään*. Helsinki: Gaudeamus, 114–130.

Greenblatt, Stephen. 1986. 'Fiction and friction', in Thomas C. Heller, Sosna Morton and David E. Wellbery (eds.), *Reconstructing Individualism: Autonomy, Individuality and the Self in Western Thought*. Stanford: Stanford University Press, 30–52

Guyer, J. & P. Peters. 1987. 'Conceptualizing the household: issues of theory and policy in Africa', *Development and Change* 18(2): 197–214.

Haatanen, Pekka 1968. *Suomen maalaisköyhälistö tutkimuksen ja kaunokirjallisuuden valossa*. Helsinki: Helsingin yliopisto.

Haatanen, Pekka 1981. 'Köyhyys Suomen maaseudulla'. In Risto Jaakkola, Antti Karisto, & J.P. Roos (ed.) *Sosiaalipolitiikka, historiallinen kehitys ja yhteiskunnallinen muutos. Juhlakirja Heikki Wariksen täyttäessä 80 vuotta 25.10.1981*. Espoo: Weilin + Göös, 134–148.

Habermas, Jürgen. 1991. *The Structural Transformation of the Public Sphere: An Inquiry into a Category of Bourgeois Society*. Transl. Thomas Burger and Frederick Lawrence. Cambridge, MA: MIT Press.

Häggman, Kai. 1994. *Perheen vuosisata. Perheen ihanne ja sivistyneistön elämäntapa 1800-luvun Suomessa.* Historiallisia Tutkimuksia 179. Helsinki: Suomen Historiallinen Seura.

Häggman, Kai. 2003. 'Suurperhe, ydinperhe, pyhä perhe?' In Anja Kervanto Nevanlinna & Laura Kolbe (eds.), *Suomen Kulttuurihistoria 3. Oma Maa ja maailma.* Helsinki: Tammi, 219–224.

Häkkinen, Antti. 1992. 'On Attitudes and Living Strategies in the Finnish Countryside in the Years of Famine 1867–1868'. In Antti Häkkinen (ed.), *Just a sack of potatoes? Crisis experiences in European societies, past and present.* Studia Historica 44. Helsinki: Finnish Historical Society, 149–166.

Hämynen, Tapio. 1984. 'Avioliitot ja niiden merkitys Heinävedellä vuosina 1750–1850'. In Laine, Antti (ed.), *Piirtoja itäsuomalaiseen menneisyyteen: Veija Saloheimolle omistettu juhlakirja.* Joensuu: Pohjois-Karjalan kirjapaino Oy, 86–112.

Hannerz, Ulf. 1967. 'Gossip networks and culture in a Black American ghetto', *Ethnos* 32: 35–59.

Hart, G. 1992. 'Household production reconsidered: Production, patronage and gender politics in rural Malaysia', *Rural Development* 20(6): 809–823.

Hart, G. 1995. 'Gender and household dynamics: Recent theories and their implications'. In M.G. Quibria (ed.), *Critical Issues in Asian Development.* Hong Kong: Oxford University Press, 39–73.

Hartmann, Heidi. 1981. 'The Family as the Locus of Gender, Class, and Political Struggle: The Example of Housework', *Signs* 6(3): 366–394.

Hastrup, Kirsten. 1995. *A Passage to Anthropology: Between Experience and Theory.* London and New York: Routledge.

Hauser, Gerard. 1998. 'Civil society and the principle of the public sphere', *Philosophy and Rhetoric* 31(1): 19–40.

Häyhä, Johannes. 1900. *Kuwaelmia Itä-Suomalaisten wanhoista tavoista. Naimistawat.* Kansanwalistus-seuran toimituksia 113. Helsinki: Finnish Literature Society.

Heikinmäki, Maija-Liisa. 1981. *Suomalaiset häätavat. Talonpoikaiset avioliiton solmintaperiaatteet.* Helsinki: Otava.

Heikinmäki, Maija-Liisa. 1988. 'Die Stellung der Schwiegertochter in Finnland', *Ethnologia Scandinavica*: 117–126.

Heikkinen, Antero. 1997. *Kirveskansan murros: elämää Kuhmossa koettelemusten vuosina 1830-luvulla.* Helsinki: Helsinki University Press.

Heikkinen, Antero. 2000. *Kirveskansa ja kansakunta. Elämän rakennusta Kuhmossa 1800-luvun jälkipuolella.* Helsinki: Finnish Literature Society.

Heikkinen, Sakari, Timo Kortteinen, Hannu Soikkanen & Arvo Soininen. 1983. *Palkat, toimeentulo ja sosiaalinen rakenne Suomessa 1850–1913.* Talous ja sosiaalishistorian laitoksen tiedonantoja 13. Helsingin yliopisto: Helsinki.

Helsti, Hilkka. 2000. *Kotisynnytysten aikaan. Etnologinen tutkimus äitiyden ja äitiysvalistuksen konflikteista.* Helsinki: Finnish Literature Society.

Herrala, R. 1999. 'Banking Crises vs. Depositor Crises: The Era of the Finnish Markka 1865–1998', *Scandinavian Economic History Review*: 5–22.

Hjerppe, R. 1989. *The Finnish Economy 1960–1985: Growth and Structural Change.* Helsinki: Bank of Finland.

Honkanen, Katriina. 1997. 'Tasa-arvoideologia suomalaisessa naishistoriassa', *Naistutkimus* 10(3): 2–15.

Honko, Lauri. 1989. 'Folkloristic theories of genre'. In Siikala, Anna-Leena (ed.), *Studies in Oral Narrative.* Studia Fennica 33. Helsinki: Finnish Literature Society, 13–28.

Ilomäki, Henni. 1998. 'The image of women in Ingrian wedding poetry'. In Satu Apo, Aili Nenola and Laura Stark-Arola (eds.), *Gender and Folklore: Perspectives on Finnish and Karelian Culture.* Studia Fennica Folkloristica 4. Helsinki: Finnish Literature Society, 143–174.

Jackson, Stevi. 1996. *Christine Delphy.* London – Thousand Oaks – New Delhi: Sage.

Jotuni, Maria. 1913. *Novelleja ja muuta proosaa I.* Edited by Irmeli Niemi. Helsinki: Otava.

Julkunen, Raija. 1994. 'Suomalainen sukupuolimalli – 1960-luku käänteenä'. In Anneli Anttonen, Lea Henriksson & Ritva Nätkin (eds.), *Naisten hyvinvointivaltio*. Tampere:Vastapaino.

Jussila, Osmo, Seppo Hentilä, & Jukka Nevakivi. 1996. *Suomen poliittinen historia 1809–1995*. Helsinki: WSOY.

Jutikkala, Eino. 1962. 'Finnish agricultural labour in the eighteenth and early 19th centuries', *The Scandinavian Economic History Review* X(2): 203–219.

Jutikkala, Eino. 1963. *Bonden i Finland genom tiderna*. Helsinki: Schildts.

Jutikkala, Eino & Pirinen, Kauko 1996: *A History of Finland*. Helsinki: WSOY.

Kaarniranta, Kim. 2001. *Elämää rahaa käärien ja velkoen. Pohjois-Karjalan maaseudun sekatavarakauppiaat ja heidän velallisensa 1860- ja 1870-luvulla*. Helsinki: Finnish Literature Society.

Kabeer, Naila. 1994. *Reversed Realities: Gender Hierarchies in Development Thought*, London: Verso.

Kähönen, Ester. 1985. Vanha Äyräpää II (Vuodet 1700–1870). Kouvola: Historiatoimikunta.

Kandiyoti, Denise. 1998. 'Gender, power and contestation: Rethinking bargaining with patriarchy', in Cecile Jackson and Ruth Pearson (eds.), *Feminist Visions of Development: Gender Analysis and Policy*. London & New York: Routledge, 135–151.

Karkama, Pertti. 1989. *J. V. Snellmanin kirjallisuuspolitiikka*. Helsinki: Finnish Literature Society.

Karonen, Petri. 2002a. 'Johdanto: moninainen patriarkaalisuus – normien ja käytäntöjen solmukohdat'. In Piia Einonen & Petri Karonen (eds.) *Arjen Valta. Suomalaisen yhteiskunnan patriarkaalisesta järjestyksestä myöhäiskeskiajalta teollistumisen kynnykselle* (v. 1450 – 1860). Helsinki: Finnish Literature Society, 10–23.

Karonen, Petri. 2002b. 'Patriarkaalisen järjestyksen monet todellisuudet'. In Piia Einonen & Petri Karonen (eds.), *Arjen Valta. Suomalaisen yhteiskunnan patriarkaalisesta järjestyksestä myöhäiskeskiajalta teollistumisen kynnykselle* (v. 1450–1860). Helsinki: Finnish Literature Society, 255–259.

Kauranen, Kaisa. 2006. 'Kansanihmisten käsikirjoitukset Suomalaisen Kirjallisuuden Seuran arkistoissa.' *Elore* 13(2). (http://www.elore.fi/arkisto/2_06/kau2_06.pdf)

Kauranen, Kaisa. 2007. 'Did writing lead to social mobility? Case studies of ordinary writers in nineteenth-century Finland.' In Lyons, Martyn (ed.), *Ordinary Writings, Personal Narratives: Writing Practices in 19th and early 20th-century Europe*. Bern: Peter Lang, 51–68.

Kinnunen, Matti. 1982. *Sanan valta Kallaveden kaupungissa I. Kuopion sanomalehdistön historia 1944–1917*. Kuopio: Savon Sanomain Kirjapaino Oy.

Klinge, Matti. 1997. *Keisarin Suomi*. Espoo: Schildts.

Koivunen, Anu. 1998. 'Suomalaisuus ja muita sitoumuksia – kommentteja Tuija Parvikon teeseihin', *Naistutkimus/Kvinnoforskning* 3: 23–30.

Korhonen, Aili. 1928. 'Karjalaisen naisen yhteiskunnallisesta asemasta'. *Kalevalaseuran vuosikirja* 8: 138–144.

Korkiakangas, Pirjo. 2005. 'Muistoista tulkintaan – muisti ja muisteluaineistot etnologian tutkimuksessa'. In Pirjo Korkiakangas, Pia Olsson and Helena Ruotsala (eds.), *Polkuja etnologian menetelmiin*. Helsinki: Ethnos Ry, 129–147.

Kortesalmi, Juhani J. 1975. *Kuusamon historia II: Kuusamon talonpoikaiselämä 1670–1970*. Helsinki: Helsingin Liikekirjapaino Oy.

Kuisma, Markku. 2006. *Metsäteollisuuden maa. Suomi, metsät, ja kansainvälinen järjestelmä 1620–1920*. Helsinki: Finnish Literature Society.

Kuismin, Anna & Kirsti Salmi-Niklander. 2008. 'Johdanto: Askelia kirjoituksen kentällä'. *Kasvatus & Aika (theme: Kirjoittamisen Historia)* 3 (http://www.kasvatus-ja-aika.fi/site/?lan=1&page_id=133).

Kumpulainen, Kalevi. 1983. *Pielaveden ja Keiteleen historia II. 1870-luvulta nykyaikaan*. Kiuruvesi: Pielaveden kunta, Pielaveden seurakunta, Keiteleen kunta, Keiteleen seurakunta.

Kuusanmäki, Lauri. 1936. 'Kulutustavarain leviäminen maalaisväestön keskuuteen'. In *Suomen Kulttuurihistoria IV*. Jyväskylä: K. J. Gummerus Oy, 96–119.

Kuvauksia kansannaisen elämästä maalla. 1890. Suomen Nais-Yhdistyksen ulosantama. Porvoo: Werner Söderström.

Lahtinen, Mikko. 2006. *Snellmanin Suomi*. Tampere: Vastapaino.

Laiho, Antto. 1936. 'Talonpojasta maanvieljelyskoulun johtajaksi', *Suomen Talonpoikaisluokan ja maatalouden historia, Historian Aitta VI*: 118–130.

Landgren, Lars. 1988. 'Kieli ja aate – politisoituva sanomalehdistö 1860–1889'. In Päiviö Tommila, Lars Landgren & Pirkko Leino-Kaukiainen (eds.), *Suomen lehdistön historia 1. Sanomalehdistön vaiheet vuoteen 1905*. Kuopio: Sanomalehtien liitto, 267–420.

Latvala, Pauliina. 2005. *Katse menneisyyteen. Folkloristinen tutkimus suvun muistitiedosta*. Helsinki: Finnish Literature Society.

Leino-Kaukiainen, Pirjo. 1988. 'Kasvava sanomalehdistö sensuurin kahleissa 1890–1905'. In Päiviö Tommila (ed.) *Suomen lehdistön historia 1. Sanomalehdistön vaiheet vuoteen 1905*. Kuopio: Kustannuskiila Oy, 421–632.

Leino-Kaukiainen, Pirkko. 1989. 'Suomen kielen käytön yleistyminen'. In Päiviö Tommila & Maritta Pohls (ed.), *Herää Suomi! Suomalaisuusliikkeen historia*. Kuopio: Kustannuskiila Oy, 329–346.

Leino-Kaukiainen, Pirkko. 2007. 'Suomalaisten kirjalliset taidot autonomian kaudella', *Historiallinen aikakauskirja* 4 (105): 420–438.

Leskinen, Tatu. 2005. 'Kansa, kansallisuus ja sivistys', *J@rgonia* 6.

Liikanen, Ilkka. 1995. *Fennomania ja kansa. Joukkojärjestäytymisen läpimurto ja Suomalaisen puolueen synty*. Historiallisia Tutkimuksia 191. Helsinki: Finnish Historical Society.

Liliequist, Jonas. 2002. 'Käänteinen vaimokuri. Diskurssi avioliittoon kuuluvasta miehisyydestä, vallasta ja auktoriteetista Ruotsissa uskonpuhdistuksesta 1800-luvun alkuun'. In Piia Einonen & Petri Karonen (eds.), *Arjen Valta. Suomalaisen yhteiskunnan patriarkaalisesta järjestyksestä myöhäiskeskiajalta teollistumisen kynnykselle* (v. 1450 – 1860). Helsinki: Finnish Literature Society, 73–99.

Linkola, Martti. 1987. 'On the history of the rural landscape in Finland'. *Ethnologica Scandinavica*, 110–127.

Löfgren, Orvar. 1974. 'Family and household among Scandinavian peasants: an exploratory essay', in *Ethnologia Scandinavica*, 17–52.

Löfström, Jan. 1999. *Sukupuoliero agraarikulttuurissa. 'Se nyt vaan on semmonen.'* Helsinki: Finnish Literature Society.

Lukes, Steven. 2005. *Power: A Radical View*. Basingstoke: Palgrave Macmillan.

Lyons, Martyn. 2007. '"Ordinary writings' or how the 'illiterate' speak to historians.' In Lyons, Martyn (ed.), *Ordinary Writings, Personal Narratives: Writing Practices in 19th and early 20th-century Europe*. Bern: Peter Lang, 13–31.

Mäkinen, Ilkka. 2003. 'Lukemisen historiaa'. In Anja Kervanto Nevanlinna & Laura Kolbe (eds.) *Suomen kulttuurihistoria 3. Oma maa ja maailma*, Helsinki: Tammi, 310–326.

Mäkinen, Ilkka. 2007. 'Kirjoitustaidon leviämisen herättämiä epäluuloja 1800-luvun Suomessa', *Historiallinen aikakauskirja* 4 (105): 402–419.

Makkonen, Anna 2002a. 'Ääni ja kirjoitus: omaelämäkertoja 1800-luvun Suomesta'. In Makkonen, Anna (ed.), *Karheita kertomuksia: Itseoppineiden omaelämäkertoja 1800-luvun Suomesta*. Helsinki: Finnish Literature Society, 7–20.

Makkonen, Anna. 2002b. *Karheita kertomuksia: Itseoppineiden omaelämäkertoja 1800-luvun Suomesta*. Helsinki: Finnish Literature Society.

Markkola, Pirjo. 1990. 'Women in rural society in the 19th and 20th centuries', in Manninen, Merja & Päivi Setälä (eds.), *The Lady with the Bow. Women in Finnish History*. Helsinki: Otava, 17–29.

Markkola, Pirjo. 1994. *Työläiskodin synty. Tamperelaiset työläisperheet ja yhteiskunnallinen kysymys 1870-luvulta 1910-luvulle*. Historiallisia tutkimuksia 187. Helsinki: Finnish Historical Society.

Markkola, Pirjo. 1997. 'Constructing and deconstructing the 'Strong Finnish woman': Women's Gender History and Gender History', *Historiallinen Aikakauskirja* 2: 129–160.

Markkola, Pirjo. 2002a. 'Vahva nainen ja kansallinen historia'. In Tuula Gordon, Katri Komulainen & Kirsti Lempiäinen (eds.), *Suomineitonen hei! Kansallisuuden sukupuoli*. Tampere: Vastapaino, 75–90.

Markkola, Pirjo. 2002b. *Synti ja siveys. Naiset, uskonto ja sosiaalinen työ Suomessa 1860–1920*. Helsinki. Finnish Literature Society.

Markkola, Pirjo. 2003a. 'Suomalaisen naishistorian vuosikymmenet', *Historiallinen Aikakauskirja* 1: 53–63.

Markkola, Pirjo. 2003b. 'Moninainen maalaisnuoriso'. In Sinikka Aapola & Mervi Kaarninen (eds.), *Nuoruuden vuosisata. Suomalaisen nuorison historia*. Helsinki: Finnish Literature Society, 129–160.

Mikkola, Kati. 2005. 'Uutuuksien pyhyys ja pahuus'. In Pekka Laaksonen, Seppo Knuuttila ja Ulla Piela (eds.) *Kansanetiikkaa. Käsityksiä hyvästä ja pahasta*. Helsinki: Finnish Literature Society, 11–41.

Mikkola, Kati 2006. 'Modernisaation vastavirrassa. Uutuuksien vastustuksen syitä ja keinoja modernisoituvassa Suomessa'. In Helsti, Hilkka, Stark, Laura & Tuomaala, Saara (eds.), *Modernisaatio ja kansan kokemus Suomessa 1860–1960*. Helsinki: Finnish Literature Society, 169–212.

Mikkola, Kati. 2009. *Tulevaisuutta vastaan. Uutuuksien vastustus, kansantiedon keruu ja kansakunnan rakentaminen*. Helsinki: Finnish Literature Society.

Mikkola, Kati & Laura Stark. 2009. 'Himotut ja halveksitut kulutustarvikkeet. Uusien kulutustottumusten vaikutukset suomalaisiin maalaisyhteisöihin 1800-luvun loppupuolella ja 1900-luvun alussa', *Historiallinen aikakauskirja* 107: 4–17.

Moilanen, Laura-Kristiina. 2008. *Talonpoikaisuus, säädyllisyys ja suomalaisuus 1800- ja 1900-lukujen vaihteen suomenkielisen proosan kertomana*. Jyväskylä Studies in Humanities 105. Jyväskylä: University of Jyväskylä.

Moore, Henrietta. 1992. 'Households and gender relations: the modelling of the economy', in S. Ortiz and S. Lees (eds.), *Understanding Economic Process*. New York: University Press of America, 131–151.

Naakka-Korhonen, Mervi & Maiju Keynäs. 1988. *Halpa hinta, pitka mitta. Vienankarjalainen laukkukauppa*, Helsinki: Finnish Literature Society.

Nainen ja naisen työ (1893). Uniooni naisasialiitto Suomessa (toim.), Helsinki.

Nieminen, Hannu. 2006. *Kansa seisoi loitompana. Kansallisen julkisuuden rakentuminen Suomessa 1809–1917*. Tampere: Vastapaino.

Nurmio, Yrjö. 1940. 'Talonpoikaiskirjailija Antti Mannisen anomus suomenkielen aseman parantamiseksi vuodelta 1854', *Historiallinen Aikakauskirja* 1–2: 149–157.

Nygård, Toivo. 2002. 'Patriarkaalisuus 1600- ja 1700-luvun lainsäädännössä'. In Piia Einonen & Petri Korhonen (eds.), *Arjen Valta. Suomalaisen yhteiskunnan patriarkaalisesta järjestyksestä myöhäiskeskiajalta teollistumisen kynnykselle (v. 1450 – 1860)*. Helsinki: Finnish Literature Society, 158–168.

Olkkonen, Tuomo. 1997. 'Modernisoiva suuriruhtinaskunta'. In *Suomen historian pikkujättiläinen*, Helsinki: WSOY, 473–543.

Ortner, Sherry. 1989. *High Religion: A Cultural and Political History of Sherpa Buddhism*. Princeton, NJ: Princeton University Press.

Ortner, Sherry. 2006. *Anthropology and Social Theory*. Durham & London: Duke University Press.

Paine, Robert. 1967. 'What is gossip about? An alternate hypothesis', *Man* 2: 278–285.

Päivärinta, Pietari. 2002/1877. *Elämäni. Perhe-elämällinen kertomus*. Helsinki: Finnish Literature Society.

Paulaharju, Samuli. 1932. *Härmän aukeilta*. Helsinki: WSOY.

Paulaharju, Samuli. 1943. *Rintakyliä ja larwamaita. Kurikan wanhaa elämää*. Helsinki: WSOY.

Peltonen, Matti. 2004. 'Uudet kaupallistumisen muodot'. In Matti Peltonen (ed.), *Suomen maatalouden historia. Osa 2. Kasvun ja kriisien aika 1870-luvulta 1950-luvulle.* Helsinki: Finnish Literature Society, 77–134.

Peltonen, Ulla-Maija. 1996. *Punakapinan muistot: tutkimus työväen muistelukerronnan muotoutumisesta vuoden 1918 jälkeen.* Helsinki: Finnish Literature Society.

Phillips, Lynn. 1989. 'Gender Dynamics and Rural Household Strategies', *Canadian Review of Sociology and Anthropology,* 26(2): 294–310.

Pietilä, Jyrki. 2008. *Kirjoitus, juttu, tekstielementti. Suomalainen sanomalehtijournalismi juttutyyppien kehityksen valossa printtimedian vuosina 1771–2000.* Jyväskylän Studies in Humanities 111. Jyväskylä: Jyväskylän yliopisto.

Piha, Kalevi. 1964. *Suurperhe karjalaisessa työyhteisössä. Karjalainen suurperhe sosiaaliantropologian ja sosiaalipsykologian valossa.* Turun yliopiston sosiologian laitos, sarja B: 6. Turku.

Pinomaa, Lennart (ed.). 1984. *Ristiinan rovastin seitsemän vuosikymmentä. A. L. Gulin 1855–1925.* Helsinki: WSOY.

Pohjola-Vilkuna, Kirsi. 1995. *Eros kylässä. Maaseudun luvaton seksuaalisuus vuosisadan vaihteessa.* Helsinki: Finnish Literature Society.

Pollak, R.A. 1985. 'A Transaction Cost Approach to Families and Households', *Journal of Economic Literature* 23: 581–608.

Pöysä, Jyrki. 1997. *Jätkän synty. Tutkimus sosiaalisen kategorian muotoutumisesta suomalaisessa kulttuurissa ja itäsuomalaisessa metsätyöperinteessä.* Helsinki: Finnish Literature Society.

Pulma, Panu (ed.). 1990. *Den problematiska familjen.* Helsinki: Finnish Literature Society.

Pylkkänen, Anu. 1990. *Puoli vuodetta, lukot ja avaimet. Nainen ja maalaistalous oikeuskäytännön valossa 1660–1710.* Helsinki: Lakimiesliiton kustannus.

Pylkkänen, Anu. 2006. 'Naisten oikeudet maatiloilla: suomalaisen modernisaatiokehityksen pitkä historia', *Historiallinen Aikakauskirja* 104(4): 382–396.

Pylkkänen, Anu. 2009. *Trapped in Equality: Women as Legal Persons in the Modernisation of Finnish Law.* Helsinki: Finnish Literature Society.

Rahikainen, Marjatta. 1996. 'Kasvot väkijoukossa. Historian kirjurit ja tekijät'. In Marjatta Rahikainen (ed.) *Matkoja moderniin. Lähikuvia suomalaisten elämästä.* Historiallinen Arkisto 107. Helsinki: Finnish Historical Society, 19–28.

Räisänen, Tauno & Kalevi Kumpulainen. 1981. *Pielaveden ja Keiteleen historia I. 1870-luvulle.* Kiuruvesi: Pielaveden kunta, Pielaveden seurakunta, Keiteleen kunta, Keiteleen seurakunta.

Rantalaiho, Liisa. 1994. 'Sukupuolisopimus ja Suomen malli', in Anneli Anttonen, Lea Henriksson and Ritva Nätkin (eds.), *Naisten Hyvinvointivaltio.* Tampere: Vastapaino, 9–30.

Räsänen, Riitta. 1992. 'Production and reproduction in burning cultivation: on the development of a gender-specific research model', *Ethnologica Fennica* 20: 35–39.

Räsänen, Riitta 1996. 'Women and marginality. Women as consumers in the agrarian modernization process in the latter half of the nineteenth century'. *Ethnologia Fennica* 24, 5–12

Räsänen, Riitta. 1998. ''Cuca cotowarcan catzo'. Kurkistuksia keskusteluihin kansannaisten himosta tavaraan'. In Jyrki Pöysä & Anna-Leena Siikala (eds.), *Amor, Genus & Familia. Kirjoituksia kansanperinteestä.* Helsinki: Finnish Literature Society, 317–336.

Räsänen, Riitta. 2008. 'Asukkaat ja asutuskuva'. In Riitta Räsänen (ed.), *Savo ja sen kansa.* Helsinki: Finnish Literature Society, 231–252.

Raussi, Elias. 1966. *Virolahden kansanelämää 1840-luvulla.* Helsinki: Finnish Literature Society.

Röhrich, Lutz. 1986. 'The quest of meaning in folk-narrative research. What does meaning mean and what is the meaning of mean?', *Arv* 40: 127–138.

Rosnow, Ralph & Gary Alan Fine. 1976. *Rumour and Gossip: The Social Psychology of Hearsay.* New York: Elsevier.

Salmi-Niklander, Kirsti. 2004. *Itsekasvatusta ja kapinaa. Tutkimus Karkkilan työläis-nuorten kirjoittavasta keskusteluyhteisöstä 1910- ja 1920-luvuilla.* Helsinki: Finnish Literature Society.

Salmi-Niklander, Kirsti. 2006. ''Kokemus varoitti, halu voitti!' Juho Kaksola ja 1800-lu-vun kirjoittavan talonpojan ajatusmaailma'. In Eija Stark & Laura Stark (eds.), *Kansanomainen ajattelu.* Helsinki: Finnish Literature Society, 165–184.

Saloheimo, Veijo. 1953. *Nurmeksen historia.* Kuopio: Savon Sanomain Kirjapaino.

Saloheimo, Veijo. 1959. *Rautalammin historia.* Pieksämäki: Rautalammin kunta & Rautalammin seurakunta.

Sauhke, Niilo. 1971. *Karjalan praasniekat.* Helsinki: Gummerus.

Scott, James C. 1990. *Domination and the Arts of Resistance: Hidden Transcripts.* New Haven & London: Yale University Press.

Scott, Joan W. 1991. 'The evidence of experience'. *Critical Inquiry* 17(4): 773–797.

Sen, A. K. 1983. 'Economics and the family', *Asian Development Review* 1(2): 599–634.

Siikala, Anna-Leena. 1990. *Intepreting Oral Narrative.* Folklore Fellows' Communications no. 245. Helsinki: Finnish Academy of Sciences.

Soikkanen, Hannu. 1981. 'Vanha ja uusi yhteiskunta' In Yrjö Kaukiainen et. al. (eds.), *När samhället förändras – Kun yhteiskunta muuttuu.* Helsinki: Finnish Historical Society, 433–453.

Soininen, Arvo. 1974. 'Vanha maataloutemme: maatalous ja maatalousväestö Suomessa perinnäisen maatalouden loppukaudella 1720-luvulta 1870-luvulle'. Historiallisia tutkimuksia 96. Helsinki: Finnish Historical Society.

Stark, Eija. 2011. *Köyhyyden perintö. Tutkimus kulttuurisen tiedon sisällöistä ja jatku-vuuksista suomalaisissa elämäkerta- ja sanalaskuaineistossa.* Helsinki: Finnish Literature Society.

Stark, Laura. 2006. 'Kansallinen herääminen ja sosiaalinen nousu maaseudulla. Tuskaa ja toivoa varhaisissa omaelämäkerroissa'. In Hilkka Helsti, Laura Stark, & Saara Tuomaala (eds.), *Modernisaatio ja kansan kokemus Suomessa 1860–1960.* Helsinki: Finnish Literature Society, 47–109.

Stark, Laura. 2008. 'Maalaisrahvaan kirjoitusmotivaatio ja asenteet kirjoitustaitoa koh-taan 1840–1890-luvun Suomessa', *Kasvatus & Aika* 3(2): 49–66.

Stark-Arola, Laura. 1998. *Magic, Body and Social Order: The Construction of Gender Through Women's Private Rituals in Traditional Finland.* Helsinki: Finnish Literature Society.

Stenius, Henrik. 1988. 'The Adoption of the Principle of Association in Finland'. *Scandinavian Journal of History* 13(4): 345–354.

Stewart, Pamela J. & Andrew Strathern. 2004. *Witchcraft, Sorcery, Rumors and Gossip.* Cambridge: Cambridge University Press.

Strömmer, Aarno. 1969. *Väestöllinen muuntuminen Suomessa. Analyyttinen kuvaous syntyvyyde, kuolevuuden ja luonnollisen kasvun tähänastisesta kehityksestä ja alueellisesta vaihtelusta.* Tornio: Väestöpoliittisen Tutkimuslaitos.

STV= *Suomenmaan tilastollinen vuosikirja* (Tilastollinen toimisto). 1883. Helsinki: Finnish Literature Society.

Sulkunen, Irma. 1986. *Raittius kansalaisuskontona. Raittiusliike ja järjestäytyminen 1870-luvulta suurlakon jälkeisiin vuosiin.* Historiallisia tutkimuksia 134. Hel-sinki: Finnish Historical Society.

Sulkunen, Irma. 1987. 'Naisten järjestäytyminen ja kaksijakoinen kansalaisuus'. In Risto Alapuro, Ilkka Liikanen, Kerstin Smeds & Henrik Stenius (eds.), *Kansa liikkeessä.* Helsinki: Kirjayhtymä, 157–175.

Suppanen, Aatto. 1888. *Kotivarkaus. Kuvaus Itä-Suomesta.* Porvoo: WSOY.

Suutarla, Zefanias. 1898. *Suomalaisen talonpojan elämänvaiheet. Kertonut tosielämän pohjalta Suomalainen Talonpoika.* Porvoo: WSOY.

Talve, Ilmar. 1997. *Finnish Folk Culture.* Helsinki: Finnish Literature Society.

Taylor, Charles. 1989. *Sources of the Self. The Making of the Modern Identity.* Cambridge: Cambridge University Press.

Tiainen, Kaija. 1975. 'Vanhat kauppaolot'. In Antti Rytkönen (ed.), *Kuopion pitäjän kirja*. Kuopio: Kuopion kaupunki, 311–332.

Toivanen, Pekka. 2000. *Kuopion historia 2. Savon residenssistä valtuusmiesten aikaan*. Jyväskylä: Kuopion kaupunki.

Tommila, Päiviö. 1979. 'Maaseutukirjeitä tutkimaan'. In Päiviö Tommila & Ari Uino (eds.), *Toimitustyön historia Suomessa*. Suomen Sanomalehdistön Historia-projektin julkaisuja no. 13. Helsinki, 2–14.

Tommila, Päiviö. 1988. 'Yhdestä lehdestä sanomalehdistöksi 1809–1859'. In Päiviö Tommila (ed.), *Suomen lehdistön historia 1. Sanomalehdistön vaiheet vuoteen 1905*. Kuopio: Kustannuskiila Oy, 77–265.

Tornberg, Matleena. 1971. 'Kuusamolainen suurperhe työ- ja elinyhteisönä'. *Sananjalka* 13: 104–131.

Tuomaala, Saara. 2004. *Työtätekevistä käsistä puhtaiksi ja kirjoittaviksi. Suomalaisen oppivelvollisuuskoulun ja maalaislasten kohtaaminen 1921–1939*. Bibliotheca Historica 89. Helsinki: Finnish Literature Society.

Tuomaala, Saara 2006. 'Kinoksia ja kivikkokankaita. Koulutie suomalaisen modernisaation kokemuksena ja metaforana'. In Hilkka Helsti, Laura Stark & Saara Tuomaala (eds.) *Modernisaatio ja kansan kokemus Suomessa 1860–1960*, 241–276. Helsinki: Finnish Literature Society.

Tuominen, Oiva. 1986. *Frans Fredrik Björnin muistelmat*. Satakunnan museon julkaisusarja nro. 5. Pori: Satakunnan museo.

Ursel, Jane. 1984. 'Toward a theory of reproduction'. *Contemporary Crises* 8(3): 265–292.

Vatanen, Pirjo. 2002. *Sääty-yhteiskunnan kirjastosta kansalaisyhteiskunnan kirjastoksi. Yleisten kirjastojemme murroskausi 1890-luvulta 1920-luvulle*. Helsinki: Finnish Literature Society.

Voionmaa, Väinö. 1915. *Suomen karjalaisen heimon historia*. Helsinki: Kansanvalistusseura.

Walby, Sylvia. 1990. *Theorizing Patriarchy*. Oxford, UK & Cambridge, USA: Blackwell Publishers.

Warde, Alan. 2005. 'Consumption and theories of practice', *Journal of Consumer Culture* 5: 131–153.

Warner, R. L., Lee, G. R. & Lee, J. 1986. 'Social Organization, Spousal Resources, and Marital Power: A Cross-Cultural Study'. *Journal of Marriage and the Family*, 48(1): 121–128.

Whatmore, S. 1991. *Farming Women: Gender, Work and Family Enterprise*. London: Macmillan.

White, Luise. 2000. *Speaking with Vampires: Rumor and History in Colonial Africa*. Berkeley – Los Angeles – London: University of California Press.

Ylikangas, Heikki. 1986. *Käännekohdat Suomen historiassa: pohdiskelua kehityslinjoista ja niiden muutoksista uudella ajalla*. Helsinki: WSOY.

Östman, Ann-Catrin. 2004. 'Samanarvoisuus ja hierarkia talonpoikaisessa työyhteisössä', *Historallinen Aikakauskirja* 3(102): 315–326.

Östman, Ann-Catrin. 2005. 'Working together? Different understandings of marital relations in late nineteenth-century Finland'. In Maria Ågren & Amy Louise Erickson (eds.) *The Marital Economy in Scandinavia and Britain 1400–1900*. Aldershot & Burlington, VT: Ashgate, 157–171.

Index of persons

General index

agency 28–37, 62, 222–223, 238
  agency as cultural projects 30–33, 221, 235–236
  agency as a game 31–33
alcohol/alcoholism 55–56, 58, 62, 84, 98–100, 135, 144, 148, 160, 203, 221, 227, 236
anonymity 58, 61, 83
antimet (see wedding gifts to groom's family)
autobiographies 38–39, 43, 45, 48, 57, 203, 209, 221
beggars 20–21, 138, 151–152, 163, 192, 224
Bible 39, 43–44, 55, 70, 72, 105, 189, 204, 209, 217
bookkeeping 128, 213–214
bride 25, 36, 122–126, 134, 159, 183, 193, 224
  faults of 143–144, 155
  valued qualities in 73, 134, 154
butter 22–23, 27, 188
  as payment to gossip women 134, 139–140, 146, 152, 161
  pilfering of 110–112, 114, 118, 128, 131, 184, 195, 206, 212–214, 228
Catechism 19, 43–44, 72, 200
cattle husbandry (*karjanhoito*) 57, 66–67, 69, 97–98, 116, 170
censorship 49, 52, 55, 66, 86
charity 21, 36, 130, 133, 163, 219, 224
child rearing 17, 120, 171, 204, 205, 209–211, 232, 238
church 19, 38, 43, 70, 72, 73, 84, 92, 123, 133, 178, 201, 215, 218, 226
civic organizations and movements (*kansalaisjärjestöt ja -liikkeet*) 16, 28, 38–39, 41
clothing 99, 103–105, 107–109, 114–117, 122–127, 131, 133–134, 171, 179, 183, 187, 197, 201–202, 208, 217–218, 229, 234–235

accumulation of before marriage 122–126, 138, 179, 192–193, 196–197, 229, 234–235
  as markers of class or estate identity 104–105, 110, 115–117, 173, 179, 224, 236
  criticism of expensive new fashions in the press 104, 114, 236
  head coverings as markers of social status 24, 103–104, 131
  of labourers and farm hands 103–104
  the appearance of factory–made cloth in Finland 103
  the appearance of sewing machines in Finland 103
coffee 27, 97–102, 107, 115, 224
  as means of bribing female gossips 134–135, 139–140, 149–153, 163–164
  purchased through pilfering 27, 111–112, 115, 131, 218, 233
  condemnation of coffee drinking in the press 102, 106
  rural poor ready to beg or go without food in order to obtain it 102
consumption 21–23, 33–34, 97–109, 114–116, 127, 200, 219, 224, 227, 233–238
  rising rural consumption leads to debt 99–100
courtship
  importance of personal reputation in 154–157
  lack of privacy surrounding 143
  parents or rivals wish to break up relations between courting couple 145–149
  role of gossip in 88, 141, 144–145, 149, 157–161
crofter (tenant farmer, *torppari*) 19, 20, 21, 28, 45, 48, 56–57, 59, 60, 80, 83, 92, 98, 103, 111, 182

STUDIA FENNICA ETHNOLOGICA

Making and Breaking of Borders
Ethnological Interpretations,
Presentations, Representations
Edited by Teppo Korhonen,
Helena Ruotsala & Eeva Uusitalo
Studia Fennica Ethnologica 7
2003

Memories of My Town
The Identities of Town Dwellers and
Their Places in Three Finnish Towns
Edited by Anna-Maria Åström,
Pirjo Korkiakangas & Pia Olsson
Studia Fennica Ethnologica 8
2004

Passages Westward
Edited by Maria Lähteenmäki &
Hanna Snellman
Studia Fennica Ethnologica 9
2006

Defining Self
Essays on emergent identities in Russia
Seventeenth to Nineteenth Centuries
Edited by Michael Branch
Studia Fennica Ethnologica 10
2009

Touching Things
Ethnological Aspects of Modern
Material Culture
Edited by Pirjo Korkiakangas,
Tiina-Riitta Lappi & Heli Niskanen
Studia Fennica Ethnologica 11
2009

Gendered Rural Spaces
Edited by Pia Olsson & Helena
Ruotsala
Studia Fennica Ethnologica 12
2009

Laura Stark
The Limits of Patriarchy
How Female Networks of Pilfering and
Gossip Sparked the First Debates on
Rural Gender Rights in the 19th-century
Finnish-Language Press
Studia Fennica Ethnologica 13
2011

STUDIA FENNICA FOLKLORISTICA

Creating Diversities
Folklore, Religion and the Politics of
Heritage
Edited by Anna-Leena Siikala,
Barbro Klein & Stein R. Mathisen
Studia Fennica Folkloristica 14
2004

Pertti J. Anttonen
Tradition through Modernity
Postmodernism and the Nation-State
in Folklore Scholarship
Studia Fennica Folkloristica 15
2005

Narrating, Doing, Experiencing
Nordic Folkloristic Perspectives
Edited by Annikki Kaivola-Bregenhøj,
Barbro Klein & Ulf Palmenfelt
Studia Fennica Folkloristica 16
2006

Mícheál Briody
The Irish Folklore Commission
1935–1970
History, ideology, methodology
Studia Fennica Folkloristica 17
2007

Venla Sykäri
Words as Events
Cretan Mantinádes in Performance
and Composition
Studia Fennica Folkloristica 18
2011

Hidden Rituals and Public
Performances
*Traditions and Belonging among the
Post-Soviet Khanty, Komi and Udmurts*
Edited by Anna-Leena Siikala & Oleg
Ulyashev
Studia Fennica Folkloristica 19
2011

STUDIA FENNICA HISTORICA

Medieval History Writing and
Crusading Ideology
Edited by Tuomas M. S. Lehtonen &
Kurt Villads Jensen with Janne Malkki
and Katja Ritari
Studia Fennica Historica 9
2005

Moving in the USSR
*Western anomalies and Northern
wilderness*
Edited by Pekka Hakamies
Studia Fennica Historica 10
2005

Derek Fewster
Visions of Past Glory
*Nationalism and the Construction
of Early Finnish History*
Studia Fennica Historica 11
2006

Modernisation in Russia since 1900
Edited by Markku Kangaspuro &
Jeremy Smith
Studia Fennica Historica 12
2006

Seija-Riitta Laakso
Across the Oceans
*Development of Overseas Business
Information Transmission 1815–1875*
Studia Gennica Historica 13
2007

Industry and Modernism
*Companies, Architecture and Identity
in the Nordic and Baltic Countries
during the High-Industrial Period*
Edited by Anja Kervanto Nevanlinna
Studia Fennica Historica 14
2007

Charlotta Wolff
Noble conceptions of politics
in eighteenth-century Sweden
(ca 1740–1790)
Studia Fennica Historica 15
2008

Sport, Recreation and Green Space
in the European City
Edited by Peter Clark, Marjaana Niemi
& Jari Niemelä
Studia Fennica Historica 16
2009

Rhetorics of Nordic Democracy
Edited by Jussi Kurunmäki & Johan
Strang
Studia Fennica Historica 17
2010

STUDIA FENNICA
ANTHROPOLOGICA

On Foreign Ground
*Moving between Countries and
Categories*
Edited by Minna Ruckenstein &
Marie-Louise Karttunen
Studia Fennica Anthropologica 1
2007

Beyond the Horizon
*Essays on Myth, History, Travel and
Society*
Edited by Clifford Sather & Timo
Kaartinen
Studia Fennica Anthropologica 2
2008

STUDIA FENNICA LINGUISTICA

Minna Saarelma-Maunumaa
Edhina Ekogidho – Names as Links
The Encounter between African and
European Anthroponymic Systems
among the Ambo People in Namibia
Studia Fennica Linguistica 11
2003

Minimal reference
The use of pronouns in Finnish and
Estonian discourse
Edited by Ritva Laury
Studia Fennica Linguistica 12
2005

Antti Leino
On Toponymic Constructions as an
Alternative to Naming Patterns in
Describing
Finnish Lake Names
Studia Fennica Linguistica 13
2007

Talk in interaction
Comparative dimensions
Edited by Markku Haakana,
Minna Laakso & Jan Lindström
Studia Fennica Linguistica 14
2009

Planning a new standard language
Finnic minority languages meet
the new millennium
Edited by Helena Sulkala &
Harri Mantila
Studia Fennica Linguistica 15
2010

Lotta Weckström
Representations of Finnishness
in Sweden
Studia Fennica Linguistica 16
2011

STUDIA FENNICA LITTERARIA

Changing Scenes
Encounters between European and
Finnish Fin de Siècle
Edited by Pirjo Lyytikäinen
Studia Fennica Litteraria 1
2003

Women's Voices
Female Authors and Feminist
Criticism in the Finnish Literary
Tradition
Edited by Lea Rojola &
Päivi Lappalainen
Studia Fennica Litteraria 2
2007

Metaliterary Layers in Finnish
Literature
Edited by Samuli Hägg, Erkki
Sevänen & Risto Turunen
Studia Fennica Litteraria 3
2009

Aino Kallas
Negotiations with Modernity
Edited by Leena Kurvet-Käosaar &
Lea Rojola
Studia Fennica Litteraria 4
2011

The Emergence of Finnish Book
and Reading Culture in the 1700s
Edited by Cecilia af Forselles &
Tuija Laine
Studia Fennica Litteraria 5
2011

www.ingramcontent.com/pod-product-compliance
Lightning Source LLC
Chambersburg PA
CBHW081737270326
41932CB00020B/3303